About the author

LANI LOPEZ is one of New Zealand's leading qualified naturopaths. She has over 15 years' experience in the field of natural medicine and appears regularly on radio and television. She has been the supplement researcher and designer for Good Health Products for the last eight years, where she is known as the Good Health naturopath. She also presents lectures and seminars for the natural food and supplement industry.

Qualified as a naturopath, Lani also has a basic knowledge of Indonesian herbal medicine and a little of Ayurvedic (Indian) herbal medicine. She has just recently found the time to learn about Maori herbal lore and medicine, and plans to specialise in natural fertility and breast cancer awareness.

Because everybody asks, her mother's father was Chinese and his wife Maori, belonging to the tribe Ngati Ranginui. Ko Ngati Ranginui te iwi, ko Huria Taurangamoana te marae. Her father is a New Zealander of mixed European descent (Scottish, French, Irish and English).

LANI LOPEZ

Natural Health
An A to Z Guide

David Bateman

Disclaimer

The information in this book does not constitute medical advice. It should not be used as a manual for self-treatment. The information herein was compiled to help you make informed choices about your health. The publisher and writer cannot guarantee the safety or effectiveness of any drug, treatment or advice mentioned. We recommend in all cases that you should consult a licensed professional healthcare provider before taking or discontinuing any medications or before treating yourself in any way. It is recommended you consult with your GP when looking at lifestyle changes, particularly if you have a medical condition. Herbs and some medications can interact. Please check with your doctor first.

If you are pregnant or breastfeeding, see your health professional for advice before starting any health programmes.

Do not come off prescription medication.

Copyright © Lani Lopez, 2004
Copyright © David Bateman Ltd, 2004

First published 2004 by David Bateman Ltd,
30 Tarndale Grove, Albany, Auckland, New Zealand
Reprinted 2004

ISBN 1-86953-545-6

This book is copyright. Except for the purpose of fair review, no part may be stored or transmitted in any form or by any means, electronic or mechanical, including recording or storage in any information retrieval systems, without permission in writing from the publisher. No reproduction may be made, whether by photocopying or by any other means, unless a licence has been obtained from the publisher or its agent.

Cover Stylist Jenna Moore
Clothing from Gergory and Muse, Newmarket, Auckland
Shoes from Molly N, Mt Eden, Auckland
Jewellery from Shellshock, Ponsonby, Auckland
Hair and make-up by Nathan Kake using Napoleon make-up
Photographer Chris Tudehope

Cover design Jag Graphics, Auckland
Design and typesetting Julie McDermid/Punaromia Publications, Auckland
Printed in China through Colorcraft Ltd, H.K.

*Dedicated to my soulmate and best friend,
my husband Steve*

Acknowledgements

Many thanks to those who have supported me.

Steve, for encouraging me to finish and achieve my goals, my step-kids Jess and James, for putting up with me and being quiet around the house, bringing laughter, tears and joy into my days and keeping me up to date with the latest styles and trends.

My family, Mum (aloha), Dad and Sri, for helping me discover my 'natural potential and many facets', my brother Jazz (love you heaps bro) and sister Chelsea. Sofi and Suki who kept me company while writing this book

My extended family, Ken Browne, Cheryl and Stewart, the Heaton and Charnley families, Nana, Aunties Winsome, Sherrie, Amy and Lois and Uncles Ernie, Dave and Bill, and the Wong families, whanau (near and far). My favourite cousins Tania and Yazz; I never realised how much I needed your love and steadfast support to keep my inner strength up.

Andrea Molloy, a life coach and author of the book *Inspirations*, who helped me set my goals and pulled me from a nasty case of writer's block.

Tracey Moxy, my best friend.

Extended thanks to:
The Blanchard family — Dave, Brian and Daren and the Good Health team — Laura, Leisa and Shelley.
Jenni Lane (naturopath), who spent many weekends editing this book.
Newstalk ZB, especially Bill Francis and radio hosts Leighton Smith, Kerre Woodham, Ruud Kleinpaste and Danny Watson.
Janice and Karin at *Healthy Options* magazine and Liz and Jenna at NEXT, for all your support.
The *How's Life* and *Good Morning* teams at TVNZ.
Peggy 'the rock' Lowndes and the inspirational Gillian Painter from South Pacific College of Natural Therapeutics.
The team from David Bateman, including my editors Tracey and Andrea, and Paul for taking me on. Doris Mousdale, who set up the meeting with Bateman.
My friends, who appropriately stayed away or kidnapped me at regular intervals to teach me balance in life while writing this book, Carolyn Leaney, Jo and Ganesh Raj.
And all the inspirational people I have met along the way including Richard Leonard, Melissa Lee, Michael Gullaway, Geoff Trainor, Wendyl Nissen, Eileen and Mike Evans.

Contents

Preface	11
Introduction	12
How to use the book	13

Part One Introduction to Naturopathy — 15–19

1	What is natural medicine?	16
	Why should we use natural medicine?	16
	What is a naturopath?	17
	How does naturopathic medicine complement orthodox medicine?	17
2	Naturopathic therapies	18
	Nutrition	18
	Supplements	18
	Herbal medicine	18
	Homeopathy	18
	Bach™ flower remedies	18
	Therapeutic body work	19
	Reflexology	19
	Aromatherapy	19
	Counselling	19
	Lifestyle recommendations	19

Part Two Naturopathic Principles — 21–62

3	Nutrition	22
4	Healthy daily nutrition	35
5	Herbal medicine	41
6	Liver detoxing and liver support	45
7	Weight loss	50

Part Three A–Z Guide — 63–284

Acne Rosacea	64
Acne Vulgaris	65
Acquired Immunodeficiency Syndrome (AIDS) and Human Immunodeficiency Virus (HIV)	68
Alcohol poisoning and adverse effects	71
Anaemia	73
Angina and Atherosclerosis	75
Anxiety	78
Arthritis (Osteo)	80
Arthritis (Rheumatoid)	83

Asthma	85
Attention Deficit Disorder (ADD) and Attention Deficit Hyperactivity Disorder (ADHD)	88
Bad Breath	92
Boils	94
Bone Spurs	96
Bronchitis	97
Bruises	100
Candida (Candidiasis)	102
Carpal Tunnel Syndrome	105
Cataracts	107
Cellulite	108
Cellulitis	110
Cervical Dysplasia	111
Chronic Fatigue Syndrome	113
Coeliac Disease	115
Colds and Flu	117
Cold Sores	120
Constipation	122
Cystitis	125
Dandruff	127
Depression	129
Detoxing	131
Diabetes Mellitus	135
Diarrhoea	138
Diverticulosis	141
Ear Infection	143
Eczema	145
Emphysema	147
Endometriosis	150
Eye Care	153
Fibroids	158
Fibromyalgia	162
Food Allergies and Sensitivities	164
Fungal Infection	169
Gallstones	172
Glandular Fever	174
Gout	177
Gum Disease	179
Haemorrhoids	180
Hayfever	182
Headaches and Migraines	184

Hiatus Hernia	187
High Blood Pressure	188
High Cholesterol	192
Hyperpigmentation of the Skin	196
Hyperthyroidism	199
Hypothyroidism	201
Indigestion	204
Infertility	205
Insomnia	210
Irritable Bowel Syndrome	212
Kidney Stones	215
Leaky Gut Syndrome	218
Lymphoedema	220
Memory Problems	223
Menopause	226
Multiple Sclerosis	231
Nerve Pain	233
Osteoporosis	236
Polycystic Ovary Syndrome	239
Premenstrual Syndrome	243
Prostate Enlargement	249
Psoriasis	252
Restless Leg Syndrome	255
Seasonal Affective Disorder	257
Seborrhoeic Dermatitis	258
Shingles	260
Sinusitis and Sore Throat	262
Sports Injuries	264
Stress	269
Sunburn	271
Tinnitus	274
Ulcers	276
Vaginitis	278
Varicose Veins	280
Warts	283
Appendices	285
Herb, supplement, drug and health condition interactions	285
Common names for herbs	289
Bibliography	292
References	293
Index	297

Preface

If you enjoy a glass of wine over dinner or a sumptuous barbecue with a few friends during summer, then this book is written for you. Life should be enjoyable and fun, but we should all learn how to strike a balance. What does this mean in relation to your health? It means being informed to a point where you can improve your health without sacrificing the things that you enjoy.

When I set out to write this book my main aim was to keep it simple and accessible for all people, including the layperson who has never been interested in natural health and the informed person who has spent many years searching for answers to improving their health, longevity and appearance.

I've often struggled to find health books that were easy to read, with trusted information that I felt was simple enough to apply to my own life, especially ones that wouldn't put me to sleep. Often the stringent health guidelines set out in these books were impossible to follow and I would feel guilty leading a normal life.

Like most people, I really enjoy a good cup of coffee or glass of wine with friends at a café or just slumping on the couch with a bag of chips watching a movie with my family. One of my nicknames is 'Lanibones' (instead of lazy bones!) and I really revel in my do-nothing moments. But when I want to improve my health, energy or physique, I get back into a healthy regime because I know what to do. I've learnt the realistic tools to optimise my health. It's really all about options — healthy, informed options.

What fantastic lives we have; we can morph our bodies, minds and health by making slight changes in our nutrition, supplement intake or bodywork. Ultimately, improving your health is all about applying common sense, but it needn't be boring or too hard. If you use just one of the naturopathic recommendations in this book, I'd be happy, but it's not about pleasing me, it's about feeling satisfied and pleasing yourself.

Once you start on your road to good health or health maintenance, the rest is actually not that difficult and eventually living healthily becomes second nature. You can create so much energy from good nutrition and lifestyles

So, here's to you and your road to a successful, healthy life.

Introduction

My first experience with natural medicine was when my 90-year-old plus grandfather — from mainland China — smeared the most vile smelling concoction of twigs and herbs on his leg after badly bruising his papery, aging skin. After interrogating him for a few minutes I gleaned that this brown, twiggy stuff was called Chinese herbal medicine and he assured me that it was going to heal his injury at a miraculous speed. In a few days his skin had repaired beautifully and my youthful thoughts at the time were 'weird, but why not if it works?'

I become more interested in naturopathy when my father was involved in natural medicine, mainly herbal medicine from Indonesia called Jamu. I thought that my dad was a complete hippy and that herbs had no place in our society. I had the mental attitude of a typical teenager when you want your parents to be 'normal'.

I have always had asthma, and one day I had an asthma scare. The inhaler I was taking didn't appear to be working, so my dad mixed me up some herbs to relieve my asthma and I was completely stunned. It felt like someone had lifted a paper bag off my head and I could breathe. That led me to follow in his footsteps to Indonesia and learn about Jamu. When I came home to New Zealand, I often helped in his practice as an apprentice. To further my education in the field of natural medicine, I went to a naturopath college and became a member of the New Zealand Charter of Health Practitioners Inc.

The South Pacific College of Natural Therapeutics in Ellerslie, Auckland, became my part-time home where I attended lectures for over four years and was granted a Diploma in Naturopathy.

More recently the South Pacific College of Natural Therapeutics amalgamated with the Charles Sturt University in Sydney, which enabled me to continue my study and complete my Bachelor of Health Science majoring in complementary medicine.

How to Use this Book

This book can be used as a comprehensive guide to basic naturopathy and naturopathic therapies to help you achieve health and well-being. It may also be used as a textbook for individuals who want to learn about natural medicine. To find information about a specific condition the reader can flick through the A–Z guide, or consult either the contents or index.

The book consists of three parts. Part One, the introduction to naturopathy, gives a basic understanding of natural medicine, defines what a naturopath is and explains how naturopathic medicine may complement orthodox medicine. It also lists different techniques that a naturopath might employ or recommend to help treat or support a health condition or concern. Part Two describes principles of nutrition, herbal medicine, detoxing and weight loss. Only the Recommended Daily Intake values of the selected vitamins and minerals are given, although some of these nutrients can be taken in amounts many times stronger than the RDI for a therapeutic use, as detailed in Part Three, the A–Z guide. The common conditions listed from A–Z follow the format below.

Introduction
The introduction gives a basic description of the condition.

Causes
This section outlines some of the common causes of the condition but may not mention all the potential causes as there are so many reasons why a disease manifests. It does not include differential diagnosis. Sometimes factors that lead to a condition are included. Risk factors are the associations between antecedent factors and disease (often established based on epidemiological factors), such as the associations between cigarette smoking and lung cancer and between hypertension and stroke.

Signs and symptoms
These are what health professionals observe to help obtain a diagnosis and create a treatment plan for the condition.
Signs are observable phenomena such as skin rashes, cough, joint deformity or elevated temperature during physical examination.
Symptoms are subjective feelings expressed by the patient such as pain, difficulty breathing, fatigue or anxiety.

Naturopathic recommendations
This section highlights general naturopathic advice given for these conditions, although for individual needs it is best to consult with a qualified naturopath before embarking on any health regimes that you are not used to. As a general rule the naturopathic recommendations are followed for three to six months. Herbs and natural therapies may take time to work so patience is necessary. If you experience any adverse reactions, discontinue the recommendations and seek the advice of a health professional. The recommendations are broken into sections that are easy to understand and apply. The sections include:
Lifestyle hints — recommendations that can be employed to help treat or support the related condition, e.g. for stress, employ meditation techniques.

Nutrition — do's and don'ts related to the specific condition. It may recommend avoidance of certain foods and beverages, advise more fluid intake and point out potential food allergens or sensitivities.

Exercise — recommendations if the condition warrants it, e.g. a typical weight loss programme should consist of cardiovascular and weight-bearing exercises carried out at least three times a week.

Supplements — with a description of how they may benefit the condition from a nutritional point of view, e.g. Folic acid, Vitamin B12, Magnesium and Zinc can be used to treat a specific condition, but also contribute to overall balanced nutrition. Supplements should be taken with a full glass of water, sometimes with food, as directed or prescribed. Many of the individual supplements recommended can be found in one product, so it is best to ask your retailer for advice. Read the food allergies and sensitivities section in this book if you suspect you are sensitive to a recommended supplement.

Herbs — with a description of how they may benefit the condition of concern, e.g. Devil's Claw — the name itself paints a vivid picture of pain, clawed fingers or the grip of some unseen malignancy — assists with the signs and symptoms of arthritis. It is a remarkable herb that relieves joint pain, reduces uric acid and inflammation. Most herbs can be taken every day, but you could take a break for one to two weeks every six months to help keep the herbs dynamic and prevent adaptation by the body as it gets used to the herbs. Read the food allergies and sensitivities section in this book if you suspect you are sensitive to a recommended herb.

Other therapies — techniques naturopaths employ to increase healing and well-being relating to the particular condition are sometimes given, e.g. using aromatherapy to relieve headaches.

Dose

The dosages or application follow the recommended herb, supplement or nutrient. Please start on the lower recommended therapeutic dose if offered or see a naturopath for more information. Doses are for adults unless listed otherwise. See Part Two: Chapter 5 on Herbal medicine for examples of proportional herbal dosages for children. (The dose will vary depending on age and body weight.)

Appendices

This section includes potential herb, nutrient, drug and condition interactions to clarify the cautions and potential dangers that may happen if these compounds are used together in certain doses. Health professionals may have a better understanding of potential adverse drug interactions, and with individual consultations and regular supervision some of these medicines may be used in combination with these supplements and drugs. If in doubt, see your health professional before taking a supplement or herbal remedy.

Part One

Introduction to Naturopathy

1 What is Natural Medicine?

Though the term naturopathy originated in 1895, this type of medicine has been practised for hundreds, if not thousands, of years.

The art of naturopathy can be traced back through Germany into Greece, to Hippocrates himself, and even beyond. Many countries have their own herbal medicine and natural healing philosophies, including herbal medicine from China, Ayurvedic medicine from India and Rongoa Maori herbal medicine from New Zealand.

In the mid and late 1800s in the United States, the standard medical schools taught herbal, homeopathic and nutritional medicine along with surgery.

Naturopathic medicine, or naturopathy, is a system of medicine that uses natural substances to treat the patient and recognises that the patient's mental, emotional and physical states must all be treated for a lasting effect.

The naturopathic ideal is 'to try to understand and treat the cause' of the disease, not simply treat the signs and symptoms. A first visit to a naturopath clinic involves understanding all the signs and symptoms presented in each body system, such as the immune system, the digestive system and so on. Then it is a matter of looking at the body as a whole and integrating any treatment to suit the whole system.

A good example is irritable bowel syndrome, a condition of the digestive system that can cause pain and discomfort. Research shows that emotional stress plays a role in triggering the symptoms. Our aim is to help soothe the digestive system and the nervous system while looking for emotional triggers, i.e. stress at work.

To accomplish these goals, naturopathic medicine incorporates many therapeutic modalities: Some of the examples are herbal medicine, homeopathy, nutrition, hydrotherapy, exercise therapy, physical therapy, manipulation of the bony and soft tissues, lifestyle recommendations and counselling.

Diagnostic techniques may help to confirm a medical health professional's diagnosis or help find the underlying cause of disease or illness. These techniques include case taking (questioning), counselling, iridology, applied kinesiology (muscle testing), quantum analysis (computerised kinesiology), body language analysis, massage, osteopathic techniques, physical examination, postural analysis and diagnostic lab reports, for example hormone levels, blood or liver enzymes testing.

Most natural medicine treatments follow the rules of common sense. The general naturopathic mantra is eat balanced meals but remove all chemicals, pesticides, additives, synthetic or processed foods, and poor lifestyle habits. Drink one to two litres of fresh water daily and create a life that balances your mental well-being with your physical fitness or health, and your spiritual or inner being. As my father (a natural therapist) says, everything in moderation, even excess.

This mantra may not suit everyone, some people still choose to smoke, or a kidney patient may be advised not to drink three litres of fluid a day. These individual needs and wants are taken into consideration. It's really all about choice, options and consequences.

Why should we use natural medicine?

If practised or used correctly, natural medicine holds the key to taking control of your own health and also creates another option for treatment if you are ill or not responding to allopathic (conventional) methods of treatment. For instance, some individuals may have vague complaints and don't feel they are 'ill' enough to see a medical doctor or take drugs, or may have used conventional medicine to no effect, or may want to start with the least possible intervention.

Natural medicine caters for individual needs and offers treatment options and preventative medicine with fewer side effects than many prescribed medications. Many natural therapies can be used in conjunction with orthodox medicine so individuals can get the best of both worlds.

To avoid drug interactions and to coordinate care, it is important for a patient to inform his or her allopathic doctor about supplements prescribed by a naturopath and vice versa. Why wait until you are sick, if you can prevent or allay age-related diseases and create better health for yourself in the present and future?

What is a naturopath?

A naturopath requires a Diploma of Naturopathy to be able to practice. The diploma takes three years of full-time study to complete and has been designed to assist students in attaining the necessary knowledge and practical skills to embark on a career as a naturopathic practitioner or to work in the natural health industry. After completing the diploma, naturopaths have the option of further study to receive a BHSc (Bachelor of Health Sciences majoring in complementary medicine). Although this is optional, many naturopaths think the BHSc provides benefits such as furthering their scientific knowledge and being more accepted into the mainstream. Although it is not required, being a member of professional industry associations and having an Annual Practising Certificate are preferred.

I always have people come up to me and ask what exactly is a naturopath and what do they do? I often say that we are a bit like doctors but we use natural methods to help heal, including herbal therapies, nutritional supplements and advice, and therapeutic body work, including osteopathic techniques. This is just a basic generalisation.

It normally takes an hour to an hour and a half for an initial consultation with a naturopath because we like to take a full history of health, rate mental well-being, do a physical examination and, if needed, we may recommend diagnostic testing. We may send a patient to a doctor to confirm a diagnosis or to offer a second opinion. The emphasis is on helping the body establish its own state of good health.

We try to empower people by helping them to create an internal and external environment that is conducive to good health, enabling the clients to make their own choices. Traditional naturopathy is not a medical practice. Major and minor surgery, prescribing drugs and pharmaceuticals, giving injections and drawing blood are limited to medical doctors and nurses only and not performed within the scope of naturopathy. However, we can support conventional treatment offered by medical establishments.

We can deal with most conditions, especially chronic conditions including acne, stress, asthma, blood pressure, diabetes, cholesterol and so on. What we can't deal with is surgery, so we leave that up to the hospitals, and we will recommend people see a doctor or go to an emergency centre if need be, again reiterating, we like to integrate with conventional medicine.

How does naturopathic medicine complement orthodox medicine?

Naturopathy works very well with conventional methods. We now have the research and resources to marry the two together. A naturopath may consult with an individual's medical doctor if they are taking prescribed medication and they can work together for the benefit of the patient.

Research into herbal and nutrient medicine, e.g. the use of vitamin and mineral supplements, has increased tenfold over the last 30 years and has lead to scientists no longer being able to deem their effects and benefits invalid because of lack of research.

This research also makes it easier for naturopaths to work with conventional methods, as it has provided more information on the care that is needed when mixing some medications with certain herbs and nutrients in some forms. Instead of being segregated, as we have been in the past, we are now becoming integrated. And it's a win-win situation for everyone, and the patient, or client, gets the best of both worlds.

Caution: Herbal medicine may interact with conventional medicine or some conditions. See the appendices for possible interactions.

2 Naturopathic Therapies

Naturopaths have many different therapies that they can use as part of a naturopathic treatment. These include changing poor lifestyle habits, such as swapping a sedentary lifestyle or a highly stressed, poorly organised lifestyle and making healthy recommendations to suit each person's needs. Types of treatment used by naturopaths may include the following:

Nutrition

This includes a diet assessment to discover environmental or food allergies or sensitivities, to identify an overload of pesticides or heavy metals, or herbs or supplements taken in incorrect doses, or potential medical prescription side effects and poor nutrition. Giving dietary advice and encouraging nutritional education is recommended to improve health. Nutritional recommendations may include taking supplements to counter deficiencies, removing potentially harmful foods and replacing them with healthier options.

Supplements

The term nutritional supplementation covers the use of vitamins, minerals and other neutraceutical food substances to support good health and treat nutritional deficiencies and health concerns.

Herbal medicine

Many plants contain potent substances that have a medicinal effect on the body. Also termed phytotherapy or botanical medicine, the use of herbs has been practised for hundreds of years by many cultures. Many pharmaceutical drugs were, and are still, derived from herbs, and modern herbal pharmacology has uncovered many chemical or nutritional constituents of plants and how they work on the body.

Homeopathy

Homeopathy works on the principle of 'like cures like.' It works on a subtle yet powerful electromagnetic level, gently acting to strengthen the body's healing and immune response. The homeopathic remedies (minerals, herbs or organic and inorganic substances) are extremely diluted and then 'potentised' (the process of diluting and then agitating the substance). When chosen correctly, homeopathic remedies have a normalising effect on the body's homeostasis (equilibrium) and the presenting illness or condition.

Bach™ flower remedies

These are plant essences that help balance emotional states. The Bach™ Flower Remedies were originally designed for self-help, but are now an integral part of homeopathic, naturopathic and herbal medicine treatments. Dr Bach (said 'batch') identified 38 remedies, each relating to a specific state of mind. For example, the plant-derived essence from olive is prescribed for mental and physical exhaustion, willow for resentment and bitterness and white chestnut for unwanted persistent thoughts. The most popular Bach™ remedy is a formula made from a combination of five remedies, known as Rescue Remedy. It is recommended in emergencies, when it can help calm after a sudden shock or panic attack. Interestingly, its benefits are not limited to humans or animals; plants respond to Bach™ Flowers too.

Therapeutic body work

This can increase circulation, decrease pain, rebalance the body, increase healing, release mental trauma and correct some structural disorders of the body. Some popular examples of body work include Swedish, Ayurvedic, Polynesian or Asian massage, sports massage, lymph massage, basic osteopathy and chiropractic techniques, dry skin brushing, applied kinesiology, Bowen technique, cranio-sacral therapy, physiotherapy, exercise recommendations (yoga), energy work, Reiki, shiatsu, pulsing, cold sitz baths, cold flannel wraps and hot or cold therapy.

Reflexology

Reflexology is a type of acupressure massage. Pressure is applied to particular points on the feet or hands with specific thumb, finger and hand techniques to determine tender or numb areas. The theory is that if certain areas are painful the corresponding organs may not be functioning properly or may be out of balance. As with other natural therapies, reflexology focuses on the body's own healing processes, using its own recuperative resources to heal and restore. Other beneficial effects include stress release, improving blood circulation and promoting the unblocking of nerve impulses to heal specific organs and areas of the body.

Aromatherapy

Aromatherapy is the art of healing with pure essential oils. These are highly concentrated extracts of plants, herbs and flowers. Aromatherapy is a way of treating mental and physical imbalances through inhalation and the external application of essential oils in massage, baths, etc. Essential oils act on the olfactory nerves that lead from the nose to the brain, having a therapeutic effect on the body.

Counselling

Having someone listen attentively is often a cathartic experience for the speaker and can result in the individual feeling more supported and nurtured, which in turn improves emotional well-being. Many physical or emotional issues can lead to poor health and can often be resolved even without the use of nutritional supplements, herbs or body work. Individuals may find support or clarification, for example, if they wish to resolve a particular problem, gain support during a crisis or need to engage in a process of personal development. Other naturopathic techniques in this area may include prayer, meditation, affirmation, stress or pain management and guided imagery.

Lifestyle recommendations

Common sense can determine many lifestyle recommendations that a naturopath might make. Poor lifestyle habits may include smoking, or using recreational drugs, 'burning the candle at both ends', ignoring signs and symptoms of ill health, stress, overexposing oneself to environmental toxins or negative thoughts. Many people find it hard to maintain a balance in life, especially when trying to meet society's expectations. Making positive, healthy lifestyle changes increases the rate of healing.

The main aim of naturopathy is to encourage people, empower them with knowledge and guide them on a path where they can heal themselves either through use of health practitioners, positive thoughts or spiritual guidance.

Part Two
Naturopathic Principles

3 Nutrition

Nutrition is one of the cornerstones of good health. However, there is a common misconception that if you eat a balanced diet you don't need any supplements. Who eats a properly balanced diet 100% of the time? Everyone is busy trying to make things more convenient and efficient these days. Try as we might, most of us find it difficult to stick to the routine of eating lean meat (or fish) with at least five servings a day of fresh fruit and vegetables, and if you have children or work late hours it can be even more difficult.

Chemicals are still added to fruit, vegetables and meat to make them look uniform and appealing. Even though organic produce tastes better and is healthier, most people are still shying away from its higher cost or tend to compromise by buying a bit of both. Modern farming methods have depleted soils of trace minerals, which leads to mineral deficiencies. Excess intake of coffee and alcohol, smoking and satisfying sweet-tooth cravings are some examples of poor nutritional habits that may lead to nutrient deficiencies.

It's obvious that having a healthy balanced diet is important, but nutritional inconsistency is a major factor in determining whether an individual may be incurring a loss of or deficiency in nutrients. The amount of nutrients required is influenced by size, age, sex, environment, physical activity, health and current nutritional status.

It ususally takes many weeks or months before signs of a vitamin deficiency appear. The cells continue to function but at reduced efficiency due to lower nutrient levels. This can lead to further cellular decline and loss of function. Scientific studies that have been conducted for decades indicate that extra supplementation helps rectify nutritional deficiencies. If you want optimal health you must take responsibility for yourself. Take extra nutrients if you need them, ask questions and do some research; this will help to empower you and, hopefully, future generations too.

The major nutrients

A nutrient is an organic substance that is utilised by the body for energy, normal growth, maintenance and repair. The major nutrients — protein, carbohydrates and fats — and the other necessities of life — water and fibre — make up the lion's share of what we consume on a daily basis.

Protein

Protein is broken down by the body into amino acids. These help to form the building blocks of the body that include the skin, collagen, tendons, bone matrix and muscles. Functional proteins (those that perform a specific function) include cell receptors, enzymes, blood components and hormones.

Sources of protein

- Complete proteins include eggs, milk products, soybean products, whey protein and meat (fish, poultry, seafood, pork, beef and lamb). These contain all eight essential amino acids.
- Incomplete proteins include legumes (beans, lentils and peas), nuts, seeds, grains, cereals and some vegetables. Incomplete proteins should be eaten in certain combinations so that the amino acids absent in one are supplied by the other. Grains can therefore be combined with legumes, for example, to form proteins that are complete and which

achieve the eight essential amino acids within a non-meat eating diet, preventing the manifestation of some diseases. When combined properly, the incomplete protein amino acids are said to be complementary since what each lacks the other supplies. This has only been recognised by researchers in the last 40 years. This led to the belief that vegetarians who didn't include milk, eggs or soy in their diets had to have the correct combination of vegetarian protein at each meal. Now this type of protein-combining at each meal is viewed as old-fashioned. As long as you eat a variety of plant foods, such as rice, nuts, cheese and legumes, within a 24-hour period, your protein needs should be met.

Carbohydrates

Carbohydrates (starches and sugars) are mainly derived from plants. Although protein and fats can be used as fuel, carbohydrates are the preferred source used for energy and cellular fuel, especially for the red blood cells and the brain (nervous system neurons). Special cellular receptors and nucleic acids also require carbohydrates for formation.

Sources of carbohydrate

- Complex carbohydrates (starches) include bread, cereals, cakes, biscuits, crackers, flour products, pasta, nuts, rice and root vegetables (e.g. potatoes).
- Simple carbohydrates (sugars) include milk (lactose), carbonated drinks, sweets, honey, sugar, molasses, fruits and fruit juice.
- Some foods, such as toasted muesli or cakes, are a combination of simple and complex carbohydrates.

Fats

Fats help the body absorb fat-soluble vitamins (A, D, E and K), are a source of fuel for the body, form cellular membranes and hormones, and insulate and cushion body organs. Prostaglandins formed from omega 3 and 6 (essential fatty acids [EFA]) play a role in smooth muscle contraction, and control blood pressure and inflammatory responses.

The modern Western diet is generally high in saturated fat and low in EFA, primarily omega 3. Research has shown that if you change from a diet high in saturated fat to a diet low in saturated fat and increase omega 3 EFA, health benefits will follow.

Saturated fats include foods containing butter, cheese, sausages, eggs, bacon (rind on), roast meats, salamis, coconut cream and milk, cream, full cream milk, ice cream, chocolate and lard. These are mainly products derived from animals.

Polyunsaturated oils include flax oil, fish oil, cold pressed vegetable oils, and some nut and seed oils.

Essential fatty acids are necessary for the body to function properly. There are two EFA, omega 3 and omega 6.

Many diets are deficient in EFA and can lead to a wide array of health problems, such as eczema and asthma, and learning problems in children. Excess intake of saturated fats from animal products, such as sausages, bacon, cheeses, steaks and fatty meats, and low intake of fish and vegetables is implicated in heart conditions and high cholesterol. Health professionals are now recommending we replace many of the 'bad fats'(solid) with non-heated 'good fats' (oils), such as flax or fish oil, to maintain a healthy heart and body.

Sources of fat

- Animal sources of fat include eggs, milk products and meat (fish, poultry, seafood, pork, beef and lamb).
- Plant sources of fats include coconut oils, nuts, seeds, corn, olive and vegetable oils.

- EFA are found in oils including, flax, hemp, evening primrose, borage and fish.
- Cholesterol food sources include organ meats (liver, kidneys, brain), egg yolk and fish roe. Smaller amounts can be found in meat and dairy products.

Water

Seventy per cent of the body is comprised of water. It is essential for rehydration and the transportation of nutrients, it keeps blood in solution and dilutes concentrations of nutrients and toxins in the body. Waste products are transferred out and excreted via water and it is involved in just about every function of the body, including regulation of body temperature. It is also necessary for the formation of joint cartilage and lubrication. It is normally recommended to drink one to two litres of pure, filtered water every day. Drinking too much water can upset your electrolyte balance. However, this is dependent on how active you are, heat and other factors.

Fibre

Fibre is plentiful in vegetables and grains, provides roughage to increase the bulk of stools and facilitates defecation. Normal bacteria found in the digestive system assist in the breakdown of indigestible fibres found in beans, cabbage, fibrous vegetables and carbohydrates (cellulose, pectins) by fermentation. Cellulose, for instance, is an important source of short chain fatty acids that are transported to the liver and used for energy production, and are the preferred energy source of the cells of the colon. Plant lignans from fibre, e.g. flaxseed fibre, are believed to be protective against cancer.

Fibre is also beneficial for conditions suuch as constipation and irregularity of bowel motions, diarrhoea and loose bowel motions, diverticular disease, weight loss support, detoxing, candida within the digestive system, coronary heart disease, cholesterol, gallstones, parasite treatment, haemorrhoids, varicose veins and diabetes.

Minor nutrients

Minor nutrients such as vitamins, minerals, antioxidants, nutritional compounds (e.g. acidophilus) and enzymes are just as important for our health, although we need smaller amounts of them. They can be derived from the food and beverages we include in our daily diet.

Key
RDI — Recommended daily intake.[1] RDIs represent the minimum amount needed to prevent deficiency and are not necessarily a therapeutic dose used to prevent and treat diseases.
mcg — Micrograms
mg — Milligrams
IU — International units

Vitamins

A vitamin is a natural substance found in small amounts in food. There are 13 vitamins that all play vital roles in cellular functions of the body. Without them we could not survive. Many people who travelled by sea in the 1700s and 1800s died from scurvy, a deficiency of vitamin C, from lack of fresh fruit and vegetables. Vitamins cannot be made by the body, except for Vitamin D, which can be made by the skin through sunlight absorption.

There are two groups of vitamins, fat-soluble and water-soluble.

Fat-soluble vitamins

Fat-soluble vitamins are digested and absorbed like fats and are stored within the liver. Excessive storage of vitamin A may lead to liver damage. The fat-soluble vitamins are A, D, E and

K, which are sourced mainly from animal or plant fats or oils. Let's look at each vitamin to understand its function.

Vitamin A is important for vision, especially in dim light, and normal bone growth and formation. It also helps maintain the skin and mucous membranes found in the digestive system.
- Vitamin A deficiency can cause night blindness, rough skin on the back of arms, acne, psoriasis and poor immunity.
- Sources include cod liver oil, palm oil, lambs' liver, carrots, spinach, sweet potatoes and egg yolk.
- Dose   Adult RDI 4000IU–5000IU.
   Pregnancy caution High doses of vitamin A — over 10,000IU daily — have been reported to increase the risk of birth defects. Doses under 10,000IU daily of vitamin A, and beta carotene sources, are a much safer option.

Vitamin D works with calcium and is important for bone remodelling and formation. Preliminary research has also shown possible benefits in seasonal depression and multiple sclerosis.
- Vitamin D deficiency can cause rickets, leading to bone deformity. Severe bow legs are characteristic of rickets.
- Sources include sun exposure and small amounts are found in fish, butter, eggs, fungi, and fortified milk and supplements.
- Dose   Adult RDI 400IU (toxicity dose is approximately 4000IU).

Vitamin E is a natural antioxidant. It helps prevent scar tissue and cholesterol oxidation, reduces inflammation, helps fertility and plays a role in the prevention of dementia and Alzheimer's disease.
- Vitamin E deficiency results in lactic acid build-up, cholesterol problems, cataracts and anaemia. Vitamin E is in every cell membrane, so it's important for every one of the body's cells and their function.
- Rich sources include unrefined soybean oil, wheat germ oil, whole grains, nuts, seeds and green leafy vegetables.
- Dose   Adults 15IU daily or RDI 10mg (alpha tocopherol equivalents) or menopausal women 50IU daily.

Vitamin K is important for blood-clotting. The most important clinical situation in which deficiency occurs is internal bleeding, which may occur in babies because fat substances don't cross the placenta easily and gut bacteria cannot yet convert fat substances to adequate amounts of vitamin K.
- Vitamin K deficiency can produce bleeding disorders.
- Rich sources include green leafy vegetables, vegetable oils, egg yolk, butter, liver and some cheeses.
- Dose   No RDI has been established.

Water-soluble vitamins

Water-soluble vitamins can be easily destroyed by cooking and are obtained from a wide variety of plant and animal sources. Water-soluble vitamins B1, B2, B3, B5, B6, B12, biotin, folic acid and vitamin C are normally flushed out in the urine if excessive amounts are consumed. The vitamin A precursor, beta carotene, does not accumulate in the liver and is safer during pregnancy.

   Vitamin B complex   All B vitamins are water-soluble and can be made from yeasts and fungi. The most important fact to remember is that B vitamins should be taken together to prevent an imbalance of one or more of the other B vitamins.

Vitamin B1 (thiamine) helps convert glucose and carbohydrates into energy, maintains a healthy nervous system and is necessary for healthy mucous membranes.
- Vitamin B1 deficiency leads to loss of appetite, constipation, fatigue, depression, sore muscles, 'pins and needles', numbness in legs and, in extreme cases, beriberi symptoms appear, including muscle weakness, weight loss, nervous disorders and ultimately paralysis and death. The need for B1 increases if eating excessive amounts of sugar (around 10% of the New Zealand and Australian populations could be deficient in B1 due to high carbohydrate intake). Raw seafood, smoking and drinking alcohol cause B1 deficiencies, and diarrhoea, fever, stress and surgery increase the need for vitamin B1.
- Tongue diagnosis   A vitamin B1 deficiency shows teeth marks scalloping the edges of the tongue.
- Rich sources include pork, brewer's yeast and molasses. Vitamin B1 is also found in the portion of grains that is normally milled to produce refined carbohydrates, e.g. the germ and bran of wheat and rice husks.
- Dose   Adult RDI 1.1mg.

Vitamin B2 (riboflavin) helps convert glucose and carbohydrates into energy and is needed for cell respiration, cellular oxygen and healthy mucous membranes. It's also great for stress, eczema, eye health and during pregnancy.
- Vitamin B2 deficiency can lead to cracks in the skin at the corner of the mouth. The skin looks oily but is scaly around the nose, mouth and forehead. The eyes appear watery and can be inflamed or irritated.
- Tongue Diagnosis   A reddish-purple tongue with lots of cracks on its surface may indicate a vitamin B2 deficiency.
- Sources include organ meats, milk, eggs and brewer's yeast.
- Dose   Adult RDI 1.7mg.

Vitamin B3 (niacin, inositol hexanoate or nicotinamide) is essential for releasing energy from carbohydrates, fats and proteins, and for healthy skin, nerves and digestive system. It also helps convert protein into serotonin, the 'happy brain' chemical. The niacin form of vitamin B3 can have an uncomfortable flushing effect in higher doses, due to its ability to dilate blood vessels, increasing blood circulation.
- Vitamin B3 deficiency leads to indigestion and poor appetite, skin sores, high cholesterol, mental imbalance and pellagra (dementia, diarrhoea, dermatitis and eventually death).
- Tongue diagnosis   A white-coated tongue with a very deep crack or fissure down the centre can indicate a vitamin B3 deficiency.
- Sources include meat (red, white, fish and poultry), brewer's yeast, peanuts and dairy products.
- Dose   Adult RDI 10mg. Doses above 2g of the niacin form may cause liver toxicity.

Vitamin B5 (pantothenic acid) assists in the metabolism of carbohydrates, proteins and fats. It also helps with cholesterol, hormone and red blood cell production. Vitamin B5 helps the body's ability to withstand stress.
- Vitamin B5 deficiency can lead to adrenal exhaustion, blood sugar imbalances, burning feet, muscle cramps and infections.
- Sources include organ meats, brewer's yeast, egg yolks and whole grain cereals.
- Dose   No RDI has been established. However, a minimum of 10mg–15mg daily has been suggested and is promoted in most vitamin B complex supplements.

Vitamin B6 (pyridoxine) is necessary for a healthy nervous system, helps convert omega 6 EFAs for beneficial effects, converts protein into serotonin and, finally, is essential for energy metabolism.

- Vitamin B6 deficiency can cause a sore mouth, sore tongue, PMS, insomnia, increased carbohydrate cravings, poor hair, skin and nail condition, weakness and irritability. A severe B6 deficiency can lead to a low red blood cell count, and numbness and tingling in the hands, legs and feet. Some patients may even experience seizures.
- Sources include eggs, brewer's yeast, avocados, bananas, soybeans, whole grains and walnuts.
- Dose   Adult RDI 2mg.

Vitamin B12 (cyanocobalamin) helps maintain healthy nerve tissue, red blood cells and is also needed to make genetic cell material. Found in protein, vitamin B12 needs to bind to a substance called intrinsic factor (IF), made by the stomach lining (mucosa), before it is absorbed into the bloodstream.
- Vitamin B12 deficiency leads to pernicious anaemia, which can cause speech difficulties, weakness or difficulty in walking, mental deterioration and other nerve disorders. Vegans may suffer from this type of anaemia if they do not take a B12 supplement. They can eventually become deficient (after two to five years) as stores of B12 are depleted.
- Sources include meats, especially organ meats, dairy products and eggs.
- Dose   Adult RDI 2.0mcg.

Folic Acid (folate) is necessary for the production and maintenance of new cells. It makes normal red blood cells, thereby preventing folic acid anaemia, and is needed to maintain proper brain, cardiovascular, immune and nervous system function and protein digestion.
- Folic acid deficiency leads to folic acid anaemia that cannot be corrected by taking the mineral iron or by vitamin B12 supplementation. Oral contraceptive intake can lead to folic acid deficiencies. Lack of folate during pregnancy increases the risk of spinal deformities. Other deficiency symptoms include diarrhoea, loss of appetite and weight loss. Additional signs are weakness, sore tongue, headaches, heart palpitations, irritability and behavioural disorders.
- Tongue diagnosis   Inflammation and soreness may indicate a folic acid deficiency.
- Sources include green leafy vegetables including spinach, liver, brewer's yeast, beans and peas, fortified cereals and grain products, and some fruits and vegetables.
- Dose   Adult RDI 200mcg–300mcg.

Other B complex vitamins include biotin and choline, inositol and para-aminobenzoic acid (PABA), B13 (orotic acid), B15 (pangamic acid) and B17 (amygdalin, or laetrile).

Vitamin C aids the formation of collagen, which is necessary for the repair and healing of wounds, strengthens the gums and teeth, and lubricates the joints. It is important for bone, blood vessel and tissue formation. It helps iron utilisation and aids the immune system during stress and infections. It also acts as an antioxidant against toxins.
- Vitamin C deficiency can show as a tendency to bruise, slow ability to heal, broken capillaries, stress, poor immunity, heart attacks, strokes and blot clots. There is an increased need for vitamin C while smoking and drinking alcohol.
- Mouth Diagnosis   Bleeding gums and weakened tooth enamel may indicate a vitamin C deficiency.
- Sources include kiwifruits, citrus fruits such as oranges, lemons, tangerines and grapefruit, cranberries, blackcurrants, strawberries, cherries, tomatoes, papaya, feijoa, capsicums and green leafy vegetables.
- Dose   Adult RDI 40mg.

Minerals

Minerals are the basic building blocks of the body and play an important role in human living tissue, building bone structures and proteins, muscle contraction, energy production and more. Calcium and phosphorus, for example, are responsible for making strong bones and teeth. Sodium, calcium and potassium are used to conduct electrical impulses along the nerves and are also responsible for transporting substances in and out of the cells. Minerals also play an important role in the blood and body fluids by maintaining the pH balance and normal blood pressure.

There are 22 essential minerals that are needed by the human body. They are divided into two categories: major minerals — magnesium, calcium, chloride, sulphur, sodium, phosphorus and potassium — and trace minerals — boron, chromium, cobalt, copper, fluoride, iodine, iron, manganese, molybdenum, nickel, selenium, silicon, tin, vanadium and zinc. Compared to the major minerals, only small amounts of these minerals are needed for cellular function.

Major minerals

Magnesium helps production of energy, muscle and nerve function, and protein synthesis.
- Magnesium deficiency can result in muscle cramps, muscle spasm and contraction (often seen as shaky hands or an uncontrollable wiggly tongue), depression and heart problems.
- Sources include dairy products, fish, meat, seafood and green leafy vegetables.
- Dose   Adult RDI 320mg.

Calcium is important for strong bones and healthy teeth, muscle and nerve function and even helps with the blood clotting process.
- Calcium deficiency can result in osteoporosis, bone malformation, teeth falling out and severe muscle contraction (tetanus).
- Sources include dairy products, tinned salmon (with bones in), egg shells (soften with vinegar, purée, then add to mayonnaise) and green leafy vegetables.
- Dose   Adult RDI 800mg.

Chloride constitutes approximately 0.15% of human body weight. It is primarily found in cerebrospinal fluid and stomach acid. Chloride is present in small amounts within bone, and aids in the maintenance of osmotic pressure and electrolytic balance.
- Chloride deficiency is characterised by a loss of appetite, lethargy, muscle weakness, and severe hypokalemic metabolic alkalosis. A chloride deficiency is most notably conspicuous in infants fed exclusively on chloride-deficient formulas. A severe deficiency affects muscle function, resulting in difficult respiration and swallowing and, on occasion, death.
- Sources include meat (red, white, seafood and poultry), table salt and dairy products.
- Dose   No RDI has been established.

Sulphur is present in every cell and is known as the beauty mineral as it keeps hair glossy and complexions clear and beautiful. It builds cells, releases energy and helps the liver release bile to digest fat.
- Sulphur deficiency may lead to skin problems and feelings of fatigue.
- Sources include meats, egg yolks, dairy, onions, cabbage and Brussels sprouts.
- Dose   No RDI has been established.

Sodium (salt) is necessary for the regulation of the body's water content and nerve function. Excess sodium has been linked to hypertension.
- Sodium deficiency may lead to fatigue, nausea and cramps. Extreme thirst may be experienced.
- Source is salt, either added to food during processing, cooking or at the table.
- Dose   No RDI has been established.

Phosphorus is an essential component of all cells and is present in bones and teeth.
- Phosphorus deficiency can cause fatigue, loss of appetite and stunted growth.
- Sources include milk, cheese, meat, fish and eggs.

- Dose   Adult RDI 1000mg.

Potassium is important for cell function and is a constituent of body fluids.
- Potassium deficiency can upset blood sugar levels and may lead to mental paranoia and extreme deficiency is linked with heart failure.
- Sources include all foods except sugars, fats and oils. Unprocessed foods have more potassium than processed foods.
- Dose   No RDI has been established.

Trace minerals

The health benefits of some of the more important trace minerals are listed below

Chromium is a component of a natural substance called glucose tolerance factor that helps to regulate the body's use of sugar and is essential for fatty acid metabolism.
- Chromium deficiency can result in elevated blood sugar levels, and possibly induce diabetes-like symptoms and weight gain.
- Sources include brewer's yeast, liver, lean meats, poultry, molasses, whole grains, eggs and cheese.
- Dose   No RDI has been established.

Copper helps to form haemoglobin in the blood and supports blood functions, regulates blood pressure and heart rate. It strengthens blood vessels, bones, tendons and nerves, and may promote fertility and reduce greying of hair, assisting with normal skin and hair pigmentation.
- Copper deficiency, although rare, may result in brittle, discoloured hair, skeletal defects, anaemia, high blood pressure, heart arrythmia and infertility.
- Sources include seafood and organ meats, molasses, nuts, seeds and green vegetables.
- Dose   No RDI has been established.

Fluoride is required for healthy teeth and bones. It helps form the tough enamel that protects teeth from decay and cavities, and increases bone strength and stability.
- Fluoride deficiency can lead to tooth decay.
- Sources include fluoride toothpaste, tap water in most large cities, cheese, meat, tea, seafood and seaweed.
- Dose   No RDI has been established.

Iodine is used as a medical antiseptic, and prevents and treats enlargement of the thyroid gland (goitre). Iodine can protect the thyroid gland from radiation exposure and is part of several thyroid hormones. They have an important role in metabolism, nerve and muscle function, nail, hair, skin and tooth condition, and physical and mental development.
- Iodine deficiency may lead to hypothyroidism, poor immunity, goitre, mental retardation, cretinism (a form of dwarfism in infants), weight gain, hair loss, fatigue and insomnia
- Sources include iodised salt, seafood and seaweed.
- Dose   Adult RDI 150mcg (maximum amount allowable 300mcg).

Iron is a component of haemoglobin, a protein in red blood cells that transports oxygen from the lungs to the various body tissues. Iron helps form myoglobin, a protein that provides extra fuel to muscles during exertion
- Iron deficiency may manifest as a waxy pallor of the face, brittle nails, smooth tongue, mouth corner sores, dysphagia (difficulty swallowing) and pica (an appetite disorder involving the desire to eat non-food substances like dirt, gravel and sand) due to epithelial atrophy. Fatigue, irritability, palpitations, dyspnea (difficulty breathing), angina and tachycardia (fast heart rate) are also related to the progression of the anaemia.
- Sources include red meat, chicken, seafood, liver (pâtés) and other animal products. Dark

green vegetables, whole grains, nuts, dried fruit and other plant foods also supply a form of iron.
- Dose   Adult RDI 12mg.

Manganese is essential for the proper formation and maintenance of bone, cartilage, connective tissue, energy and protein synthesis. It forms part of an important antioxidant enzyme and assists in normal blood clotting.
- Manganese deficiency may lead to diabetes, tendon sensitivity and thickened skin.
- Sources include bananas, oranges and strawberries. Brown rice, nuts, seeds, wheat germ, whole grains, beans and peas are also good sources.
- Dose   No RDI has been established.

Selenium stimulates the metabolism, acts as an antioxidant, supports immune function and protects against degenerative diseases.
- Selenium deficiency may lead to an increased risk of cancer, cardiovascular disease, inflammatory diseases and age-related diseases.
- Sources include whole grains, asparagus, garlic, eggs, mushrooms, lean meat and seafood.
- Dose   No RDI has been established.

Zinc plays a role in immunity, bone development, cellular growth and formation, energy, detoxification, and regulating blood pressure.
- Zinc deficiency may lead to loss of taste, poor hair, skin and nail condition, low immunity and inability to heal, infertility, ADD, white spots on nails, appetite loss, fatigue, diabetes and prostate problems.
- Sources include oysters, seafood, lean meat, eggs, soybeans, peanuts, bran (wheat), seeds, Brewer's yeast and cheese.
- Dose   Adult RDI 12mg.

Antioxidants

If you are exposed to the sunlight, eat processed foods or even exercise, you are being exposed to free radicals. Free radicals are responsible for some diseases as well as aging, and may increase the risk of cancers.

A free radical is a rogue molecule with an unpaired electron. Free radicals cause oxidation, a chemical reaction that involves the loss of an electron from an atom.

During its evolution, the human species developed its own free radical defence system to combat the effects of UV radiation. Various antioxidants and enzymes from the fruit and vegetables we eat form the basis of this defence system, including vitamins E and C, superoxide dismutase (SOD), catalase and glutathione enzymes.

Unfortunately, our natural defence system finds it increasingly difficult to cope with the levels of UV radiation, pollution, chemicals and toxins we are exposed to today. The body needs a greater antioxidant supply than it can receive even from the most 'ideal' diet. That's why everybody needs plenty of antioxidants from fruits and vegetables as well as effective antioxidant supplements to further quench and neutralise free radicals.

The body makes its own antioxidants, which include enzymes such as SOD and glutathione peroxidase. These enzymes can scavenge several thousand free radicals at a time. To make SOD or glutathione, the body's enzyme levels need to be increased by a number of dietary antioxidants. Supporting the body with supplemental vitamins, minerals and plant antioxidants can bolster its own natural antioxidant defence system, therefore reducing free radical damage which leads to age-related diseases.

Antioxidant synergism

A combination is better than a single antioxidant. Although some antioxidants are more important than others, compelling evidence supports the intake of a diverse selection of antioxidants. David Heber, M.D., Ph.D., of the University of California, and others have suggested that humans and other mammals co-evolved in a dietary environment rich in antioxidants, fostering a genetic dependence on a diverse dietary supply of antioxidant vitamins, minerals and phytonutrients. Al L. Tappel, Ph.D., of the University of California, compared the free radical quenching ability of one antioxidant with that of many. These studies suggest that a broad-spectrum range of antioxidants (nutrients) will be more effective in neutralising free radicals than a single antioxidant ingredient.

Who should take antioxidants?
Everybody, especially those who fit into any of the following categories: people who exercise intensely, the elderly, those susceptible to infection, those who suffer from psychological stress, people taking medication, people with cancer and degenerative diseases or a history of degenerative diseases, people exposed to chemicals (hairdressers, car painters, floor finishers, etc.), and those living near airports and overhead power lines.

Antioxidants may be beneficial for people who suffer from arthritis (rheumatoid and osteo), collagen and tendon disorders, gum disease, osteoporosis, glaucoma, dry age-related macular degeneration, hepatitis, multiple sclerosis aging, chronic fatigue syndrome, high cholesterol, arteriosclerosis, heart attacks, strokes, chronic immune disorders, Alzheimer's disease and atherosclerosis.

Antioxidant supplementation
For many people, supplements are an important part of an overall health programme, along with eating antioxidant-rich foods and avoiding stresses that generate free radicals. Because free radical damage accumulates with age, people should start supplementing with antioxidants early to achieve long-term benefits. Think of antioxidants as weapons for combating free radicals. We may be able to live longer and healthier lives.

Phytoantioxidants are antioxidants that come from plants (phyto means plant). There is a lot of research available on plant antioxidants and how truly effective they are against free radicals. Some of the stronger phytoantioxidants are referred to as oligomeric proanthocyanidins (OPCs). The OPC compounds have been isolated and found to exist in far higher concentrations within certain fruits and plant extracts.

Helping to counteract free radicals
There are many positive steps that we can take to help to fight damaging free radicals. Nutrition plays a large role in protecting against chronic and age-related diseases, and in improving health. A healthy diet includes plenty of vegetables and fruit (organic where possible) that are rich in beta carotene and flavonoids, and foods rich in protein, selenium, zinc and vitamin C. Good dietary sources that may increase antioxidants within the body are listed below.

Dietary sources of antioxidants
Vitamin C is found in high quantities in kiwifruits and citrus fruits, such as oranges, lemons, tangerines, grapefruit, etc. Other foods such as cranberries, blackcurrants, strawberries, cherries, tomatoes, papaya, capsicums and green leafy vegetables are also good sources.

Carotenoids are potent phytochemicals found in abundance in yellow, orange, red and green fruits and vegetables. Beta carotene and related carotene foods include spirulina, carrots, squash, yams, sweet potatoes, apricots and raw carrot juice. Alpha carotene and lutein are found in green leafy vegetables and lycopene is found in tomatoes.

Cruciferous vegetables such as cabbage, broccoli, Brussels sprouts and cauliflower have antioxidant capabilities because of their high vitamin C and flavonoid content. They also contain plant chemicals called indoles and isocyanates that help liver cells detoxify chemical carcinogens. Indeed, some studies consistently show that eating cruciferous vegetables protects against several forms of cancer, including colon, prostate and breast cancer.[2,3]

The onion family (garlic, onions, shallots, spring onions and leeks) contain flavonoids, vitamin C, selenium and sulphur-containing substances. In experimental models, garlic extracts protect against free radical damage and inhibit low-density lipoprotein (LDL, or 'bad' cholesterol) oxidation.[4] Observations in Italy and China show an association between a high consumption of garlic and onions and low rates of cancer.[5,6,7]

Selenium is found in garlic, onions, shallots, leeks, asparagus, seafoods and fish, meats, brewer's yeast, wheat germ and bran, whole grains and sesame seeds.

Zinc is found in pumpkin and sunflower seeds, oysters and meats, including seafood.

Manganese is found in whole grains, green leafy vegetables, legumes, nuts, pineapples and egg yolks.

Methionine and **cysteine** are found in beans, fish, liver, eggs, brewer's yeast and nuts. As we age we become deficient in sulphur-containing amino acids. Studies have suggested that supplementation with cysteine may promote longevity in humans.[8] These amino acids also help to make antioxidant enzymes. Dietary methionine and cysteine levels are a major ingredient in the free radical scavenging enzyme glutathione peroxidase. When increased levels of toxic compounds or free radicals are present in the body, the body needs higher levels of cysteine and methionine. One study shows that cysteine acts as a radio-protective agent on X-ray induced damage.[9] Cysteine can also help protect the body from harmful metals as well as destructive free radicals that are formed by smoking and drinking alcohol.

Flavonoid fruits and **vegetables** contain plant pigments (red, blue, violet, yellow). Grapes, berries (especially red coloured), blueberries (also known as bilberry, providing antioxidant anthocyanidins), plums, strawberries, corn, tomatoes and capsicums are rich in flavonoids.

Antioxidant condiments and **herbs** include garlic, turmeric, onions, ginger and rosemary.

Plant sources of antioxidants

Ginkgo biloba leaf For thousands of years, the Chinese have known the virtues of ginkgo. Modern research focuses on using ginkgo tree leaf extracts to improve brain function. Ginkgo also contains quercetin, ginkgo flavone glycosides and terpene lactones that prevent oxidative damage to LDL cholesterol, blood vessels and damage to cell membranes. It helps maintain blood circulation to the peripheral areas of the body, such as legs, hands and feet.

Green tea is a favourite drink in Asia, and has powerful tannins called catechins, which act as antioxidants. A lot of green tea would need to be drunk throughout the day to receive its benefits, however, and it is now easier to find green tea in concentrated supplement form.

Grape seed contains bioflavonoids and powerful antioxidants that protect cells and blood vessels from damage. The bioflavonoids reduce capillary fragility, increase the integrity of the venous wall and increase muscular tone of veins.

Bilberry is also known as blueberry, or *Vaccinium myrtillus*. Bilberry extracts (25% anthocyanidin content) are widely used for opthalmological applications, including poor day and night vision, glaucoma, diabetic retinopathy and macular degeneration. The anthocyanosides of *Vaccinium myrtillus* have a very strong affinity for the pigmented epithelium of the retina, which composes the optical or functional portion of the retina. They reinforce the collagen structures of the retina and prevent free radical damage.

Pine bark extract has been marketed under the name pycnogenol. Pycnogenol was discovered in the 1950s and contains well-known OPCs or flavonoid antioxidants, as do ProenOthera®, grape seed and green tea.

Kelp is a seaweed containing a rich store of minerals, particularly iodine, which is used by the thyroid gland. Iodine is used to make the hormone thyroxine, which is responsible for basal metabolic rate, carbohydrate, lipid and protein metabolism and other functions of the body. Iodine can be protective against radiation.

Chlorella, Spirulina and **Chlorophyll** are powerful antioxidants and free radical quenching agents. They have been shown to reduce radiation-induced DNA damage within cells.

Other plant antioxidants include turmeric, St Mary's thistle, rosemary, red ginseng, hawthorn berries, soy, dong quai and slippery elm. There are many more discovered and undiscovered plant flavonoids — in fact some cultures have antioxidant formulas that have been around for centuries.

Other antioxidants

Antioxidant enzymes The body makes SOD, glutathione peroxidase and catalase by using precursor ingredients such as vitamins, minerals and sulphur containing amino acids taken from the food we eat. Studies show people taking a tablet containing SOD do not appear to have increased levels of SOD in their blood or tissues.[10] As yet, we cannot supplement these enzymes, but we can make sure we eat plenty of these precursor foods and nutrients, including protein and selenium.

Co-enzyme Q10, like other antioxidants, can engulf free radicals and prevent cellular damage. The antioxidant activity is noteworthy because it enhances the regeneration of vitamin E and therefore acts as a complementary antioxidant to help trap free radicals alongside vitamin E.

Beta 1.3 glucan is an extract derived from the cell walls of yeast. Besides having superior antioxidant effects with free radical scavenging activity, this food derivative has radio-protective effects. Beta 1.3 glucan binds on to macrophage receptors, stimulating the macrophage into action. Beta 1.3 glucan supports our natural defence against infection and, although it is derived from yeast, the proteins have been removed to avoid yeast-allergic reactions.

Free radical sources

External sources of free radicals include:

Tobacco smoking (including herbal cigarettes and recreational drug smoking). This may be one of the most damaging sources of free radicals to load the body. The detrimental effects of smoking are actually related to an extremely high number of free radicals being inhaled (this includes passive smoking).

Radiation, such as UV radiation from the sun, tanning and sun-beds. Wear appropriate sun block and sunglasses when spending extended periods of time under the sun, as this may help to reduce cataracts, skin damage, wrinkles and skin cancers. Other radiation sources include microwaves, televisions, VDU computer screens, X-rays, radiation therapy and mobile phones. In fact, recent news sources suggest mobile phones may be a particularly high-risk source, the full implications and dangers of which are yet to be fully understood.

Air pollutants, such as smog, vehicle exhaust fumes, acid rain, industry pollutants and 'burn off'.

Water pollutants. These may be caused by lead or copper pipes. Water may have too much chlorine or fluoride added and other potential toxins may make it less than desirable.

Non-organic pesticides, such as garden sprays, local and council spraying, fruit and vegetable sprays, chemical lawn sprays, garden insect sprays, weed killers and fungal sprays.

Medical sources including anesthetics, some drugs and medication, radiotherapy and chemotherapy.

Aromatic hydrocarbons, such as air fresheners, oven cleaning sprays and aerosols.

Petroleum-based products, such as lip glosses, some lipsticks, topical petroleum jellies, some skincare baby products and industrial greases.

General products, such as perfumes, make-up, hair and skin products (chemicals and parabens).

Solvents, such as formaldehyde, toluene and benzene are well-known ingredients of cleaning products.

Dietary sources of free radicals include:

Dietary carcinogens, caused by burnt, grilled, fried, smoked, barbecued and cured foods.

Beverages, such as alcohol, coffee, carbonated soft drinks, drinks with artificial flavours and sweeteners.

Oxidised fats (fats which have been exposed to oxygen or heat processes), such as aged cheeses and some dairy products, some oils (oxidised rancidity), cured and smoked foods.

Trans fatty acids like margarine, shortenings and convenience foods.

Added chemicals in food, such as colouring, preservatives, emulsifiers, antibiotics, nitrates, food enhancers, some sweeteners and any sort of synthetic additive.

Heavy metals, such as aluminium pots, foil and utensils, and deodorants and other products with aluminium in them. Aluminium is often used as an additive to make food flow better during processing (free-flowing agent). Copper or lead piping for drinking water and mercury fillings in teeth are other sources.

Internal sources of free radicals include:

Heavy labouring and **exercising**. If you exercise, whether you are a casual gym member or a serious athlete, you need to supplement with antioxidants. Increased exercise places a heavy free radical load on the body.

General recommendations

Obviously some of these free radical sources are very difficult to avoid. To help reduce free radicals within the body, and therefore slow down the physical effects of aging, follow the lifestyle, dietary and supplement recommendations. The body's natural defence force of free radical quenchers needs to be fortified with positive dietary steps, involving both food and supplements.

4 Healthy Daily Nutrition

These are basic recommendations to improve your health by using nutrition as a tool. If you don't currently employ any of the recommendations below, start off by trying one nutrition principle, and then increasing it to two. Pretty soon you should be feeling an increased sense of well-being, lose excess weight and have a lot more energy.

Basic naturopathic nutrition principles
Body weight
Maintain an ideal body weight and don't skip meals. Eat three small meals and two to three snack-sized meals daily to assist metabolism, digestion and blood sugar levels. Oscillating blood sugar levels will make you tired, and crave fats, salt or carbohydrate foods.

Fat
Reduce saturated fat and trans fatty acid intake. This means eating less fried foods, lard, heated oils and fats, solid fats (animal and coconut) and margarine. Substitute these with polyunsaturated (plant oils), monounsaturated (olive oil) and essential fatty acids (EFA). EFA are more beneficial and are sourced from fish oil, flaxseed oil, evening primrose oil, hemp oil and borage oil. You can add these to your diet, as they are easy to come by in supplement form. My favourite is flax oil because it contains omega 3, 6 and 9. Simply take 1–2 tablespoons per day. Flax oil connoisseurs can take it directly from a tablespoon or for those who enjoy scrumptious salads, replace the olive oil with flax oil and mix with lime, garlic, lemon juice or balsamic vinegar for a decadent salad dressing. Besides these tasty dressings, flax oil can be mixed into smoothies, mayonnaise, butter and yoghurt or drizzled over vegetables, toast and baked potatoes. Never heat or fry flax oil, as it will spoil due to its fragility. Once opened, keep it refrigerated for up to three months.

Sugar and carbohydrate intake
Decrease refined carbohydrate intake. These are foods such as sugar, pastries, cakes, biscuits and refined flour products, which give you a sense of fullness and provide calories but contain very little nutritional value (empty calories), vitamins, minerals or fibre. High sugar and saturated fat intake is linked to Alzheimer's disease, obesity, heart problems, diabetes and rheumatoid arthritis. Substitute with adequate, but not excessive, amounts of whole grains and unprocessed forms of carbohydrates from vegetables, corn, potatoes, kumara (sweet potatoes), pumpkin, tomatoes, carrots and rice (basmati, wild, brown, short and long grain white). Eat whole foods that are prepared from scratch rather than heavily refined and processed foods. Try nourishing foods including hot meals, stews, casseroles, vegetables and fruit (cooked or raw). Eat canned, unsweetened fruit in moderation and dried fruits sparingly.

Fibre
Modern Western diets contain much less fibre than is desirable. Increase your intake of fruit, vegetables, legumes and whole grains to assist general health, including bowel complaints. High fibre diets also reduce the risk of cancer.

Indole-3-carbinol and sulphoraphane
These are found in plants including broccoli, cauliflower, cabbage, Brussels sprouts and kale.

Indoles activate detoxification enzymes in the liver, bind to chemical carcinogens, rendering them inactive, and improve oestrogen balance, reducing the risk of breast and prostate cancer.

Protein

Consume adequate amounts of lean protein, either from meat or vegetarian sources, regularly at meals. Avoid eating an excessive amount of animal protein by combining it with vegetarian proteins — this can make meals interesting and provide fibre. Mix lean meats with grains (rice, chickpeas, couscous) or beans to reduce meat intake. For example, add refried beans to mincemeat for a Mexican dish or chickpeas to a tuna casserole, and dhal (legumes) to a chicken meal, for tasty dishes. If you're iron deficient, add liver to the diet or an iron supplement. Eat fish at least 3–4 times weekly including salmon, tuna and sardines as they are also rich in omega 3 oils.

Dairy

Dairy products should be eaten in moderation and not at all if you are sensitive to them. Eating certified organic, natural sugar-free acidophilus yoghurt daily (avoid if allergic) can help the natural gut flora convert plant oestrogens into usable oestrogen and progesterone in your body, and to balance hormones. Some people are dairy-sensitive or lactose-intolerant. A dairy-free diet contains no milk, cheese, butter, cream cheese, cottage cheese, sour cream, ice cream, chocolate or whey. If you eliminate all dairy products, ensure you have an adequate amount of calcium from supplements or calcium-fortified foods. To see if dairy suits your chemical make-up, read the section on food allergies and sensitivities or see a naturopath for testing.

Digestion enhancers

Enjoy a bitter aperitif, such as vermouth or soda, lime and bitters, before dinner to encourage digestive juices. Alternatively take 50ml of aloe vera juice before every meal to increase absorption and digestion of nutrients from food. Most people over the age of 55 have reduced stomach acid, which affects the proper digestion of tablets, certain foods and minerals (e.g. calcium).

Fluids

Depending on how active you are, your underlying health conditions and your rate of perspiration, it's recommended that you drink one to two litres of water, herbal teas and diluted vegetable or fruit juices daily. The water can be filtered, purified, distilled or can be derived from fresh water collection or springs. Medical and herbal diuretics or common beverages including alcohol, tea (black leaf tea) and coffee stimulate the excretion and flow of urine, so they don't count as your one to two litres of fluid intake. Fresh, juicy fruits and vegetables, such as melons and cucumbers, can also increase fluid intake. Drink green juices, such as spirulina, chlorella, barley or wheat grass, or vegetable and fruit juices, such as carrots, apple, silverbeet and beetroot, daily.

Nutrition hints

Eat a variety of foods, especially those that are in season. This helps to reduce the development of food sensitivities and supports your local produce community.

Eat smaller amounts of food to enhance digestion. Eating food too quickly or consuming too much food in one go creates indigestion, gas and sometimes fatigue.

Chew your food thoroughly to help your digestive enzymes properly break down foods and assist your digestive process. Finish each mouthful of food before attempting another.

Eat in a relaxed environment. This aids digestion and assimilation of food nutrients. Imagine you are eating your meal blindfolded. Feel the texture of the food, taste every flavour and savour each mouthful.

Eat more fresh (organic) vegetables and fruit, and unprocessed foods. Pesticides, herbicides and food stabilisers are likely to put more stress on the body. Eat citrus fruits that supply vitamin C and bioflavonoids. Try three pieces of fruit and two to four cups of vegetables daily.

Clean vegetables to remove, neutralise and eradicate bugs and insecticides. Soak vegetables in 1 Tbsp of hydrogen peroxide (3% food grade) and or nine drops of Lugol's iodine per four litres of water for five to ten minutes. Drain and rinse thoroughly, store or use.

Preferred forms of food preparation include eating foods raw, steaming, pressure cooking, flash stir-fry cooking, boiling, grilling or baking. Barbecuing is fine occasionally. Frying and microwaving are my least favourites. Do not use plastic containers or plastic food wrap to heat food in the microwave as plastics contain unwanted, potentially harmful oestrogens that can leach into the food and contribute to oestrogen overload. Use glass or porcelain instead. Avoid cooking with aluminium cookwear or utensils.

Supplements

You should take a high quality, high potency multi vitamin and mineral formula as well as an antioxidant formula or 1 tsp of a super green food, such as spirulina or barley grass every day with juice. One tablespoon of flaxseed oil or 3g of fish oil daily is also recommended.

Indulge a little not a lot!

While it's fine to indulge in your favourite foods now and then, the aim of naturopathy is to find a healthy balance while feeling mentally positive about your lifestyle, nutrition and yourself. Reduce the following foods and beverages.

Caffeine, found in black and green tea, chocolate, cola and coffee, prolongs the action of adrenaline, increases pain and stimulates the action of the heart muscle. I use coffee as a stimulant when I'm tired, but I try not to become addicted to it. If you must have coffee every day, drink a maximum of one to two cups and avoid instant coffee.

Carbonated soft drinks and **alcohol** should be reduced. Alcohol and mixers are usually high in sugar. Alcohol is a substance that many people include in their diets. However, it depletes the body of vitamins B1, B2, B3, B6, folic acid, calcium, magnesium and zinc. It slows down the brain, nervous system, heart, liver, stomach and kidneys. It increases urination, depleting electrolytes, and in the long-term can cause the liver to become fatty, leading to poor liver function, high blood pressure and high cholesterol. It can also lead to diabetes, psychological dependence and alcoholism.

It is recommended that men and women eat a large meal and drink water if they are consuming alcohol and that men drink no more than 3–5 servings and women no more than 2–4 servings over a period of several hours. One serving equals 300ml of beer, 60ml of sherry, martini or port, 30ml of spirits, or 100ml of wine. If you drink alcohol on a regular basis try to have at least three alcohol-free days per week. See the section on alcohol poisoning and adverse effects for further recommendations.

Processed foods should be limited in your diet. Try to prepare meals from whole foods, starting from scratch. Processed foods include processed meats, cheese, prepackaged sauces, soups and flavour mixes, and artificial components that have been added to foods.

Food sensitivities and allergies seem to play a major role in fatigue, poor digestion, pain and inflammation. One theory suggests that partially undigested proteins are absorbed into the system, creating an allergic response, which may lead to an autoimmune reaction. Identify your food sensitivities and then avoid them. These days there are plenty of food or beverage substitutes to keep your meal tasty and delicious. See the section on food allergies and sensitivities for further recommendations.

Pesticides, monosodium glutamate (MSG), food colouring, preservatives and additives prolong a food's shelf life, improve colour, enhance flavour, change food texture and appearance and facilitate food processing. We are ingesting an increasing amount of these artificial substances, which may cause chemical interactions within the body resulting in inflammation, allergies and toxicity.

Avoid artificial sweeteners including saccharin, cyclamate, aspartame and acesulfame K. Substitute with natural sugars, although use these sparingly. Natural sugar sources include sucrose, glucose, fructose, dextrose, lactose, sugar (brown, cane, white, icing and castor sugar), honey, malt, dried fruit and maple syrup. Stevia is a natural leaf extract that imparts a sweet taste without the calories that sugar contains, and is appropriate for diabetics.

Naturopathic lifestyle recommendations

Changing your lifestyle to include habits that increase your well-being is just as important as embarking on, and maintaining, a healthy diet. Naturopathy takes a holistic approach to health. Try following the guidelines recommended below. If adding these to your lifestyle all at once seems daunting, try one at a time and note the effects the lifestyle change has on your general well-being.

Stop smoking and avoid recreational drugs

These substances increase toxicity within the body, lower testosterone levels (affecting sperm production), increase the risk of early menopause and lung damage, and rob your body of essential nutrients. Smoking is associated with increased risk of osteoporosis, coronary heart disease and lung cancer. If you choose to use these substances, limit their effects by moderating your intake and increasing antioxidants, wholesome food, vitamins (B and C) and minerals in your diet. Use herbs to help your liver's detoxification processes to avoid liver and cellular damage. Milk thistle and dandelion root are marvellous liver-protecting herbs, and you should consider a gentle herbal detox twice a year.

Prescription medication

Do not take yourself off any prescription medication until you have discussed the consequences with your doctor. As your health improves you may not need the same drug, or as much of the drug, as you are currently using. A naturopath can work with your doctor to try and reduce these drugs and if possible, with medical supervision and follow-ups, omit the use of prescription drugs if appropriate.

If you are taking antibiotics for a bacterial infection, finish the course. If you don't finish it you may develop bacteria that is resistant to antibiotics. These super bugs are dangerous and can cause a major bacterial infection that doesn't respond to treatment, which can be life-threatening. After finishing a course of antibiotics, take acidophilus yoghurt and supplements to help repopulate beneficial bacteria in the bowel.

Get plenty of high quality sleep

Sleep helps regenerate your body and refresh your energy levels. Most people need five to eight hours of quality sleep each night. See the section on insomnia for further recommendations.

Dry skin brush

Before you shower or bathe rub a dry flannel, soft brush or loofah over your body in a circular motion to help remove dead surface skin, sweat and toxins. Then hop into the bath or a shower to rinse. This will also improve circulation, energy and your sense of well-being. Do this three to seven times a week.

Exercise

Exercise strengthens the supporting structures (muscles, tendons, ligaments), increases the range of motion, shock absorption and flexibility of joints, and also prevents muscle wasting. While exercise produces free radicals, light, regular exercise provides long-term health benefits for the mind and body. To maintain strong muscles mix aerobic exercise with muscle strengthening exercises like weight training. Stretching helps to maintain and increase flexibility.

Cardiovascular exercise increases the heart rate and improves circulation, cardiovascular and respiratory function. A minimum of 15–20 minutes of exercise at your training heart rate (consult a health professional) at least three times a week is necessary to gain any significant benefit from exercise.

Resistance exercise helps increase bone strength and density. Training with light weights helps keep muscles toned and the body taut and trim. Train two to three times a week on average.

Stretching and **yoga** helps to maintain and increase flexibility. It is also a peaceful time for body and mind. Train two to three times a week on average. A healthy posture will aid your joints, breathing and organ function.

Mental strengthening and protection

Cognition, memory and comprehension are all-important functions of the brain. Aging can reduce these abilities and may even progress to Alzheimer's disease and senility. Exercise can be related to mental fitness. Researchers performed a study showing that older people who exercise regularly performed better on cognitive tests than those who didn't.[11] This may be due to better circulation, as exercise increases blood flow to the brain. Other beneficial factors may include brain exercises, such as memory tests or crossword puzzles, and taking Ginkgo biloba, a specific herb that research has proved can increase brain cognition and memory. The most recent research concludes that elderly people who have higher levels of antioxidants in their blood have better memories than those who do not.[12]

Relaxation and de-stressing techniques

Taking time out for a relaxing holiday is an ideal way to reduce stress. As the body relaxes, muscles may release their tension, increasing blood flow and a sense of well-being. Many people use meditation as a conscious form of relaxation for the mind, body and spirit. Meditation may be a regular way for the mind to get a small holiday. The simplest form of relaxation is settling down in a quiet place and just listening to your breathing while relaxing your muscles.

Tub therapy is excellent for relaxation. Mix one handful of Epsom salts in a bathtub of hot water and soak for a maximum of 15 minutes. The magnesium within the Epsom salts will relax tense muscles and help ease the pain of sensitive joints.

Therapeutic massage can help remove toxins from joints and ease muscle tension, increasing blood circulation and mobility. See a professional massage therapist for the best results. For home therapy try reflexology. Firmly massage the soles of your feet for two to five minutes every day or roll your foot over an old broomstick handle, concentrating on tender areas. Reflexology is an ancient Chinese therapy that helps to heal the body. This simple technique has improved many people's health. Do not rule out other body therapies. These include deep massage (at least six sessions), Rolfing, the Bowen technique, osteopathic techniques and daily stretching exercises.

5 Herbal Medicine

Until the advent of prescription drugs, herbal medicine was the most popular form of treatment worldwide. Herbal or botanical medicine has been used by many cultures for many centuries. Like most consumables, herbal medicine gained its reputation for healing through observation and trial and error. Even animals use forms of herbal therapy to treat digestive illnesses.

Some herbal mixtures are still prepared in exactly the same way as they were hundreds of years ago. Asian herbalists prepare formulas that contain a combination of herbs to remedy the cause of the illness and balance other body organs or systems that may not even seem related to the illness presented. This is because herbalists and naturopaths treat the body as a whole system, not individual organs. Traditionally the herbs are measured, weighed, combined and put into a paper parcel. The patient then takes the dry herbs home and infuses them with hot water by steeping for 20 minutes, or boils the herbs if the active constituent comes from the bark or dried berry of a plant. After preparation, the herbal mixture is then sweetened and drunk as prescribed.

Many parts of plants are used: flowers, leaves, roots, bark, rhizome, fruits, inner bark and seeds all contain the active constituents that herbalists and naturopaths use to restore balance to the body and treat some health conditions.

Information on herbs has been methodically collected and developed over the centuries and fills thousands of pages in herbal pharmacopoeias. Many drugs commonly used today are of herbal origin, containing either plant extracts or chemicals synthesised to replicate a plant's active principle. The foxglove plant, for example, is used to make the cardiac stimulant digitalis, and keeps millions of heart patients alive worldwide.

The interest of conventional medicine in the herb St John's Wort has increased because of the positive testimonials from individuals who have been using it for mild depression. Doctors in many European countries prescribe it because it is effective and does not have the nasty side effects associated with antidepressants.

When I studied Jamu (Indonesian medicine), I learned a very large part of the population took herbs every day. Some would visit the herbal cafés, choose the desired herbal remedy of the day from a menu and drink it at the café counter while chatting to friends. Others would wait until the herbalists — with big baskets on their backs — came to their workplace or home before pouring freshly prepared herbal remedies into a glass.

If you visit a naturopath you are more likely to take home a combined herbal formula that is made from herbal fluid extracts or tinctures. A 100ml–200ml bottle may contain two to nine herbs that have been extracted by alcohol. The general recommendation will be to take 5ml of this mixture three to four times daily.

The modern use of herbs differs from traditional methods, with herbal extracts available in capsules or tablets bought over the shop counter and/or prescribed by a naturopath.

Usual forms of herbal medicine

Herbs can be prepared or used in a variety of ways. It is important to use the correct amount of the herb prescribed and the right part of the plant. For example, dandelion has several uses according to the different parts of the herb: the leaves can be used to provide potassium and increase urine flow as a diuretic, the flowers can be used in salads to aid digestion and the dried root is used to help liver function.

Herbal tinctures

The dried or fresh parts of plants are steeped in alcohol (usually ethyl or vodka) to extract the herbs' active constituents at a higher concentration than can be achieved by infusion (tea) or decoction in water. Tincturing will extract and preserve both the water-soluble and alcohol-soluble properties of a herb. Alcohol is an ideal medium for extracting fats, resins, waxes and most alkaloids from herbs.

Fluid extracts

Fluid extracts are used both to concentrate and preserve the active ingredients of a herb. A water-based herbal extract is often used, as water is a good medium to extract gums, mucilage, saponins and tannins. An equal amount of vegetable glycerine is added to a decoction or infusion of herbs to preserve and sweeten the mixture. Fluid extracts are considered by many herbalists to be the preferred way to preserve water-soluble active ingredients. When properly made, one fluid ounce of extract equals one ounce of fresh herb (1:1).

Decoctions

Roots, barks and fruits are thicker and need to be boiled rather than infused to release their active properties. The material is cut or broken into small pieces, covered and boiled. After cooling and straining the liquid from the boiled twigs, fruits or roots (the decocted liquid) can be taken hot or cold.

Water infusions

You've probably had a herbal tea infusion if you have drunk peppermint or chamomile tea. The tea is made by pouring boiling water over a herb and allowing it to steep for 15–20 minutes, covered, with no additional heat source. Infusions generally have a short shelf life of two to three days if kept in the refrigerator, and are prepared as needed.

Oil infusions

Pure vegetable oils like sunflower, almond and olive oil dissolve the active, fat-soluble principles of medicinal plants and herbs, like garlic or chilli. This process is called infusion and is carried out at room temperature or higher. Infusion is a slower process than alcohol extraction but has the advantage of resulting in an oil-based solution of medicinal constituents that can easily be used to make creams and ointments. Hot infusion is recommended for the harder parts of the plants, while cold infusion is more suitable for flowers and leaves.

Dry herbs

Drying herbs makes them more concentrated It also makes them last longer. Dried herbs and powders are added to teas, capsules and tablets. Sometimes the herbs are extracted and concentrated to get the benefit of a strong dose without having to use a large amount of the herb. For example, you may get 10g worth of grape seed in a 1g capsule, but it has been concentrated ten times so it can fit inside the capsule.

Standardised extract

A standardised extract is a recognised and accepted herbal constituent that has been isolated from the herb and is concentrated to an amount not naturally found in the plant. Sometimes it is the method of preparation that guarantees the amount of active constituent.

Syrup simplex

Often used for children or as cough mixtures, syrups have the added benefit of being soothing to locally inflamed areas like sore throats. One part water and one part dissolved sugar or honey is normally used for cough mixtures or to sweeten children's herbal formulas, making them taste more appealing.

Herbal vinegars
Apple cider vinegar (preferably organic) can also be used as a herbal carrier. Look for vinegar with 5.7% acetic acid (or thereabouts) for a long shelf life. It is also a digestive tonic and can be used to season food.

Poultices and compresses
Herbs that have been crushed, mixed into a mulch, chilled or gently heated to release their active properties can form a poultice or compress. These are applied onto the site of the injury, rash, boil, etc.

Salve
A salve contains the herb, an oil (e.g. almond), beeswax and a preservative (e.g. benzoin). Salves reduce moisture evaporation from the skin and are soothing to cuts, scrapes and rashes.

Creams and ointments
Herbal infusions, oils or tinctures are added to petroleum jelly, soft paraffin wax, beeswax or aqueous cream to form an oily barrier on the surface of injuries and carry the active principles to the affected area.

Essential oils
Essential oils are the volatile, oily components of aromatic plants, trees and grasses. They are located in the flowers (e.g. neroli), leaves (e.g. eucalyptus), roots (e.g. calamus), wood (e.g. sandal) and resins (e.g. frankincense). Essential oils are extracted by three main methods: steam distillation, expression and solvent extraction.

Dosages
The dosages given in this book are adult doses unless otherwise specified. To calculate dosages for other ages see below. It is recommended you consult a health professional for guidelines before giving herbs and supplements to children.

Examples of proportional herbal doses

Age	Amount (g)	Amount (ml)	% of adult dose
Adults (70 years +)	0.5g	0.5ml	50%
Adults (12–70 years)	1.0g	1.0ml	100%
10–12 years	0.5g	0.5ml	50%
8–10 years	0.4g	0.4ml	40%
4–8 years	0.25g	0.25ml	25%
2–4 years	0.125g	0.125ml	12.5%
1–2 years	0.0625g	0.0625ml	6.25%
6 month	0.0220g	0.0220ml	2.2%
3 month	0.0180g	0.0180ml	1.8%
1 month	0.0145g	0.0145ml	1.45%
Newborn	0.0125g	0.0125ml	1.25%

Duration of treatment
It is hard to determine the duration of treatment because it depends on the condition that

you are using the herbs for. It also depends on any other underlying health conditions, your mental and emotional state, rate of healing and compliance, your lifestyle and nutrition.

Combining prescription drugs and herbs

The belief that herbs are natural and not harmful is only partially true. All medicines, herbal and prescription, affect the body. However, in general, herbs are far safer, i.e. they have fewer side effects and are healthier, than prescription medications.

It's important to understand that, just because herb-drug interactions can occur, this doesn't indicate a widespread problem. Most herbs can be taken safely with medical drugs. However, there are some that should not be combined unless under strict medical and naturopathic supervision. It is recommended you see a herbalist or naturopath for further advice if you would like to try herbal therapy and are taking medical drugs. Medical doctors are not trained to understand herbs and may not advocate their use due to lack of knowledge.

St John's Wort (SJW) has come under fire because it has been shown to reduce the level of immunosuppressant drugs and some HIV medications in the blood. This presents a potential danger to users of the drug, i.e. HIV patients and people who have had organ transplants. This has also led to the belief that it should not be taken with any medicine as it would appear SJW speeds up enzymes that metabolise certain drugs in the liver. However, certain drugs, alcohol and food, such as grapefruit juice, broccoli and Brussels sprouts, affect the same enzyme system — should they also be banned? As a precaution, one doctor wouldn't let his patient take a multi vitamin supplement that contained 25mg of SJW. Let me tell you, 25mg of SJW isn't even therapeutic and would not have had an effect on the medication she was taking. Knowledge and understanding is the key to gaining maximum benefit from prescription and herbal medicines.

You will be happy to know that every day I receive phone calls from specialists and doctors who are willing to learn about herbs, and are accepting them. Pharmacists seem to be more willing to find out about herbal therapies than doctors.

See the appendices for herb-drug interactions.

6 Liver Detoxing and Liver Support

It is important to think of your liver as a detoxifying organ. The liver filters the blood, forms bile for fat digestion and metabolises toxins for excretion. If the liver is not functioning properly and assisting removal of toxins, you may feel tired, irritable and, no matter how much sleep you get, you may never feel completely rested. The liver function can be altered by a variety of causes.

Causes
- Viral hepatitis A, B and C
- Glandular fever
- Alcohol
- Toxins, heavy metal, pesticides, food additives, solvents
- Hereditary disorders
- Pregnancy
- Steroidal hormones, oral contraceptives
- Chemicals, smoking and drugs
- Hyperthyroidism, hypothyroidism
- Gallstones
- Excessive production of bowel toxins
- Poor nutrition and a high-fat diet
- Parasites.

Signs and symptoms
- Coated tongue, dark circles under eyes
- Hormonal imbalances, PMT
- Longitudinal ridges in the nails
- Raised liver enzymes
- Raised cholesterol levels and high blood pressure
- Diminished bile flow (cholestasis)
- Fluid retention
- Poor digestion
- Floating pale stools
- Abdominal bloating
- Nausea and jaundice (symptoms increase after eating fatty foods and drinking alcohol)
- Weight gain
- Constipation
- Depression, emotional swings, brain fog
- Allergies, eczema, psoriasis, rashes and itchy skin
- Bad breath and body odour
- Headaches and migraines
- Blood sugar fluctuations
- Cancer
- Asthma
- Inflammatory conditions
- Liver spots and more than seven clusters of spider veins — a cluster may have several spider veins in one grouping.

How to cleanse your liver

Once you get into the swing of it, cleansing your liver through dietary and lifestyle changes isn't as hard as you might think. Just follow the recommended guidelines below for two to three months and you may expect to lose excess weight, have bright white eyes, more energy, fewer allergic reactions and gorgeous, clear skin. It's your chance to let out the goddess or god in you!

Lifestyle hints

Lifestyle changes may include exercise, quitting smoking (or as my friend says, having a long break) and seeking counselling.

Exercise

Increase your activity to get your heart rate and circulation going. This will help dislodge toxins in your body and move them through your system. Include power-walking daily to help gently detox your body.

Set time aside for activities such as Pilates, meditation, massage, yoga, deep relaxation techniques, bubble baths, listening to music and reading. In today's busy world you have to take time out for yourself. These activities don't generally do a lot for weight loss but are great for your state of mind and sense of well-being, and are important for balance and health.

If you have limited time for training, yoga and Pilates not only cover relaxation but also strength and flexibility.

Fasting

This is optional. If you think it is too hard to attempt, move on to the general nutrition guidelines for supporting liver function.

Fasting is one of the quickest ways to cleanse the body, remove toxins and aid liver function. The three-day Gall Bladder Flush Fast is fairly easy to attempt compared to most fasts because of the constant supply of sugar obtained from drinking apple juice every hour; however, it is not for the faint-hearted. The liver produces bile which the gall bladder stores. At the end of day three, if you have gallstones, they will be excreted. Do not attempt to drive or do any strenuous activity on the third day of the gall bladder diet, as you may experience cramps, pain and dizziness. I know this from personal experience. It is recommended you consult with a health professional or check with your doctor before attempting a fast.

Gall bladder flush fast

Day One: Drink one cup of pure, organic apple juice every hour. Apple juice contains malic acid which may help dissolve stones. At night drink one tablespoon of dissolved Epsom Salts with half a cup of warm water and flavour it with half a cup of apple or orange juice. Epsom salts help to dilate the gall bladder duct by releasing muscle contraction.
Day Two: Follow above instructions.
Day Three: Follow above instructions until the evening. Then whip up one cup of cream and eat the cream with a small bowl of fruit salad. After 15 minutes drink the Epsom salts mixture. The cream will make the gall bladder contract and the Epsom salts makes the duct relax, allowing stones to go through. Immediately go to bed and lie at a 45° angle, or lie on your right side with your knees drawn up either for the first 30 minutes, or until you go to the toilet or go to sleep.

What will happen? As the gall bladder releases the gallstones by contracting in response to the cream, you should excrete stools and gallstones. Some green jelly lumps will be evident and can be mistaken for stones, but that's just the cream and bile mixing together.

Liver Detoxing and Liver Support

Do not resume eating your normal meals until the fourth day. If you have any serious medical conditions that may be affected by this diet, please see a naturopath who may assist you with advice before embarking on the three-day programme. Do not stop taking any prescribed medication.

Nutrition

Follow a liver-supporting, gentle detoxing diet as follows.

'Wake up call' Drink one large glass of hot water and a squeeze of lemon, lime or orange juice when you wake up in the morning. Initially some people may feel nauseous after drinking hot water and lemon juice. This is the action of the liver working and the nausea should stop after three days as your liver function improves.

'Nutrient lift' Supply your body with extra nutrients to help with detoxing the liver and improving energy levels. Drink one glass of fresh vegetable juice (carrot, celery, spinach or fruit juice (cranberry, grape, pear, pineapple), or one teaspoon of spirulina with vegetable or fruit juice, or take a multi vitamin and mineral formula supplement.

Consume carrots, beetroot, alfalfa, barley grass, cabbage, broccoli, Brussels sprouts, capsicums, tomatoes, citrus fruits (except grapefruit), brewer's yeast, brown rice, whole grains, soy flour, buckwheat flour, oats, corn, pumpkin, kumara or sweet potatoes, fresh fruit and vegetables (organic where possible). A small amount of ground nuts and seeds is recommended.

Increase your intake of green leafy vegetables, water-filled fruits, prunes loaded in fibre, and apples. Use the antioxidant properties of berries to protect your body from the cell damage caused by the build-up of free radicals.

Fibre is important for detoxing. Eat plenty of fibre from fruit (e.g. apple pectin), grains (bran, ground flaxseed and oat bran) and vegetables. It is known that a diet high in fibre intake (traditionally from vegetables, grains, gums, etc.) can produce some benefits to general health. These particular fibres work by absorbing water, cholesterol and toxins, and remain undigested as they pass through the body, improving stool transit time and bulk.

Digestion enhancers increase absorption and digestion of nutrients from food. Enjoy a bitter aperitif, such as vermouth or soda, lime and bitters, before dinner to encourage digestive juices. Alternatively take 50ml of aloe vera juice with every meal.

Do not cook in or with aluminium utensils, foils, pots and pans. Aluminium is linked with Alzheimer's disease, although this is not yet proven.

Include ginger in your diet to increase the circulation of nutrients around your body, and tumeric for antioxidants and liver protection.

Eat fish at least three to four times weekly as it's rich in omega 3 oil. Good sources include tuna, sardines and other types of oily deep-sea fish.

Avoid smoking as it constricts blood vessels, reducing blood flow to the brain and increases toxicity within the body.

Consume three meals daily and include two healthy snack meals in between.

Protein contains amino acids that are important to help with the detoxing process. However, too much protein places a strain on the digestive system and kidneys. Eat 2–3 servings (100g–200g) of lean, organic white meat, fish, poultry, seafood or vegetarian protein per day.

Dairy products should be eliminated for one month. Small amounts of butter 2 tsp daily forcooking or spreads) and yoghurt (4 Tbsp daily) for those who are not sensitive to dairy is fine. A variety of goat's, rice or soya milk products are recommended as substitutes. Ensure you get an adequate amount of calcium from supplements or calcium-fortified foods.

Water is essential for excreting toxins. Drink two litres of pure, filtered water throughout the day, every day. As you increase your fibre intake, your water intake must also be increased to avoid dry constipation. Avoid diuretics and antihistamines, and reduce tea, caffeine, coffee and alcohol.

Saturated animal fats should be avoided as they aggravate the liver and gall bladder more than saturated vegetable fats, such as coconut milk. Poly and mono unsaturated fats help fat metabolism and reduce inflammation, so substitute for animal fats with these beneficial fats and oils, e.g. olive oil, avocado oil, flaxseed oil and evening primrose oil. Do not deep-fry any foods. Instead use the flash pan technique. Heat the pan until hot. Add 1 tsp of olive oil or coat with olive oil spray. Add meat or vegetables then a little water to steam-fry your food.

High sugar and refined carbohydrate intake increases cholesterol production and the blood triglyceride levels of the liver, triggered by the pancreas's response to the sugar. Reduce sugar intake to prevent cholesterol metabolism problems involved with gallstones. Avoid eating sugary foods including sweets, desserts, cakes, biscuits and fatty crackers.

Food sensitivities to the following foods can lead to inflammation and immune system reactions. Eliminating eggs, pork, onions, milk, coffee, oranges, corn, beans and nuts has been shown to reduce symptoms dramatically. See the section on food allergies and sensitivities to identify your possible sensitivities.

Eliminate junk food, roasted foods, takeaway meals, fatty fried foods, charcoal-cooked meats and foods, artificial foods, sodas, excessive amounts of sugar, and non-essential medication, drugs and smoking.

Restrict alcohol to four serves per week. Try to avoid coffee and black tea. Drink a maximum of two cups of coffee or three cups of tea daily, if you feel you must.

Supplements

Lecithin helps to keep cholesterol soluble and acts as a fat emulsifier, helping the digestion and breakdown of fats. Take 1000mg–5000mg daily. Or if you are not food sensitive to eggs, eat one to two free range eggs, three to four times per week. If you have high cholesterol, limit this to two egg yolks per week.

Antioxidant formulas that include vitamin E, the amino acid proteins methionine, cysteine and taurine and the mineral manganese are beneficial, as deficiencies in antioxidants (particularly these ones) are thought to contribute to liver disease. Take a broad spectrum antioxidant formula as directed.

Liver nutrients include magnesium (450mg daily), choline (30mg daily) copper (2mg daily), zinc (15mg daily) and vitamin C (1.5g daily). These are the main nutrients needed for liver detoxification.

Calcium supplementation is important for those avoiding dairy products. Take 1500mg daily.

Fibre is important as it helps to chelate (grab onto) toxins for evacuation and reduces toxic reabsorption when the toxins are unloaded into the digestive tract. Fibre supplements from flaxseeds, psyllium, pectin or slippery elm help to bind onto excess dietary cholesterol for excretion. Take 1 tsp–3 tsp of flaxseed fibre, psyllium husk or other fibre products daily.

Herbs

Liver-cleansing and regenerating herbs are important for supporting the liver's enzymatic processes and bile flow.

Dandelion   Take 3g–5g of dried root daily.

Yellow dock   Take 2ml–4ml daily.

Milk thistle   Take a standardised Milk Thistle product (420mg of silymarin content) daily to enhance bile flow and detoxify the liver.

Globe artichoke   Take 1.5g–4g of dried leaf daily to promote the flow and discharge of bile.

Turmeric   Take 2g–3g daily to act as a liver antioxidant.

Other beneficial therapies

Baths, showers, lymphatic massage, reflexology, sports massage and deep tissue massage facilitate the removal of toxins from the skin and muscles. Self-massage before you shower, by gently scrubbing your body all over with a dry flannel. Then have a warm shower. At the end of your shower have a blast of cold water to stimulate your body and the removal of toxins. A handful of Epsom salts (magnesium) or rock sea salt added to your bath for the last 15 minutes can aid removal of toxins and relax fatigued muscles.

Detoxing observations

During the cleansing process you may experience some symptoms of detoxing, such as headaches, hidden skin blemishes like pimples rising to the surface and an increase in bowel movement. If symptoms persist, or if any unusual changes occur, discontinue the detox and seek professional health advice.

If you have problem pimples, you may need to use liver herbs to help clear any blind spots or erupted pimples. The herb burdock is brilliant for this. Otherwise, read the Acne section in Part 3, the A–Z guide of health conditions.

7 Weight Loss

Smart girls and guys don't diet! They know that choosing a healthy, balanced lifestyle is the key to successful weight management. Let's face it, yo-yo dieting and quick-fix pills simply don't work. That's not to say you should live a miserable existence by forgoing a glass of wine, chocolate biscuits or desserts.

If being overweight and having a poor body image is affecting your self-esteem, making you feel unhappy and unhealthy, it's time to take responsibility and regain control over your body. Sure, it would be great if we could all live the lifestyles of the rich and famous. We too could be slim, if we had a daily personal fitness trainer and healthy ready-made meals served six times a day by an in-house chef, but, for most of us, a lifestyle like that is just a dream. However, with the right attitude and a little bit more effort in planning, you can get your body into the shape you want and achieve your goals — and you don't have to be a movie star or go under the knife. Your weight depends on the following important factors.

Your **genetic make-up**, inherited from your parents, is a significant factor in determining the number and size of fat cells you have, your weight and body shape.

Metabolism is the rate at which your body breaks down the nutrients in food to produce energy. Did you know that for long-term successful weight loss, calorie-restricted diets alone don't work? Sooner or later your body's calorie and food requirements will lessen as you lose weight, due to a decrease in your basal metabolic rate (BMR), so exercise is essential to keep your metabolism functioning at its peak.

BMR is the number of calories your body uses to run normal cellular processes. For instance, if you have a slim build your BMR will be lower than if you are a plus-size. It's important to include exercise to increase your BMR.

What and how much you eat or exercise. It has been shown that people who are overweight eat more food than they admit. Even small daily excesses can lead to a large accumulation of fat. If you are not doing enough exercise and your intake of food (or calories) is in excess of your body's daily requirements, your weight will increase.

Low serotonin (the 'happy' brain chemical) levels may have a major influence on eating behaviour. Diets low in protein (amino acids), a source of serotonin, increase the appetite and result in binge eating or a preference for 'comfort' carbohydrate foods.

Nutritional deficiencies in essential fatty acids, chromium, protein, fibre and coenzyme Q10 may lead to an increase in body fat and a decrease in lean toned muscle.

Hormonal imbalance, including steroidal, thyroid, oestrogen and progesterone imbalance and insulin sensitivity may increase weight either by an increase in fat or water retention.

Psychological factors also play a role in weight gain. People generally tend to snack on high sugar, fat or carbohydrate foods while watching television or videos, or if they are bored or upset. Couple this with lack of activity and exercise, and these poor habits can lead to obesity. Eating for emotional comfort increases weight if the underlying issues are not dealt with. Some counsellors believe obesity may be brought on by the need to create a shield of protection from emotional hurt and psychological trauma.

What is a healthy weight range?

The **BMI** (body mass index) can determine if you are within the healthy weight range for your height. To establish this, divide your weight by your height squared (height multiplied by height). For example, 63kg divided by 2.89 (1.7m x 1.7m = 2.89) equates to a BMI of 21.7. A BMI less than 19 indicates that you are underweight, 19–24 is a healthy weight, 25–29 is overweight, 30–34 is obese and 35–39 is classified as being grossly obese.

While the BMI is a good guide, some ethnic groups (e.g. Asians) may be at the lower end of the scale and while others (e.g. Polynesians) may be naturally heavier. As the BMI does not differentiate between muscle and fat, athletes may weigh more than the 'normal' range, but still be healthy due to increased muscle mass.

The 4-step success plan

Get smart! Stop fad dieting and look at your weight management from a new perspective. Successful weight management is all about bringing long-term healthy lifestyle changes and exercise into your daily routine. It doesn't matter whether you want to lose 5kg or 30kg, gain lean muscle or drop body fat — when you start on your nutrition and exercise regime you will feel more positive simply by taking the first steps towards your goals. The 4-Step Success Plan encompasses positive goals to shape your mind and body through mental affirmation, quality exercise, nutritional support and great-tasting nutrition.

Step 1. Gain a head start — Mental commitment and goal setting

A change of diet alone will not help a person lose weight if they do not change their thoughts. Achieve the mental commitment for successful weight management by using these simple techniques.

Visualisation is a very powerful tool that you can use every day to get results. First visualise how you want your body to look. Imagine your body being the healthy shape and size you want it to be. Picture buying clothes that are a smaller size, eating healthy food, feeling energised, confident and wanting to exercise regularly. Use a healthy role model or mentor to act as an inspiration to you and set a reasonable date you would like to achieve your goal by.

Get over excuses and your own personal objections. Ask yourself, 'What are the obstacles I will come across?' For instance, a common excuse is that you don't have enough time in the day. You know you can find the time if you really want to. Deal with these obstacles and make the changes necessary to provide a workable solution.

Start acting now like the healthy slim person you are going to be. Lift your energy and think positively about your appearance and confidence. Fake it to make it. Eventually you will start to feel positive about your whole body image.

Write down your goals. Writing and drawing pictures or talking to a friend may help to activate these goals. This is essential. Look at these questions and write down the answers.

Ask yourself, 'Why do I really want to lose weight?' and give a list of reasons. Lifestyle changes start with taking an honest look at your eating habits and daily routine. To assess your eating behaviours, ask yourself if you tend to eat when you're bored, angry, tired, anxious, depressed or socially pressured. Look at your eating style, shopping and cooking techniques. Were you taught to clean your plate? Do you eat too fast? Do you eat while watching TV? See if any patterns emerge to identify possible triggers for overeating. Are there emotional issues involved? Do you need counselling to help achieve your goals? If so, ask for professional help to deal with these issues.

State how much weight loss or shape change you want to achieve. For example: I will lose 'x' inches off my waist, or I will weigh 'y' kilos by 'z' date. Now, again, visualise yourself having the body you want and act as though you have that body.

Where do you want to be in three, six or nine months? For instance, you might make the goal that you will weigh 70kg by 1 March. The general average weight loss is around 500g to 1kg each week if you are exercising, eating healthy, balanced meals and drinking plenty of water. If you are losing more than this you may not be eating enough calories per day or you may be losing muscle and water along with fat. Losing too much muscle may reduce your metabolism, affecting your long-term body shape.

Ask yourself, are my goals realistic and achievable? If yes, congratulation. Go for it and don't look back. If they're not, reduce your expectations to make them achievable. Don't be afraid to recruit your friends and draw support from others.

Write up a daily meal, exercise and supplement diary chart. This will help you to achieve your weight loss and body-shaping goals by making you accountable to yourself, giving you a sense of commitment and control.

Affirmations are positive sayings and prayers, which can be important for your success. Rather than dwelling on negative thoughts that may sabotage your results, repeat daily affirmations, e.g. 'I am a size 12, I am healthy, energised and fit.' Simple short statements send positive messages to your body and mind, making you feel great. Just try saying, 'I love my body and myself.' Write your own punchy affirmation for your new positive mental attitude and body.

Health professionals can help you with your goals. A personal trainer, naturopath and/or nutritionist will cost $40–$60 per hour. If you can't afford this, invest in an exercise video, or see the health professional once every six to eight weeks. Get your friends or family to buy you a session for a birthday or Christmas present.

Fight procrastination. Prioritise your weight loss goals and daily 'to-do' list. Make a commitment to accomplish your weight-loss goal and then do it! If it's not realistic and still seems overwhelming, reconstruct your goals and to-do list again until they truly are achievable. Use positive affirmations and visualise yourself eating healthy, exercising and being happy. Write down at least one thing that you have achieved today and be thankful or positive about that experience. Pat yourself on the back. Reward yourself with something you really want, like a luxurious facial or new clothes.

Get rid of the guilts. If guilty emotions come occur when you eat chocolate, for example, on a day that you haven't specified as a 'free day' (the one day a week chosen to rest from exercise and the meal plan), or when you can't be bothered exercising, ask yourself, 'How will I benefit from feeling guilty? How would I prefer to feel? What changes do I need to make to feel positive and healthy?' Then do it!

Step 2. Exercise

Exercise can make you feel energised in more ways than one. Whether it's pounding the pavement or swimming amongst the waves, exercise is guaranteed to get your heart pumping, blood flowing through your body, and just think what it can do for your libido! As we exercise, our body uses up energy from calories provided by the food we eat. Exercise is the key to burning stored fat, toning the stomach and thighs and helping to trim the bat wings from the backs of the arms.

Some of the benefits of exercising include healthy weight management, better sleep, an increase in your body's BMR, and an improved mood state because it decreases anxiety and stress. Exercise keeps you fit, strong, lean and toned while decreasing the risk of diabetes and cardiovascular disease. A balanced exercise programme should contain cardiovascular, resistance and relaxation training.

Cardiovascular training

Cardiovascular exercise, so named because of the effect it has on the heart and circulation, includes jogging, running, belly dancing, aerobics and even exercising to specialist fitness videos. Other favourable forms include kickboxing, walking the dog, exercising with friends or playing an individual or team sport. It's important to make cardiovascular exercise an enjoyable experience by finding an exercise that you really enjoy and doing it regularly.

People may associate an exercise with negative thoughts if they are doing it because someone told them to. Richard Leonard BSc (Sports and Exercise Science), my personal fitness trainer, remarks that cardiovascular exercise should be fun. 'Exercise should be something you enjoy and should include lots of variation to avoid repetition.' Remember, even dancing can be a form of exercise. Your body needs a balanced amount of cardiovascular exercise to be a healthy weight. Cardiovascular exercise is all about burning calories. Exercise, along with the weight loss meal plan, will help you to burn accumulated body fat.

HINTS

- Trying to burn more fat? Do your cardiovascular exercise on an empty stomach first thing in the morning. Your body uses up carbohydrate energy stores while you are sleeping, which forces your body to burn more stored fat for energy during morning exercise than at night.
- Keep your intensity high, set goals that challenge your body, and move out of your comfort zone. To make changes in your body shape you will have to do more exercise than normal, so your body doesn't plateau or become immune to its effects.
- Running is free, convenient, burns fat fast and gives your body a long, lean look over time. You can run at your favourite places and even learn more about your neighbourhood, beaches and parks. If you're a beginner, run from one lamp post to the next, then walk briskly to the next lamp post, then run to the next and so on. If you don't relish the thought of running straightaway, start by power-walking (by pumping your legs and arms) to get your heart rate up and break into a sweat.

Resistance exercise

This is all about contracting your muscles against an external load. Resistance can include exercises such as free weights, machines, body weight exercises (press ups and lunges), Swiss ball exercises, Pilates and yoga. Contrary to popular folklore, if you touch a weight you won't bulk up. It takes years of dedicated training to look like a bodybuilder. Nor will your muscles turn to fat when you stop. If you stop training your muscles will actually shrink in size — it's the fat that makes you look fat. When your goal is weight loss, resistance training is a must. It's all about increasing your metabolism. As you increase your lean muscle mass by weight training, your BMR is boosted. Great news! As you increase your lean muscle mass your body burns more calories without having to exercise.

A person with a fast metabolism will utilise calories more quickly, making it easier to stave off excess kilos. The more fat-free mass you have, such as your muscle, bones and organs, the higher your resting metabolic rate will be. In fact, some plus-sized women could have a resting metabolic rate up to 50% higher than that of women who are thin, as their mass is greater. Personal trainer Richard Leonard specialises in weight loss and body toning and often reminds me that weight training is the best way to preserve and build lean muscle, thereby increasing the metabolic rate for weight loss, fitness and strength.

HINTS

- Vary your routines and intensity. This will surprise your body and keep up positive changes by preventing it from finding its comfort zone.
- Don't use momentum when exercising, keep your movements controlled and slow while visualising the muscle group you are working on.
- Imagine your ideal exercise regime and talk it through with a personal trainer or friend. If you can't afford a trainer use the latest library books on exercise recommendations and develop your own programme.

Relaxation

This includes activities such as Pilates, meditation, massage, yoga, deep relaxation techniques, bubble baths, listening to music and reading a book. Although these activities don't generally do a lot for fat loss they are great for your state of mind and a sense of well-being. Taking time out for yourself is important for balance and health.

> **HINT**
> - If you have limited time for training, yoga and Pilates not only cover relaxation but also strength and flexibility.

Exercise programme

It is recommended you seek advice from a medical practitioner and a qualified fitness professional before designing or commencing any exercise regime.

Resistance training 40 minutes 2–3 days per week
Cardiovascular training 20–40 minutes 3 days per week
Relaxation training 60 minutes 1–2 days per week

	Monday	Tuesday	Wednesday	Thursday	Friday	Saturday	Sunday
Resistance	40 mins		40 mins		40 mins		
Cardiovascular		20–40 mins		20–40 mins		20–40 mins	
Relaxation			60 mins				60 mins

Step 3. Nutrition and lifestyle recommendations

The main reason most of us are overweight is because we take in more food or calories per day than we actually need. If you can't eat as much as you used to without putting on weight, it probably has more to do with lack of activity and exercise than a slow metabolism. After the age of 30, the average person's resting metabolic rate decreases 2%–3% every 10 years or so, mainly due to inactivity and muscle loss.

Healthy, balanced nutrition must be undertaken together with adequate, consistent exercise for long-term weight management to be successful. We all know that a healthy, balanced diet should consist of a variety of quality carbohydrates, protein, fats, plenty of fruit, vegetables, nutrients and one to two litres of clean water daily. But the truth is nutrition can often come down to the habitual choices we make on a day-to-day basis.

Adopting a new eating style that promotes a healthy body must include lowering your total calorie intake. Decreasing calories need not mean decreasing taste, satisfaction or even ease of meal preparation. One way you can lower your calorie intake is by eating more plant-based foods — fruits, vegetables and whole grains. Increasing dietary fibre and antioxidants sourced from fruits, grains and vegetables may help to protect against cancer, heart disease and diabetes, and reduces the appetite by giving a sense of fullness.

Strive for a variety of quality foods to help you achieve your goals without compromising taste or nutrition. Cutting back on calories is easier if you focus on limiting saturated fat, but increase your dietary intake of 'good fats' — essential fatty acids (EFA). Omega 3 and 6 EFA from nuts, seeds, plant oils and fish help the body burn fat while building lean muscle.

There are some general guidelines you can follow to gain the bodyshape and health you want. Eat small meals frequently, five to six times a day. This includes three main meals and two to three snack-size meals. Eating this way makes you feel satiated, thus helping avoid food cravings, bad food choices and food binging. It also maintains a steady source of energy through blood sugar balance. Reduce refined white sugar and processed foods and moderate your intake of saturated fat.

If you're not into cooking, or are on the run a lot, it's preferable to choose a protein bar or sushi over a chocolate muffin or a bag of potato chips. The following Nutritional Meal Plan outlines the daily nutritional recommendations, cooking techniques and food choices for your weight management programme.

It's not enough to eat healthy foods and exercise for a limited period of a few weeks or months. You have to incorporate these behaviours into your life. To do that, you have to change the habits that made you overweight in the first place.

Step 4. Nutritional support — The scoop on the key nutrients for weight loss

Nutritional supplements offer support for successful weight loss. Nutritional deficiencies from poor diet can promote weight gain. Corrective supplementation ensures optimum nutrition and can increase metabolic rate and affect appetite. My absolute favourite supplements are the following.

5HTP (5-Hydroxy tryptophan), sourced from the *Griffonia simplicifolia* plant, converts safely in the body into serotonin. Many people may be overweight due to low serotonin levels, as the 'happy' chemical in our brain (serotonin) literally turns off hunger, and decreases cravings for carbohydrates and fatty foods. When we don't have adequate amounts of serotonin we may feel tired, anxious and depressed, and reach for comfort foods high in saturated fat or sugar to make us feel better. One of the most exciting weight management nutrients to be discovered is 5HTP. Research showed that women taking 5HTP daily reported earlier satiety (or a feeling of satisfaction) after their meals than the placebo groups.[13, 14, 15]

Bitter Orange creates thermogenesis (the production of heat by metabolic processes), which helps increase the metabolism and burn stored body fat. Stimulating thermogenesis is one of the keys to increasing fat loss and the effectiveness of diet and exercise regimes. Synephrine is the main compound derived from bitter orange. Researcher Dr. Dennis Jones, of Bariatrix International and patent holder of bitter orange extract Advantra 2, found that taking a concentrated extract of 4%–6% synephrine stimulates beta 3 receptors in the body's muscle and fat cells that help to increase the rate at which fat is released from the body's stores. This leads to an increase in thermogenesis and the resting metabolic rate. Synephrine only stimulates beta 3 receptors responsible for increasing metabolic rate, without stimulating alpha or beta 1 and 2 receptors that change heart rate or blood pressure. This is another advantage Synephrine has over potentially harmful ephedrine stimulants that can affect the heart.

Black Pepper's key component is piperine. Modern science has found that when piperine is used in conjunction with other nutritional supplements, it helps to enhance absorption and bioavailability. In fact, research has shown that a daily dose of 5mg of piperine resulted in a 60% increase in absorption of nutrients.[16] The heating effect of peppers also increases satiety directly after a meal, helping to reduce the appetite after eating.

Caffeine stimulates hormone-induced fat burning by increasing free fatty acid concentrations and adrenaline levels. This results in greater lipolysis (oxidation of fats for energy), which can drain your fat stores over time. Caffeine also heightens mental alertness, which can positively affect your motivation to exercise, decrease your appetite and create the caloric deficit needed to lose body fat. Although caffeine works well, it does have a down side. Some people can experience an increase in blood pressure, anxiety and insomnia if they are sensitive to caffeine or suffering from adrenal exhaustion. Starch carbo blockers, B complex vitamins and adrenal tonics are preferable to caffeine for these individuals.

L-Carnitine is an amino acid that transports dietary fat into the 'furnace' (mitochondria) of each of the body's cells to increase the rate of oxidation of fats, which in turn increases body fat loss by facilitating the utilisation of fatty acids as fuel.

Chitosan is a natural marine fibre extracted from New Zealand squid pen. Nutritionists agree that healthy diets can include a treat now and then, so dieting doesn't become a chore. There's only one problem…it's so easy to slip into old habits and eat more than you planned. Ideally you should get straight back into your new healthy dietary regime. However, if you have the occasional lapse, chitosan may be able to help. Chitosan fibre attracts the dietary fat that has just been eaten, binds to it and stops it from being absorbed into your blood stream to be stored as excess fat. Like normal fibre it can make you regular, but the bonus is that the fat is eliminated and excreted as well.

Chromium is an essential trace mineral that plays an important role in normal carbohydrate metabolism and normal glucose tolerance. Chromium increases the body's sensitivity to insulin. Without chromium, blood sugar levels are increased, thermogenesis is inhibited and the insulin action can become blocked. When blood sugar levels are unbalanced, this may lead to cravings and a preference for carbohydrates and sweets. Chromium deficiencies may lead to obesity and weight gain.

EFA ('good fats') should be included in your diet to help burn stored fat. Sounds too good to be true? The body burns EFA for energy only when an excess of them is present. They speed up the rate at which our bodies burn fat and glucose. They also help with muscle repair by reducing inflammation and helping balance hormone processes. Replace saturated fats with EFA, which also help with satiety and reducing cravings. Excellent sources include fish oil, flax oil, evening primrose oil and borage oil.

Fibre reduces the appetite and gives you a sense of fullness. Choose fruit, grains, grainy brown breads, cereals and fibre supplements to increase your dietary fibre.

Green tea is a natural source of caffeine and antioxidants to help neutralise toxins.

Guarana contains guaranine, a compound that is similar in make-up and action to caffeine. (See caffeine.)

Gymnema is a woody climbing plant found in the tropical forests in central and southern India. When chewed, the gymnema leaves interfere with the sugar taste buds on the tongue and inhibit the ability to taste sweetness. Taken internally, gymnema may have a positive effect on damaged pancreas cells, helping regeneration and therefore helping to balance normal blood sugar levels. In Hindi its name is Gurmar, which means, 'destroyer of sugar'.

Hydroxycitric acid (HCA) is naturally sourced from the rind of the Garcinia cambogia fruit found in India and is used to help block fat production. In therapeutic doses HCA temporarily inhibits an enzyme (ATP citrate lyase) that converts dietary carbohydrates into fat, helps increase energy, decreases cravings for sweets and works on the body's own satiety signal, so you feel a sense of satisfaction and fullness.

Iodine helps to nourish the thyroid gland, which is responsible for metabolic rate. Seaweeds such as kelp are a rich source of iodine. Multi vitamin and mineral formulas supply daily iodine dietary requirements.

Lecithin is a dietary fat emulsifier and works like a detergent to break down fats to aid their digestion.

Liver-cleansing herbs include dandelion root, milk thistle and burdock root. Cleansing the liver helps it produce a better quality of bile to emulsify and break down fat. Excessive toxins within the body may also lead to congestion and water retention. Liver function is disturbed in a large percentage of overweight people, or those who have a slow metabolism.

Protein regenerates lean muscle, which improves the resting metabolic rate, and preserves lean muscle mass, important for staying in shape, toning and looking great. Insufficient amounts of protein trigger hunger. Complete quality protein should be part of a healthy balanced diet, and one way to ensure this is to eat whey. A combination of proteins — whey isolate, whey concentrate and caseinate protein — provides benefits over single whey proteins as it enhances tissue repair, muscle recovery, growth and fat loss. Although whey has superior absorbability and induces muscle repair and growth, it cannot maintain this state of muscle growth. Casein tends to coagulate before it is digested, providing the body with slow amino acid release, consequently helping to maintain muscle growth, which tones and strengthens muscles and eventually increases the metabolic rate. Combining these proteins provides a high quality, time-released protein for sustainable muscle repair and growth.

Starch blockers, from White Kidney Bean extract (*Phaseolus vulgaris*), block dietary starch absorption preventing starch calories turning into fat. The natural protein compound from the white kidney bean is called phaseolamine. It temporarily blocks the digestive enzyme (alpha amylase) that breaks down starch, so starches pass through the body without releasing calories. If a diet is one quarter starch from bread, rice, pastas and starchy vegetables, studies show that up to 25%–30% of this caloric intake can be neutralised.

White willow contains the active constituent salicin, similar to the chemical make-up of aspirin. Effective ECA fat-burning stacks (a combination of ephedrine or ma huang, aspirin and caffeine) were used to decrease appetite and increase energy and metabolic rate to burn fat, but recent discoveries reported that ephedra has detrimental effects on health and the heart. Natural combinations of bitter orange, white willow and guarana or caffeine are now replacing the ECA stacks because they have a similar effect but are ephedrine-free.

Weight management programme

This is a low fat nutritional plan based on a high protein to carbohydrate ratio. Pick one 'free' day a week to rest from exercise and the meal plan. Choose a weekday as your free day instead of Saturday or Sunday. This may help to help prevent food binging on your free day.

Healthy food choices

Make the right choices when it comes to food for successful weight loss and nutrition. Here are some examples of healthy food options. Each is equivalent to one serving.

Fruit
- 1 whole fruit.
- Or ½ a medium-sized banana.
- Or ½ a cup of fruit pieces.
- Or 20g–40g of dried fruit. (A small amount of extra dried fruit in cereals is acceptable.)

Vegetables, fungi and herbs
Eat lots of vegetables (at least 2–3 cups) every day. Choose a wide variety, especially leafy, dark green, red and orange coloured vegetables. It's preferable to eat organic; otherwise wash your produce thoroughly to avoid pesticide residue. Add chopped fresh herbs and sprouts in your salads, e.g. parsley, watercress, fennel, mint and alfalfa.

Complex or starchy carbohydrates
You will notice a lot of vegetables and legumes cross over into this list, and are not officially complex carbohydrates. Choose a mixture of:
- Bananas, beetroot, bulgur wheat, carrots, corn, couscous, daikon radish, eggplant, kumara, legumes, lentils, noodles, parsnip, pasta, peas, potatoes (avoid green potatoes), pumpkin, rice (brown, white and wild), squash, taro, turnip and yams.
- Breads

2 toast size slices of dense bread, rye, sour dough, wholemeal, whole grain or pita bread. Dense bread is full of seeds and grains, and fairly heavy compared to white breads.
- Cereals
    ½ a cup of rolled oats
    or two wheat biscuits
    or 1 cup of corn flakes or bran flakes.
- Crackers
    4 crispbread, rice cakes, Ryvita or Vita Wheat (2 if large size)
    or 1 cup of unsalted, unbuttered popcorn.

Good fats

Healthy fats and oils that contain omega 3, 6 and 9 are important in your diet as you reduce the amount of saturated fat from animal produce. Actually some of these items contain carbohydrates along with protein and fat. When stated in the meal plan choose from either:
- ¼ of an avocado
- Or 25g of feta or parmesan cheese
- Or ½ cup of cottage cheese.
- Or 1 tsp of nuts and seeds (including almond, linseed, peanut, pumpkin, sunflower, walnut, 1 tsp of peanut or nut butter)
- Or 1 tsp of low-fat mayonnaise
- Or 4 large olives
- Or 1 Tbsp of organic flax oil. Use cold pressed organic oils such as olive oil, and organic flax oil on salads, vegetables, toast, in protein shakes, yoghurt, homemade mayonnaise. (Healthy oils include sunflower, safflower, sesame and small amounts of walnut oils). Add lemon, balsamic, apple cider, red wine or white wine vinegars with pepper, garlic, dried or fresh herbs, spices or mustard to dressing.
- Use butter sparingly — no more than 1 tsp. Avoid margarine as it can create trans fatty acids which the body cannot metabolise properly, leading to cholesterol problems and disease. Try also avocado, banana, hummus, nut spreads, homemade mayo and pesto.
- Dairy products including full milk, cream, cream cheese, sour cream and butter should be used as little as possible. Goat's, soya or trim milk, and yoghurt are suitable substitutes.

Protein

- Choose 150g of uncooked (fish or beef) or 100g of cooked lean protein (beef, pork, lamb and ham). The white meat of chicken or turkey is preferable to the fatty, brown meat or skin.
- Or 100g of tuna or sardines (fresh or drained)
- Or 50g of salmon (fresh or drained)
- Or 100g of fish or seafood. If choosing tinned fish or seafood select those in natural or spring water.
- Or 1 yolk and 3 egg whites (organic free range)
- Or 150g of tempeh or tofu along with legumes.
- Avoid processed meats including salami and sausages.

Sugar

Avoid artificial sugars, processed sugar and undiluted fruit juices and use small amounts of honey or Stevia.

Water
Drink at least 2–3 litres of fresh water daily, depending on your thirst and exercise rate.

Alcohol
If you are committed to your weight management it is best to avoid alcohol as it contains lots of 'empty' calories. However, if you have decided to continue drinking alcohol, you may drink 1 glass of alcohol per day (1 medium size beer, wine, or 1 double spirits), but you must take out your mid-afternoon snack and dessert, and make sure you keep up your cardiovascular exercises. You can drink more on your 1 free day per week — it's up to you — but a free day doesn't mean bingeing. Remember you have a goal to reach. Try to have at least 3 alcohol-free days per week.

Daily plan
'Wake-up call'
Drink one large glass of hot water with a squeeze of lemon, lime or orange juice.

'Get moving to burn'
Go for a 15–30 minute power walk or run (3–4 times weekly) or complete your weight resistance programme (3 times weekly is your goal) to help tone and shape the body.

'Nutrient lift'
- Drink one glass of fresh vegetable juice (carrot, celery, spinach) or fruit juice (cranberry, grape, pear, pineapple).
- Or add one tsp of spirulina to vegetable or fruit juice.
- Or take a multi vitamin and mineral formula supplement.

Breakfast
- Eat 1 protein bar with 1 piece of fruit or ½ banana.
- Or 2 scoops of protein powder with ½ banana or 100g of fruit (either berries, apple, pear, peaches or kiwifruit) blended with ½ cup of ice and 200ml of cold water or milk. (See the list of dairy products in the Good fats section above for choices.)
- Or mix ½ cup of cereal (above) with 200ml of cold water or milk (see above). Add 100g of fruit (apple, kiwifruit, pear, peach, pineapple), ½ a banana, 40g of raisins or 'lite' acidophilus yoghurt. Add 2 scoops of protein powder to cereal after it is prepared.
- Or eat two pieces of bread (above) with:
    1 poached egg or 1 omelette made with 1 egg yolk and 3 egg whites
    Or 50g of tuna, sardines or salmon
    Or 200g of baked beans
    Or ½ a large grilled tomato with 1 steamed flat mushroom.
    Optional: Spread 1 tsp of organic flax oil, avocado or cottage cheese on toast and eat 1 piece of fruit.
- Or eat 2 oat bran muffins or buckwheat pancakes (see recipes below).
- Or have a light breakfast of fresh fruit salad sprinkled with 1 tsp of nuts and seeds (above) and 1 'lite' or acidophilus yoghurt (add 1 tsp of manuka honey or 1 tsp of organic flax oil if desired). Use 3–4 pieces of preferably organic fruit.
- Drink 1 large glass of water, herb tea, black tea or coffee (add a dash milk [above] if desired).

Mid-morning
- Drink a protein powder smoothie. Add 2 scoops of protein powder, with water or 200ml

of water or milk (above). Add fruit, fruit juice and ice if desired.
- Or eat 50g of protein, e.g. tuna or ½ a cup of 'lite' cottage cheese, with one of the cracker options (above). Spread a little Marmite on crackers if desired.
- Or eat a protein bar or drink 200ml of milk (above) or eat a small tub of low fat yoghurt and a fruit option (above).
- Drink 1 large glass of water.

Lunch

Choose 1 serving of protein (above) and 150g of cooked complex carbohydrates (above) with ¼ of an avocado or 1–2 Tbsp of flax oil or other good fat option (above) with two cups of salad or vegetables and drink 1 large glass of water

For example:
Combine 150g of cooked potatoes or pasta with 100g of cottage cheese and 2 Tbsp of tomato salsa, soya sauce or Thai chilli sauce.
Or choose 2 slices of dense bread with 150g of mussels (fresh, steamed or marinated).
Or eat 6 average size pieces of sushi (if there is avocado in the sushi it will count as your fat option).

Mid-afternoon

Any choices from mid-morning section

'Get moving to burn'

If you didn't exercise this morning, do it now.

Dinner

Avoid carbohydrates at night, mainly to reduce the temptation to binge, but make sure you have an after-dinner snack. If you must have carbohydrates eat 150g of cooked complex carbohydrates.
- Eat 150g of cooked lean protein.
- Or eat 150g of mussels (steamed, marinated or raw) or 1 omelette made with 1 egg yolk and 3 egg whites with 200g of 'lite' cottage cheese.
- Eat an unlimited amount of vegetables — raw, boiled, microwaved, baked or, preferably, steamed.
- Add 1 Tbsp of flax oil to 1 tsp of lemon juice or balsamic vinegar and a condiment (e.g. mustard), salt and pepper for a salad dressing.
- Limit stir-frys to once a week using 2 tsp of olive oil.
- And remember to drink 1 large glass of water

After dinner (optional)

- If you have a sweet tooth, eat a pure fruit juice ice block.
- Or 1 cup of custard made with trim milk.
- Or a small tub of low fat plain yoghurt with 100g of fruit.
- Or two pieces of fruit.
- Or drink a protein powder smoothie.

HINTS

- Maintain your food and exercise diary.
- Don't wait for Monday. Start now.
- If you have to drink alcohol take out your mid-afternoon snack and dessert. Try to have a least 3 alcohol-free days.
- Avoid any foods you are allergic or sensitive to. To discover any potential food

sensitivities, visit your local herbalist or naturopath.
- Eat 6 meals a day (not 3 square meals) to burn fat and balance sugar levels.

Preparing healthy food

Healthy ways to prepare food can include baking, steaming, boiling, broiling, barbecuing (limit to once a week) grilling and poaching.

Limit stir-fry cooking to once a week using 2 teaspoons of olive oil. To flash pan or stir-fry, heat pan up then when hot cover the surface with olive oil spray (approximately ½ tsp). Throw vegetables or thinly sliced meat in the pan and cook for 1–2 minutes then add a little water to 'steam-fry'.

Avoid deep-fried food and if you use a microwave to heat or cook food, put the food in a glass or ceramic dish. Try to avoid heating food with plastic wrap and plastic cookwear. This helps to reduce xeno-oestrogens in your diet. These may affect water retention and your weight management results.

Recipes
Buckwheat Pancakes
Mix 1 cup of buckwheat flour, 1 cup of water and 1 egg white. Cook pancakes in a non-stick pan coated with a little oil. Before cooking, add (to the pancake mix) fruit, cinnamon and vanilla to make sweet varieties, or tomato, onion, ham, tofu, mushroom and even salad greens or broccoli for a savoury filling.

Oat Bran Muffins
Preheat oven to 180°C. Mix 2¼ cups of oat bran cereal, 1 Tbsp of baking powder, ¼ cup of brown sugar, and ½ cup of dried fruit, 1 chopped banana or 1 cup of cooked fruit (peaches, pears, etc.). Combine 1¼ cups of skim milk, 2 egg whites and 2 Tbsp of vegetable oil mix with dry ingredients. Fill 12 medium-sized muffin tins with mixture and bake for 15–17 minutes. Consume within 3 days and keep in fridge for freshness.

Fish
Make a tin foil parcel of 150g of raw fish fillet and a handful of chopped fennel, chilli, lemon rind and juice, parsley, and a dash of white wine or fish stock. Bake in a preheated oven at 180°C for 15 minutes.

Salad
Mix 2 cups of mixed leaf salad greens with 1 chopped carrot, 1 stick of celery, ½–1 cup of cooked, torn pieces of pumpkin or fluffy couscous, a small amount of thinly sliced red cabbage and red onion. Add 4 spoonfuls of light cottage cheese, 1 tsp of shaved parmesan cheese and ⅛ of a sliced avocado to the salad. Serve with a flax oil salad dressing. Add 100g of cooked chicken, tuna or lean meat for protein.

Salad dressings
Shake up 2 Tbsp of flax oil (or 1 Tbsp of olive oil with 1 Tbsp of flax oil) with 3 Tbsp of either vinegar, lime or lemon juice, and add salt and pepper to taste. For variation add mustard grains, mustard powder, chilli sauce, pesto or fresh or dried herbs, e.g. tarragon.

Protein shakes
My favourite protein shakes are the Good Health Body Burn™ Whey Less shakes. Blend 2 scoops of Body Burn™ Whey Less, 1 Tbsp of flax oil, 200ml soya or trim milk and a spoonful of acidophilus yoghurt with ½ a banana, ½ a cup of frozen blueberries and 2–3 ice cubes.

Daily meal, exercise and supplement chart

Keep a weekly record of your food, exercise and supplements to help chart your progress and keep you on track to achieve your goals and a new lean, toned body (see next page).

Date:	Example	Monday	Tuesday	Wednesday	Thursday	Friday	Saturday	Sunday
Exercise	Power-walk 30 minutes							
Lemon or spirulina drink	x 1 x 1							
Supplement	1 tsp spirulina							
Breakfast	1 cup of oats with 200ml skim milk, 100g fruit and 1 glass water							
Mid-morning	1 x protein shake with ½ banana 1 glass water							
Supplement								
Lunch	100g of tuna, 2 cups of salad 1 small potato with 2 tsp cottage cheese and 1 Tbsp flax oil dressing 1 glass water							
Supplement								
Afternoon tea	4 Vita Wheat with Marmite, ½ cup cottage cheese							
Exercise	None – exercised in the morning							
Dinner	100g lean steak 2 cups of vegetables 1 Tbsp flax oil salad dressing							
Supplement								
Snack	1 x yoghurt and 100g of fruit							

Part Three

A to Z Guide

Acne Rosacea

Acne rosacea is a chronic inflammatory disorder involving the skin (and sometimes the eyes). The skin of the face looks extremely red, especially on the cheeks, nose and chin. While it is mainly seen in adults (30–60 years), it is known to start in the early pubescent years in those who are prone to blushing or flushing.

Causes

The causes of acne rosacea are largely unknown, although possible factors include:
- Poor or low hydrochloric acid or gastric acid output in the stomach. Stress or worry, possibly due to stress mechanisms leads to reduction in gastric acid output.
- A special skin mite (*Demodex folliculorum*) that feeds on the skin's sebum pore oil, reducing the quality of the sebum and causing hair follicle irritation, swelling and redness.
- Food allergies.
- Fungal infections may aggravate acne.
- Blushing or flushing can cause the face to look redder, especially around the T-Zone area. Consuming alcohol, hot drinks, spicy foods and niacin, a form of vitamin B3, can cause flushing as the veins around the face become dilated. The other form of B3, termed niacinamide, nicotinamide or nicotinic acid, does not cause flushing and, contrary to the way the name sounds, is not associated with nicotine.
- Exposure to extreme heat or cold may also aggravate acne rosacea.

Signs and symptoms
- Blotchy or diffuse red spots on the skin.
- Spider veins and dilation of facial veins are responsible for the reddish colour of the skin.
- The face has an oily appearance and, rather than having acne that is blocked by sebum plugs (comedones), the acne has normally erupted.
- The lesions affect the blush areas of the face and the T-zone — nose, cheeks, chin and central area of the forehead — where there is the greatest number of sebaceous glands. Acne rosacea for some individuals includes the neck and chest areas.
- Migraine headaches are experienced by many individuals suffering from acne rosacea.

Naturopathic recommendations

Lifestyle hints
Don't expose your face and neck to extreme hot and cold temperatures or to the sun.

Exercise
To improve blood flow and to reduce your stress levels exercise at least 3 times a week.

Nutrition
- If prone to flushing, avoid hot drinks, spicy foods, alcohol and the niacin form of vitamin B3.
- An unrefined, wholefood diet is best, rather than eating heavily processed foods.
- Food sensitivities may aggravate or cause acne rosacea. These include chicken, eggs, dairy, wheat, citrus and nightshade vegetables (tomatoes, potatoes, eggplant, capsicum, tobacco and chillies). It can be difficult to find out what your food sensitivities are, and, rather than jump to conclusions, consult with a naturopath to discover these.
- Remember to avoid deficiencies if you cut out certain food groups, such as dairy, and

to take correct supplementation (e.g. calcium). Increase dietary fibre from fruit and vegetables and eat lean meats and fish for protein. Reduce saturated fat and excessive salt intake and use herbal salt, Celtic or sea salt rather than iodised salt. Remember to drink 8–9 glasses of fresh, pure water daily.

Supplements

Vitamin B complex   Lack of Vitamin B2 may cause acne rosacea. Take 50mg–100mg of B2 daily. If you take a specific B Vitamin you should also take a Vitamin B complex to avoid B Vitamin imbalance. Any regular Vitamin B complex product will be suitable.

Betaine or Hydrochloric acid (HCL) supplements   Lack of stomach acid may contribute to acne rosacea. HCL initiates the conversion of pepsinogen to pepsin and assists protein digestion. HCL renders your stomach sterile against orally ingested pathogens, prevents bacterial and fungal overgrowth of your small intestine, encourages the flow of bile and pancreatic enzymes, aids the absorption of Folic acid, Vitamin C, Beta Carotene, Iron, Calcium, Magnesium and Zinc. Betaine Hydrochloric acid increases digestive juices for protein digestion and aids in killing some bacteria in foods. Take 100mg–200mg 3 times daily with meals.

Bioflavonoids   Hesperidin, Rutin and Quercetin increase the strength of the blood vessels and help to regulate their permeability, reducing the red appearance of dilated veins and capillaries. They also assist the role of Vitamin C to help strengthen collagen structures of the skin, are essential for the proper absorption and use of Vitamin C, and prevent its destruction by oxidation. In combination with Vitamin C they help to prevent haemorrhages and ruptures in the capillaries and connective tissues, and reduce the appearance of redness and the dilation of facial veins. Take 400mg of Quercetin 3 times daily, or 1000mg of mixed Bioflavonoids daily.

Aloe Vera juice   Helps rebalance the pH level in the skin, acting as a gentle astringent, firming and toning, as well as protecting against blemishes. Aloe Vera also acts as a moisturiser in two ways. First, it creates a barrier that prevents moisture loss and second, it carries nutrients and moisture through the many layers of the skin down to the dermis. This stimulates fibroblasts, the cells responsible for the manufacture of collagen. Drink 100ml daily and gently wipe onto skin as a toner before moisturising.

Vitamin A (Retinol), C and **Bioflavonoid creams**   These creams have a strong reputation for toning broken capillaries. Try to purchase a water-based cream with at least 5% of Vitamin C and Bioflavonoids. Use as directed.

Acidophilus and **Bifidus**   Good bacteria that help to keep the digestive system healthy. If you have taken antibiotics as a treatment for acne rosacea, you will need to take 1 billion of the Acidophilus and Bifidus species in capsule form daily on an empty stomach to repopulate your digestive system.

Herbs

Parasite-cleansing herbs   To help eradicate the *Demodex* mite, take two 3-week courses of **Cloves** (1800mg) combined with **Wormwood** (2000mg) and **Black Walnut** (2000mg) daily. You may also follow acne vulgaris herbal guidelines.

Acne Vulgaris

Whether acne involves a single pimple that pops out on an important date or chronic clusters associated with hormones or puberty, most people will experience the condition in their lives. Unlike some other health conditions, acne is visible and can affect the self-esteem of many. Acne vulgaris is the most common form of acne. It affects both sexes and occurs mainly during puberty, although many women can experience pimples around menstruation and up to 6% of adults (25–40 years) may end up with chronic (ongoing) acne. This is generally due to the production of excess androgens (male sex hormones) within the body. These stimulate cells to produce more sebum which can plug the hair follicle and sebaceous gland, collectively known as the pilosebaceous duct.

Causes

- When the pilosebaceous duct is blocked, normal bacteria found on the skin (e.g. *Propionibacterium acnes*) may stimulate inflammation around the area, which is why antibiotics are normally given by doctors to treat this condition. However, long-term use of oral (by mouth) antibiotics can cause an overgrowth of *Candida albicans* within the intestine, which in turn may lead to systemic candida, vaginal thrush or intestinal toxaemia.
- Naturopaths believe acne may be due to a wide variety of causes, such as hormonal imbalances, food sensitivities and excessive consumption of some foods, including iodised salt and saturated fats found in cooked meats and dairy products. Additionally, stress, intestinal toxaemia and nutritional deficiencies may cause acne.
- An increase of androgens due to hormonal imbalance or stimulation. Even stress can cause acne, by causing an increase in androgen levels.
- Blockage of the pilosebaceous duct.
- Presence of normal bacteria microflora that is found on the skin and within the pilosebaceous duct.
- Nutritional excess of iodised salt, saturated fats from animal produce, dairy (milk protein), and deficiencies, including Omega 6 (essential fatty acid), vitamin A, B6 and the minerals zinc and chromium. Food sensitivities including chicken, eggs, dairy, citrus and nightshade vegetables, e.g. tomatoes, potatoes, eggplant, capsicum, tobacco and chillies.
- Toxins within the bowel and/or an excess of toxin overload within the body.
- Make-up products (e.g. mineral oil-based products and foundation) that clog up the skin.
- Constant skin trauma from squeezing, leading to spread of bacteria.

Signs and symptoms

- Pimples are slightly raised inflamed pilosebaceous ducts, topped with a pustule.
- Blind spots or cysts are deeper pimples that do not rise to the surface of the skin.
- Whiteheads are formed by the plugging of sebum in the pilosebaceous duct.
- Blackheads are actually whiteheads, but the melanin pigment from the hair causes the typical black plug.
- Scarring, redness and inflammation normally surround the pimple area.
- Acne is most commonly found on the face, chest, buttocks and/or back.
- Acne conglobata is a more chronic form of acne with deep cysts and scarring.

Naturopathic recommendations

Lifestyle hints

Exercise
To improve blood flow and to reduce your stress levels exercise at least 3 times a week.

Skin hygiene

- Wash skin carefully with pH balanced lotions and avoid soaps. Avoid mineral oil-based makeup or makeup altogether if you can, as it may clog skin pores. Wash makeup sponges

Acne Vulgaris

and brushes regularly in antibacterial shampoo or tea tree oil and hot water, and blow-dry carefully. Dirty utensils may contain bacteria which aggravates and inflames acne.
- Tea tree oil, lavender oil and calendula products (diluted oil or creams) will not stop pimples but will help prevent infection making them worse, and may improve the appearance of inflammation and redness. Dilute with water and test a patch on your skin first, as these oils in high concentration can burn some sensitive skins. Apply to skin with a clean cotton ball. Apply tea tree and/or calendula cream or infused water with a cotton ball onto the skin daily.
- Washing skin too often can cause it to produce even more oil. Using vitamin E, calendula oil, evening primrose oil, jojoba or rosehip mixed with appropriate essential oils (e.g. sandalwood or lavender) can balance the skin's oil production.

Nutrition

- An unrefined, wholefood diet is best, rather than eating heavily processed foods.
- All refined carbohydrates (sugary foods, white flour products and soft drinks), milk and milk products, fried foods and margarine should be avoided. Foods that cause allergies (e.g. chicken, eggs and dairy) should be eliminated and, although it can be difficult to find out what your food sensitivities are, it's best not to jump to conclusions. Consult a naturopath to discover your potential food sensitivities instead.
- Remember to avoid deficiencies if you cut out certain food groups, such as dairy, and to take correct supplementation (e.g. calcium). Increase dietary fibre from fruit and vegetables and eat lean meats, vegetarian protein and fish for protein. Reduce saturated fat and excessive salt intake and use herbal salt, Celtic or sea salt rather than iodised. Remember to drink plenty of fresh, pure water, 8–9 glasses daily.

Supplements

Vitamin A   Retinols, including oral Vitamin A, have been shown to reduce sebum production of the sebaceous follicles. To dry up acne, dosages of Vitamin A must be relatively high and are potentially toxic to the liver, and during pregnancy, unless supervised by a medical doctor or an experienced health professional. Take a safer dose of 5000IU–8000IU daily.

Zinc   The importance of Zinc for skin health is well-recognised. Studies show Zinc supplements improve and increase skin healing and health within 12 weeks.[17, 18, 19, 20] Take up to 45mg of Zinc amino acid chelate daily. Non-oily Zinc cream is also known to be beneficial.

Vitamin B6   Women with premenstrual aggravation of acne often respond to B6 supplements. Take 100mg daily and combine with a B complex. If the PMS symptoms are severe, increase the dose to 200mg daily for 7 days leading up to menstruation and 3 days during.

Selenium and **Chromium**   Assist with healing of the skin. Take 200mcg of Selenium and 300mcg of Chromium daily and combine with the Vitamin B complex.

Flax oil and **Evening Primrose oil** (EPO)   These plant seeds supply Omega 6 oil (linoleic acid) which is often deficient in the sebum. This may contribute to the disruption of healthy sebum secretion. Take 1 Tbsp of Flax oil (or 10 1000mg capsules) and 3000mg of EPO daily.

Herbs

To treat acne, in addition to adopting a nutritious diet and drinking lots of water, start with a programme to detoxify the body from the inside out. Many nutritional, dietary and botanical factors have been shown to be important in the maintenance of a healthy liver.

Liver-cleansing herbs   Important for supporting the liver's enzymatic processes. **Dandelion** (3g–5g of dried root daily) and **Milk Thistle** (9g–10g of seed daily) enhance bile flow and detoxify the liver. **Burdock** (2g–6g of dried root daily) helps to cleanse the blood and is a specific herb indicated for acne.

Bowel toxaemia Lack of **Acidophilus** and **Bifidus** bacteria, and a low fibre diet, contribute to excessive toxins within the bowel. Elimination of toxins and the introduction of good bowel bacteria increase bowel health. Dietary fibre is important because it absorbs the toxins excreted by the liver, including hormone products. Acidophilus and Bifidus are good bacteria that help to keep the digestive system healthy. If you have taken antibiotics as a treatment for acne you will need to take 1 billion of the Acidophilus and Bifidus species in capsule form daily on an empty stomach to repopulate your digestive system.

Hormone balancing Excess androgens (male hormones) can cause acne, especially during puberty. Some women also experience acne in conjunction with their monthly menstrual cycle. Typically the acne starts just before the period is due or during the period, and heals as the period is finished. The herb **Chaste Tree** can be used internally to balance hormones causing acne. Take 750mg 2 times daily.

Stress Can aggravate acne, perhaps either because stress increases production of androgens from the adrenal glands, or because stress can disrupt the normal hormonal balance. Take a **Vitamin B** complex with **Ginseng, Liquorice** and **Passionflower** herbs daily to help adrenal stress.

Echinacea (1200mg daily), **Olive Leaf extract** (270mg 3 times daily) and **Calendula** (1ml–4ml of tincture daily) These herbs are used to enhance the skin's regeneration, for blood purification and to help reduce excessive bacterial processes within the skin.

Finally, a simple remedy that helps to improve acne: Don't touch your face. A lot of people don't realise that repeatedly touching the acne lesions can make them worse. Squeezing the lesions can force the bacteria and sebaceous material into the adjacent skin, forming a cyst and an inflammatory reaction, eventually leading to scarring.

Scarring Apply a mixture of Vitamin E and Rosehip oil to the scar.

Acquired Immunodeficiency Syndrome and Human Immunodeficiency Virus

Acquired Immunodeficiency Syndrome (AIDS) is the final stage of the spectrum of disease caused by the Human Immunodeficiency Virus (HIV). HIV attacks and depletes the immune system, which is the body's natural defence system. People infected with HIV become increasingly likely to develop certain infections or some forms of cancer, which the body would normally resist easily.

HIV and the immune system

HIV is classified as a retrovirus that escapes the initially highly effective immune response. The immune system becomes damaged and depleted, as HIV is both immune suppressive and aggressively opportunistic. HIV actively replicates in white blood cells, especially when they are activated to mount a response to an infection. The profound immune suppression seen in AIDS relates to the infection replication process. The immune system's T-cells (CD4+) cease to function, their numbers are dramatically reduced and eventually they are destroyed.

Three main phases of HIV infection

To understand the possible treatment strategy, an understanding of the HIV progression to full-blown AIDS will be helpful. There are three main phases of HIV infection.

Initial phase Follows infection where HIV replicates itself in lymphocytes and macrophages, which would normally assist the body in fighting against this infection. The earliest symptoms appear 5–10 days after infection and patients complain of a mild cold-like or glandular fever-like disease, very slight fever, headache, malaise, aseptic meningitis, rash, lymphadenopathy (enlarged lymph glands), sweating and dry throat that usually lasts for 2–4 weeks. This period is known as the window period of seroconversion. The HIV antibodies are not detectable at this stage.

Asymptomatic phase   The immune system response causes the HIV to replicate more slowly. This phase may last 2–10 years. There is slow, persistent erosion of the immune system, with a progressive decline in CD4+ lymphocyte counts. Individuals with HIV infection often appear healthy, but they are infectious and may pass the virus on to others. A mild general enlargement of lymph nodes may be the only feature of infection.

Symptomatic phase   Occurs 2–10 years after initial infection as the virus growth starts to accelerate, leading to rapid viral replication and high antigenic variability. Eventually CD4+ cells are so depleted they can't prevent development of opportunistic infections or certain forms of virus-induced cancers, and the person develops an AIDS-defining illness. Gradual weightloss, fatigue and weakness, headaches, nightsweats and continued bouts of diarrhoea may be experienced. Anaemia and decreased T-cell counts in the bloodstream, with more suppressor T-cells than helper T-cells, will likely occur. This phase is associated with the beginning of many infections.

AIDS (full blown)

The individual will experience debility, emaciation, enlarged lymph nodes, severe continual dry cough and diarrhoea. Purplish lesions will appear on the skin, and the patient may exhibit a white furry tongue, sore throat, fever, night sweats and a decreased appetite. AIDS-associated dementia, neurological disorders, multiple infections and cancers develop and eventually lead to death.

Naturopathic recommendations

Lifestyle hints

- HIV-positive individuals should monitor their immune function by having CD4+ counts determined every six months if levels are above 500 and every three months if levels are below 500.
- Adopt naturopathic practices of healthy lifestyle choices, including avoiding excess toxins from chemicals, cigarettes and alcohol.
- Use meditation to reduce stress and depression, listen to relaxing music and avoid hustle and bustle or noise if you find these things stressful.
- Include regular exercise and get plenty of rest — 7–8 hours of sleep every night.
- Apply safe sex strategies. See your local HIV/AIDS Foundation for more information.

Nutrition

- Certain vitamins are required by the immune system to fight off the myriad of infectious agents that challenge our bodies. It is very important for people with HIV to maintain a healthy body and immune system for as long as possible through good nutrition and a healthy diet.
- Food hygiene must be adhered to as a prevention against opportunistic infections and as a tool for supporting a healthy immune system.
- Eat whole, organic fruits, vegetables, grains, seeds, beans and nuts. Avoid high levels of saturated fats, fried fats and refined sugars but substitute with large amounts of essential fatty acids (flax, fish and evening primrose oil) and polyunsaturated fats (vegetable oils). Avoid food intolerances and allergies. Drink 8 glasses of purified, boiled water daily.

- Whey protein shakes. Individuals with HIV/AIDS need at least 2g of protein per 1 kilo of bodyweight. Whey protein benefits include the ability to heal the digestive tract and to help prevent progressive muscle wasting.

Supplements

Antioxidant formula   HIV and opportunistic infections can generate high levels of free radicals and oxidative stress. These highly reactive free radicals have been associated with more rapid progression to AIDS as they stimulate the virus. ProenOthera® (EPO seed husks), Pine Bark, Green tea, Grape Seed, Ginkgo, Kelp, Lipoic acid, Beta 1.3 Glucan, Vitamins A, C, and E, minerals Zinc and Selenium, and amino acids Cysteine and Methionine are good antioxidant combinations that help reduce free radicals.

Vitamins and **minerals**   A comprehensive supplement programme may provide an effective approach to slowing or inhibiting the progression of HIV to AIDS. Since just about all vitamins and minerals are involved in enhancing immunity, a good high potency vitamin/mineral supplement is recommended.

Vitamin C   Studies show Vitamin C intake slows progression of HIV to AIDS. Take 500mg–1000mg 3 times daily.[21]

Vitamin E   Shows the most promise at slowing down the progression of HIV to AIDS of all the antioxidants. Low Vitamin E levels correlate with low T-cell numbers, while high levels of Vitamin E stimulate T-cell activity.[22] It may also increase the therapeutic effect of the drug therapy AZT and reduce the drug's toxicity to bone marrow cells. Take 400IU daily.

Acidophilus and **Bifidus**   Good bacteria that help to keep the digestive system healthy. Take 1 billion of the Acidophilus and Bifidus species in capsule form daily on an empty stomach to repopulate your digestive system.

Colostrum   Contains insulin-like growth factor-1 and growth hormones that studies show help increase muscle mass and, therefore, help prevent muscle wasting. Colostrum has immunoglobulin factors that are effective against pathogens, such as bacteria, viruses, fungi and parasites. Epithelial growth factor, a constituent of Colostrum, is also indicated for leaky gut syndrome and diarrhoea because it helps to heal damaged digestive tract mucosa. Take 4g daily and combine with 2 Tbsp of Flax oil.

Herbs

Turmeric   A powerful antioxidant that may help reduce viral replication. Its activity is over 300 times greater than Vitamin E. For a potent curcumin dosage source, choose pure curcumin rather than the crude dry root form, or curry used in food. It is best taken in combination with Bromelain, an enzyme from pineapple, as this has been shown to increase absorption. Take 1g–3g daily.

Bromelain   A natural product from pineapple, which has been investigated as a cheaper source of protease inhibitors and shows fewer side effects. Protease inhibitor drugs are popular in the fight against HIV replication. Dosage equates to 2000mg (1200mcu–1800mcu or 'milk clotting units') per day, divided into five doses taken on an empty stomach, or 250mg–750mg twice daily.

Liquorice   Glycyrrhizin, one of the active constituents in Liquorice Root, has prevented deterioration of the immune system and prevents progression from HIV to AIDS.[23] Take 1g–5g of Liquorice Root daily.

Olive Leaf extract   Profoundly researched by the St Upjohn Pharmaceutical company, Kalamazoo, Michigan, for its numerous effects against fungi (candida), viruses, bacteria and parasites.[24, 25, 26] Numerous case studies dated from 1995 report that standardised Olive Leaf extract (OLE) 12% oleuropein contains antioxidants and natural protease inhibitors. Used in combination with Naltrexone, both dissolved in a whole lemon/olive oil drink, it has been shown to reduce HIV viral load from a high count of 58,000 to non-detectable levels in two weeks. Case reports published by Keep Hope Alive indicated drinking Olive Leaf tea improves lab test readings, from viral counts of 380,000 falling to 129,000, in six-and-a-half weeks. A course of 6 capsules of approximately 270mg of OLE taken over a period of at least 17 weeks shows promise as a herbal treatment for HIV/AIDS.[27,28]

Other treatments
Other complementary treatments include naturopathic and herbal medicine, nutrition, homeopathy and vitamin therapy. Pain control therapies include hydrotherapy, Reiki, acupuncture, meditation, chiropractic treatments and therapeutic massage.

Alternative therapies can also be used to help with side-effects of the medications used in the treatment of AIDS. A survey carried out on HIV patients showed 54% were using complementary therapies. These included vitamins, minerals, protein supplements, massage, Reiki and acupuncture. The most common nutrients and herbs were Echinacea, Acidophilus, Ginseng, Ginkgo, St John's Wort, Goldenseal, Garlic, Saw Palmetto, Chinese herbs, Milk Thistle and Yohimbe. The average viral loads of HIV patients using complementary therapies were a quarter the load of those who were not using them.[29]

Herbal caution
St John's Wort (SJW)   SJW in therapeutic doses (2g–5g daily) interacts with the prescribed HIV treatment drug indinavir by increasing the rate at which the liver eliminates indinavir from the body. Resistance to indinavir can decrease the response to other protease inhibitors such as nelfinavir, amprenavir, ritonavir and saquinavir.

Alcohol Poisoning and Adverse Effects
How many times do we hear 'One glass of wine per day is healthy for you'? Scientists are discovering some wines and beers contain compounds (antioxidants) that are heart protective and may prolong life. The fact not mentioned is these compounds are isolated from the wine and the alcohol content is not used in these studies, and we all know that alcohol affects the liver. Although drinking alcohol is legal and can help soothe the mind and body and release inhibitions, the subsequent nutritional negatives outweigh the benefits. Again, the advice is everything in moderation.

Alcohol depletes the body of vitamins B1, B2, B3, B6, folic acid, calcium, magnesium and zinc. It slows down the brain, nervous system, heart, liver, stomach and kidneys. It increases urination, acting as a diuretic and depleting electrolytes and, in the long-term, can cause the liver to become fatty, leading to poor liver function, high blood pressure and high cholesterol. It can lead to diabetes, breast cancer, psychological dependence and alcoholism.

Signs and symptoms
- Alcohol poisoning occurs when an individual has consumed too much alcohol (usually from binge drinking, inexperience and/or teenage parties).
- They will look pale and feel clammy.
- If they have become unconscious they will not respond to being talked to, shouted at or pinched.
- They may have laboured breathing and have vomited.
- Even if the individual has finished drinking, blood alcohol levels will continue to rise as the alcohol left in the stomach is absorbed into circulation. The alcohol keeps affecting the brain and the detoxifying pathways of the liver and liver cells.

Medical care

If the individual is unconscious, if possible seek assistance, put them in the recovery position to aid breathing, and call emergency services immediately for more advice. Keep checking on their breathing. Avoid giving them a cold shower, liquids such as coffee to sober them up, or aspirin — at this point they may need medical care.

Naturopathic recommendations

Lifestyle hints

After you have been given the all-clear by your doctor, follow the naturopathic recommendations to help recovery.

Nutrition

- Cut down on fatty food for 3 weeks as the liver has been affected and you may feel nauseous when you try to eat fatty food. This is a sign you need to have a break from fatty fried foods, cream, butter and heated fats. Good fats are fine and will even assist liver recovery. These include olive, flax and evening primrose oil.
- Eat healthy foods, such as lean meats, complex carbohydrates, fresh fruit and vegetables, and avoid junk food for at least 3–4 weeks. Drink 8–9 glasses of fresh, clean, water daily.
- If you still choose to drink alcohol, learn to drink in moderation. Males should drink no more than 3–5 servings and females 2–4 servings over a period of several hours (1 serving equals 300ml of beer, 60ml of sherry, martini or port, 30ml of spirits or 100ml of wine).
- Eat a moderate-sized healthy meal and include a glass of water with every glass of alcohol as the French and Mediterranean people do — a lot more sophisticated.
- Don't be afraid to turn down drinks, and even think about educating your friends on the measures to help someone in need in an alcohol poisoning situation. Your experience is not the first, and it will not be the last.

Supplements

Multi vitamin and **mineral formula**   Take a Multi that contains all the vitamins and minerals, especially B1, B2, B3, B6, Folic Acid, Calcium, Magnesium and Zinc. This will help make up for the deficiencies caused by alcohol. Take a high strength Multi daily for at least 3 months.
Vitamin B complex   Vitamins are required in larger amounts during alcohol consumption and stress. Take a B complex daily to help boost B Vitamin levels.
Essential fatty acids   Take Omega 3, 6, 9 found in **Flax oil**, **Fish oil** capsules (not cod liver) and **Evening Primrose oil**. Alcohol inhibits the conversion of the essential oils within the body. They are essential for the good health of the cardiovascular system, skin and even fat metabolism. Take 3 1g capsules daily for 2 months.

Herbs

As the liver is severely affected by alcohol, the main aim is to help the body cleanse itself to improve the health of the liver. The liver can become fatty and damaged due to years of alcohol intake. The liver area may feel painful and poor liver function can affect fat, protein and glucose metabolism. This may lead to heart disease, liver disease and diabetes.
Liver-cleansing herbs   Take **Milk Thistle** (9g–10g of dried seed daily) and/or **Dandelion root** (3g–5g of dried root daily).

Aloe Vera juice   If the stomach is still delicate, drink Aloe Vera juice (50ml 2–3 times daily) with soothing stomach herbs such as **Slippery Elm** and take the nutrient **Colostrum** (8 500mg capsules daily).

Anaemia

Anaemia is a condition that occurs when the number of circulating red blood cells (RBCs) or the haemoglobin (iron-containing) part of red blood cells is abnormally low.

There are 3 main types of anaemia caused by nutrient deficiencies:
- Iron deficiency anaemia
- Vitamin B12 deficiency anaemia (pernicious anaemia)
- Folic acid deficiency anaemia.

Causes
- Deficiency of nutrients, for example, iron, B12 or folic acid. Vitamins B12 and folic acid are required for production of RBCs and deficiencies may cause abnormally enlarged RBCs. Iron deficiency anaemia arises from dietary deficiency and is common in deprived populations, where meat is not available, or in vegetarian diets, as meat is a rich source of iron. Infant iron deficiency may occur if there is a maternal deficiency and if infants are fed on a diet consisting mainly of cow's milk, as the iron in cow's milk is poorly absorbed. Infant iron deficiency can occur in up to 30% of low income populations.
- Increased demands for iron, due to diarrhoea, pregnancy, lactation, menstruation and from a child's extra nutritional growth needs, may cause anaemia.
- Excessive blood loss from trauma, peptic ulcer, fibroids or excessive menstruation. Gastric ulcers, aspirin use, haemorrhoids and intestinal polyps may also cause excessive blood loss leading to anaemia.
- Red blood cell destruction.
- Poor red blood cell production.
- Hereditary conditions e.g. sickle cell anaemia and thalassemia.

Signs and symptoms
Iron deficiency anaemia
- May manifest as fatigue, irritability, dizziness, loss of appetite, brittle nails, smooth tongue and mouth corner sores.
- Lack of oxygen from poor red blood cell circulation reduces tissue oxygenation leading to night cramps, abdominal pain, pale skin, pale eyelids (underside of lower lid) and nails.
- Angina, palpitations (tachycardia) and heart murmurs can occur as the heart tries to compensate for low circulating oxygen in the elderly, or in severe cases of anaemia.

B12 deficiency anaemia (pernicious anaemia)
- Can result from poor intestinal absorption of vitamin B12 or lack of B12 in the diet. Meat and animal produce are rich sources of B12. Poor absorption may be a result of damage to the stomach lining (mucosa), as a substance called the 'intrinsic factor' is produced by gastric mucosa. The intrinsic factor increases B12 absorption, protecting the lining from destruction from digestive enzymes as it binds to dietary B12.
- Nerve disorders can manifest, such as symmetric numbness in the feet or fingers, loss of position sense and nerve deterioration, which may be fatal.

Folic acid deficiency anaemia

- Arises from malnutrition, alcoholism, dietary lack, specific drugs (i.e. methotrexate), alcoholism and malabsorption syndromes, and other intestinal disorders.
- Signs and symptoms include diarrhoea, a swollen red tongue, and birth defects in the babies of pregnant women. Depression can manifest with folic acid deficiency.

Naturopathic recommendations

Lifestyle hints

- The cause of your anaemia must be determined for the success of your treatment. If the cause is not identified, the condition will be ongoing, no matter how much supplementation you take.
- Avoid taking aspirin and ask your doctor about certain drugs, e.g. cholestyramine and tetracycline, that also inhibit absorption of iron.

Nutrition

- If possible introduce more red meat into your diet, such as liver (pâté), Chinese stir fries with red meat, and beef soup, and plenty of green, leafy vegetables. Red meat contains iron, vitamin B12 and folic acid.
- Avoid drinking tea (black) and wine, as they contain tannins that have an ability to inhibit iron absorption.
- Some vegetarians tend to have vitamin B12 deficiencies because high levels of folic acid can mask this, and it can take months or years for the stored B12 to run out, which makes it difficult to diagnose B12 deficiency early on. Some vegetarians and vegans without proper dietary awareness, and who eat non-organic produce, miss out on eating insects and bug residue that can be an essential part of the diet, providing minute amounts of B12. Try to include iron and B complex supplements, milk, fish or eggs in the diet. If this isn't suitable, consult with a naturopath to research other options.

Supplements

Spirulina A group of eight women, who had been limiting their meals to stay thin, were showing hypochronic anaemia (lower than normal blood haemoglobin content). They took 4g of Spirulina after each meal. After 30 days, their blood haemoglobin content increased 21%, from 10.9 to 13.2.[30] This was a satisfactory level and they were no longer considered anaemic. Take 4g of Spirulina 3 times daily with meals for at least 30 days for iron deficiency anaemia.
Vitamin C 1500mg daily encourages iron absorption.
Schuessler Tissue Salt Ferr Phos Take 1 tablet every 30 minutes for 5 days, then take at least 4 tablets daily to help balance iron deficiency.
Natural liquid Iron formulas Take 10ml 2 times daily before morning and evening meals.
Digestive enzyme capsules Iron absorption is enhanced by digestive acid secretion and low stomach acid may affect iron absorption. Take digestive enzyme capsules that include Phytase and Betaine hydrochloride, ingredients to help digest phytates found in grains, seeds and nuts that also inhibit iron absorption. Increasing stomach acid output helps to absorb iron. Take 2 capsules 3 times daily with meals or as professionally advised.
Iron Succinate or fumartate are the preferred iron forms. They are highly absorbable, do not appear to upset the stomach or cause constipation. Take 30mg 3 times daily with meals.
Vitamin B12 Methylcobalamin is preferred over the cyanocobalamin form. Take 1g daily with Folic acid and a Vitamin B complex for better absorption if B12 deficiency is due

to dietary lack. B12 deficiencies may need to be treated with intravenous injections by a doctor to reverse anaemia and nerve damage. If you suspect severe anaemia, consult your naturopath or doctor.
Folic acid   Take 400mcg–800mcg daily.
Multi vitamin and **mineral formula**   Take a Multi that includes Vitamins B1, B2, B3, B5, Choline and B6, Vitamin C, Calcium and Copper. These are needed for red blood cell formation, to increase iron absorption and aid nutrient deficiencies.

Herbs
Gentian   A bitter herb that helps increase stomach acid, which helps absorb iron and B12, and increases your appetite. See bottle for dose details.
Nettle tea   Helps to build blood and supplies a natural source of iron. Take Nettle tea liberally throughout the day, perhaps in place of black tea and coffee.

Angina and Atherosclerosis

Angina conjures up images of an older person clutching their chest with one hand as they fall into a foetal position, face a pained and clammy. However, it's not only older people who can suffer from this particular affliction. To understand angina, we have to look at the possible reason for the development of this disease: Atherosclerosis.

Angina   Occurs when not enough oxygen reaches the heart muscle. It can sometimes be brought on by vascular spasms, excessive eating, exercise or stress.

Atherosclerosis   Our body manufactures cholesterol to produce hormones and other compounds that are essential to good health. High blood cholesterol, especially LDL (low-density lipoprotein) 'bad' cholesterol, is a prime cause of blockage in the coronary arteries. A heart attack, stroke or, less seriously, leg cramps (intermittent claudication) can occur when these 'pipelines' to the heart get too narrow and cut off the blood supply.

Causes
- Obesity and lack of activity
- Stress, high blood pressure and elevated blood cholesterol
- Poor fat and cholesterol metabolism, LDL/HDL (high density lipoprotein) ratio, elevated lipoproteins and fibrinogen
- Viral, bacterial and parasitic infections, causing blood vessel, heart muscle and valve damage
- Raised homocysteine (an amino acid compound) levels
- Heavy metal toxicity and smoking
- Oxidised lipoproteins (a) due to low levels of antioxidants in the diet
- Poor nutrition, including high fat and elevated sugar consumption, leading to nutrient deficiencies.

Signs and symptoms
- Angina: a crushing sensation of pain, which can last from 1–20 minutes, in the chest. The pain may also be felt in the left jaw, shoulder blade or arm.
- Atherosclerosis: a deep vertical crease in the earlobe may develop. Angina or leg cramps (intermittent claudication) can occur as oxygen supply to the muscles decreases due to partially blocked blood arteries. Forgetfulness or mental confusion may develop due to lack of oxygen to the brain.

Naturopathic recommendations

Lifestyle hints
Doctors must monitor angina as it is a serious condition.
- Eliminate smoking. This is an absolute must. Smoking damages the blood vessels and causes constriction and atherosclerosis. If you do choose to continue, take supplements, such as vitamin C and a multi containing vitamins, beta carotene and minerals.
- Relax. Stress exacerbates angina, poor fat metabolism and high blood pressure. Learn to relax by using yoga or meditation, or use relaxing techniques to suit your needs.

Exercise
- Start off gradually and lightly if exercise is not already a regular habit. Walking 3–4 times weekly is a good start. Increase your speed if it becomes too easy. You should walk for 40 minutes to 1 hour. Intensity of speed or exercise can reduce the length of time you need to exercise, to 20–30 minutes.
- If you have bone, joint or muscle injuries seek professional personal training advice to establish an adaptive exercise programme to suit you.

Nutrition
- Avoid alcohol as it increases cholesterol and triglycerides. If you do choose to drink, never binge and limit yourself to 5 servings a week (1 serving equals 300ml of beer, 60ml of sherry, martini or port, 30ml of spirits or 100ml of wine, preferably red). Reduce or eliminate coffee, caffeine, salt and soft drink intake.
- Avoid excessive intake of cholesterol. Cholesterol is an odourless, white waxy substance found in all animal foods, fish, offal, seafood and eggs. The type of fat you eat can affect your blood cholesterol level more than the amount. Eating a lot of foods that are high in saturated or trans fatty acids, such as butter, cream, coconut cream, squid, prawns, palm oil, take-away foods, fatty meats or fried foods, can raise your blood cholesterol. Limit eggs to 2 egg yolks per week and choose mostly white meat, fish and organic poultry. Cholesterol is not present in fruits or vegetables.
- Avoid excessive intake of saturated fats and trans fatty acids (TFAs). Saturated fats are fats that go hard at room temperature, such as lard, animal fats, dripping, butter, coconut and palm oil. Reduce saturated fat intake by removing visible fats and skin from meat, choosing grilling, steaming, broiling, baking or microwaving over frying and roasting. TFAs should also be avoided. TFAs are contained in margarine, shortenings, shortening oils and some salad oils, butter, milk and heated meats or fats.
- On the other hand, non-heated polyunsaturated or monounsaturated fats found in vegetable oils (olive oil or avocado) can actually lower cholesterol. Use omega 3 and 6 essential fatty acids or 'good fats' including flax oil or small amounts of olive oil and avocado as a substitute for butter and margarine. Use small amounts of olive or avocado oil to stir-fry foods.
- Reduce refined carbohydrates, such as white flour, white rice, croissants, toasted muesli, cakes, biscuits, pastries, pies, breadcrumbs, man-made carbohydrates and soft drinks.
- Consume complex carbohydrates. Halve the amount you normally have or eat 3 servings the size of your fist daily. Include dense grainy breads, lots of whole grains, oat bran and textured wholemeal or white sourdough, long grain white, basmati or brown rice, kumara, taro, yam, pasta, noodles, barley and bulgur wheat, porridge, untoasted muesli, Special K and All-Bran. Choose low-fat, low-sugar biscuits made with oats.

Angina and Atherosclerosis

- Sparingly use sugars, even those in honey, fruit juices, dried fruits and maple syrup. Avoid artificial sweeteners or processed sugar.
- Eat more fibrous carbohydrates like salads, celery, onions, garlic, asparagus, and beans and legumes, rather than starchy carbohydrates like potatoes, corn, rice, pasta and breads. Eat more dietary fibre and natural antioxidants found in vegetables (leafy greens, yellow and red), cherries and berries.
- Eat six small meals daily to help balance blood sugar levels, which may have a positive effect on fat metabolism.

Other dietary hints

- Increase non-sweetened yoghurt intake and choose low-fat dairy products, such as low-fat yoghurt, cottage and ricotta cheese, quark or feta.
- Eat at least 3 fish meals weekly. Sardines, tuna and salmon are great sources of omega 3 oils. Tinned fish may be more affordable, but grilled or steamed fresh fish is preferable.
- Consume copious amounts of ginger, garlic and onions with meals to help break down fibrous deposits (fibrinogen) on the arteries and thin the blood, and eat soy products, oat bran, whole grain cereals, legumes, alfalfa and sprouts, nuts and linseeds to help reduce cholesterol levels.
- Drink 2 litres of pure, fresh water daily and include a cup or two of green tea daily. Low in caffeine and rich in catechin antioxidants, green tea helps lower cholesterol and improve fat metabolism.

Supplements

Vitamin E (400IU daily), **Vitamin C** (500mg 3 times daily) and **Bioflavonoids** (30mg–450mg daily)   These act as antioxidants and prevent deficiencies which may lead to angina attacks and atherosclerotic build-up.

Vitamin B6, (15mg daily) **B12** (25mcg daily), **Folic acid** (200mcg–400mcg daily) and **IP6-Phytase** (50mg daily)   Reduce Homocysteine amino acid complex levels.

Lecithin   Helps emulsify and break down dietary fat. Take 3000mg daily or 3 tsp of granules on breakfast cereal daily.

Omega 3 oils   Help to thin the blood and improve cholesterol levels and poor heart function. Take 3000mg of **Fish oil** or 2 Tbsp of **Flax oil** daily. Avoid taking with the prescribed medication warfarin, as these oils in large amounts may magnify the drug's blood-thinning effect.

Magnesium   Helps prevent blood vessel spasm. Take 450mg 2 times daily.

Coenzyme Q10   Supports healthy cholesterol (HDL) and prevents the excess oxidation of LDL. Take 75mg–300mg of CoQ10 daily.

Antioxidant formulas (full spectrum)   Include ProenOthera® from Evening Primrose Seed husk, Green tea, Grape Seed, Pine Bark, Beta Carotene, Vitamins E, A and C, oligomeric proanthocyanidins, flavonoids and adjunctive minerals (Zinc, Selenium, Manganese and Iron). These are essential to help prevent oxidation and stickiness of LDL, and to reduce inflammation and atherosclerotic formation within the blood vessels. One of my favourite choices for heart and cholesterol conditions. Take as professionally advised or as supplement labels suggest.

Bromelain   An enzyme from pineapple that helps to break down clots. Dosage equates to 2000mg (1200mcu–1800mcu 'milk clotting units') per day divided into 5 doses taken on an empty stomach or 250mg–750mg 2 times daily.

EDTA (Ethylene diamine tetra-acetic acid)   Chelation therapy is an intravenous treatment that extracts Calcium deposits from plaqued arteries in patients with heart disease, improving heart and blood vessel function. Consult a health professional.

Fibre   Flax, Pysllium, Pectin or **Slippery Elm** should be taken to increase fibre and chelate onto heavy metals and cholesterol. Take 1 tsp–3 tsp of these fibres, singly or in combination, daily.

Herbs

Hawthorn Beneficial for high cholesterol and blood pressure, and angina. Acts as an antioxidant, therefore is protective with atherosclerotic conditions. Can be used in conjunction with aspirin and beta-blockers. Take 1.5g–3g of dried flower, leaf or berry daily.

Garlic Reduces triglycerides and LDL cholesterol, and prevents LDL oxidation. In addition to using fresh Garlic in your cooking, you can also take a therapeutic dose of Garlic in supplement form. A 400mg Garlic extract, or one clove of fresh Garlic a day, is suggested to reduce cholesterol. Look for Garlic supplements with standardised allicin. Avoid with the prescribed medication warfarin, as Garlic in large amounts may magnify the drug's blood-thinning effect, although adding to food in its natural form should be fine.

Milk Thistle (210mg–630mg daily, 80% silymarin), **Artichoke** (500mg daily, 15% cynarin) and **Curcumin** from Turmeric (900mg daily), are specific antioxidant herbs to help the liver metabolise fats.

Guggul The refined extract of this resinous herb native to India is called Gugulipid. It has been shown to decrease both LDL cholesterol and triglycerides. Take Guggul standardised to contain 25mg of guggulsterones 3 times daily.

Dan Shen Has been researched for angina and appears to dilate blood vessels, helping increase oxygen levels to the heart and reduce blood clotting. Take 3g–5g daily.

Ginger Helps circulation and breaks down fibrous deposits on blood vessels and arteries. Take 500mg 2–4 times daily, and add Ginger to foods and teas. Avoid with the prescribed medication warfarin, as Ginger in large amounts may magnify the drug's blood-thinning effect. Ginger tea and adding to food should be fine.

Passionflower (4g–8g of dried herb daily) and **Valerian** (1g–3g daily) Have muscle relaxant and anti-anxiety effects, helping to reduce stress symptoms.

Ginkgo Biloba Helps reduce risk of stroke, heart attack, intermittent claudication, mental deterioration and acts as an antioxidant. Beneficial for cholesterol problems. Take 4g–8g of whole leaf or 24mg–30mg of standardised extract of Ginkgo flavone glycosides daily. Avoid with the prescribed medication warfarin, as Ginkgo in large amounts may magnify the drug's blood-thinning effect.

Anxiety

Anxiety is when an individual feels extreme nervousness. It is relatively common and can be a wonderful survival mechanism when our brain perceives we are in danger. However, long-term anxiety or acute anxiety panic attacks can be severely debilitating.

Causes

- Stimulants, such as caffeine, alcohol and recreational drug abuse
- Mental or physical trauma
- Relationship, work and financial problems
- Deaths, divorce, marriage, moving house, public speaking and job stress
- Deficiencies of Omega 6 and 3, calcium, potassium, magnesium, B vitamins and brain chemicals serotonin and/or melatonin
- Food sensitivities may include preservatives, artificial sugars, dairy and gluten
- Insomnia as poor regeneration and rejuvenation may lead to raised anxiety levels
- Chronic health problems
- Low blood sugar levels.

Anxiety

Signs and symptoms
- Panic attacks, claustrophobia, agrophobia or nervousness
- Intense emotions, fear, irritation, tearfulness or anger
- Heart palpitations, shaking hands and tense muscles
- Headaches, breathlessness and low libido
- Insomnia, fatigue and high blood pressure
- Sweating and dizziness
- Nausea, weight loss and diarrhoea
- Lowered immunity.

Naturopathic recommendations

Lifestyle hints
- Ring a counselling service or if appropriate seek spiritual guidance or talk to a health professional or communicate with helpful friends or family.
- Learn how to relax by trying yoga, receiving a massage, or learning meditation or breathing techniques.
- Get plenty of restful sleep. Make sure the room is completely dark to help ensure sleep.

Exercise
- Exercise 4 times weekly, e.g. power-walking, jogging, swimming, dancing or gym.
- If you are not mobile, bounce on a trampoline and seek assistance if needed.

Nutrition
- Eat 6 small meals spread throughout the day.
- Drink 1–2 litres of fresh water daily.
- Avoid caffeine including coffee, cola drinks, chocolate, black and green tea.
- Alcohol, tobacco and recreational drugs should be avoided.

Supplements
Vitamin B5   The specific vitamin required for adrenal function. Take 50mg–100mg daily.
Vitamin B complex   Required for adrenal function. Take as directed.
Vitamin C   Studies show Vitamin C levels are reduced by stress, which may lead to poor immunity against disease. Take 1500mg daily.
Calcium and **Magnesium**   Deficiencies of these are common and may lead to muscle cramps, anxiety and depression. Take 1500mg of Calcium at night after a meal for better absorption and 450mg–900mg of Magnesium daily.
Flax oil, Fish oil, Evening Primrose oil and **Borage oil**   Provide rich sources of Omega 3 and 6 essential fatty acids. Deficiencies in these 'good fats' will cause anxiety, aggression, confusion, postnatal depression and clinical depression in some people. Take 3g of Evening Primrose oil, Borage, Fish oil and/or 2 Tbsp of Flax oil daily.
5-Hydroxy tryptophan (5HTP)   A serotonin precursor, made naturally by the body and also sourced from the plant *Griffonia simplicifolia,* helps boost serotonin levels, reducing anxiety and insomnia. Take 150mg–300mg daily.
Melatonin   Levels may be reduced by anxiety, leading to insomnia. Seek a prescription from your doctor and take 1mg–3mg at night before sleep. Not recommended for children as their levels are generally adequate.

Herbs

Skullcap Relaxes nervous tension, helps soothe the nervous system and combines well with the herb Valerian. Take 750mg 3–5 times daily.
Valerian Has muscle relaxant and anti-anxiety effects. Taken during the day for anxiety and/or at night may also help with insomnia. Very occasionally, some people can find this herb stimulating. Take 1g–3g daily.
Kava Its sedating and muscle relaxing effects aid anxiety symptoms for those who can't seem to slow down. Take 1.5g–3g of dried root daily.
Passionflower Aids nervousness, restlessness and digestive disturbances brought on by anxiety. Its action is magnified when combined with 5HTP. Take 4g–8g of dried herb daily.
Liquorice The specific herb for adrenal exhaustion. Take 2g–4g daily or as prescribed. (See Appendices for more information.)
Ginseng (*Panax*) Increases stamina and stress resistance. Take 600mg–10g of dried root daily unless otherwise prescribed.
St John's Wort For mild depression, anxiety and nervousness. Take 2g–5g of dried herb daily.
Lemon balm A gentle relaxing herb with possible pain relieving effects; may be taken as a tea and has a mint lemon flavour. (Avoid taking in large doses if you have low thyroid function). Take 5g–10g of dried leaf daily.
Californian Poppy Has a relaxing effect on the mind and potential mood elevating actions without addictive side effects. Take 900mg daily.
Hormone balancing herbs Some women experience anxiety in conjunction with their monthly menstrual cycle.
  Chaste Tree The herb Chaste Tree can be used internally to balance hormones. Take 750mg 2 times daily.
  Vitamin B6 Women with premenstrual aggravation are often responsive to Vitamin B6 supplementation. Take 100mg daily, double dose if premenstrual, and combine with a Vitamin B complex.

Bach™ flower remedies

Choose a single remedy or a combination recommended by a health professional. Take 4 times daily or as recommended.
Mimulus For those who have a feeling of fear (of known things).
Vervain For workaholics who are highly strung-out and over-achieving to the point of perfection and exhaustion.
Rescue Remedy For shock or grief.

Arthritis (Osteo)

It is an alarming fact that 1 in 3 people may be affected by joint degeneration or inflammation during their lifetime. It is also a fact that more older women are afflicted with arthritis than men. Arthritis is the single greatest cause of disability, with osteoarthritis being the most common type. Predisposing factors include a family history of the disease, obesity or joint injuries from accidents or sport.

Causes

A lot of people over the age of 50 years will start to experience some joint discomfort, with creaky 'popping' knees and reduced flexibility. This may be due to the gradual deterioration of cartilage, a super-slick padding that protects bones from rubbing together. This 'wear and tear' on our joints is what causes some of the commonly experienced symptoms of osteoarthritris. Age, sex, inflammatory joint disease, genetics, diet, obesity and structural damage or trauma to the joints are also factors leading to osteoarthritic disease.

Signs and symptoms

Osteoarthritis causes pain in the hips, hands or knees, which is worse in the evening due to aggravation throughout the day, and is relieved by rest. The joints will feel stiff in the morning and will be eased by movement. Swelling, joint popping sounds and limitation of movement are associated with osteoarthritis.

Naturopathic recommendations

Lifestyle hints
- The naturopathic aim is to help the joints stay supple and healthy to maintain mobility.
- The major therapeutic goal appears to be enhancing repair processes of the various connective tissue cells, especially those of the joints.
- Dietary factors are essential as this is a weight-bearing condition, and losing excess weight, for some people, can greatly relieve the pain of osteoarthritis.
- Other considerations include the potential triggers of pain. Some say checking food allergies may help.
- Alcohol, tobacco and heavy use of painkillers, anti-inflammatory medication and/or drugs can deeply affect the body's healing process and it is advised that these be avoided as much as possible.
- Aspirin and non-steroidal anti-inflammatory drugs, for example ibuprofen, may suppress pain symptoms but on the downside they suppress cartilage regeneration and thereby accelerate the progression of osteoarthritis.

Exercise
- Increase your activity to get your heart rate and circulation going. This will help dislodge toxins in your body and aid removal of waste from the joints and body.
- Walking is a good start, or if this is not possible, stretch isolated muscle groups to aid flexibility and strength, and lymphasize, i.e. bounce on a small trampoline which can be done easily while sitting on it. Please do not underestimate the effectiveness of the apparatus and its benefits in helping you towards mobility.

Other therapies
- Seek therapeutic massage once a week and use cold compresses to reduce acute swelling or hot compresses to relieve aches and pains using the anti-inflammatory essential oils chamomile and lavender.
- Soak for 15 minutes in hot to warm baths with a handful of magnesium (Epsom) salts to assist muscle relaxation.

Nutrition
- Attention to weight has significance for osteoarthritis. Excess weight and obesity tend to increase stress on weight-bearing joints.
- Avoid all food additives, pesticides and chemicals.
- Foods high in sugar and refined carbohydrate, and high-fat foods, including all hydrogenated oils and fried foods, should be reduced to a bare minimum.
- Gluten in foods like bread, muffins, cakes and caffeine, especially instant coffee, may increase pain and inflammation for those who are sensitive to gluten.

- Other common allergy foods include wheat products, dairy, nightshade vegetables such as eggplant and tomatoes, tobacco, bell peppers and potatoes, and lamb, seafood, onion and garlic.
- After checking your food allergies with a naturopath to determine what to avoid, start enjoying foods you can include in your diet, such as fresh fruits and vegetables, whole grains, beans, nuts and seeds (organic when possible). Include garlic (if not sensitive) and ginger in your dishes.
- Enjoy moderate amounts of lean meat including lots of fish. Healthy dietary fats such as cold pressed olive oils, flax oil, fish oil, borage oil and nut oils help to reduce inflammation, as can removal of heated fats and trans fatty acids, such as margarine, from the diet. It is better to eat butter instead. However, this is not a recommendation to spread it an inch thick on breads and crackers. Use it sparingly.
- Drink plenty of fresh pure water and green tea daily.

Supplements

Glucosamine and **Chondroitin**   Current research shows that these natural nutrients sourced from sea crustaceans, sea cucumber or cartilage are used by the body for the support of healthy joint tissue, assisting with lubrication and articulation. They help to reduce the pain and inflammation of arthritis and give the body the ingredients necessary to rebuild damaged joint cartilage. They may slow down progression of the disease considerably and prevent cartilage being worn away.[31, 32, 33] Take 1500mg of Glucosamine and 1200mg of Chondroitin daily.

Flax oil, Fish oil and **Evening Primrose oil**   To help reduce inflammation within the joints take 3000mg of Evening Primrose oil or Fish oil daily, or 1 Tbsp (13,000mg) to 2 Tbsp of Flax oil daily.

Antioxidant formulas   ProenOthera® (EPO Seed), Pine Bark, Green tea, Grape Seed, Ginkgo, Kelp, Beta 1.3 Glucan, Vitamins A, C, E, minerals Zinc and Selenium, and amino acids Cysteine and Methionine are good antioxidant combinations to help reduce free radicals and excessive bone and joint-chewing enzymes. Take a combined antioxidant formula as recommended.

Herbs

Parasite-cleansing herbs   Use these herbs first. Parasites can inflame, irritate and perforate the intestinal lining resulting in 'leaky gut'. This can lead to undigested food particles entering the bloodstream creating food allergies and inflammation. Parasites can settle in the joints and muscles, form cysts and create joint inflammation. Take two 3-week courses of **Cloves** (1800mg daily) combined with **Wormwood** (2000mg daily) and **Black Walnut** (2000mg daily) to help eradicate parasites.

Devil's Claw   Contains two active ingredients, Harpogoside and Betasitosterol, with anti-inflammatory properties that help to reduce swelling and pain while also improving the mobility of the joints. One study found that its anti-inflammatory effects equalled those of the commonly prescribed anti-arthritic drug phenylbutazone.[34] Take 500mg of dried root daily.

Celery Seed   Most widely used to help reduce pain and swelling of arthritis. Celery Seed is a natural diuretic so it can be helpful in preventing fluid build-up. Take 500mg–3g daily.

White Willow Bark   Has an ingredient similar to aspirin, which supplies natural relief from pain. Take 1g–2g daily.

Creams, ointments and gels

Aloe Vera gel   Mixed with oil of Wintergreen, Menthol or balms, such as Tiger balm, may increase circulation and heat to joints, relieving pain.

Arnica, Ginger, Basil and **Capsaicin** from **capsicum** Just a few examples of herbs that may be used topically on the skin over the joints to relieve pain and inflammation.

Arthritis (Rheumatoid)

Rheumatoid arthritis (RA) is considered to be an autoimmune disease. RA is an inflammatory joint disease in which the inflammation causes ongoing damage to the joint. The body's natural defence mechanisms are somehow put into reverse, and attack the cartilage instead of protecting it.

Causes
- Autoimmune response. Joint inflammation occurs when the individual's own antibodies (immune system) create inflammatory reactions within the joint itself.
- Food sensitivities and leaky gut syndrome. These antibody responses may be triggered by foods and thus food sensitivities are a factor to discover. Most people with arthritis show some food reactions on testing. However, in most cases there are other factors and avoiding foods is not a cure although it may greatly relieve pain and inflammation.
- Genetic, race and sexual factors are involved in RA, which affects 3 times as many women as men. It is more common in younger people (than osteoarthritis), and can involve one joint or the whole body.
- Other factors in RA can include a history of poor nutrition, increased physical or emotional stresses or recent infections. One suggestion is that rheumatoid arthritis can be caused by bacterial, parasitic and viral infections. Diets high in saturated fats are inflammatory and may lead to clogging of the arteries leading to decreased circulation in the joints and other vital tissues.

Signs and symptoms
- Pain and stiffness in the joints, particularly in the morning, and general fatigue and tiredness are often experienced.
- Swelling is seen around joints and the individual will feel increased warmth, tenderness and limitation of movement surrounding the joints.
- Deformities may occur later with this disease and it commonly affects the neck, shoulders, elbows, wrists, hands, knees, ankles, feet and toes.

Naturopathic recommendations

Lifestyle hints
Exercise
- Increase your activity to get your heart rate and circulation going. This will help dislodge toxins in your body and aid removal of waste from the joints and body.
- Walking is a good start or if this is not possible, stretch isolated muscle groups to aid flexibility and strength, and lymphasize, i.e. bounce on a small trampoline, which can be done easily while sitting on it. Please do not underestimate the effectiveness of the apparatus and its benefits in helping you towards mobility.

Other therapies
- Seek therapeutic massage once a week and use cold compresses to reduce acute swelling

or hot compresses to relieve aches and pains, using anti-inflammatory essential oils chamomile and lavender.
- Soak for 15 minutes in warm to hot baths with a handful of magnesium (Epsom) salts.

Nutrition
- Common allergy foods are wheat (gluten), dairy, nightshade vegetables such as eggplant, and tomatoes, tobacco, bell peppers and potatoes, and lamb, seafood, onion and garlic. Gluten in foods such as bread, muffins and cakes may increase pain and inflammation.
- Avoid high-sugar, refined carbohydrate and excessive high-fat diets. Reduce alcohol intake and eliminate smoking.
- A vegetarian diet has been shown to improve onset of RA flare-ups.
- Drink plenty of fresh water daily.
- Omega 3 and 6 are anti-inflammatory. Increase intake of omega 3 oil by including deep-sea fish such as tuna, salmon and sardines in your diet on a daily basis or take 3g of omega 3 fish oil daily. Alternatively add 1 tsp–1 Tbsp of ground linseed to your cereal in the morning to boost omega 3 and 6 dietary intake.
- Adding ginger to food increases circulation and also helps to reduce inflammation.
- Consume a lot of berries, cherries, and blue, red, yellow and green-coloured fruit and vegetables to increase antioxidants and fibre in the diet.

Supplements
Glucosamine and **Chondroitin**   Current research shows that these natural nutrients sourced from sea crustaceans, sea cucumber or cartilage are used by the body for the support of healthy joint tissue, assisting with lubrication and articulation.[35, 36, 37] They help to reduce the pain and inflammation of arthritis and give the body the ingredients necessary to rebuild damaged joint cartilage. These nutrients do not affect the cause of RA, which is the immune system response. However, the progression of the disease may be slowed down considerably as these nutrients help prevent cartilage being worn away. Take 1500mg of Glucosamine daily and 1200mg of Chondroitin daily.

Flax oil, Fish oil and **Evening Primrose oil**   To help reduce inflammation within the joints take 3000mg of Evening Primrose oil or Fish oil daily, or 1 Tbsp (13,000mg) to 2 Tbsp of Flax oil daily.

Antioxidant formulas   ProenOthera® (EPO Seed), Pine Bark, Green tea, Grape Seed, Ginkgo, Kelp, Beta 1.3 Glucan, Vitamins A, C, E, minerals Zinc and Selenium, and amino acids Cysteine and Methionine are good antioxidant combinations to help reduce free radicals, and excessive bone and joint-chewing enzymes. Take a combined antioxidant formula as recommended.

Leaky gut syndrome   Linked to rheumatoid arthritis. Heal the gut lining with **Colostrum** (4g daily) combined with **Acidophilus** (1 billion daily), **Bifidus** (1 billion daily), **Flax oil** (2 Tbsp daily), **Vitamin A** (5000IU daily), **Zinc** (45mg daily) and **Folic acid** (300mcg daily).

Fibre   Flax, Pysllium or **Slippery Elm** should be taken to increase fibre and protective lignans in the diet. Take 1 tsp–3 tsp of these fibres, singly or in combination, daily.

Betaine or **Hydrochloric acid supplements**   Lack of stomach acid may contribute to rheumatoid arthritis. Take 100mg–200mg 3 times daily with meals.

Herbs
Parasite-cleansing herbs   Use these herbs first. Parasites can inflame, irritate and perforate the intestinal lining resulting in 'leaky gut'. This can lead to undigested food particles entering the bloodstream creating food allergies and inflammation. Parasites can settle in the joints and muscles, form cysts and create joint inflammation. Take two 3-week courses of

Cloves (1800mg daily) combined with Wormwood (2000mg daily) and Black Walnut (2000mg daily) to help eradicate parasites.

Devil's Claw   Contains two active ingredients, Harpogoside and Betasitosterol, with anti-inflammatory properties that help reduce swelling and pain while improving the mobility of the joints. One study found that its anti-inflammatory effects equalled those of the commonly prescribed anti-arthritic drug phenylbutazone.[38] Take 500mg of dried root daily.

Celery Seed   Most widely used to help reduce pain and swelling of arthritis. Celery Seed is a natural diuretic so it can be helpful in preventing fluid build-up. Take 500mg–3g daily.

White Willow Bark   Has an ingredient similar to aspirin, which supplies natural relief from pain. Take 1g–2g daily.

Ginseng (*Panax*)   Take 500mg of standardised extract 3 times daily or 10g–30g of dried, uncured **Rehmannia glutinosa** root daily or 2g–4g of **Liquorice Root** daily to help reduce steroid medication and restore adrenal glands (see Appendices for more information). See a naturopath for advice before using these herbs if you are taking steroid medication.

Bupleurum   Helps to modulate immune system and protect the liver. Take 3g–12g of dried root daily.

Other valuable herbs   Cleavers to cleanse the lymphatic system (including glands) and Pokeroot for any infectious processes. However, care must be taken when using Pokeroot, although effective it can be toxic if used incorrectly. Valerian and Cramp Bark help to restore nerves, relieve pain and spasms, and Ginger increases circulation. For more information consult a naturopath.

Creams, ointments and gels

Aloe Vera gel   Mixed with oil of **Wintergreen**, **Menthol** or balms, such as **Tiger balm**, may increase circulation and heat to joints, relieving pain.

Arnica, Ginger, Basil and **Capsaicin** from **capsicum**   Just a few examples of herbs that may be used topically on the skin over the joints to relieve pain and inflammation.

Asthma

Asthma occurs when the airways are narrowed and restricted due to spasms in the bronchial tubes. There is inflammation and excessive mucus production, causing plugging of the airways, and expiratory flow rates are reduced.

Causes

- Triggers include allergens such as pollen, mould, dust, cat hair, cat saliva, animal fur and bed and dust mite faeces.
- Perfumes or strong odours, and inhaled chemicals and gases.
- Respiratory tract infections or candida.
- Food sensitivities, food colouring, excessive salt intake and preservatives, especially yellow dye and sulphites. Asthmatics are often allergic to common foods such as citrus fruits, dairy products, eggs, soy, wheat and yeasts.
- Dry climate, cold air, exercise, emotional states and stress, some drugs, i.e. aspirin and non-steroidal anti-inflammatory drugs (NSAIDs), gastroesophageal reflux, exposure to cigarette smoke and hyperventilation may also trigger asthma.
- Low hydrochloric acid (stomach juice) production.
- Deficiencies in Omega 6 or 3 leading to atopic asthma and eczema.
- Hyperventilation or excessive mouth breathing.
- Blood sugar fluctuations

Signs and symptoms
- Wheeze on expiration (breathing out) is caused by mucosal oedema, excess mucus and obstructive secretions and bronchospasm, and is a result of air squeezing past greatly narrowed airways.
- Breathlessness or a tight feeling in chest with or without mucous congestion in chest.

Medication: In acute circumstances always seek medical attention
Take your preventive medication from the doctor as recommended. If your asthma inflammation in the bronchial tubes increases to a point where you find it increasingly difficult to breathe, talk to your doctor about taking a very short course of corticosteroids, e.g. prednisone medication to reduce inflammation and prevent long-term scarring of airways. However, try to avoid long-term use of prednisone, which has some nasty side effects if taken over a long period.

Naturopathic recommendations

Lifestyle hints
- Avoid triggers such as animal fur, smoke or chemical inhalation.
- Vacuum as often as possible and wipe surfaces with a damp cloth. Clean mould from household surfaces.

Incorrect breathing, hyperventilation or excessive mouth breathing
Buteyko breathing tutors teach asthmatics to breathe correctly through the nose with a set of exercises to reduce phlegm, bronchial tightness, asthma and even snoring. I have tried this technique and it works wonderfully if I continue the exercises. No herbs, medication or need for supplements and a lifetime of techniques to help with asthma and breathing problems. When I don't practise the exercises medication, supplements and herbs are a genuine life-saver, especially around allergy season. See your local directory or website (www.buteyko.co.nz) for more information on the Buteyko breathing method, if you wish to buy the book or to source Buteyko breathing tutorial classes in your area.

Nutrition
- Food intolerances should be avoided including food colouring and preservatives, especially yellow dye and sulphites. Asthmatics are often allergic to common foods such as citrus fruits (lemons, oranges, mandarins, limes, tangelos), dairy products, eggs, soy, wheat and yeasts. Seek naturopathic testing for food sensitivities.
- The Buteyko method (see above) includes the following nutritional advice: Do not over-eat, instead eat 6 smaller meals daily. Eat plenty of raw vegetables, especially dark green leafy varieties, and fruit. The Buteyko method holds that cooked food, including meat, increases hyperventilation and, therefore, asthma. Eliminate all meat, fish, dairy and eggs until your breathing improves. Meats that are difficult to digest, such as steak, pork and beef, are preferable to easily digested animal proteins such as dairy, fish and eggs if you do choose to eat meat. Take 1 tsp of lemon juice in hot water three times daily. Reduce salt intake and protein intake (short term) if asthma frequency is increasing, as these tend to increase hyperventilation. Goat's milk may be a dairy alternative or if you are not allergic to soy use calcium-enriched soy milk.
- Consume omega 3 oils such as fish oil and flax oil to reduce inflammation and, if not allergic, liberal amounts of garlic and onion. (Also see bronchitis dietary instructions).
- Drink green tea daily as it has antioxidant and anti-asthmatic properties.

Supplements

Vitamin A   Helps to heal any damage to the lining of the airways. Take 5000IU–8000IU daily.
Vitamin E   Internal scarring may occur with severe asthma. Vitamin E may help break down internal scarring. Take 400IU daily
Magnesium   Helps to relax the smooth muscles that constrict the air passages (bronchials). Take 200mg–450mg 2 times daily.
Flax oil and **Evening Primrose oil**   Deficiencies of the essential fatty acids or 'good fats' are often linked with eczema incidence within the family, or an individual with asthma. This may be due to essential fatty acids deficiency in the diet. Take 3000mg of Evening Primrose oil daily and/or 1 Tbsp–2 Tbsp of Flax oil daily. Increase oily fish in your diet such as tuna, salmon and sardines on a daily basis or take 3g of Omega 3 from **Fish oil** daily.
Digestive enzyme formulas   Lack of stomach acid may contribute to asthma. Take 100mg–200mg of **Betaine HCL** 3 times daily with meals. Or alternatively, drink the tincture of the bitter herb **Gentian** daily with meals to help to increase stomach acid.
Calcium   If you are avoiding dairy products, take 1500mg daily to avoid deficiency.

Other helpful supplements

These may help reduce the immune inflammatory response that causes airways to react by constricting, causing asthma.
Vitamin B complex   Take as directed.
Vitamin C   Take 1500mg daily.
Selenium   Take 200mcg–400mcg daily.
Bromelain (the enzyme from pineapple) or the bioflavonoid **Quercetin**   Take 400mg 3 times daily.
Ginkgo Biloba   Take 80mg 3 times daily or **Grape Seed** extract (50%–95% active Oligomeric Proanthocyanidins [OPC] content) 100mg–1g daily.

Herbs

You must take some of these herbs and wait for at least 2 weeks to gain anti-allergy effects. Take during your seasonal allergy months or every day if needed.
Lobelia   Reduces inflammation, acts as a respiratory stimulant and relieves congested mucus. Take 50mg–200mg of dried Lobelia herb 3 times daily. Start at the lower dose first and build up. High doses can cause vomiting.
Marshmallow Root   Has soothing actions on the bronchi, reducing inflammation of the airways and decreasing the stickiness of mucus while helping the body to expel the mucus from the lungs. Take 2g–5g daily, and the dried flowers or leaves of **Mullein** (2g–5g daily).
Liquorice   Soothing to the airways, and reduces mucous congestion and inflammation in the airways. Stress can trigger asthma, but Liquorice helps the body adapt better to stress and has a mild action against viral infection, such as colds and flu. Take 1g–5g of Liquorice Root daily. Take as directed by a naturopath or herbalist as Liquorice causes high blood pressure in certain doses or with long-term use. See the Appendices for further information.
Boswellia   An anti-asthmatic, anti-inflammatory herb (gum resin). Take 3g daily. One of my favourite remedies, Boswellia has a long history of use and is added to many ancient Indian Ayurvedic formulations. It is also known as Frankincense.
Perilla   Reduces the histamine allergy reaction, helpful in eczema, asthma and psoriasis. Take 900mg daily. The longer you take Perilla the more effective it is, and it's also effective for hayfever symptoms and rheumatica (muscle pain).
Eyebright   Helps with upper respiratory mucus build-up, watery eyes, sneezing, blocked nasal passages or profuse watery nasal flow. Take 300mg–900mg daily.

Fenugreek Selected for its congestion-relieving and airway-soothing properties. Take 300mg–900mg daily. Alternatively add 1 tsp of slightly crushed Fenugreek Seeds to 1 cup of hot water. Cover for 15 minutes then drink the Fenugreek tea after discarding seeds.
Olive Leaf extract and **Echinacea** Take 270mg of Olive Leaf extract 3 times daily and 1200mg–6g of Echinacea daily for 10–30 days for signs of microbial, viral, bacterial or fungal infection. These herbs also help to improve the body's immune system.

Attention Deficit Disorder
Attention Deficit Hyperactivity Disorder

These are classified as disorders generally characterised by 'depression, irritability, restlessness, hyperactivity, impulsiveness and an inability to sustain attention or concentration'.

Causes
Attention deficit disorder (ADD) and attention deficit hyperactivity disorder (ADHD) affect both adults and children. A number of factors may influence ADD, such as possible brain dysfunction (information transfer problems), frequent ear infections, exposure to drugs or alcohol in utero, impaired cerebral cortex, overactive limbic system within the brain, blood sugar fluctuations, brain trauma, genetic influences, environmental toxins (lead, food additives and colouring), food allergies and, most importantly, nutrient depletions. Orthodox treatment utilises stimulant and depressive medications as well as behavioural modifications, however, nutritional supplementation has been presenting some very positive results.

Babies and Infants
Even before we are born, specific nutrients are required for brain development and brain functions. Essential fatty acids found in fish oil such as DHA (Docosahexaenoic acid) and EPA (Eicosapentaenoic acid) are vital for healthy growth and development of babies.

A baby's supply of nutrients is totally reliant on the levels present in the mother's diet. The extra requirements during pregnancy may also lead to the mother's and baby's levels being depleted.

Children
Children developing without, or with diminished levels of, these nutrients may develop their own problems, for example, ADD, ADHD, hyperactivity, lack of concentration, depression, degenerative disorders of the brain, and comprehension and learning disorders. Studies show that children supplemented with DHA had higher IQs and learning abilities than children who did not.

Signs and Symptoms
ADD, ADHD and Hyperactivity should be diagnosed properly by a health professional. Signs and symptoms may include one or a combination of the following;
- Head knocking
- Self destructive behaviour
- Emotional instability, temper tantrums and impatience
- Learning disabilities, disorders of speech and hearing
- Extreme distractibility, forgetfulness and absentmindedness
- Inability to sit still, clumsiness and sleep disturbances
- Failure in school despite average or above average intelligence.

Naturopathic recommendations

Nutrition
Studies show ADHD boys having DHA deficiency, a compound found in Omega 3, which produced symptoms including allergies, eczema, excessive thirst, frequent urination, brittle nails and dry skin. ADHD and ADD sufferers may not be able to convert dietary essential fatty acids (Omega 3 and 6) found in plant oils. However, they can convert DHA found in Omega 3 fish oils. So direct intake of Omega 3 sourced from fish oil as opposed to Omega 3 sourced from plant oils may be more effective.

Include essential fatty acids Omega 3 (fish oil and flax oil) and 6 (evening primrose oil) along with nutrients including vitamin E and phosphatidylserine oil from lecithin or soy in the daily supplementary intake.

Naturopathic nutritional suggestions
- Refer to a naturopath for testing for food allergies (gluten, dairy, chocolate, oranges, eggs, peanuts, sugars, phosphate and salicylate foods) and heavy metal toxicity.
- Phosphate, salicylate, gluten, refined carbohydrate and, if necessary, dairy-free diets have proved to make a substantial change in ADD and ADHD individuals.
- To avoid low blood sugar levels which have been linked to aggressive and hyperactive behaviour eat 5–6 times daily. This means breakfast, morning tea, lunch, afternoon tea, dinner and a snack, or 3 main meals with two to three snacks in between. Ensure a combination of protein and carbohydrate is eaten at least 3 times daily, and try to use fresh organic produce to improve nutrition. Whole grains such as brown rice, oats and millet are low-glycaemic and full of nutrients.
- Eliminate all foods and drinks that contain artificial colourings, sweeteners, flavours and preservatives, as these may aggravate ADD and ADHD symptoms.
- Avoid phosphates and salicylates (as included below) as these may aggravate. Many health professionals recommend removing gluten and dairy products as these may aggravate food allergies, resulting in ADD and ADHD symptoms.
- Adults must reduce alcohol to a minimum and avoid stimulants such as caffeine and recreational drugs.

Diet
This diet may seem pretty intimidating but it gives you a basic idea of how far you may have to go. Food sensitivities play a large part in ADD and ADHD. This diet excludes common phosphates, salicylates, gluten and dairy as these are common allergy components of foods.

Protein
- Eat fish, especially salmon, tuna and sardines, as these provide good amounts of fish oil (rich in DHA and EPA) which studies show may be beneficial for ADD and ADHD symptoms.
- Include well-boiled beans and legumes, bean sprouts, lentils, peas, soya, all meats, all fish, all shellfish, and all dairy (unless there is a dairy sensitivity — see a naturopath for testing).
- Some children and adults are allergic to dairy products, which include milk, yoghurt, cream, ice-cream and butter. If dairy is avoided, soya products may be a suitable substitute, although some people are also sensitive to soya, and this should be tested too. If soya is taken as a substitute, choose calcium fortified soya or calcium supplements to reduce calcium deficiencies. Rice, goat's and nut milk can be alternatives to soy milk.
- Avoid cheese, and canned and processed meats, as these are high in phosphates.

Carbohydrates
- Cereals and grains. Eat gluten-free products (gluten-free cookies, pasta and bread) and rice products (Japanese rice crackers, rice cakes and rice porridge). Other gluten-free cereals, grains and flours include pea, millet, kamut, buckwheat, cornflour, cornmeal, maize, polenta, potato, rice and soy. Use rice flour, corn flour or arrowroot for thickening.
- Avoid wheat, rye, oats, barley, pasta, semolina or foods that contain these products, due to gluten. See your naturopath to test for gluten sensitivity and reactivity.
- Sugars. Studies suggest there is a connection between hyperactive behaviour and the consumption of sugar. Sugars may also increase intestinal candida (thrush), which may cause symptoms similar to ADD and ADHD.
- Avoid refined and processed carbohydrate foods such as sugar, cakes, lollies or sweets, biscuits, buns, desserts, puddings and toppings. Try palm sugar, beet sugar, molasses, honey, Stevia and maple syrup as alternative sweeteners.
- Fruit. Low salicylate fruits include apple (golden delicious), banana, paw paw, peeled pear and pomegranates. Moderate salicylate fruits are apple (red delicious, ripe splendour), fresh figs (not dried), lemon, loquat, mango, persimmon, tamarillo (ripe) and bananas.
- Reduce intake of apples (especially Granny Smith, Jonathan and Gala) avocado, rockmelon, watermelon, stone fruits (apricots, nectarines, peaches, plums, prunes), dried fruit, all berries, cherries, kiwifruit, canned lychees, passionfruit, guava, grapes, oranges, grapefruit, mandarins, tangelos and tomatoes. Avoid vinegars except malt. These contain salicylates, which may set off aggressive behaviour.
- Vegetables. Low salicylate vegetables include bamboo shoots, cabbages, celery, choko, leeks, lettuces and swedes. Asparagus (fresh only), beetroot (fresh or boiled), broccoli, carrots, cauliflower, corns, marrows, mushroom, onion, parsnip, turnip, cooked unpeeled potatoes, kumara or sweet potato, pumpkin, yams, rhubarb and spinach are suitable too.
- Avoid capsicum, pickled vegetables, olives, chillies, radishes, tomatoes, especially concentrate, zucchini, canned asparagus, broad beans, cucumber, eggplant and watercress.

Fats
- Avoid almonds, peanuts and water chestnuts.
- Do have fish oils, flax oils, phosphatidylserine oil, borage (starflower) oil, evening primrose oils, safflower and cold pressed unheated oils. Use small amounts of olive oil heated with stir-frys.

Dairy
- Eat ghee (small amount), rice milk, goat's milk and yoghurt, white cheese, such as feta, quark, cottage cheese or ricotta, and nut milks.

How to make nut milk

Soak ½ cup nuts (cashew) overnight in ½ litre of water and add a small vanilla pod. Blend and add ½ tsp of cold pressed oil (flax, apricot kernel and safflower oil).

Drinks
- Drink water, cocoa, Milo (use as a treat and sparingly only), carob and chamomile tea.
- Avoid all brands of tea and cordial drinks.
- Avoid carbonated beverages that contain a large amount of phosphates, which may be responsible for hyperkinesis (exaggerated muscle activity).

Herbs and spices
- Garlic, parsley, vanilla, tamari Japanese soy sauce (because it is gluten-free) and malt vinegar.

- Avoid all other vinegars, Vegemite, Marmite, Promite, Worcestershire sauce, tomato sauce, mustard, curry, and large amounts of mint.

Other
- Use natural toothpaste to avoid preservatives and artificial sugars.
- Reduce phosphate intake by avoiding soft drinks, canned and processed meats, cheeses, instant soups, puddings and toppings.

Supplements

Minerals **Magnesium**, **Zinc** or **Iron** deficiencies can trigger ADD or ADHD symptoms. Take these supplements as professionally advised.

Vitamin E Aids essential fatty acid metabolism and acts as an antioxidant against fatty degeneration. A deficiency is linked to many neurological problems such as muscle weakness and visual defects. Take 100IU–200IU daily.

Phosphatidylserine From **Lecithin**; an important fatty lipid found in the brain that aids brain and nerve function, including memory, concentration, cognition, attention and behaviour. Take 50mg–150mg daily.

Fish oil Provides Omega 3 oil that contains the essential fatty acids EPA and DHA, important building blocks for the nervous system and brain, which aid brain signals and cell communication. Those with ADD or ADHD may be deficient in these nutrients. Take 3000mg daily.

Flax oil Provides plant sources of Omega 3 and 6, although it may not convert quite as well as Fish oil, it's still a great substitute for olive oil salad dressings. You can also mix it into butter or mayonnaise on sandwiches or add to health shakes to increase Omega 3 and 6 supplementation. Take 1 Tbsp–2 Tbsp daily.

Spirulina A natural source of nutrients, including Iron, Zinc and B Vitamins, to boost nutrition. Take 1 tsp–3 tsp daily, and add to a shake.

Colostrum Helps to heal the gut, reduces reactivity to foods and helps boost immunity by fighting infections. Take 4g daily.

5-Hydroxy tryptophan (5HTP) A serotonin precursor made naturally by the body and also sourced from the plant *Griffonia simplicifolia* that helps boost serotonin levels reducing anxiety and insomnia. Take 150mg–300mg daily. Due to a lack of research, for safety I can only recommend it for children above 12 years of age.

Schuessler Tissue Salts **Kali Phos**, **Mag Phos** and **Silica** act as nerve tonics, to aid relaxation and irritability and improve memory and thinking. Dissolve 1 tablet in mouth every half hour until symptoms reduce, then 4 tablets daily to maintain.

Herbs

Parasite-cleansing herbs Parasites and intestinal candida may be linked with ADD and ADHD causing irritation, food sensitivities, chronic inflammation and brain fog. Take 2 3-week courses of **Cloves** (1800mg daily) combined with **Wormwood** (2000mg daily) and **Black Walnut** (2000mg daily) to help eradicate parasites. Children above 6 years, take half of the adult dose.

Herbal detoxing Heavy metal toxicity, e.g. Lead, Mercury, Cadmium, Copper and Aluminium, can be a factor leading to ADD or ADHD. See Detoxing for further details.

Herbs for anger, aggression, tension, anxiety and stress

Bach™ flower remedies Choose a single remedy or a combination recommended by a health professional. Take 4 times daily or as recommended.

Relaxing herbs Valerian, Lemon Balm, Hops, Chamomile, Passionflower, Wood Betony and Skullcap may be beneficial. Children 6–12 years, take 1/2 the dose as directed on bottles.

Herbal teas Mixed with natural pear juice as a sweetener (and to cool them down), herbal teas can be soothing to the nervous system. Try Chamomile, Lemon Balm, Skullcap, Nettle (for iron) and Oatstraw to help relax or use before bed to aid sleep.

Relaxing essential oils Lavender, Chamomile, Lemon Balm or Vanilla (2–3 drops of each). Add to 100ml of Olive oil or a massage oil, such as Almond or Jojoba, and massage into the body, or add 2–3 drops of the essential oils to a basin filled with hot water and breathe in deeply. Children must be supervised during this process, or drop the oil into an essential oil burner or dehumidifier designed for this purpose.

Other treatments
Some children and adults respond well to osteopathic treatment.

Further Reading
No More Ritalin: Treating ADHD Without Drugs by Mary Ann Block (Kensington Publishers, New York, 1996)

Ritalin-Free kids: A Safe, Natural, and Effective Program for Treating ADD and Other Learning Problems by Judyth Reichenberg-Ulman and Robert Ulman (Prima Publishing, Rocklin, CA, 1996)

Re: Food intolerance, *Fed Up* by Sue Dengate (Random House, Australia, 1998)

For more information please contact the ADHD society or support group in your area.

Bad Breath

Bad breath, or halitosis, is when a distinct unpleasant smell comes from the mouth. Those with bad breath can sometimes be oblivious to their own mouth odour although it is obvious and unpleasant to those around them. A person's self-esteem can suffer and they may not smile as much or talk closely with their friends and family, and they can even become depressed. If you find that you have bad breath, whether it's ongoing or short and intermittent, find the cause then treat it successfully.

Causes
Bad breath may be due to an underlying health problem. See your doctor for a thorough check up.

- Heavy metal build-up, such as arsenic, lead, bismuth and methane.
- Mucus build-up from sinusitis, post nasal drip and throat infection can cause excess mucus in the back of the throat, leading to an overabundance of anaerobic bacteria that causes breath problems.
- Dental issues, such as gum disease, poor oral hygiene, mouth bacteria and tooth decay. See a dental professional for proper diagnosis and treatment.
- Digestive system issues, such as improper diet, constipation, indigestion, low hydrochloric acid, protein maldigestion, liver malfunction, pathogenic digestive tract infection, candida and overgrowth of stomach bacteria.
- Smoking (tobacco) dries out the mouth and promotes overgrowth of anaerobic bacteria that create a sulphurous smell. Nicotine smoke leaves an unpleasant odour too.
- Diabetes can cause a fruity acetone smell from ketosis.
- Stress or nervous tension.
- Foods and food sensitivities. Dairy products and tea or coffee together will cause instant bad breath.
- Dry mouth due to excessive talking, breathing through your mouth rather than your

nose, snoring and alcohol (wine, beer and even commercial mouth rinse containing alcohol) can cause your saliva to thicken and anaerobic (no oxygen) bacteria to produce volatile sulphur compounds.
- Drugs, medication and some chronic illnesses, such as osteoporosis, diabetes, intestinal adhesions and candida.
- Poor nutrition.

Signs and symptoms
- White tongue
- Sour metallic taste or an acidic taste
- Odorous breath
- Bloating, flatulence and burping.

Naturopathic recommendations

Lifestyle hints
Many people give up too early and need to persevere to clear halitosis. Some people need to concentrate on their programmes longer than others for positive results.

Nutrition
- Drink plenty of water, at least 8 glasses daily, to avoid dehydration, especially if you talk a lot, exercise a great deal or if you are on a high protein diet. See a dental hygienist to check your teeth and gums, a naturopath for food sensitivities or your G.P. for a full check up.
- Alcohol makes the mouth extremely dry and will cause instant bad breath. Wine, beer and even commercial mouth-rinse cause dehydration. In addition, several studies have shown that too much alcohol over a period of time can destroy oral tissue.
- If you suspect candida is the cause, follow the anti-candida diet because all bacteria thrive on sugar. Peppermint candies may give you a false sense of having lovely, minty breath, but bad breath can still be smelled by others.
- Reduce or avoid coffee, tea, eggs, red meat and dairy products, including ice cream, milk, cheese and yoghurt (organic unsweetened is the exception). Onions, leeks and garlic will create bad breath instantly because they contain sulphur compounds. To help you get rid of bad breath after eating onion or garlic, eat plenty of carrots, parsley and celery.
- Consume plenty of green leafy and crunchy vegetables, berries, cherries, apples and pears.
- Brush your teeth and tongue thoroughly after each meal. Floss every day and rinse your mouth with warm water with 1 tsp of apple cider vinegar and 3 drops of Lugol's iodine with a little salt, dissolved in it, then follow up with a glass of fresh water to avoid thirst after the salt rinse.

Supplements
Coenzyme Q10   Deficiencies lead to poor gum health and eventually gum disease. Take 75mg daily and apply oil topically to the gums.
Zinc   Can help reduce bad breath by inhibiting the bacteria that create the sulphur compounds. Take 50mg with food daily.
Vitamin C and **Vitamin A**   Essential for gum and digestive tract health. Take 1500mg of Vitamin C daily and 5000IU of Vitamin A daily.
Fibre   **Flax, Pysllium** or **Slippery Elm** should be taken to support the good bacteria in the digestive tract, to aid regularity during constipation or diarrhoea, to coat the digestive tract to aid healing, and to increase fibre and protective lignans in the diet. Take 1 tsp–3 tsp of these fibres, singly or in combination, with a large glass of water daily.

Digestive enzymes Improve digestion by taking digestive enzymes, especially Papaya (Papain), Bromelain, Betaine, Pepsin, Cellulase and Lactase. These enzymes break down the protein and lactose from meats and dairy products and break down sulphur in vegetables (broccoli, cabbage, cauliflower) as improper digestion can lead to bad breath. Take a digestive enzyme formula as directed.

Acidophilus and **Bifidus** Good bacteria that help to keep the digestive system healthy and overcome candida or fungal overgrowth within the digestive system. Take 1 billion of the Acidophilus and Bifidus species in capsule form daily on an empty stomach to repopulate your digestive system.

Bioflavonoids Hesperidin, **Rutin** and **Quercetin** help build resistance to infection, and aid in preventing and healing bleeding gums. Take 400mg of Quercetin 3 times daily or 1000mg of mixed Bioflavonoids daily.

Nutrients Help to gently cleanse and deodorise the body and supply the 'greens' found in green leafy vegetables. Take **Chlorophyll** (5ml 3 times daily), **Aloe Vera** juice (20ml daily), **Spirulina** (1 tsp 3 times daily) and **Chlorella** (1 tsp 3 times daily).

Herbs

Cleansing Excellent for halitosis, as it aids the digestive and internal systems of the body. Take Vitamin C, Garlic, Shark Liver oil and total body cleansing herbs Milk Thistle, Red Clover, Yellow Dock, Burdock and Liquorice. See Detoxing, page 131.

Bacterial, viral and **fungal infections** Take 270mg of **Olive Leaf** extract 3 times daily and 1200mg–6g of **Echinacea** daily for 10–30 days for signs of microbial, viral, bacterial or fungal infection.

Myrrh or **Bee Propolis tincture** Brush the tincture directly onto the gums, gargle and take internal amount as directed on the bottle. It will not taste very nice, but due to its antiseptic and astringent qualities myrrh is very effective against gum disease.

Parasite-cleansing herbs Parasites can inflame, irritate and perforate the intestinal lining, resulting in 'leaky gut'. This can lead to undigested food particles entering the bloodstream and creating food allergies, candida and gut toxicity. Take two 3-week courses of **Cloves** (1800mg daily) combined with **Wormwood** (2000mg daily) and **Black Walnut** (2000mg daily) to help eradicate parasites.

Boils

Boils are tender and often painful abscesses caused by blockages of the hair follicle that have become infected and are most commonly found on the neck, under the arms, thighs and buttocks. If they spread to other hair follicles the collected mass is called a carbuncle.

Causes

- The common skin bacteria *Staphylococcus aureus* is found to cause boils.
- Boils may also be a symptom of low immunity.
- Poor nutrition, such as diets high in junk food and sugar, and low in vegetables and fruit.
- Poor hygiene leads to spread of infectious boils.

Signs and symptoms

- The tip of the boil will be smooth and round or with a white pinpoint pus head with a deeper hardened centralised core.

Naturopathic recommendations

Lifestyle hints
- See your doctor if the boils spread, if they do not reduce within three days, if bluish reddish veins become more pronounced, if the area feels extremely painful and tender, or if a mild fever develops.

Hygiene
- Hygiene is extremely important to prevent the spread of boils. Wash and dry hands often and thoroughly. Clean the area with tea tree oil and warm water before applying the recommendations below.
Lugol's (aqueous) iodine   Swab 'boil' area with a clean cotton bud soaked in iodine and take 4 drops of Lugol's iodine daily for 7 days. Do not confuse this type of iodine with BP tincture of iodine. If BP tincture of iodine is all you can source, apply this to the boils, but do not consume. Add Lugol's iodine to a glass of hot water, 1 tsp of manuka honey and 1 tsp of apple cider vinegar. Avoid taking iodine internally if you are allergic to iodine, or taking thyroid medication.
Tea tree oil   To help eradicate the infection apply antiseptic tea tree oil over the top of the iodine twice daily.

Nutrition
- Ensure a well-balanced diet by eating plenty of raw and steamed green leafy vegetables, carrots, celery, broccoli and fresh fruit.
- Reduce sugar and refined carbohydrate intake.
- Avoid alcohol and coffee and drink 8 glasses of pure, fresh water daily.

Supplements
Vitamin A (5000IU daily), **Vitamin C** (1.5g daily) and **Zinc** (45mg daily)   Help to increase the body's ability to resist infections and heal wounds.
Acidophilus, Bifidus   Replacement is needed for a healthy digestive system after medical antibiotic therapy. Take 1–2 capsules (active 1 billion) daily for at least 10–20 days.

Herbs
If taking antibiotics and the treatment does not appear to be working you may combine these herbs with antibiotic therapy if the *staph* spp. bacteria appears to be slightly resistant.
Olive Leaf extract (270mg 6 times daily), **Goldenseal** (1500mg dried root daily), **Myrrh** (30 drops of tincture daily) and **Echinacea** (1200mg–6g daily)   Help to eradicate skin infections
Red Clover flowers (2g–4g daily), **Cleavers** (2g–4g daily) and **Burdock** (2g–6g of dried root daily)   Blood purifiers that help to cleanse out the toxins within tissues and the bloodstream. These work extremely well for boils, especially if they are ongoing or recurring.
I can't help but recommend two particular products for boils because I have had a lot of success with them. **Jamu Gadong Gadok** coupled with **Jamu Bersih Darah**, are Indonesian blood cleansing herbal formulas produced by an Indonesian herbal company, Nonya Meneer. Try the internet to purchase these products. I admit it takes a while to get used to the taste, but they work wonders. Take as directed.

Drawing compresses and poultices
Apply an **Epsom mineral compress** by mixing 2 Tbsp of Epsom salts with hot water and

soaking a clean flannel in this mixture. Apply onto the area of the boil to bring it to a head. **Burdock poultices** can help reduce inflammation and boils.

> *How to make a Burdock poultice*
>
> Wash a handful of Burdock leaves and roots, and crush. Boil in hot water and simmer for 15 minutes. Strain the fluid, and drink it or add to vegetable stock. While warm place the mashed roots and leaves directly onto the boil. Cover with a clean cloth and rest for 30 minutes. Apply twice daily.

Bone Spurs

Bone spurs or osteophytes are a natural response of the human body to stress placed upon bone. The bone will grow where excessive forces or trauma have been applied. Normally found on the heel, bone spurs are calcium deposits that form a pointed growth and cause pain and discomfort when weight is applied during activity, such as walking.

Cause

- Physical stress or trauma to the area causing formation of calcium deposits as the body tries to heal the damage.
- Individuals with bone spurs are normally over 40–50 years of age, or experience arthritis and obesity.
- Ill fitting shoes may lead to bone spurs.
- An excess of joint-chewing enzymes can cause the joint cartilage to break down faster than your body can rebuild it. This can lead to the formation of bone spurs around damaged cartilage and joints, most often on hands and feet.

Signs and symptoms

- An X-ray will show formation of bone spurs.
- Tenderness when walking or applying weight onto the area of the bone spur.

Naturopathic recommendations

Lifestyle hints
Exercise

- Gentle water exercise, such as swimming, is practical and important for your heart, health and fitness. Weights can strengthen your body and stretches will allow your body to become more flexible and feel relaxed. Exercise 4–5 times a week.

Nutrition

- Some food sensitivities may trigger the pain, including chocolate, oranges, tomatoes, potatoes, eggplant, tobacco, paprika and chilli. Use corn, sweet potato (kumara), pumpkin, squash and turnips in place of potatoes
- Avoid caffeine, soda, cooked spinach and rhubarb.
- Eat fresh fruit, especially pineapple, cherries, berries and apples. Other beneficial foods include broccoli, cabbage and cauliflower.
- Drink 8 glasses of pure, fresh water daily.

Supplements

Schuessler Tissue Salt Combination U One of my favourite homoeopathic mineral combinations for the balanced assimilation of Calcium. Take 4 tablets 4 times daily for 3 months.
Magnesium Take 450mg 1–2 times daily to help reduce nerve pain and balance Calcium absorption.
Bromelain Helps break down protein and reduce inflammation. Take 450mg 2–3 times daily.
Betaine or **Hydrochloric acid supplements** Stomach (Hydrochloric) acid is often deficient in people above 50 years of age. It is important for the absorption of Calcium and other minerals that are needed for bone growth, metabolism and repair. Take 100mg–200mg 3 times daily with meals.
Also see the arthritis (Osteo) recommendations for other supplementary recommendations.

Herbs

See the arthritis (Osteo) recommendations for herbal recommendations.

Bronchitis

Bronchitis is so debilitating that a lot of people can really feel quite down in the dumps due to the lack of oxygen, the extra effort to breathe, and fatigue. People with bronchitis really need to learn to slow down and look after themselves with a bit of tender loving care, as is the case with most illnesses. Bronchitis describes irritation and inflammation of the bronchi, the airways and passages within the lungs.

There are two types of bronchitis

Acute bronchitis Occurs when there is inflammation of the airways normally as a result of a viral infection, such as the common cold or the flu, spreading from the sinuses and throat into the lungs. This can produce a dry irritating cough which can become productive in several days with phlegm ranging from clear to yellow, green and with streaks of fresh blood, if coughing is particularly violent. Sore throat, mild fever, sore chest and excess mucus often accompany the coughing. With treatment you can normally expect a speedy recovery.
Chronic bronchitis More ongoing or recurring, and can be related to damage from inhaled smoke, environmental pollution, chemicals and microbial infections, such as viruses or bacteria. Excessive mucus build-up and production occurs within the lungs (bronchi) with inflammation of the airways and sometimes fibrosis. Chronic bronchitis results in a very 'wet' cough and a sore chest and throat from constant coughing. The mucus can be difficult to cough up and can be slightly yellow-green in colour. The individual can feel emotional and tired, as not enough oxygen is circulating through the body or the brain. If left untreated, chronic bronchitis may lead to more serious complications, such as pneumonia.

Causes

- Bacterial infection
- Viral infections
- Smoking, environmental pollution or chemical inhalation
- An inherited deficiency of α_1-antitrypsin.

Signs and symptoms

- Runny nose, mild fever, cold or flu is usually experienced before the onset of bronchitis.
- Dry or slightly productive cough and a sore throat.
- Chest tightness or breathlessness and associated insomnia.
- Excessive mucus (bacteria thrive in these mucus collections).
- Tiredness, malaise and mild depression.

Naturopathic recommendations

Lifestyle hints

If symptoms persist, abnormal neck stiffness occurs, a rash appears, blood in mucus appears, fever increases or if breathing becomes difficult, see your doctor in case of other complications, such as meningitis or influenza. A visit to your doctor may be necessary to rule out any secondary bacterial infections, heart complications or pneumonia. Oxygen therapy may need to be applied if short of breath or dizzy.

- Stop smoking or working with environmental pollutants and harsh chemicals.
- You need plenty of rest — try to rest in bed for a least three days if you are not doing so already. Without rest you are likely to relapse. It may be best for you to rest sitting up to prevent aggravating your cough.
- Apply heat to help loosen mucous secretions. Cover a heated wheat bag or filled hot water bottle with a thick towel to prevent it burning you and place on your chest or back.

Incorrect breathing, hyperventilation or excessive mouth breathing

Buteyko Breathing tutors can teach people with chronic recurring bronchitis to breathe correctly through the nose with a set of exercises to reduce phlegm, bronchial tightness, asthma and even snoring. I have tried this technique and it works wonderfully if I continue the exercises. See your local directory or website (www.buteyko.co.nz) for more details.

Exercise

- While exercise is normally recommended, do not exercise too strenuously while you have bronchitis, or if you suspect bacterial or viral infection, as this may lead to further complications. In rare circumstances viruses and bacteria can damage the heart. Extra stress on the body reduces the body's capacity to heal itself, when you should be resting.
- When you are well enough, exercise consistently, but start off gently to maintain good health.

Nutrition

- Drink plenty of fluids, including diluted vegetable and fruit juices such as carrot, beetroot, silverbeet and apple, vegetable soups and herbal tea preparations. This will help to rehydrate your body, lessen the stickiness of the mucus and relieve dry irritated mucus membranes.
- Avoid sugar...did you now that too much simple refined sugar can lower the ability of your immune system, namely the white blood cells, to function properly? However, if you simply must have sugar, eat a maximum of 2 tsp of Manuka honey or 3 servings of fruit daily, but do not include any more simple refined sugars in your diet until you are better. If you are diabetic follow your health professional's diabetic guidelines.
- Do not eat refined carbohydrates, sugar, dairy products and egg whites — this will help reduce the body's ability to produce mucus. Substitute with soy or rice milk, soy cheeses, stevia (a natural sweetener) and egg substitute. Check out your local health food stockist.

- If you are breathless, opt for a vegetarian diet (no meat, fish or eggs). If this does not suit you, reduce the amount of meat and include beans, chickpeas and lentils to boost your meat dishes. Use organic meats, vegetables, including parsley, basil, green capsicum, broccoli, Brussels sprouts, tomatoes (lots of them) and fruit, and increase horseradish, wasabi, cinnamon, fenugreek, garlic, ginger and onions in your diet. You might like to add more culinary herbs to your diet or try drinking honey-sweetened thyme or rosemary tea. Avoid alcohol, tea and coffee.

Supplements

Vitamin C Enhances white blood cell activity and immune support. Take 500mg every 2–3 hours.

Zinc Requirements are increased during poor immunity. Take 45mg daily.

Vitamin A or its precursor **Beta Carotene** Helps to heal any damage to the lining of the airways. Take 5000IU–8000IU daily.

Bromelain An enzyme from pineapple that helps to break down and reduce the stickiness of mucus congestion. Take 450mg 2–3 times daily.

Herbs

Lobelia Reduces inflammation, acts as a respiratory stimulant and relieves congested mucus. Take 50mg–200mg of dried Lobelia herb 3 times daily. Start at the lower dose first and build up. High doses can cause vomiting.

Liquorice Soothing to the airways and reduces mucous congestion and inflammation in the airways. Stress can trigger asthma, and Liquorice also helps the body adapt better to stress and has a mild action against viral infection such as colds and flu. Take 1g–5g of Liquorice Root daily. Take as directed by a naturopath or herbalist as Liquorice causes high blood pressure in certain doses or with long-term use. (See appendices for more information.)

Fenugreek Selected for its congestion-relieving and airway-soothing properties. Take 300mg–900mg daily. Alternatively add 1 tsp of slightly crushed Fenugreek Seeds to 1 cup of hot water. Cover for 15 minutes, strain then drink.

White Horehound (1g–2g daily), **Thyme** (1g–2g daily) and **Hyssop** (1g–2g daily) Act as expectorants for non-productive coughs, dry coughs, coughing spasms and excess mucus within the respiratory tract.

Wild Cherry Bark Particularly good for coughs that cause the individual to become exhausted. Indicated for dry and wet coughs. Take 3g–7g daily

Marshmallow Root (2g–5g daily) and the dried flowers or leaves of **Coltsfoot** (2g–5g daily) and **Mullein** (2g–5g daily) Have soothing actions on the bronchi, reducing inflammation of the airways and decreasing the stickiness of mucus while helping the body to expel the mucus from the lungs.

Elecampane A warming expectorant (mucus clearer) that also stimulates the cilia hairs of the bronchi to eliminate mucus congestion from the lungs. Take 1g–4g of dried root daily.

Olive Leaf extract (270mg 3 times daily) and **Echinacea** (1200mg–6g daily) Take for 10–30 days if signs of microbial viral, bacterial or fungal infection are present. These herbs also help to improve the body's immune system.

Other popular herbs for bronchitis include **Mouse Ear**, **Kumerahou**, **Euphorbia** and **Wild Indigo** for infection, coughs and mucus build-up. The herbs **Sundew**, **White Willow**, **Wood Betony** or **Yarrow** help to reduce the fever and pain. Take as directed by a naturopath or health professional.

Aromatherapy

Menthol, **Pine**, **Eucalyptus**, **Basil**, **Wintergreen**, **Chamomile**, **Thyme**, **Lavender** and **Rosemary** essential oils are useful in aromatherapy oil burners or in steam inhalation (1–2

drops in a basin filled with hot water) to help clear the sinuses and airways while reducing inflammation of the sinuses and bronchi. Mix 3–10 drops in 100ml of olive oil or a base oil (almond or jojoba or unscented sesame oil) and massage onto the throat, chest and back.

Reflexology

Apply aromatherapy oils to the base and top of the foot, working in areas that appear sensitive or tender. These reflect acupressure points of the feet that may benefit the corresponding areas of the body. The ball areas of the feet are the main areas for the lungs. I use a lot of reflexology, especially when I'm working on myself. Try it gently on yourself if no one volunteers and then work at the area for around 5 minutes. If you can bear it, try adding a little more pressure the next time round to stimulate healing reflexes.

Bruises

Bruises or haematomas are clots of blood that have accumulated in the tissues after an injury or trauma. Corners of coffee tables are my number one enemy when it comes to bruises — I wonder what yours are?

Causes

Bruising often occurs when body parts are banged against hard objects, although some people bruise much more easily. Factors that contribute to bruising include surgical operations, poor nutrition, anaemia, Von Willebrand's disease or anti-clotting conditions, Vitamin C deficiency, smoking and cancer.

Von Willebrand's disease is the most common hereditary bleeding disorder. The disease is estimated to occur in 3 or 4 people per 100,000. There are no racial or ethnic associations for this disorder. A family history of a bleeding disorder is the primary risk factor. It is transmitted by an autosomal gene and affects both sexes. Most cases are mild and bleeding may occur after a surgical procedure or tooth extraction.

The condition is worsened by the use of aspirin and other non-steroidal anti-inflammatory drugs.

Signs and symptoms

- When underlying skin tissues are damaged, blood collects under the skin causing swelling, pain and black and blue marks. These marks start out red, but as the blood gets reabsorbed into the tissues the marks may turn dark blue and then yellow before they disappear.
- Von Willebrand's disease presents as nose bleeds, bleeding gums, abnormal menstrual bleeding, bruising and skin rash. Children with Von Willebrand's disease should avoid unnecessary trauma, and those with severe disease should avoid contact sports. During menstruation, adolescent females may want to take extra precautions to avoid embarrassing accidents as Von Willebrand's disease may cause excessive bleeding. During bleeding episodes, elevate and apply cold compresses and gentle pressure to the area. During nose bleeds, apply pressure to the soft tissue under the bridge of the nose, and have the child lean forward until bleeding stops, to prevent blood running down the back of the throat and being swallowed.

Naturopathic recommendations

Lifestyle hints
- Apply pressure and cold compresses initially to help reduce bleeding and swelling. After the first day, apply hot compresses to help speed the absorption of blood. Massage can help clear some bruises. However, the correct techniques to help clear the blood and not create more bruising are essential.

Nutrition
- Eat fruits that contain vitamin C and bioflavonoids to help strengthen and tone blood capillaries. These include berries, cherries, capsicum, citrus fruit and kiwifruit.

Supplements
There are many nutrients that help prevent bruising by improving blood clotting and strength of capillary walls. Other nutrients may help eliminate deficiencies that make people more prone to bruising.

Vitamin B12, Folic acid and **Iron**   Help the formation and regeneration of red blood cells, thus helping prevent anaemia or bruising related to anaemia.

> **Vitamin B12**   Methylcobalamin is preferred over the cyanocobalamin form. Take 1g daily with Folic acid and a Vitamin B complex for better absorption if B12 deficiency is due to dietary lack. B12 deficiencies may need to be treated by intravenous injections by a doctor to reverse anaemia and nerve damage. If you suspect severe anaemia, consult your naturopath or doctor.
>
> **Folic acid**   Take 400mcg–800mcg daily.
>
> **Iron succinate** or **fumartate**   These preferred iron forms are highly absorbable and do not appear to upset the stomach or cause constipation. Take 30mg 3 times daily with meals.

Vitamin K   May help tissues reabsorb blood more quickly. See your health professional for Vitamin K dosage advice.

Multi vitamin and **mineral formula**   Take a multi that includes Vitamins B1, B2, B3, B5, choline and B6, Vitamin C, Calcium and Copper, which are needed for red blood cell formation, to increase Iron absorption and aid nutrient deficiencies. Take as directed.

Vitamin C (Ascorbic Acid)   Helps heal wounds and strengthen blood vessels as it is required for the synthesis of collagen, the intercellular 'cement' which holds tissues together. Take 1500mg daily.

ProenOthera® (Evening Primrose Seed Husk), Bilberry, Grape Seed, Green tea and **Pine Bark extracts**   Tiny blood vessels (capillaries) can become fragile, especially in older people, producing capillary fragility. This can lead to more frequent bruising. Oligomeric Proanthocyanidins (OPCs) are the active components of these nutrients and strengthen capillaries by protecting them from free radical damage and by stimulating the formation of healthy connective tissue and aiding in the formation of new capillaries, or regeneration. Take 1000mg of a mixed combination of these antioxidants daily.

Bioflavonoids   **Hesperidin, Rutin** and **Quercetin** increase the strength of the blood vessels and help to regulate their permeability, reduce the red appearance of dilated veins and capillaries. They also assist the role of Vitamin C to help strengthen collagen structures of the skin, are essential for the proper absorption and use of Vitamin C and prevent its destruction by oxidation. In combination with Vitamin C they are beneficial in hypertension, help prevent haemorrhages and ruptures in the capillaries and connective tissues, assist with immunity during infections and aid in preventing and healing bleeding gums. Take 400mg of Quercetin 3 times daily or 1000mg of mixed Bioflavonoids daily.

Glucosamine (1500mg daily) and **Chondroitin** (1200mg daily)   Play a role in wound healing by providing the necessary ingredients called glycosaminoglycans (GAGs) for the capillary walls.

Schuessler Tissue Salts   Calc Fluor is a homoeopathic preparation of minerals to strengthen veins and create tissue tone and elasticity. Take as directed.

Herbs

Gotu Kola extract, Horse Chestnut extract and **Butcher's Broom**   Strengthen connective tissue structures within the veins and capillaries. Take 30mg of Gotu Kola extract (Triterpenes) daily, 10mg–20mg of Aescin (standardised Horse Chestnut extract) 3 times daily and 300mg of standardised Butcher's Broom (11% Ruscogenin) daily.

Arnica   A traditional herbal and homoeopathic remedy for bruising. Take an acute dose of Arnica homoeopathic pillules as directed until condition is alleviated and then use a maintenance dose. Apply Arnica cream or oil in the morning and at night.

Bach™ Rescue Remedy   Apply 2 sprays or 4 drops on bruise immediately to prevent formation of bruise and to ease shock.

Witchhazel cream or **lotion**   Applied twice daily works as an astringent toning broken blood vessels.

Von Willebrand's disease

Avoid the following if you have Von Willebrand's disease (does not apply for normal bruising).

Medicines   Avoid any drugs with antiplatelet or anticoagulant actions unless prescribed by your health professional.

Herbs   Avoid high doses of **Ginkgo, Red Clover, Feverfew, Meadowsweet, White Willow Bark** and **Garlic.**

Nutrients   Avoid taking large doses of **Vitamin E, Flax oil, Fish oil, Evening Primrose oil** and **Borage oil**, unless prescribed by your doctor, as in high doses they have a blood-thinning effect.

Candida (Candidiasis)

Candida is caused by an overgrowth of yeast, leading to fungal infection. This commonly occurs within the mouth, ears, nose, gastro-intestinal tract or genital tract, e.g. vagina. Candida is part of our normal microflora, meaning that it is supposed to be residing harmoniously within our bodies. However, due to the causes outlined below, candida can become opportunistic, thriving, growing and causing an imbalance in our normal internal microflora. Candida overgrowth produces toxins (canditoxins) that travel through the bloodstream affecting all of our body's organs and tissues.

Causes

- High sugar or refined carbohydrate diets
- Poor immunity, diabetes, gall-stones, liver dysfunction, HIV, AIDS, immune diseases acquired or genetic
- Overuse of antibiotics, thyroid hormone use, some medications including asthma steroids
- Nutrient deficiencies
- Excessive alcohol intake
- Immunosuppressive drugs including steroids
- Pregnancy

- Hormonal imbalance and oral contraceptives
- Stress
- Poor gastric acid output
- Poor liver function and toxicity
- Infection.

Signs and symptoms
- Chronic fatigue, muscle fatigue or pain, joint pain, anxiety, dizziness, poor libido, memory fog, attention deficit disorder (ADD), attention deficit hyperactivity disorder (ADHD), autism, headaches, gritty sore eyes, irritability, poor concentration, craving for sweet foods, foods containing yeast, carbohydrates or alcoholic beverages.
- Acne, itchiness, nappy rash (babies), allergies, asthma, eczema and psoriasis.
- Diarrhoea or constipation, heartburn, abdominal cramps, colic, mucus in stools, rectal itching, bloating, gas, bad breath, irritable bowel syndrome, colitis and Crohn's disease.
- Oral or genital thrush, vaginitis, vaginal itching or labia redness, chronic cystitis, PMS, fluid retention, hot flushes and night sweats.
- Sore throat, dry cough, glue ear, sinusitis, blisters in mouth, mouth ulcers, burning tongue and round, white plaques on tongue.

Naturopathic recommendations

Lifestyle hints
Naturopaths like to treat candida conditions within the patient from top to toe. This includes helping nutrient deficiencies, repopulating the gut with beneficial gut flora, killing excess candida and lots more. The mistake a lot of self-treating people make is that they concentrate on only one of these items when a whole series of treatments must be used at the same time for success. Believe me, if naturopaths could recommend only one or two treatments and they worked, we would.
- If necessary, reduce or avoid the following drugs, with substitute measures put in place by health professionals first: anti-ulcer drugs, corticosteroids, oral contraceptives, oestrogen replacement therapy and antibiotics.
- Also avoid chemicals (including bubble baths, deodorant, tampons or pads and scented toilet paper) contacting candida-affected areas. Buy organic cotton pads and tampons.
- Wear loose 100% pure cotton underwear. Avoid nylon and tight pantyhose. Sterilise all underwear and towels that have contacted fungal areas after each use in extremely hot water and Dettol or Napisan to avoid cross-contamination.
- Speaking of cross-contamination, it is likely that any sexual partners who have come into contact with candida will have an overgrowth too, especially men who are prone to athlete's foot. This is common, and partners may carry fungal infections that are not symptomatic for many years. If you or your partner has athlete's foot, apply echinacea herbal liquid tincture to the fungal areas 2 times daily, but not on broken skin. Apply tea tree oil twice daily (may be added to shampoo and conditioner for dandruff). Dilute with water if too strong. Dry skin and toes properly twice a day and you may also paint iodine onto the fungal area. Always use a towel cleaned with bleach (old ones are good), do not let it get wet and musty smelling, use a fresh one daily and never let anyone else use it.
- Avoid sexual intercourse while symptoms persist. Condoms will not give much protection, due to infected fluids around the pubic area, which may irritate the vaginal area. However, if you do have sex, wash and dry thoroughly after intercourse. Wipe toilet paper from front to back after elimination and thoroughly dry the vaginal area after

bathing or swimming, possibly with a blow dryer on a low setting, to avoid warm, moist breeding grounds for external candida.
- Avoid smoking nicotine and recreational drugs.

Nutrition

- Identify and eliminate food sensitivities. The most common are wheat, gluten, citrus and dairy foods.
- Until the candida is under control, avoid sugary foods, yeast, foods made with yeast and sugar, and fermented foods or beverages (this includes beer, wine, alcohol, cheeses, peanuts, mushrooms, lollies, chocolate, cakes, etc., breads, fizzy drinks, eating too much fruit or fermented soy, etc., beetroot, Marmite, Vegemite, Promite, honey, maple syrup, etc.). Avoid fresh and dried fruit and juices because of fructose sugar content — these foods feed thrush. Take the herb gymnema and/or the mineral chromium to reduce sugar cravings.
- Avoid milk and milk products due to lactose content, possible food sensitivity and antibiotic content. Dairy products may increase yeast growth due to antibiotic content and high lactose (milk sugar) content. The exception to this is unsweetened, unflavoured, non-processed (organic, if possible) yoghurt.

How to make your own yoghurt

1 large jar
1 tea-towel or muslin cloth to cover and a rubber band
De Winkel natural unflavoured yoghurt with acidophilus
Blue-top milk (organic if possible)
Heat 1 pint of organic blue-top milk until it rises (don't let it boil or it won't work very well), then take it off the heat and cool to a lukewarm temperature. Get a large jar and pour in enough De Winkel natural yoghurt to cover ¼ of the jar. Pour the lukewarm milk on top to fill the jar. Cover the jar rim with a clean tea towel or muslin cloth and secure with a rubber band. Put into the hot water cupboard on top of the cylinder overnight. The next morning, put in the fridge. It's now ready to eat.

- Include garlic, onions, ginger, culinary herbs and spices (oregano, basil, parsley, coriander, cinnamon, aniseed and cloves), fresh green leafy vegetables, legumes, nuts and seeds, and fresh, unprocessed organic meat.

Supplements

Fibre Flaxseeds, **Psyllium** or **Slippery Elm** increase dietary fibre, absorb the toxins and aid the balance of beneficial gut bacteria or microflora. Take 1 tsp–1 Tbsp of these fibres, singly or in combination, with plenty of fluid, daily.

Acidophilus and **Bifidus**   Repopulate good bacteria with these species, including *Lactobacillus acidophilus, L. bulgaricus, Bifidobacterium bifidum* and *B. longum*. Take 1–10 billion daily. You can also insert 2 capsules into the vagina to help combat thrush. Remember to thoroughly wash and dry your hands before and after inserting the capsules.

Caprylic acid   A short-chain fatty acid from coconut oil that has an anti-candida effect. Take 1g–2g of slow release Caprylic acid daily.

Multi vitamin and **mineral formula**   A high potency multi vitamin and mineral will help with nutrient deficiencies.

Digestive enzymes   Lack of stomach acid is linked with candida. Improve digestion by taking digestive enzymes, especially Papaya (papain). Take as directed.

Flaxseed oil (2 Tbsp daily) and **Colostrum** (4g daily) May help reduce leaky gut syndrome and inflammation associated with candida.
Vitamin B complex Enhances liver repair and reduces deficiencies caused by oral contraceptives and oestrogen therapy. Take as directed.

Herbs

Reduce overpopulation of candida and increase immune function without killing beneficial bacteria with **Olive Leaf extract** (270mg 3 times daily), **Goldenseal** (1500mg of dried root daily), **Garlic** (400mg–2g daily), **Pau D'Arco** (1.5g–3.5g daily), **Beta 1.3 Glucan** (400mg 2 times daily) and **Astragalus** (500g–10g daily).
Liver-cleansing herbs Take 9g–10g of dried **Milk Thistle Seed** daily and 3g–5g of dried **Dandelion Root** to support the liver and help it withstand candida toxins.
Parasite-cleansing herbs Help eradicate candida, accelerate the healing process and kill microscopic parasites that proliferate with candida infections. Take two 3-week courses of **Cloves** (1800mg daily) combined with **Wormwood** (2000mg daily) and **Black Walnut** (2000mg daily) to help eradicate parasites.
Bach™ flower remedies Choose a single remedy or a combination recommended by a health professional. Take 4 times daily or as recommended to speed up the healing process and emotional aspects associated with candida. Add **Crab Apple** to aid cleansing.
Hormone balancing The herb **Chaste Tree** can be used internally to balance hormones by women who have thrush triggered by their menstrual cycle. Take 750mg 2 times daily.
Stress Take a Vitamin B complex as directed with **Ginseng** (600mg–10g daily), **Liquorice** (2g–4g daily) and **Passionflower** (4g–8g daily) to help adrenal stress.

See a naturopath for more advice if you have ongoing, chronic candida or if you are pregnant or breastfeeding.

Carpal Tunnel Syndrome

A painful condition of the wrist, hand and/or fingers. The median nerve, which is the main nerve to the fingers, becomes compressed as it travels through a canal made by the bones and ligaments of the wrist.

Causes

- Injury or trauma to the wrist area.
- Repetitive strain, or occupational overuse, of the wrist area. Typing, strenuous work with the hands or continuously using pinching or gripping motions and movements can cause repetitive strain, leading to carpal tunnel syndrome (CTS).
- It may be a feature of other diseases, such as diabetes, rheumatoid arthritis and hyperthyroidism.
- Tumours, bone spurs, swelling or inflammation of the tendons can cause compression.
- Can occur during pregnancy, in menopausal women, in patients on haemodialysis or in those who use oral contraceptives, as their requirement for vitamin B6 is higher.

Signs and symptoms

- Numbness and or pain in the wrist and hand
- Pain in the first three fingers or a burning sensation which is worse at night
- Weakness in precision gripping
- Worsened with ongoing, repetitive use and relieved by rest.

Naturopathic recommendations

Lifestyle hints
- Rest your wrists often or apply good working practices and posture if you continue with these movements.
- Bowen technique, self-massage, professional massage or acupuncture can treat CTS, reducing pain and inflammation.
- Hot and cold compresses can reduce inflammation. Alternate between a heated or ice cold flannel on the wrist and fingers that are numb, painful or burning.

Exercise
- Stretching the wrist and fingers daily, yoga, meditation and relaxation will help reduce compression of the nerve and reduce stress associated with CTS.

Nutrition
- Avoid high protein diets and food colouring, especially yellow dye in foods. This has been linked with CTS. Include adequate, but not excessive, amounts of protein.
- Whole raw and cooked, organic fruits, vegetables, grains, seeds, beans and nuts can be beneficial.
- Reduce caffeine, especially instant coffee as intake can increase pain.
- Reduce alcohol, saturated fat and refined sugar intake.
- Avoid food intolerances and allergies.
- Drink 8 glasses of fresh water per day.

Supplements
Vitamin B6   Important for nerve function. Deficiencies of B6 are linked to CTS. You may need to take Vitamin B6 for as long as three months before benefits can be seen. Take 25mg–50mg 3 times daily.

Vitamin B complex   Essential to aid B6 absorption and for proper nerve function. Take 1–2 tablets daily.

Vitamin C   Reduces inflammation within muscles and tendons and aids healing. Take 1500mg daily.

MSM (Methyl Sulphonyl Methane)   This natural sulphur compound is helpful for relieving compression-type pain. Take 2g daily.

Bromelain   An enzyme from pineapple that reduces inflammation and bruising, and aids healing. Dosage equates to 2000mg (1200mcu–1800mcu 'milk clotting units') per day divided into five doses taken on an empty stomach or 250mg–750mg 2 times daily.

Flax oil, Fish oil and **Evening Primrose oil**   Help reduce inflammation within the joints. Take 3000mg of Evening Primrose oil daily, 3000mg of Fish oil daily or 1 Tbsp–2 Tbsp of Flax oil daily.

Herbs
Devil's claw   Contains two active ingredients, Harpogoside and Betasitosterol, with anti-inflammatory properties that help reduce swelling and pain while also improving the mobility of the joints. One study found that its anti-inflammatory effects equalled those of the commonly prescribed anti-arthritic drug phenylbutazone.[39] Take 500mg of dried root daily.

Celery Seed   Most widely used to help reduce pain and swelling. Celery Seed is a natural diuretic so it can be helpful in preventing fluid build-up. Take 500mg–3g daily.

White Willow Bark   A natural pain reliever with an ingredient similar to aspirin. Take 1g–2g daily.

St John's Wort   Normally popular for its positive effects concerning anxiety and mild depression, SJW is also anti-inflammatory, especially for nerve conditions, such as CTS and sciatica. Take the equivalent of 2g–5g of dried root daily.

Other anti-inflammatory herbs that may be helpful for relieving pain include **Aloe Vera** juice or gel, **Yucca**, **Yarrow**, **Ginger**, **Turmeric** and **Cayenne**.

Aromatherapy and essential oils

Rub or massage Wintergreen oil, Chamomile, Basil or Tiger balm, Arnica oil, or Cayenne (Capsaicin) onto wrist, hand and forearm.

Homoeopathics

Rhus Tox or Ruta Grav homoeopathic drops are indicated to treat CTS. Take as directed.

Cataracts

Cataracts are the most common condition related to age-associated visual loss. The normally transparent lens of the eye becomes cloudy and this interferes with the light transmitted to the retina, reducing vision.

Causes

- Cataracts are common in sportspeople or those who spend a lot of time outdoors without protective eyewear, due to excessive sunlight from either sun glare or snow glare. Ultraviolet rays from the sun cause damage to the proteins that make up the lens.
- Poor metabolism of glucose or galactose.
- Some drugs are linked to cataracts including Dinitrophenol (a weight loss drug used in the 1930s), Triparanol, chlorpromazine and corticosteroid drugs.
- Injury or trauma to the lens.
- Congenital cataracts (present at birth) and senile cataracts associated with aging.
- Elevated salt and fat intake.
- Diabetes mellitus.
- Heavy metal build-up or toxicity, smoking and poor nutrition.

Signs and symptoms

- Gradual vision loss, blurred vision or visual distortion, sensitivity to light and glare, fading or yellowing of colours, poor night vision and halos around lights.
- Gross opacity of the lens on examination.

Naturopathic recommendations

Lifestyle hints

Early cataract formation can be reversed or halted. Unfortunately, well-formed cataracts or excessive damage to the lens is near impossible to reverse. Medical (surgical) intervention involves extracting the cataract lens and replacing it with an intraocular lens. A recent study on patients over 70 years of age showed that inhaled use of corticosteroids for more than 3 years produced a higher risk of cataract formation.

- Undertake a detox. (See page 131.)
- Avoid smoking.
- Wear protective sunglasses or eyewear when exposed to UV light or the sun.

Nutrition

- Increase your nutrients by taking spirulina and eating a diet rich in antioxidants from fruit and vegetables. Berries, carrots, capsicum, citrus fruits, broccoli, spinach, tomatoes, corn, kale, and all red and yellow pigment fruits, vegetables and legumes. These colourful pigments contain antioxidants critical to protecting and restoring vision.
- Avoid fried food and a diet heavy in saturated fats.
- If you are diabetic avoid sugars or products containing glucose and dairy products as they contain lactose, a combination of galactose and glucose. Glucose enters the lens and is metabolised into an alcohol (sorbitol) which passes back out of the lens distorting the lens fibres and creating cataracts.

Supplements

The following are recommended for early stage cataracts.

Antioxidant formula Reduces the free radical damage to the lens and encourages the body to make antioxidants, enzymes which mop up thousands of free radicals that damage the lens. Antioxidants include ProenOthera® from Evening Primrose Seed husk, Green tea, Grape Seed, Pine Bark, Beta Carotene, Vitamins E, A and C, Amino Acids Methionine and Cysteine, oligomeric proanthocyanidins, Flavonoids and adjunctive minerals (Zinc, Selenium, Manganese). Take a combined antioxidant formula as recommended.

Vitamin A Take 5000IU–8000IU or **Beta Carotene** 200,000IU daily

Vitamin C Long-term high intake of Vitamin C reduces the risk of cataracts and protects the lens of the eye. Take 1g 3 times daily.

Vitamin E Take 400IU daily, Selenium 400mcg daily and Zinc 45mg daily.

Amino Acids Take 200mg–400mg of Methionine daily and 200mg–400mg of Cysteine daily to encourage the body to make antioxidant enzymes superoxide dismutase and glutathione.

Melatonin A prescriptive synthetic hormone of the pineal gland that has been shown to inhibit formation of cataracts, act as an antioxidant and also help insomnia by regulating the sleep-wake cycle. Available by prescription only. Take 1.5mg–3mg daily

Herbs

Bilberry, Ginkgo and ProenOthera® have special compounds called flavonoids or oligomeric proanthocyanidins (OPCs) that protect the eye lens and eye capillaries, and reduce cataract formation.

Bilberry extract (25% anthocyanidins) Take 40mg–80mg 3 times daily.

Ginkgo Take 24mg–30mg of standardised extract of Ginkgo flavone glycosides daily.

ProenOthera® extract (75% oligomeric proanthocyanidins) Take 40mg–100mg daily.

Cellulite

Cellulite is not a disease or health condition, although it causes a great deal of discussion for many Australasian, European and American women. The term cellulite is used to describe a cosmetic defect, an 'orange peel look', i.e. pitting, bulging and deformation of the skin. Cellulite is the irregular pockets of fat that cause the area around hips and thighs to appear dimpled. 90–98% of cases occur in women, whether they are thin or overweight — even supermodels can have cellulite.

Cellulite

Understanding the structures of cellulite within the skin

The orange peel appearance, or cellulite, is seen on the thighs, calves, stomach, arms and buttocks. As women age, the skin surface layers (which are already thinner in women than in men) become progressively thinner and looser. This allows fat cells to migrate into these layers. In addition the connective tissue walls between the fat cell chambers also become thinner, allowing the fat cell chambers to enlarge excessively.

The breaking down or thinning of connective tissue structures is a major contributor to the development of cellulite and is responsible for its dimpled look and feel.

Water retention from fluctuating hormone levels can also often exacerbate the appearance of cellulite. Symptoms may include the feeling of tightness and heaviness in areas affected (particularly the legs).

Causes

- Break down of connective tissue. Damage from exercise, incorrect massage and physical trauma lead to cellulite. Poor connective tissue may be caused by a genetic predisposition, which may also be evident if the individual suffers from haemorrhoids and varicose veins.
- Thin skin, aging and poor circulation to the cellulite areas.
- Basic vitamin/mineral deficiency, such as fat metabolising vitamins and minerals.
- Excess fluid retention from hormonal influence or inflammation, pushing the irregular-looking fat cells towards the skin's surface.
- Large fat cells with excessive fat storage.
- Toxins from an overload of food chemicals, coffee, tea, smoking and medication.

Naturopathic recommendations

Lifestyle hints

- Avoid all toxin consumption including alcohol, caffeine and cigarettes or tobacco, and drink at least 8 glasses of clean fresh water daily.

Exercise

- Exercise, exercise, exercise! Toning muscular areas and increasing fat burning helps reduce the appearance of cellulite. Power-walking, jogging and toning with weights are the most effective exercises for cellulite.

Nutrition

- For large fat cells with excessive fat storage, reduce excessive consumption of animal fats, dairy products, heated fats, synthetic fats such as margarine, and semi soft butters, and substitute with oils such as flax oil, walnut, safflower, evening primrose oil, borage oil, olive oils and fish oils (all unheated).

Supplements

Evening Primrose oil (EPO) and **Fish oil** (3 1g-capsules daily), **Kelp** (the equivalent of 75mcg of Iodine daily), **Lecithin** (1 3g-capsule daily) and **antioxidants** such as **Grape Seed** (500mg–10g daily) and **Bioflavonoids** (50mg–100mg of mixed Bioflavonoids daily) Help the effects of aging, keeping the skin smooth and supple while helping the body metabolise excess stored fats.
Vitamin B6 and **EPO** Help reduce excess fluid retention from hormonal influence or inflammation. Take 15mg–50mg of B6 daily.

Herbs

The herbal compounds below have shown impressive clinical results and confirmed effects in the treatment of cellulite. Take these herbs consistently for at least 3 months (12 weeks), give them time to work and include detoxing regimes, good diet and exercise.

Detox first Use a herbal detox regime that includes **Milk Thistle**, **Red Clover**, **Dandelion Root**, **Burdock Root** and **Yellow Dock**. Detoxing opens up and clears congested or toxic tissues at the surface of the skin. See Detoxing, page 131.

Gotu Kola extract and **Horse Chestnut extract** Clinical studies have shown the positive strengthening effects on damaged connective tissue and the reduction of excess fluid pooling in the legs. These are my two favourite herbs for cellulite. Take 30mg of Gotu Kola extract (Triterpenes) 3 times daily and 10mg–20mg of Aescin (standardised Horse Chestnut extract) 3 times daily.

For poor circulation Take the circulatory and warming herbs **Ginger** (500mg 2–4 times daily), **Turmeric** (900mg daily) and **Hawthorn berries** (1.5g–3g of dried flower, leaf or berry daily).

External applications and massage

Shower massage Massage cellulite areas with a loofah every day.

Aromatherapy essential oils **Juniper, Lavender, Fennel, Lemon, Ginger** and **Geranium** act by clearing excess fluid and toxins, and by increasing circulation. Mix 2 drops of each with 100ml of Olive oil or a 'base oil', such as Almond oil, and massage over cellulite areas twice daily with a flat hand to increase circulation and fat metabolism of cellulite areas.

Gotu Kola, Kelp and **Cola Vera extract** (14% caffeine) Studies show that applied in cream or gel form to the cellulite area, these help improve the cosmetic appearance of cellulite.

Cellulitis

Not to be confused with cellulite, cellulitis is a severe inflammation of tissues just beneath the skin or certain deeper structures (such as connective tissue that surrounds the uterus).

Cause

- Bacterial infection, which can spread through the tissues producing sheets of pus.

Signs and symptoms

- In addition to the local pain and discomfort, toxins (poisons) are released by the infection and produce a high fever and a general feeling of being unwell (malaise). The infecting bacteria normally enters the skin through a small scratch or wound.
- Erysipelas, in which there is little pus but the skin is raw, red and painful, is a form of cellulitis caused by bacteria (*Streptococcus pyogenes*). The bacteria that cause cellulitis are spread by small lymph vessels. Patients with lymphatics blocked by disease or with congenital blockage of the lymph system are at particular risk of recurrent cellulitis.

Naturopathic recommendations

Lifestyle hints

Due to possible life-threatening complications it is recommended that the patient with cellulitis has medical supervision and treatment with antibiotics.

- To support medical treatment, avoid caffeine, smoking and alcohol, which will help the immune system fight the infection.

Nutrition
- A diet rich in raw and cooked whole natural organic foods, such as fruits, vegetables, grains, seeds, beans and nuts, is beneficial to assist with nutrition.
- Reduce saturated fats and refined sugars.
- Consume adequate but not excessive amounts of protein.
- Avoid food intolerances and allergies.
- Drink 8 glasses of fresh water per day.

Supplements
Vitamin A   Enhances the skin's ability to heal. Take 20,000IU daily (unless you are pregnant or have liver problems).
Vitamin C   Enhances wound healing, skin collagen repair and aids the white blood cells' fight against infection. Take 1000mg 3 times daily.
Zinc   Helps to reduce the infection and heals the skin. Take 45mg daily.
Garlic   Helps to inhibit *Streptococcus* bacteria and aids the immune system. Take 400mg of standardised allicin content Garlic extract daily.
Acidophilus   Take a course of Acidophilus to repopulate beneficial gut flora after antibiotic courses. Take this separately from **Goldenseal** (below). Acidophilus and Bifidus are good bacteria that help to keep the digestive system healthy. Take 1 billion of the Acidophilus and Bifidus species in capsule form on an empty stomach to repopulate your digestive system.

Herbs
Echinacea (1200mg daily), **Olive Leaf Extract** (270mg 3 times daily) and Calendula (1ml–4ml of tincture daily)   Prescribed by herbalists to enhance the skin's regeneration, for blood purification and bacterial processes within the skin.

Use antibacterial herbs against *Streptococcus* bacteria and increase immune function without killing good bacteria with **Goldenseal** (1500mg of dried root daily), **Garlic** (400mg–2g daily), **Pau D'Arco** (1.5g–3.5g daily), **Beta 1.3 Glucan** (400mg 2 times daily) and **Astragalus** (500g–10g daily).

For best results, see a herbalist to obtain the following recommended formula. Take simultaneously with the herbs above.   **Cleavers, Pokeroot, Myrrh** and **Wild Indigo**. These herbs will assist with the bacterial infection while acting as a blood cleanser (clean blood heals skin injury quickly), tissue regenerator and lymphatic cleanser.

Cervical Dysplasia

Cervical dysplasia is a condition in which a woman has abnormal changes in the top layer of cells of her cervix. Abnormal cervical cells with disordered development or growth are normally discovered by a Pap smear test. Catching and treating cervical dysplasia early may help to prevent cancer of the cervix.

Causes
- Sexual intercourse at an early age.
- Not using condoms during sexual intercourse with new male sexual partners.
- A promiscuous male partner or numerous male sexual partners (it's rare among celibate women).

Cervical Dysplasia

- Herpes simplex Type 2, Human papilloma viruses and *Candida* spp.
- Smoking.
- Oral contraceptive use.
- Poor nutrition.
- Weakened immune system.
- Genetic.

Signs and symptoms
- There are usually no symptoms associated with cervical dysplasia. If there are symptoms, they may be vague, such as vaginal discharge or abnormal vaginal bleeding.

Naturopathic recommendations

Lifestyle hints
- Often cervical dysplasia can be healed after early detection through a Pap smear. Women should start to have Pap smears and pelvic exams when they reach the age of 16, or as soon as they become sexually active.
- Avoid cigarette smoke, quit smoking.
- Wait to have sexual intercourse until age 18 to 20.
- Limit sexual partners.
- Use latex condoms and practice safe sex with each sexual encounter.
- Avoid high-risk sexual partners.
- Reduce the long-term use of oral contraceptives.

Nutrition
- Eat a diet rich in raw and cooked organic wholefoods, such as fruits, vegetables, grains, seeds, beans and nuts.
- Reduce saturated fats and refined sugars.
- Consume adequate but not excessive amounts of protein.
- Avoid food intolerances and allergies.
- Drink 8 glasses of fresh water per day.

Supplements
These nutrient deficiencies are associated with cervical dysplasia.
Vitamin B complex   Essential to aid B6, B12 and Folic acid absorption. Take 1–2 tablets daily.
Vitamin B6   Take 25mg 3 times daily.
Vitamin B12   Take 1mg daily.
Folic acid   Take 10mg daily for 3 months, then 2.5mg daily until your pap smear becomes normal.
Vitamin A (5000IU–8000IU daily) or **Beta Carotene** (25,000IU–50,000IU daily)
Vitamin C   Take 500mg–1000mg 3 times daily.
Vitamin E   Take 200IU–400IU daily.
Selenium   Take 400mcg daily along with 45mg of **Zinc** daily.

Herbs
Olive Leaf extract   Studies show that Olive Leaf extract (standardised 12% Oleuropein) reduces the high grade cervical dysplasia caused by *Candida* spp. Olive Leaf extract has several antiviral properties that help to boost the immune system and can also destroy the protein coating of the herpes virus, also linked with cervical dysplasia, helping to fight

on-going infection. Take 270mg of Olive Leaf extract 3 times daily.
Goldenseal   Contains berberine which has broad spectrum antimicrobial activity against viruses, bacteria and fungi and gently tones and heals the mucous membranes in the vagina. Take 2g–4g daily.
Cleavers (2g–4g daily) and **Red Clover** (2g–4g daily)   Help to cleanse the blood and clear the lymphatics to aid healing of abnormal cervical tissue.

Chronic Fatigue Syndrome

Chronic fatigue syndrome (CFS) describes a collection of symptoms, principally a disabling, constant feeling of fatigue, but excluding other illnesses that may cause fatigue, e.g. iron deficiency anaemia.

Causes
- Viral infections e.g. Epstein-Barr virus, herpes, hepatitis B, papovaviruses, Ross River virus, Barmah Forest virus, Cox-sackie B virus, retroviruses, cytomegalovirus and pseudorabies virus, HIV and post viral syndromes.
- Immune system dysfunction and glandular fever.
- Parasite infections, eg., giardia.
- Fungal infections, eg., candidiasis.
- Bacterial infections and toxic by-products.
- Overload of toxins, chemicals or heavy metals.
- Allergies and leaky gut syndrome.
- Adrenal exhaustion from stress.
- Chronic illness, including lung, heart, liver or kidney disease, chronic pain, hypothyroidism, endocrine dysfunction, mental illness, diabetes, hypoglycaemia (low blood sugar) and cancer.
- Nutrient deficiencies, e.g. iron, folic acid, vitamin B12 and magnesium.
- Prescription medication, e.g. sedatives, anti-depressants, blood pressure medication, anti-inflammatory medication, steroids, oral contraceptives and antihistamines.
- Multiple chemical sensitivity, electrical sensitivity, vaccination reactions, carbon-monoxide poisoning, radiation poisoning and Fibromyalgia all have symptoms similar to CFS. See a health professional who specialises in these conditions for consultation and advice.

Signs and symptoms
- Disabling fatigue, excessive post-exercise fatigue, weight gain and weight loss.
- Stomach upsets, diarrhoea, nausea, PMS, decreased libido, lack of appetite or vomiting.
- Sore throat, swollen lymph glands, cough, recurrent fever, dry eyes and mouth.
- Muscle aches, fatigue, numbness or pins and needles, light sensitivity, night sweats and/or pain.
- Headaches, stress, insomnia, irritability, need for excessive sleep, anxiety, poor concentration and depression.

Naturopathic recommendations

Lifestyle hints
- Save yourself time and money by consulting with your health professional, e.g. naturopath

or doctor, for examination, tests and diagnosis. With correct diagnosis and supervision you will be able to have your health back on track. It is likely to take many months, so try to be as patient as possible.
- Avoid smoking tobacco and/or recreational drugs.
- Counselling, homeopathy and craniosacral therapy are other therapies to investigate to increase your rate of healing.
- Be gentle on yourself — CFS is extremely frustrating and is often misunderstood. Take plenty of bed rest when needed.

Exercise
- Take light to moderate exercise, such as Tai Chi, yoga, stretches, walking, swimming and reflexology.

Nutrition
- Eliminate food sensitivities (e.g. dairy), alcohol and caffeine.
- Drink 8–9 glasses of pure fresh water daily.
- Drink green juices or vegetable juices daily. Try spirulina, chlorella, barley or wheatgrass drinks. Other varieties are freshly juiced carrots, apple, silverbeet and beetroot.
- Eat three small meals and three snack-sized meals daily to assist metabolism, digestion and blood sugar levels. Oscillating blood sugar levels will make you tired and fatigued.
- Avoid refined carbohydrates, excessive consumption of sugar, saturated fats or fried foods, including fast foods.
- Eat organic fruits, vegetables and meats. Pesticides, herbicides and food stabilisers are likely to put more stress on the body.
- Eat whole foods prepared from scratch rather than heavily refined and processed foods.
- Consume adequate amounts of protein either from meat or vegetable protein. Obviously a combination of both is beneficial too — for instance, add chickpeas to a tuna casserole or dhal (legumes) to a chicken meal for interesting, tasty dishes.

Supplements
Magnesium   Deficiency can cause symptoms similar to CFS. Take 500mg–1200mg daily
Multi vitamin and **mineral formula**   A high potency multi vitamin, multi mineral formula, **Chlorella** or **Spirulina** (3 tsp daily or 6 500mg tablets 3 times daily) enhance nutrition.
Kelp   This is seaweed and contains a high level of minerals including a rich store of iodine. This is particularly nourishing for the thyroid and energy levels, having a gentle rather than dramatic action. Take as directed. Avoid if you have hyperthyroidism or sensitivity to iodine.
Coenzyme Q10   Also known as Ubiquinone, this plays a major role in energy production. Deficiencies can lead to chronic fatigue and lowered cellular energy levels. Take 75mg–300mg of CoQ10 daily.
Vitamin B complex with extra **Vitamin B5** (250mg daily) and **Vitamin C** (3g daily in divided doses).

Depending on your diagnosis, complete the detoxing, depression, candida, anaemia, leaky gut syndrome, hypoglycaemia, hypothyroidism or stress release recommendations in this book. If you think you may need to complete several of these suggestions see a naturopath for further recommendations.

Herbs
Olive Leaf Extract   Studies show that Olive Leaf extract (standardised 12% Oleuropein) fights viral, bacterial and fungal infections. Take 270mg of Olive Leaf extract 3 times daily.
Burdock (2g–6g of dried root daily), **Cleavers** (2g–4g daily) and **Red Clover** (2g–4g daily)

Help to cleanse the blood and clear the lymphatics to aid healing of abnormal cervical tissue.
Liver-cleansing herbs   Important for supporting the liver's enzymatic processes. **Dandelion** (3g–5g of dried root daily) and **Milk Thistle** (9g–10g of seed daily) enhance bile flow and detoxify the liver.
Bowel Toxaemia   Lack of **Acidophilus** and a low-fibre diet contribute to excessive toxins within the bowel. Elimination of toxins and the introduction of good bowel bacteria increases bowel health. Dietary fibre is important because it absorbs the toxins excreted by the liver, including hormone products. Take 1 billion of the Acidophilus and Bifidus species in capsule form daily on an empty stomach to repopulate your digestive system.
Astragalus   Balances the immune system and is especially indicated for chronic long-standing fatigue. It has a positive effect against stress, viruses and has protective effects for the heart, liver and adrenal glands. Take 10g–30g daily
Pau D'Arco   Effective against viruses and candida. Take 1.5g–3.5g daily.
Liquorice (1g–2g daily), **Siberian Ginseng** (2g–4g daily) and **Korean Ginseng** (600mg–10g daily)   Common examples of herbs that have supportive effects against adrenal exhaustion, depression and microbial infections.

Coeliac Disease

Coeliac disease (CD) is typically regarded as associated with small bowel damage from eating gluten-containing foods. Consequently, nutrients are not absorbed normally because of damage to the small bowel, and a wide spectrum of different symptoms result.

Causes
- Susceptibility to Coeliac disease is genetic. When you have certain genes, there is a higher likelihood of CD. However, those particular genes alone are not sufficient to produce the disease. There are other factors involved as well, but we still do not fully understand them.
- Environmental Factors. Certain dietary grain proteins activate Coeliac disease. These include wheat (gliadin), barley (hordeins), rye (secalins) and oats. The 'toxic' proteins (those in brackets) that these cereals provide are commonly referred to as gluten.

Signs and symptoms
As a result of ingesting gluten the villi of the stomach lining are attacked by the immune system and are eventually destroyed. This results in malabsorption, leading to severe gastrointestinal disturbances. Nutrient malabsorption, vitamin and mineral deficiencies often lead to anaemia and thin bones (osteoporosis). Other signs and symptoms include:
- Muscle cramps, fatigue, poor appetite, colitis, bloating, abdominal pain, diarrhoea and flatulence.
- Weight loss, inflamed tissues and headaches due to systemic antibody response.
- Delayed growth and failure to thrive in infants.
- Pain in the joints and possibly seizures.
- Tingling numbness in the legs (from nerve damage).
- Pale sores inside the mouth, called aphthous ulcers.
- Painful skin rash, called dermatitis herpetiformis.
- Tooth discolouration or loss of enamel, and thyroid dysfunction.
- Missed menstrual periods (often because of excessive weight loss).

Coeliac Disease

Naturopathic recommendations

Lifestyle hints
Exercise
- Exercise moderately four times a week.
- Include power-walking, gentle jogging, yoga and aerobics.

Nutrition
- Adhere to a gluten-free diet for about six months. It takes that long for the immune activated antibodies to be eliminated.
- Avoid oats, barley, rye, wheat, durum flour, couscous, semolina, spelt, kamut, bulgur and triticale.
- Beware of terms like starch, which could indicate the presence of corn starch or wheat starch.
- Other terms to watch out for are dextrin, malt, maltodextrin, modified food starch, fillers, natural flavouring, hydrolysed vegetable protein (HVP) and hydrolysed plant protein (HPP) because these may also contain gluten.
- Substitute gluten grains with carbohydrates such as rice, corn, potato, kumara, pumpkin, cornmeal, quinoa, millet and soyflour. It may be necessary for some Coeliac patients to remove dairy products from the diet due to a deficiency in the enzyme lactase, which digests milk sugars. If nervous system disorders are present, such as numbness, it may be possible to reverse the damage by avoiding gluten for a year or two.

Supplements
The first nutrient to show signs of deficiency is Iron. Sometimes all you see in some Coeliac patients is iron deficiency anaemia. Other nutrients that may become deficient are Calcium, Magnesium, Vitamins B1, B2, and B6, Folic acid, Vitamins C, D, E, A, and K, proteins, and fat. It may take many months to reverse symptoms and may be impossible to reverse if gluten is not totally removed from the diet.

Multi vitamin and **mineral formula**   Due to malabsorption of vitamins and minerals you will need to take a potent Multi vitamin and mineral supplement daily.

Spirulina   Take 1 tsp 3 times daily to boost nutrients and iron.

Colostrum   Encourage healing of the stomach lining and villi by using 4g of Colostrum daily combined with **Flax oil** (2 Tbsp) or **Fish oil** (3000mg), **Vitamin A** (5000IU), **Zinc** (45mg daily) and **Folic acid** (300mcg daily) to heal cell membranes in the stomach wall.

Papain   Papain (from papaya) and pancreatic enzymes have been known to improve digestion and absorption of nutrients. Take 1g of Papain with each meal, and 10,000IU of **Lipase**, 6000IU of **Amylase** and 600IU of **Protease** with each meal.

Glutamine   An amino acid that helps heal the stomach lining area. Take 10g–40g daily.

Probiotics   Acidophilus and Bifidus are good bacteria that help to keep the digestive system healthy. Take 1 billion of Acidophilus and Bifidus species in capsule form daily on an empty stomach to repopulate your digestive system.

Herbs
Slippery Elm   Acts as a gentle, nutritious coating to the digestive system allowing healing to take place. Mix 1 tsp (3g) in a glass of water and drink quickly to heal inflamed gastric membranes. This should be taken separately from the other herbs.

Aloe Vera juice   Can speed up the healing time of the digestive tract and increase absorption and digestion of nutrients from food. Take 50ml with every meal.

Chamomile Assists recovery from inflammatory processes in the digestive tract. Drink the herb tea or take 2g–4g of dried flowers daily.
Liquorice Soothes as it coats digestive tract, assists adrenal function, and is excellent to heal digestive system. Do not take Liquorice without naturopathic supervision if you have hypertension or extreme water retention. Take 1g–5g of Liquorice Root daily. (See appendices for more information.)
Wild Yam Reduces internal digestive inflammation. Take 2ml–4ml of liquid extract daily.

Colds and Flu

I've always had the opinion that having a mild cold or flu at the beginning of autumn or winter prepares the immune system for the viral (colds and flus) onslaught. Ongoing colds or flus are a concern though. It may signify that the immune system isn't strong enough to combat the surrounding bugs, or that stress levels are too high or it may be a simple matter of burning the candle at both ends. People who have 'chest' weaknesses, such as asthma, people over the age of 65, the chronically debilitated, care-givers and health care professionals are more susceptible to these viruses. Children often come into close contact with other children, which can make them very vulnerable and more likely to catch the dreaded cold and flu bugs. However, these are good for their developing immunity.

Causes

Colds are viral infections that give us that horrible feeling of head and sinus congestion, coughing and fatigue. In order to catch a cold or flu, respiratory tracts must be exposed to the virus, simply by breathing it in, possibly from a sneeze or cough, via air conditioning, or surface contact.

Cold and flu viruses can live on surfaces like telephones, hand railings and even money for up to six hours, which makes it easier for these viruses to go from one person to another. So it's important to wash and properly dry hands frequently, cover mouth while sneezing, use disposable tissues to blow noses rather than germ carrying hankies and avoid sharing cups and food utensils.

Severe influenza virus infection may develop into viral or bacterial pneumonia or bronchitis, e.g. *Mycoplasma pneumoniae, Haemophilus influenzae* or *Streptococcus pneumoniae*. Other complications include secondary bacterial infection, which is more likely in patients who already have respiratory conditions such as chronic obstructive pulmonary disease (COPD), asthma, emphysema, cystic fibrosis or bronchiectasis. These infections are mostly caused by *Moraxella catarrhalis, S. pneumoniae*, staphylococci, pneumococci and *H. influenzae*. Secondary infection may also aggravate these conditions. *Staphylococcus aureus* may cause a rare but potentially fatal pneumonia.

Signs and symptoms

Cold The classic symptom of a cold is a constantly runny nose. Colds produce sneezing at the beginning, and a low-grade fever may develop with fatigue and perhaps a headache. Other symptoms include sneezing, general muscle weakness, sore throat, dry or productive cough, mild malaise or fatigue and tiredness. People may seem more restless and grumpy than usual and the appetite can be poor because of a blocked nose.
Flu A flu virus produces a higher fever, chills, red face and is usually accompanied by generalised aches and pains which develop 1–3 days after the incubation period. Runny nose, headache, persistent dry cough and sore throat can occur as the virus proliferates. Children

may feel tired, weak and may become overly clingy and tearful. Contact a physician, especially if chills and shortness of breath occur or an accompanying fever goes above 38.3°C (101°F) for more than three days, or any fever above 39.4°C (103°F).

Most people recover in a space of 1–3 weeks, but if the infection is severe enough it may develop into pneumonia or bronchitis and secondary bacterial infection may occur, especially in those who already suffer from COPD. Persons may also suffer from post-viral syndrome weeks later, indicated by fatigue or mild depression.

How can I tell if it's meningitis?

Meningitis is an extremely dangerous condition that causes inflammation of brain tissue and also the spinal cord. The individual will typically develop a severe headache and stiff neck where any movement of the neck causes pain. This is the key for doctors to differentiate meningitis from other infections. Additionally, meningococcal meningitis can also cause a very distinctive rash, which looks like small purple to red spots on the body. If either of these symptoms occur, one should seek immediate medical treatment.

Naturopathic recommendations

Lifestyle hints

- Avoid smoking and drinking excessive alcohol and coffee.
- Ensure you get adequate nutrition, fluids for hydration and sleep.
- Dehydration is a concern with a mild fever. Drink plenty of fluids, including diluted (with water) vegetable juices such as carrot, beetroot and silverbeet, diluted organic fruit juices such as apple; vegetable soups, herbal tea preparations, homemade ice-blocks and pure water. This will help to rehydrate your body and lessen the stickiness of the mucus and mucous membranes. High intakes of sugar (even from fruit) depresses immunity, so keep sugar intake low.
- A cool cloth or chilled wheat bag applied to the forehead and/or back of the neck can help lower a fever and relieve headaches.

Exercise

- I don't recommend exercise if someone has a cold or flu. In rare circumstances the virus can damage the heart. Extra stress on the body reduces the body's capacity to heal itself, when you should be resting.
- When you are well enough, exercise consistently, but start off gently to maintain good health.

Nutritional assistance

- To help overcome cold and flu viruses, it is important to strengthen the immune system and use anti-viral and antibiotic herbs to help eradicate the virus that is causing the cold or flu symptoms.

Nutrition

- Mild foods, such as soups, soft stewed fruits and vegetables are recommended. Include foods high in Vitamin C, such as citrus fruits, green capsicum, strawberries and tomatoes.
- If you are breathless opt for a vegetarian diet (no meat, fish or eggs). If this does not suit you include beans, chickpeas and lentils to boost your meat dishes.
- Use organic meats, vegetables, including parsley, basil, green capsicum, broccoli, Brussels sprouts, tomatoes (lots of them), and fruit, and increase horseradish, wasabi, cinnamon, fenugreek, garlic, ginger and onions in your diet. You might like to add more culinary

herbs to your diet or try drinking thyme or rosemary tea.
- Avoid mucus-forming foods, such as bananas, dairy products, refined carbohydrates, egg whites and excessive amounts of wheat. Supplement with small amounts of calcium-fortified soy or rice milk. Avoid food sensitivities and, if you are not allergic or sensitive, substitute dairy products with soy, e.g. soy cheeses. You can also try stevia (a natural sweetener), sugar substitute and egg substitute. Your local health food stockist can help replace mucus-forming foods until you are better.
- Avoid sugar…did you know that too much simple refined sugar can lower the ability of your immune system, namely the white blood cells, to function properly? If you simply must have sugar, eat a maximum of 2 tsp of Manuka honey or 3 servings of fruit daily, but do not include any more simple refined sugars in your diet until you are better. If you are diabetic, follow your health professional's diabetic guidelines.

Supplements

Vitamin C Enhances white blood cell activity and immune support. Take 1500mg daily.
Zinc Requirements are increased during poor immunity. Take 45mg daily. Zinc gluconate lozenges (5mg–10mg) dissolved every 2 hours help to coat the throat and mouth, improving Zinc levels and helping to inhibit viral replication.
Vitamin A or its precursor **Beta Carotene** Helps to heal any damage to the lining of the airways. Take 5000IU–8000IU daily.

Herbs

Natural medicines are not like manufactured drugs. Herbal preparations work gently, so they take time to act internally.
Olive Leaf extract (10g daily) and **Echinacea** (1200mg–6g daily) Take for 10–30 days for signs of viral, bacterial or fungal infection. They also help improve the body's immune system. Echinacea is very safe to take even while breastfeeding and helps modulate and correct the immune system. Take a maximum of 1200mg daily if you are pregnant or breastfeeding.
Astragalus (500mg–10g daily) and **Pau D'Arco** (1.5g–3.5g daily) Help to enhance the body's resistance and are antiviral herbs effective for cold or flu viruses.
Eucalyptus, Lavender, Friars Balsam (steam inhalants) Add 2–3 drops of each in a bowl of hot water and inhale the steam to help clear the sinuses. Add essential oils to olive oil or a popular base, such as almond or jojoba oils, and massage into the feet and chest for congestion relief.
Herbal cough mixtures May include **Mullein** (2g–5g daily) **Elecampane** (1g–4g daily), **Hyssop** (1g–2g daily). These are soothing and help suppress an ongoing cough while helping to clear mucus build-up.
Homemade herbal teas Simmer a handful of fresh **Sage** and **Thyme** herbs for 15 minutes. Strain the herbs and add manuka honey to sweeten and drink to help relieve coughs and sore throats. Additionally simmer a handful of **Catnip** herb to help reduce fevers.
Lavender and **Chamomile** tea help kids calm down, especially if coughing or breathing is affected and they start to panic.

Antibiotics

Long-term use of antibiotics may affect the beneficial bacteria in our bodies, which allows fungal infections, such as candida, to multiply rapidly producing symptoms of bloating, fatigue and vaginal or oral thrush. Colds and flu are caused by viruses, not bacteria. In these cases antibiotics are ineffective, although secondary bacterial infections, such as strep throat, bronchitis and pneumonia, can be treated with antibiotics. See you doctor for medical treatment or advice.

After antibiotic use

If antibiotics have been prescribed (for a bacterial infection) take Acidophilus after the treatment.

Acidophilus and **Bifidus** Beneficial bacteria that help to keep the digestive system healthy. If you have taken antibiotics as a treatment for a secondary bacterial infection you will need to take 1 billion of the Acidophilus and Bifidus species in capsule form daily on an empty stomach to repopulate your digestive system after the antibiotic course.

Children When you give your child a herbal preparation, begin with a small amount or use children's formulas only. Watch closely for signs that symptoms are easing. Observe how the preparation makes your child feel. Using herbal treatment requires observation, coupled with good judgment. If you wish to lessen the amount of alcohol in a herbal alcoholic tincture before giving it to your child, mix the appropriate dose with one-quarter of a cup of very hot water. After about five minutes most of the alcohol will have evaporated and the mixture should be cool enough to drink. Small, hard lozenges or vitamin tablets should be crushed and applied with food, or dissolved in water for children under 5 years, to reduce the risk of choking.

Cold Sores

It's funny that blisters on the lips are called cold sores. It is true that the extreme cold can trigger cold sores on the face, but sun, stress and mainly viruses stimulate cold sore occurrence.

Cold sores on the lips can be embarrassing and often painful. Apart from walking around with a paper bag on your head, it's nearly impossible to hide them. Here are some naturopathic tips to help reduce the occurrence and frequency of cold sores.

Causes

- Cold sores, herpes 1 and 2 are all related to the herpes virus, as are shingles (herpes zoster) and chickenpox. For some people the herpes virus may be dormant for many years or asymptomatic (there, but without symptoms).
- Cold sores can be triggered by excess sun or wind exposure, low immunity, stress and menstruation (all of which affect the immune system), high protein diets or illness, perhaps from another virus.
- There are many areas that can be affected by this virus, such as the lips, eyes, genitals, anus and nose. All these areas are made up of mucous membrane-type tissue.
- Yes, they are contagious. Contact with any mucous membrane when the virus is active may ultimately cause the virus to spread. Herpes may also spread to other skin areas. Avoid touching other mucous membrane areas (lips, eyes, genitals, anus and nose) after you have touched your blister, and wash hands thoroughly. To prevent contamination, avoid kissing or intimate contact with others.

Signs and symptoms

- Cold sores, or fever blisters, first appear 3–10 days after exposure to the virus. The first sign is local tingling and tenderness with a small bump. The small bump then turns into a blister and more tenderness, itchiness and irritation surrounds the area.
- Cold sores are found generally on the lips, around the mouth or in and around the nose, although some blisters can affect the eyes.

Cold Sores

- Getting rid of symptoms related to the viral infection doesn't mean the virus is eliminated. The virus can remain dormant and break out again when the host's immunity becomes compromised.

Naturopathic recommendations

Lifestyle hints
- Because a run-down condition can bring on cold sores, treatment aims to restore vigour and immune function.
- Avoid extreme weather changes

Nutrition
- Eat fresh fruit and vegetables that have been thoroughly washed, then boiled or steamed, or eat them raw. Choose green leafy vegetables and reduce use of tomatoes, potatoes and eggplant in the diet.
- Reduce use of all processed foods. Eat foods that are prepared from scratch and increase intake of yoghurt.
- If eating protein, reduce as much as possible and eat only organic meats. Protein can encourage herpetic blisters and symptoms. If you do eat protein take the amino acid supplement Lysine to counteract the arginine amino acid found in protein, which is linked to cold sore activation.
- These foods may trigger cold sores: chicken, eggs, salmon, tuna, bacon, beef, milk, stocks, almonds, peanuts, nuts and chocolate. Some naturopaths also recommend wheat and gluten be avoided.

Orthodox treatment
- There is a product called Zovirax (acyclovir) — a pharmaceutical drug that you can purchase from your chemist — which is a cream that you can use on the little blisters or tingling feeling without them spreading too much. Zovirax internal medication may be obtained with a prescription. Use under medical supervision.
- Herbal topical cream is available for those who do not want to use chemicals and wish for a herbal or natural alternative. Try herbal creams with Lysine and Lemon Balm herb. This may be available from health stores and some pharmacies.
- Some creams may spread the cold sore blisters. Avoid creams that are not antiviral as they may have this effect.

Supplements
Vitamin C   Provides antioxidant protection against pollution and toxins. Take 1500mg daily.
Lysine   An amino acid that helps reduce blisters and aids healing. Take 1g–6g daily.
Zinc   Helps the body fight off a range of viral infections, from strep and influenza to herpes and the common cold. Take 45mg daily.

Herbs
These herbs help reduce the viral attack and heal cold sore blisters. Without treatment, viruses can be immortal. Many orthodox treatments treat symptoms, but cannot penetrate the viral host cell.
Olive Leaf extract   Has several antiviral properties that help to boost the immune system and may also help to eradicate viruses. Research shows that Olive Leaf extract with oleuropein can destroy the protein coating of the herpes virus helping to reduce symptoms and ongoing infection. Take 270mg of Olive Leaf extract 3 times daily.

Astragalus The antiviral action of Astragalus is mainly due to increased immunity and interferon production. Take 500mg–10g daily.

Pau D'Arco Effective against viral activity, including herpes 1 and 2 and influenza. Take 1.5g–3.5g daily.

St John's Wort Antiviral action against cold sores and herpes outbreaks. Take the equivalent of 2g–5g of dried root daily.

Lemon Balm Add 1 handful of leaves to a pot of hot water. Cover with a plate and leave to steep for 15 minutes. Drink as a substitute for coffee or tea. You can also buy it as a tincture, add it to baths, or use it as a gargle, etc. Best to use as a preventative or when the first symptoms are felt or appear.

Constipation

Constipation is experienced when evacuation of waste material from the colon is sluggish and stools are hard and difficult to pass, making evacuation of the bowel difficult and uncomfortable. Bad breath, nausea, fatigue, colicky pain, bloating, mucus around stools and headaches are associated symptoms of constipation.

Causes

- The main cause of constipation is a diet high in animal fats (meats, dairy products, eggs) and refined sugar (rich desserts and other sweets), but low in fibre (vegetables, fruits, whole grains), essential fatty acids (Omega 3 and 6) and water.
- Weakness of abdominal muscles, stress, anxiety or fear, inactivity and excessive bed rest and immobility may cause constipation.
- Irritable bowel syndrome (IBS). Spasms of the colon slow down the elimination of waste, leading to constipation.
- Poor bowel habits, such as ignoring the urge to go to the toilet, children who habitually neglect going because it interferes with play, fear of public toilets, and busy lifestyles, can create constipation.
- People who habitually take laxatives, such as magnesium (high doses), senna, cascara sagrada (doses above 100mg daily) or whole aloe vera leaf, become dependent upon them and may require increasing dosages until, finally, the intestine becomes lazy and won't function without them.
- Many medications can cause constipation. These include painkillers, aluminium antacids, antispasmodic and antidepressant drugs, diuretics, tranquillisers, iron supplements and anticonvulsants for epilepsy.
- People often experience constipation when travelling long distances, which may relate to changes in lifestyle, stress, parasites, schedule, diet, and drinking water.
- Certain hormonal disturbances, such as PMS, and an underactive thyroid gland, can produce constipation.
- Hormonal changes and increasing anatomical changes as the womb enlarges can lead to constipation during pregnancy.
- Fissures and haemorrhoids. These conditions can be painful during elimination of stools so individuals repress the urge to eliminate.
- Specific diseases that affect the body tissues, such as low hydrochloric acid, scleroderma, lupus, certain neurological or muscular diseases, multiple sclerosis, Parkinson's disease and stroke.
- Loss of body salts through the kidneys or through vomiting or diarrhoea is another cause of constipation.

- Scarring, inflammation around diverticula, cysts, tumours and cancer can produce mechanical compression of the intestine and result in constipation.
- Nerve damage. Injuries to the spinal cord and tumours pressing on the spinal cord can produce constipation by affecting the nerves that lead to the intestine.
- Lack of beneficial bacteria, such as bifidus and acidophilus species including *Lactobacillus acidophilus, L. bulgaricus, Bifidobacterium bifidum* and *B. longum*.

Naturopathic recommendations

Lifestyle hints
Set a time after a main meal to defecate and relax. Massage your stomach clockwise to stimulate the movement of faecal matter and gas. It does not matter if it doesn't work straight away — this is part of reprogramming your bowel. Massage with carminative essential oils. Use almond oil mixed with a few drops of fennel, dill, aniseed, cajuput and lavender.

Exercise
- Sedentary lifestyles can cause the musculature surrounding the intestinal system to grow lazy, exacerbating the problem.
- Physical activity, such as walking, jogging, yoga, aerobics, abdominal exercises and even abdominal massage, helps tone the intestinal muscle system.
- Exercise for at least 30 minutes 3 times a week just to maintain good health.

Nutrition
- Certain foods may need to be removed from the diet. Wheat and dairy, especially cheese, may cause constipation. Avoid fried foods, white and glutinous rice, white bread and heavy protein, such as red meat. Try gluten-free foods and soy or rice milk substitutes.
- It's important to add fibre to the diet, whether in food form or as a supplement. Inadequate fibre is, of course, a primary cause of constipation. Consume more fibre, whole grains, brown rice (mixed with a little white rice for taste), cereals, green leafy vegetables, acidophilus yoghurt, fruits including grapes, prunes and kiwifruit, ground flaxseeds (1 tsp–1 Tbsp daily) and raw, green leafy vegetables.
- Drink more raw juices including apple, carrot, beetroot and spinach. Fibre has an extensive history of use in the relief of constipation. Include psyllium husks, apple pectin, flaxseed, slippery elm, marshmallow root and chitosan as supplemental fibres. Flaxseeds are great for PMS-onset constipation.
- The main feature of this diet is eating up to 6 times daily. This helps to balance sugar cravings as the food gets broken down and used for energy, and also helps keep very regular bowel movements as faecal matter is pushed through at regular intervals.
- You must drink 8–10 glasses of warm water daily. When constipation is corrected you may switch back to cold water.

Supplements
Fibre **Flaxseeds, Psyllium** or **Slippery Elm** increase dietary fibre, absorb toxins and aid the balance of beneficial bacteria or microflora in the digestive tract. Take 1 tsp–3 tsp of these fibres, singly or in combination, with plenty of fluid daily.
Bifidus and **Acidophilus** Repopulate good bacteria with these species including *Lactobacillus acidophilus, L. bulgaricus, Bifidobacterium bifidum* and *B. longum*. Take 1–10 billion daily.
Digestive enzymes Lack of stomach acid is linked with constipation. Improve digestion by taking digestive enzymes, especially Papaya (papain). Take as directed.
Aloe Vera juice Helps digestion and absorption of nutrients which in turn can normalise bowel evacuation. Take 50ml with each meal.

Mild Constipation

Chamomile tea, **Peppermint tea**, **Ginger tea**, **Wild Yam**, **Swedish** or **Bush Bitters**, and **Dandelion Root** coffee. These beverages may be drunk to act as gentle, bitter stimulants, producing bile and stimulating bowel movement.
Vitamin C   Take 1500mg every 5 minutes until diarrhoea results. (This could be as much as 20g–35g in total.) Vitamin C causes diarrhoea as the body becomes saturated completely with Vitamin C. Take the Vitamin C with adequate amounts of water and continue to drink water until bowels are clear. Stop taking Vitamin C when you experience loose bowels; at this point you have reached saturation. Do not undertake without asking your doctor if you are pregnant, breastfeeding or taking medicines.

Constipation

The next step is taking fumitory *Fumaria officinalis*, which has similar effects to **Chamomile** and **Dandelion Root**, but is stronger and more dynamic. See your naturopath or herbalist for your prescription.
Dandelion Root (3g–5g daily), **Black Walnut** (2000mg daily), **Barberry**(2ml–3ml of tincture up to 3 times daily), **Boldo** (3g–4g of powered leaf daily) and a combination of bitter stimulants and fibre gently aid in detoxing the body, helping to normalise good bowel function.
The main cause of concern is chronic constipation, which may be due to a weak colon muscle movement. This may lead to dry, impacted stools if not enough fluid is consumed.
Magnesium works to draw water into the bowel area from the body, thus dissolving the stool mass and causing diarrhoea. Take 2g 3 times daily until stools liquefy or for a maximum of 3 days. Do not rely on Magnesium as a long-term laxative, as it may cause a weak or lazy bowel.

Chronic bound-up constipation

Faecal impaction may require manual manipulation to remove or loosen waste. Often oil enemas are employed to loosen stool matter and create lubrication. Laxatives, enemas and colon flushes should be used as prescribed by your health practitioner and should be avoided in simple constipation as they can encourage the colon (large bowel) to become lazy, or they may interfere with the defecation reflex.
Magnesium works to draw water into the bowel area from the body, thus dissolving the stool mass and causing diarrhoea. Take 2g 3 times daily until stools liquefy or for a maximum of 3 days. Do not rely on Magnesium as a long-term laxative as it may cause a weak or lazy bowel.
For something stronger, although harsher, take **Castor oil, NZ Flax Root, Alder Buckthorn, Senna, Rhubarb Root, Cascara Sagrada**. These herbs increase irritation and a milking action in the bowel (peristalsis) causing diarrhoea. We never recommend using Cascara Sagrada or Senna — another strong laxative — for more than 30 consecutive days. We don't want to create an addictive situation where the bowels get reliant on stimulus. Due to the overstimulating nature of these herbs, you should consult a naturopath for dosage and supervision.
If you are taking a fibre supplement, discontinue use until the dry congested matter is cleared. Continue detoxing the liver with herbs, such as **Burdock, Dandelion Root, Yellow Dock, Cascara Sagrada** (0.25g–1g daily, limited to short periods) and **Liquorice**, which have a mild but healthy laxative effect. See Detoxing, page 131, for dosages.

Cystitis

Cystitis is inflammation of the bladder. The most common cause of cystitis is bacterial infection that travels up the urethra (urine tube) or ureter. Interestingly, cystitis is more common in women because the female urethra is short and close to the vagina and anus, making it is more vulnerable to pathogens, such as accumulated bacteria from the anus. *Escherichia coli (E. coli)* bacteria are normally transferred from the anal area, but other bacteria, including *Proteus, Klebsiella, Enterobacter* and *Serratia* species, are also found to cause cystitis.

Interstitial cystitis is a chronic, long-term type of cystitis where certain inflammatory factors (perhaps food sensitivities, lowered immunity and stress) break down a protective layer of the bladder lining, allowing harmful substances to come in direct contact, causing ongoing inflammation and lesions of the bladder lining.

Causes
- The most common cause of cystitis is bacterial infection that travels up the urethra or ureter.
- Interstitial cystitis due to breakdown of the glycosaminoglycan (GAG) layer protecting the bladder lining.
- Imbalances in gut flora, for example, lack of *Lactobacillus acidophilus*, or candida (thrush).
- Pregnancy, due to anatomical and hormonal changes.
- Sexual activity may cause normal rectal bacteria to enter the urethra.
- Age-related changes in the urinary tract and bacterial infection can lead to cystitis. It is often difficult to diagnose in the elderly because those who are not infected commonly show similar signs and symptoms — urgency, frequency and incontinence — and sometimes no symptoms are evident until the infection is well advanced.
- Urine retention caused by bladder ischaemia and poor bladder emptying.
- Obstruction. Kidney stones or tumours, endometriosis, urinary obstruction, functional disability or prostate hyperplasia can cause bladder outflow obstruction.
- Sexually transmitted infections, such as herpes, chlamydia, vaginitis and gonorrhoea.
- Senile vaginitis, diabetes, urinary catheter insertion, immunosuppression and constipation.
- Diminished bactericidal activity of urine and prostatic secretions.
- Bacteria entering the kidneys through the bloodstream is potentially life-threatening and should be treated and monitored by a doctor.
- Antibiotics, certain contraceptives, hormone imbalances caused by stress or fear, diet, food allergy, hygiene and underwear irritation.

Signs and symptoms
- Urge to urinate frequently, sometimes as often as every 20 minutes.
- Lower abdominal pain and temporary relief from passing urine.
- Burning, stinging or scalding sensation during urination.
- Pain on urination or strong smelling urine.
- Constant pressure and discomfort in the bladder.
- Mild fever or general fatigue and a feeling of being unwell.

See your doctor if the symptoms last longer than 24 hours (this is because infection can spread to the kidney); there is vomiting, fever, back pain, or blood in the urine; you are pregnant (pregnant women are more at risk of kidney infection); there are repeated attacks or attacks occur following a change in sexual partners; or if the attacks have occurred in a child or a man. Early diagnosis and treatment of cystitis is essential to prevent kidney scarring and permanent damage.

Naturopathic recommendations

Lifestyle hints
- During frequent or chronic cystitis it is best to use supplements that enhance the bladder lining strength and support the immune system.
- Urinary habits. To avoid bacteria transfer, women should wipe their bottom from front to back.
- Curling up with a hot-water bottle or ice-pack clasped to the lower abdomen offers relief.

Nutrition
- It is best to alkalinise the urine by taking alkalinising preparations (barley grass and green juices) and following a diet high in fruit and vegetables.
- Avoid tea, coffee, alcohol, animal protein and high-sugar foods to reduce acidity.
- To reduce acidity of urine (responsible for the stinging and scalding) and to flush infected urine out of bladder as quickly as possible, drink one-quarter of a litre (½ a pint) of cold water, barley water, or water with bicarbonate of soda in it every 20 minutes. Don't overdo the bicarbonate — 1 tsp per hour for up to 3 hours is the maximum you should take. Avoid these suggestions if you have a heart condition, stick to plain water or barley water.
- Foods known to aggravate cystitis and related conditions are asparagus, spinach, beetroot, raw carrots, potatoes, tomatoes, citrus fruits and strawberries, red meat, milk and ice-cream, condiments and junk food in general. Chlorinated water and alcohol are also aggravating. Adzuki and kidney beans are said to be beneficial.
- Drink 2–3 litres of water per day.

Supplements
Vitamin A or its precursor **Beta Carotene** Important for boosting the immune system, and for the maintenance and repair of epithelial tissue. Prevents and helps heal infections, especially colds, flu, bladder, kidney, lung and mucous membrane problems. Beta Carotene is necessary for immune function and mucous membrane integrity. Take 5000IU–8000IU of Vitamin A daily, or Beta Carotene equivalents.
Zinc Important for healthy immune function and healing. Take 15mg–45mg daily.
Vitamin C Immune boosting and aids in production of healthy connective tissue. Vitamin C supports the immune system, which inhibits bacterial growth. Take 1500mg of non-acid Vitamin C daily.
Shark Cartilage, **Methyl Sulphonyl Methane** (MSM) and **Glucosamine** Repair the bladder lining if inflammation has caused small lesions, commonly associated with interstitial cystitis. Take 1000mg of each daily.
Aloe Vera juice An anti-inflammatory that can help reduce the hold that bacteria can have on the bladder lining. Like Cranberry extract, its action helps to clear bacteria from the urinary tract. Take 1–2 cups daily and then 50ml daily to maintain your health.

Herbs
Cranberry Cranberry juice and Cranberry extract contain oligomeric proanthocyanidins, chemicals which inhibit the activity of *E. coli* (the bacteria most often responsible for cystitis) by stopping the bacteria from sticking to mucosal surfaces, which line the bladder and bowel. This helps to clear bacteria from the urinary tract. Those who suffer from kidney stones should avoid taking Cranberry extracts due to high oxalic content. Take 10g of Cranberry extract up to 3 times daily.
Bearberry Has a marked antiseptic and astringent effect on the membranes of the urinary

system, soothing, toning and strengthening them. Arbutin is the principal constituent leading to antibacterial activity, inhibiting the growth of *E. coli, Citobacter, Enterobacter, Escherichia, Klebsiella, Proteus, Pseudomonas* and *Staphylococcus* (Kedzia). Bearberry leaves are used in inflammatory diseases of the urinary tract, urethritis and cystitis. Avoid Bearberry use during pregnancy and lactation. Not for children under the age of 12 years. Take 250mg–500mg of powdered solid extract (10% arbutin) daily or 1.5g–4g of dried leaves as a tea.

Buchu Acts as a mild diuretic aiding urine flow while disinfecting the urinary tract. Buchu may be used in any infection of the genito-urinary system, such as cystitis, urethritis and dysuria. Its healing and soothing properties indicate its use together with other relevant remedies in any condition of this system. It is particularly useful in painful and burning urination. The herb's diuretic activity is due to the presence of diosphenol, which may also be antibacterial. Avoid Buchu use during pregnancy and lactation. Take 1g–2g of dried leaf 3 times daily as a tea or 0.5ml–1.5ml of a liquid extract (1:1) 3 times daily.

Goldenseal One of the most effective herbal antimicrobial agents against microbes such as *E. coli, Proteus* spp., *Klebsiella* spp., *Staphylococcus* spp., *Enterobacter aerogenes* and *Pseudomonas* spp. It is the alkaloid berberine that is responsible for Goldenseal's effectiveness against bacteria, protozoa, and fungi. Goldenseal also has a reputation for healing mucous membranes, the tissue that lines the urinary tract. Avoid Goldenseal use during pregnancy and lactation. Take 1g–2g of dried root daily.

Gotu Kola The most specific herb for interstitial cystitis. Glycosaminoglycans (GAG) protect the lining of the bladder. Certain factors lead to a breakdown of this protective GAG layer allowing harmful substances to come in direct contact with the bladder lining, leading to inflammation and interstitial cystitis. Gotu Kola contains three different triterpenes (Asiatic acid, Madecassic acid and Asiaticoside) that protect the GAG layer by promoting healing, regeneration and growth, and by preventing lesions of the bladder lining. Take 30mg of Gotu Kola extract (Triterpenes) daily.

Olive Leaf extract Olive Leaf is effective against *E. coli* and helps boost a low immune system providing a protective effect. Take 270mg of **Olive Leaf extract** 3 times daily and 1200mg–6g of **Echinacea** daily for 10–30 days for signs of viral, bacterial or fungal infection. These also help to improve the body's immune system. Echinacea is safe to take even while breastfeeding and helps to modulate and correct the immune system. Take a maximum of 1200mg daily if you are pregnant or breastfeeding.

Dandruff

Black clothes are a definite no-no when it comes to dandruff. Dandruff is a fairly common scalp condition that occurs when the scalp skin is shed, producing white or greyish flakes of dry skin that can be easily brushed from the scalp to settle on the shoulders. Dandruff may be a symptom of seborrhoeic dermatitis, an inflammatory scalp disease, as a result of overactive sweat (sebaceous) glands. Dandruff has even been linked to hair loss and baldness.

Causes
- Stress, trauma or illness.
- Hormonal imbalances.
- Seborrhoeic dermatitis, psoriasis, eczema and cradle cap (infants).
- Too much simple carbohydrate or sugar consumption or food allergies.
- Impaired long chain fatty acid synthesis.
- Deficiencies in nutrients, vitamins, essential fatty acids and selenium.

- Constipation or toxic build-up.
- Overproduction of a naturally occurring fungus known as *Pityrosporum ovale*.
- Sensitivity. Your scalp might be reacting to harsh ingredients in shampoo or conditioner.

Signs and symptoms
- Small, white flakes of dead skin fall from the scalp — this becomes worse in winter.
- Normally the scalp is not itchy.
- Excessively dry or oily scalp.
- Seborrhoeic dermatitis can appear as scales, lumps or crusts on the scalp. Often there is itching as well and the scalp may become red from scratching.
- May come from the scalp, eyebrows, hairline and, in males, the beard.

Naturopathic recommendations

Lifestyle hints
- Hair products, shampoos and conditioners can prevent the natural shedding of skin leading to dandruff. Use a clarifying shampoo to rid the scalp of build-up and be sure to rinse very thoroughly every time you wash and condition. Keep very oily or greasy products away from your scalp.
- Dry scalp is a common occurrence, especially in winter. When washing your hair, use a mild shampoo and massage your scalp to loosen flakes.
- Tricologists (hair and scalp specialists) recommend massaging 2 Disprin dissolved in water through the hair and scalp to clear already shed skin flakes. Aspirin or Disprin contain salicylic acid that lifts and rinses dead skin from the scalp. Use once a week. Rinse with apple cider vinegar as another alternative.
- Use a shampoo with both antifungal and antibacterial ingredients (tea tree) plus a shampoo containing zinc to calm the inflammation. Use on alternate days.

Nutrition
- Identify food sensitivities and avoid. Common food sensitivities include dairy, wheat, tomatoes, citrus, peanuts, eggs and chicken.
- Avoid excess fried food, sugar and raw egg white consumption to reduce biotin (a B vitamin) deficiency, which triggers dandruff.
- Include acidophilus yoghurt, fresh vegetables and small amounts of raw fruit in your diet, and eliminate coffee.

Supplements
Fish oil, Flax oil, essential fatty acids (EFAs)   Take 1 Tbsp–2 Tbsp of Flax oil daily or mix with lemon juice, salt and pepper for a salad dressing alternative to reduce EFA deficiency, which is linked to dandruff.

Vitamin B complex   Including Para-aminobenzoic acid (PABA), B6, B12 and Biotin. Deficiencies are linked to dandruff. Any regular Vitamin B complex will be suitable. Take as directed.

Selenium (200mcg daily) and **Zinc** (45mg daily)   Deficiencies are linked to dandruff.

Acidophilus and **Bifidus**   The normal gut bacteria helps to produce B Vitamins and Biotin. B Vitamin and Biotin deficiency has been linked to dandruff, cradle cap and seborrhoeic dermatitis in babies. Take 1 billion of the Acidophilus and Bifidus species in capsule form daily on an empty stomach to repopulate your digestive system.

B6 ointment   Mix 5g of B6 into 100g of aqueous cream. Use 1–2 times daily.

Sulphur   Tablets and aqueous cream are beneficial to the scalp. Use as directed.

Herbs

Detox First detox the body with herbs including **Milk Thistle** (9g–10g of seed daily), **Dandelion Root** (3g–5g of dried root daily), **Burdock Root** (2g–6g daily) and **Red Clover** (2g–4g daily) to help the liver and lymph system, and to purify the blood.
Aloe Vera juice Take 20ml–50ml with each meal to encourage healthy digestion and absorption of nutrients.
Spirulina Take 1 tsp with each meal to help increase nutrients in your diet.
Hair rinse An infusion of **Chamomile**, **Thyme** and **Rosemary** may be beneficial.

> *How to make a hair rinse*
>
> Steep a handful of these herbs in a pot with just-boiled water for 20 minutes and then strain out the herbs. Add a pinch of Ascorbic acid (Vitamin C powder obtained from the chemist) to the rinse and dissolve. After shampooing and rinsing hair, use this as a secondary rinse, carefully avoiding the eyes.

Depression

Depression is the most common mood disorder and can affect one in every seven people. A low mood can persist for many weeks, months or even years. Depression can range from mild, where life is hard to enjoy, to severe, where it can be very debilitating. Other conditions may cause depression, including bipolar disorder in which the mood swings from intense highs to lows with normal mood levels in between. Other types of depression may be indicative of seasonal changes — a condition labelled seasonal affective disorder (SAD). The most important thing is to identify that there is a depression problem, and then make changes or seek treatment to enjoy a better quality of life.

Causes

- Seasonal affective disorder, postnatal depression, bipolar disorder, or dysthymic disorder.
- Stress, adrenal exhaustion, sleep disturbance, long-term illness, physical or mental trauma.
- Hormonal imbalance, candida, reduced serotonin levels, long-term disability or frustration.
- Relationship, financial or family issues.
- Biochemical changes within the body and brain. This is normally a genetic predisposition.
- Alcohol abuse, medication or drug use.
- Nutrient deficiencies, including vitamin B complex, vitamin C, amino acids, minerals, essential fatty acids (DHA), toxicity or heavy metal build-up.
- Allergies or food sensitivities, parasites (or microbial infection) and low blood sugar.

Signs and symptoms

- Crying easily, irritability, lack of motivation, concentration or interest.
- Withdrawal from social contact, low libido and energy.
- Weight loss or weight gain from a change in eating habits.
- Muscle tension, headaches and unexplained body pain.
- Feelings of worthlessness, low self-esteem or guilt.
- Recurrent suicidal thoughts (seek professional medical attention).
- Constant tiredness, insomnia or wanting to sleep more than usual.

Naturopathic recommendations

Lifestyle hints

- Find someone who you can trust to talk to. Counsellors are trained therapists who may offer assistance. A friend, family member, doctor or health professional may offer guidance. If you do not feel understood the first time, you do have options to try another friend or counsellor.
- Learn as much as you can about depression and your treatment options. Seek support and treatment as soon as you can.
- Try to avoid stimulants, such as caffeine, cigarettes, drugs and alcohol. Start by cutting down a little every day to help wean yourself off them. Check with your doctor if you are taking any prescribed medication. Some medication is linked to depression.
- Try to keep your mind positive and don't dwell on negative thoughts.
- Keep active. Whether your activity is stimulating or relaxing, it can help improve sleep, increase fitness and keep your mind at ease.
- Watch out for triggers that make your depression worse or increase the possibility of a relapse. Write notes and possible triggers in a daily diary to help identify these factors.
- Take nutritional supplements to aid the adrenal glands and immune system.
- Learn how to relax by trying yoga, receiving a massage, or learning meditation or breathing techniques.
- Get plenty of restful sleep. Make sure the room is completely dark to help ensure sleep.

Exercise

- Attempt to have a balanced exercise regime. Exercise 3–5 times a week for 15–60 minutes, e.g. power-walking, jogging, swimming, dancing or going to the gym.
- If you are not mobile, try bouncing on a trampoline or lymphasizer (small trampoline) and seek assistance if needed.

Nutrition

- Avoid any identified food allergies or sensitivities. Have your hormonal levels checked out including your thyroid, reproductive hormones and cortisol levels. Blood tests and liver enzyme tests may be appropriate too. See your doctor.
- Depression can rob you of hunger or drive you to eat or drink foods laden with fat or sugar. The basic nutritional approach to stress management is to eat 5–6 times per day to keep metabolism and sugar levels balanced. This is important as blood sugar imbalances can affect mood.
- Potassium can be depleted during adrenal-exhaustion; a diet rich in potassium is critical to maintain adequate levels within the body. Foods rich in potassium include: fresh vegetables such as asparagus, avocado, raw carrots, corn, cooked lima beans/spinach, potatoes and raw tomatoes; also fresh fruits like apples, dried apricots, banana, oranges, peaches, plums and strawberries. Unprocessed cooked fish and meats such as flounder, salmon, drained tuna, chicken (the white meat), pork, roast lamb and beef. Eat porridge for breakfast because oats are nourishing for the nervous system.
- Avoid unnecessary stressors, including outside (environmental) factors, e.g. processed foods, pollution, etc. Don't take too much on, as this could be a potential trigger.
- Drink 1–2 litres of fresh water daily.

Supplements

Vitamin B5 The specific vitamin required to help reduce stress. Take 50mg–100mg daily.
B complex Vitamins Help reduce stress and support the nervous system. Take 15mg–50mg of each daily.

Vitamin C Studies show that Vitamin C levels are reduced with stress and depression which may lead to poor immunity against disease. Take 1500mg daily.

Calcium and **Magnesium** Deficiencies of these are common and may lead to muscle cramps, anxiety and depression. Take 1500mg of Calcium at night, after a meal for better absorption, and 450mg–900mg of Magnesium daily.

5-Hydroxy tryptophan (5HTP) A serotonin precursor made naturally by the body and also sourced from the plant *Griffonia simplicifolia*, helps boost serotonin levels reducing anxiety and insomnia. Take 150mg–300mg daily.

Melatonin Levels may be reduced leading to insomnia and anxiety. Seek a prescription from your doctor and take a 3mg tablet at night before sleep. Not recommended for children as their levels are generally adequate.

Flax oil, Fish oil, Evening Primrose oil and **Borage oil** Provide rich sources of Omega 3 and 6 essential fatty acids. Deficiencies in these 'good fats' will cause anxiety, postnatal depression and clinical depression in some people. Take 3g of EPO, Borage oil, Fish oil and/or 2 Tbsp of Flax oil daily.

Herbs

St John's Wort For mild depression, anxiety and nervousness. Take 2g–5g of dried herb daily.

Ginkgo Increases blood flow and oxygen to the brain. Take 80mg 3 times daily of standardised extract with 24% flavone glycosides.

Oats (0.6ml–2ml daily), **Vervain** (2ml–4ml daily) and **Damiana** (2g–4g daily) Gentle tonics to revive a depressed nervous system.

See **Anxiety** page 78 and **Detoxing** page 131 for other herb recommendations.

Schuessler Tissue Salt Kali Phos This homoeopathic mineral is excellent for nerves and depression, and can work very quickly without being contraindicated for other medication. Take 1 tablet a minimum of 4 times daily or if needed take 1 tablet every 5 minutes.

Bach™ flower remedies

Choose a single remedy or a combination recommended by a health professional. Take 4 times daily or as recommended, or choose from any of the other 38 remedies. Mix your specific remedy and take 4 drops a minimum of 4 times daily, or if needed take 4 drops every 5 minutes.

Elm For depression due to a feeling of being overwhelmed.
Gorse If you cannot see the light at the end of the tunnel.
Rescue Remedy For depression from shock.
Pine For depression caused by guilt.
Cherry Plum For a sense of losing control almost to the point of feeling suicidal.
Rock Rose For extreme panic and fear.
Gentian If you are aware of what causes the depression, but get despondent when things don't turn out right.

Detoxing

A toxin is any compound that has a detrimental effect on the body's cells. Toxins are found in our food as pesticides, additives and colourings, and are found in our make-up, cleansers and moisturisers. Some toxins have minimal effects, but a build-up of toxins can damage the body in an insidious and cumulative way. When the body's ability to clear toxins is impaired, your health may be compromised, leading to chronic health problems.

Causes

- Industrial waste, car fumes, chemicals and smoke.
- Grooming chemicals found in make-up, hair products, shower gels and detergents.
- Pesticides, colouring, stabilisers, preservatives found in food.
- Medicine, such as aspirin, painkillers, asthma drugs, heart medication, etc.
- Toxic heavy metals from dentistry work, lead, mercury, cooking utensils and aluminium.
- Alcohol, solvents and herbicides.
- Bacteria, viruses, fungi and parasites release toxins into our bodies.

Signs and symptoms

- Fatigue, sluggish metabolism, headaches, muscle pains, sore, red eyes, paleness, dizziness, impaired ability to concentrate, indigestion, tingling in hands or feet, inflammation, allergies and cancers, and constipation. As toxicity increases, so does the severity of the signs and symptoms.

Who should do a detox?

Those who:
- are overweight, have cellulite or have excess fluid retention
- are diabetic, have high blood pressure or cholesterol
- have gallstones
- drink alcohol or smoke
- have skin problems, psoriasis or asthma
- use steroids (prednisone) or preventer inhaler for asthma
- take oral contraceptives or HRT
- are exposed to solvents, pesticides, antibiotics and thyroid drugs
- have liver problems or hepatitis
- have more than 4 of the signs and symptoms above.

Naturopathic recommendations

Lifestyle hints

- Lifestyle changes may include exercising, quitting smoking (or as my friend says, having a long break) and counselling.

Exercise

- Increase your activity to get your heart rate and circulation going. This will help dislodge toxins in your body and help move them through your system. Include power-walking daily to help gently detox your body.
- Include activities such as pilates, meditation, massage, yoga, deep relaxation techniques, aromatherapy baths, listening to music and reading a book. In today's busy world you have to take time out for yourself. These activities don't generally do a lot for weight loss but are great for your state of mind and sense of well-being, and important for balance and health. If you have limited time for training, yoga and pilates not only cover relaxation but also strength and flexibility.

Nutrition

- Consume fish, brown rice, pumpkin, kumara or sweet potato, and fresh fruit and vegetables (organic where possible). Increase green leafy vegetables and water-filled fruits, prunes loaded in fibre, apples, etc. Use berries as a form of antioxidant protection from a build-up of free radicals that cause damage to cells.

- Eat non-gluten foods, and beans cooked without animal fat or salt that have been soaked and prepared before cooking.
- Limit breads and similar products to 3–6 servings per week, choosing non-gluten produce and breads over gluten (oats, rye, barley and wheat) products.
- Large amounts of organic vegetables and fruit may assist with detoxing. These include cabbage, broccoli, Brussels sprouts, capsicum, tomatoes, and all fruits. Small amounts of nuts and seeds are recommended.
- 1–2 servings per day of vegetarian protein (beans, legumes, etc.), lean organic meat, fish, poultry and seafood is fine. Protein contains amino acids that are important to help with the detoxing process.
- Avoid non-essential medication, drugs, smoking, alcohol, coffee, junk food, takeaway meals, artificial foods, sodas, excessive amounts of sugar and fatty, fried foods.
- Small amounts of butter and yoghurt for those who are not sensitive to dairy products are fine. If sensitive to dairy, try a variety of goat's, rice or soya milk.
- Drink 2 litres of filtered water throughout the day, every day. As you increase your fibre intake the water intake must be increased to avoid constipation. It is known that a diet high in fibre (traditionally from vegetables, grains, gums, etc.) is extremely beneficial to general health. These particular fibres work by absorbing water and toxins as they pass through the body, improving stool transit time and bulk.
- For more suggestions see the weight management section of this book, or see a naturopath for fasting recommendations and supervision.

'Wake-up call'
- 1 large glass of hot water and a squeeze of lemon, lime or orange juice.

'Nutrient lift'
- Drink 1 glass of fresh vegetable juice (carrot, celery, spinach) or fruit juice (cranberry, grape, pear, pineapple).
- Or 1 tsp of Spirulina with vegetable or fruit juice, or 1 tsp of Supreme Greens (chlorella, barley grass, chlorophyll), shaken with water.
- Or take a multi vitamin.

Supplements
Antioxidant formula and a **Multi vitamin** and **mineral formula**   Needed to support the general detoxification process. Vitamins B2, B5, B12, Folic acid, Copper, Selenium, Magnesium and Zinc are required by detoxification enzymes to function. Antioxidants found in Turmeric, Milk Thistle, Ginkgo, Grape Seed, Pine Bark, ProenOthera® (Evening Primrose Seed Husk) and Green tea reduce free radical damage. Take a combined antioxidant formula as recommended.

Aloe Vera juice (20ml 3 times daily) and **Spirulina** (1 tsp 3 times daily)   These and green powders, consisting of broccoli, chlorella, barley grass, acerola and sprouted wheat grass powder, are gentle nutrients that help to cleanse the body.

Acidophilus and **Bifidus**   Good bacteria that help to keep the digestive system healthy. Take 1 billion of the Acidophilus and Bifidus species in capsule form daily on an empty stomach to repopulate your digestive system with good microflora.

Vitamin C   Provides antioxidant protection against pollution and toxins. Take 500mg 3 times daily to maintain Vitamin C levels.

Shark Liver oil   Chelates onto heavy metals. Take 6 1000mg capsules daily.

Cysteine, Methionine and **Taurine**   Amino acids required by the liver to remove toxins. They also produce antioxidant enzymes that help scavenge for free radical toxins. Take 1g of each amino acid daily.

Fibre **Flaxseeds, Pectin** or **Slippery Elm** increase dietary fibre, absorb toxins and aid the balance of beneficial gut bacteria or microflora. Take 1 tsp–3 tsp of these fibres, singly or in combination, with plenty of fluid, daily.

Herbs

What keeps the body from becoming too toxic? The circulatory and lymph system, colon, liver, urinary system, lungs and skin. Blockage of any of these systems can ultimately result in toxicity. The liver must neutralise toxins into safe by-products for elimination.

It's virtually impossible to escape toxins in our modern lifestyles. However, by working with traditional cleansing herbs and nutrients at least twice a year, we may assist the body in the normal clearing of toxin accumulation. Detoxing the liver, purifying the blood and gently cleansing the kidneys helps to avoid toxic gridlock while supporting other crucial systems, such as the lungs, adrenal and lymphatic system.

Dietary fibre is equally important as, when the toxins are unloaded into the digestive tract, fibre helps to chelate (grab onto) toxins for evacuation and reduces toxic reabsorption.

Liver-cleansing and **regenerating herbs** Important for supporting the liver's enzymatic processes and bile flow. **Dandelion** (3g–5g of dried root daily), **Yellow Dock** (2ml–4ml daily) and **Milk Thistle** (9g–10g of seed daily) enhance bile flow and detoxify the liver.

Blood cleansing and **purifying herbs** Red Clover flowers (2g–4g daily), and **Burdock** (2g–6g of dried root daily) are blood purifiers that help to clean out the toxins within tissues and the bloodstream.

Lymphatic cleansing herbs The lymphatic system often goes unnoticed but is an essential part of detoxification, immunity and fluid removal from tissues. Use **Pokeroot** (herbalist supervision only), **Echinacea** (1200mg daily), **Cleavers** (2g–4g daily), **Calendula** (1ml–4ml of tincture daily) and **Queens Delight** (2ml 3 times daily). Pokeroot cleanses the lymphatic glands and is used to treat mastitis. *Caution:* large doses of Pokeroot are emetic and purgative (cause vomiting), and should be taken in low doses for short periods of time.

Adrenal support **Liquorice** (2g–4g daily or as prescribed) offers adrenal protection and helps the body adapt to stress.

Circulation **Turmeric** (1.5g daily), **Ginger** (50mg–250mg daily) and **Cayenne** (5mg daily) enhance the impact of herbs and increase circulation, improving absorption of herbs in peripheral tissues. They also reduce inflammation.

Lung support **Irish Moss** is good for excessive mucus in the lungs, and protects and soothes the digestive tract. Take 2g–3g daily.

Parasite-cleansing herbs **Cloves, Wormwood** and **Black Walnut** kill over 120 different types of parasites, improving digestion and energy levels, and reducing toxicity release from parasites. Take two 3-week courses of Cloves (1800mg daily) combined with Wormwood (2000mg daily) and Black Walnut (2000mg daily) to help eradicate parasites. You may also follow acne vulgaris herbal guidelines.

Massage, baths and **showers** Lymphatic massage, reflexology, sports massage and deep tissue massage facilitate the removal of toxins from the skin and muscles. Self-massage-gently scrub your body all over with a dry flannel, and then have a warm shower. At the end of your shower have a blast of cold water to stimulate your body and removal of toxins. A handful of Epsom salts (Magnesium) or rock salt added to your bath for the last 15 minutes can aid removal of toxins and relax fatigued muscles.

Detoxing observations During the cleansing process you may experience some symptoms of detoxing. These may include headaches, an increase in bowel movement, and hidden skin blemishes like pimples may rise to the surface. If symptoms persist, or if any unusual changes occur, discontinue detoxing and please seek health professional advice.

If you have problem pimples, you may need to use liver herbs to help clear any blind spots or erupted pimples. The herb Burdock is brilliant for this. See Liver detoxing on page 45 or the Acne section on page 64.

Diabetes Mellitus

Diabetes is a metabolic disorder in which the body cannot properly manage carbohydrates that have been broken down into glucose. Diabetes sufferers also have fat or protein metabolism dysfunction. The pancreas releases the hormone insulin in response to raised glucose levels in the blood. Insulin assists the entry of glucose into the cells and if there is too little insulin or poor insulin receptor activity, glucose cannot be easily absorbed into tissues and glucose levels can then increase markedly in the blood and spill over into the urine.

Insulin dependent diabetes mellitus (IDDM or Type I)
IDDM is generally early-onset diabetes (adolescence) and involves insulin administration, as beta cells of the pancreas are destroyed leading to loss of insulin production.

Non-insulin dependent diabetes mellitus (NIDDM or Type 2)
NIDDM may be present sub-clinically for years, but is usually associated with age (above 50 years old) and degree of obesity. People with type 2 diabetes have tissue resistance to insulin and may also have reduced pancreas secretion of insulin, causing an increase in blood sugar.

Other forms of diabetes include impaired glucose tolerance, gestational diabetes (glucose intolerance in pregnancy) and secondary diabetes, which is due to pancreatic disease, hormonal disturbances, malnourishment or drugs. Feeding cow's milk to babies under the age of one may trigger juvenile diabetes.

Causes
- Genetic predisposition or autoimmune dysfunction
- Viral attacks or infections of the pancreas and diseases or damage to the pancreas
- Poor nutrition and nutrient deficiencies
- Diet high in refined carbohydrates and saturated fat
- Hormone dysfunction conditions, and pregnancy.

Signs and symptoms
- Weight loss
- Obesity (80% Type 2 diabetics)
- Polyuria (excess urination), polydipsia (excess thirst) and polydysphagia (excess hunger)
- Chronic hyperglycaemia (high blood sugar levels)
- Glucose intolerance
- Disturbances in carbohydrate, fat and protein metabolism
- Glucosuria (excess sugar in urine)
- Recurrent blurred vision
- Fatigue, nausea, vomiting
- Parathesias, numbness and tingling, especially in the extremities of the body
- Frequent infections, including bladder, vagina and skin. Skin infection can include yeast infection, for example, vulvovaginitis in women or jock itch in men.
- Diabetic ketoacidosis is a complication of diabetes mellitus caused by the build-up of by-products of fat metabolism (ketones), which occurs when glucose is not available as

a fuel source for the body. A fruity odour to the breath occurs as the body attempts to get rid of excess acetone. This is a characteristic sign of ketoacidosis (including diabetic ketoacidosis), a potentially life-threatening condition.

Naturopathic recommendations

Lifestyle hints
Exercise
- Exercise 4 times weekly to increase your heart rate and cardiovascular fitness e.g. power-walking, jogging, weight training, swimming, dancing or going to the gym. If you are not mobile, bounce on a trampoline and seek assistance if needed.
- Exercise improves insulin sensitivity.

Nutrition
- Consider seeking nutritional counselling with a naturopath or nutritionist to aid your understanding of eating the right foods for you and to determine food sensitivities.
- Avoid foods with a high Glycaemic Index (GI). The GI is a method of classifying foods according to their potential to increase blood sugar levels. Eating high GI foods results in higher and more rapid increases in blood glucose levels compared with eating low GI foods. For example, if your blood sugar is low and continuing to drop, causing fatigue during exercise, carbohydrates that raise your blood sugar quickly or those that have a high GI are favourable. To keep your blood sugar from dropping during a few hours of mild activity, carbohydrates that have a low GI are better to balance your blood sugar. High GI foods include sugars, including glucose, maltose, honey and sucrose; white bread; puffed, short grain and jasmine rice; most varieties of potatoes; pumpkin and beetroot; most breakfast cereals; most biscuits and crackers; tropical fruit, such as mango and pineapple; and some dried fruits, including raisins.
- High GI foods also increase cravings for carbohydrates. After eating high GI foods the blood sugar quickly rises, which triggers the pancreas to release a bolt of insulin. The insulin reduces the blood sugar levels, which creates the craving for sugars and carbohydrates. It can be a vicious cycle that results in weight gain and continual frustration, with blood sugar levels leading to diabetic overdrive.
- Avoid refined carbohydrates, such as white flour, white rice, pasta, cakes, biscuits, pastries, pies, breadcrumbs, man-made carbohydrates and soft drinks.
- Low GI alternatives include eating half the amount of carbohydrates you normally have, or 3 servings the size of your fist, daily of the following foods: dense breads, lots of whole grains, oat bran and textured wholemeal; long grain white, basmati and brown rice; kumara, taro and yam; pasta and noodles; barley and bulgur wheat, porridge, muesli, Special K and All-Bran; biscuits made with oats that are low in sugar; and stone fruit, citrus fruit and orange juice. Some foods have a low glycaemic index but are high in fat, such as ice-cream and sausages. The combination of fatty (e.g. fried, saturated fats) and sugary foods should also be avoided.
- Avoid alcohol (especially bingeing), smoking, coffee, and high levels of caffeine, salt and softdrink intake. Reduce saturated fat intake and animal fats, including lard, dripping, butter, coconut and palm oil, butter, cream, fatty meats with nitrates including salami, processed meats and fried foods. Avoid trans fatty acids, such as margarine, shortenings and shortening oils.
- Use sugars sparingly, even those in honey, molasses, fruit juices, dried fruits and maple syrup. Avoid artificial sweeteners or processed sugar, substitute with stevia, a natural

sweetener that does not increase blood glucose levels. Reduce your intake of carbohydrates to half the original level. Eat more fibrous carbohydrates, like salads, celery, onions, garlic, asparagus, beans and legumes, than starchy carbohydrates, like potatoes, corn, rice, pasta and breads.

- Eat six small meals daily to help balance sugar levels. This has a positive effect on fat metabolism. Eat more non-sweetened yoghurt, dietary fibre, vegetables, cherries and berries.
- Eat at least 3 fish meals weekly. Sardines, tuna and salmon are great sources of Omega 3 oils. Tinned fish may be an affordable option, but grilled or steamed fresh fish is preferable. Eat lean meats and include Spirulina in your diet.
- Consume copious amounts of ginger, garlic and onions with meals, and eat soy products, oat bran, whole grain cereals, legumes, alfalfa sprouts, nuts and linseeds.
- Drink 2 litres of pure, fresh water daily and include a cup or two of green tea daily. Due to the milk sugar content, avoid dairy products, but supplement with calcium to prevent calcium deficiencies. Avoid sodas and carbonated drinks.

Supplements

Can I still take Insulin with these herbs and supplements?

Yes, there have been many scientific studies with the use of these herbs for Type 1 insulin dependent and Type 2 non-insulin dependent diabetes mellitus. These herbs and supplements may reduce blood sugar levels, so these levels should be closely monitored by the patient and, if they do reduce, consult with your health professional to correct your insulin dose. Do not take yourself off insulin unless recommended by a medical practitioner.

Multi vitamin and **mineral formula** Take a well balanced Multi daily to reduce any nutrient deficiencies and maintain a basic level of nutrition.

Antioxidant formulas Will help protect against cholesterol, eye conditions, nerve problems and poor circulation. Antioxidants include **Vitamin C** with Bioflavonoids (2g daily), **Lipoic acid** (60mg daily) **Vitamin E** (400IU daily) and **Bilberry extract** 25% anthocyanidins (40mg–80mg 3 times daily).

Evening Primrose oil and **Borage oil** (Starflower oil) Contain Gamma Linolenic acid (GLA). **Fish oil** and **Flax oil** contain Omega 3, Docosahexaenoic Acid (DHA) and Eicosapentaenoic Acid (EPA) and Omega 6. These essential fatty acids offer protection against cholesterol, high blood pressure, circulation and fat metabolism problems associated with diabetes. Take 3000mg of Evening Primrose oil or Borage oil daily, 3000mg of Fish oil daily and 1 Tbsp–2 Tbsp of Flax oil daily. Substitute Olive oil with Flax oil in your salad dressing, add to yoghurt or mix in with a smoothie for a creamier taste.

Chromium (Chromium Picolinate) This essential trace element is required for normal insulin functioning. Chromium stimulates the activity of enzymes involved in the metabolism of glucose for energy and the synthesis of fatty acids and cholesterol. Adequate amounts of Chromium can significantly reduce insulin requirements and play a physiological role in promoting insulin tissue sensitivity. Various lines of evidence suggest that good Chromium nutrition may protect cardiovascular health. Take 300mcg–400mcg daily.

Fibre Flax, Guar Gum, Pysllium, Pectin or **Slippery Elm** should be taken to increase fibre and to chelate onto heavy metals and cholesterol. Fibre improves glucose tolerance, causing food to be released slowly into the intestine allowing blood glucose to rise gradually. Take 1 tsp–3 tsp of these fibres, singly or in combination, daily.

Herbs

Detox Complete a gentle detox herbal programme and a parasite-cleansing programme to balance the internal body organs and prepare for a healthy start. Detox herbs should include **Burdock** (2g–6g of dried root daily), **Cleavers** (2g–4g daily) and **Red Clover** (2g–4g daily) to help cleanse the blood and clear the lymphatics. **Dandelion** (3g–5g of dried root daily) and **Milk Thistle** (9g–10g of seed daily) enhance bile flow, detoxify the liver, and reduce diabetic signs and symptoms. Do not food-fast without health professional supervision or recommendations.

Parasite-cleansing herbs Take two 3-week courses of **Cloves** (1800mg daily) combined with **Wormwood** (2000mg daily) and **Black Walnut** (2000mg daily) to help eradicate parasites.

Gymnema The leaf is well-known for its ability to remove the taste of and cravings for sugars when chewed. Clinical studies have shown remarkable results in reduction of glucose levels.[40,41] Gymnema 25% Gymnemic acids is thought to increase insulin production by stimulating the pancreas and may repair the (Islet of Langerhans) pancreas, which facilitates the use of glucose in the body. It also increases the activities of the enzymes, which facilitate the use of glucose by insulin dependent pathways and increases intake of glycogen by liver and muscles. Take 200mg 2 times daily and put a small amount of powdered leaf on your tongue to stop sugar cravings.

American Ginseng New findings support this herb's effectiveness as a blood-glucose modulator.[42] Take 1g–3g 3 times daily.

Bitter Melon Lowers blood glucose in diabetic patients and may exert a direct insulin-like action, stimulating the release of insulin. Take 1g 2 times daily.

Fenugreek The uses of defatted Fenugreek Seeds (known as Fenugreek powder) have been known since ancient times, and in Greek and Latin Pharmacopoeias, the seeds were recognised for their anti-diabetic properties. Recently preclinical and clinical studies have confirmed the anti-diabetic and anti-cholesterol action.[43,44,45] Take 1 tsp 3 times daily.

Turmeric Traditionally used in Asia as an antioxidant and to enhance the properties of other herbs and help circulation, which is necessary in the treatment of diabetes. Take 4g daily.

Ginkgo Biloba Increases blood flow within the body, including the extremities and the brain, reduces circulatory disease and improves cholesterol by acting as an antioxidant. Take 4g–8g of whole leaf or 24mg–30mg of standardised extract of Ginkgo flavone glycosides daily. Avoid taking with the prescribed medication warfarin, as Ginkgo in large amounts may magnify the drug's blood-thinning effect.

Diarrhoea

Most people will experience diarrhoea in their lifetime. Some people view it as 'a good clear out', but excessive diarrhoea can have dire consequences. Diarrhoea is an excessive passing or elimination of stool matter, including an increase in volume, frequency, urgency and fluidity of stools.

Causes

- Increased water content in stools caused by magnesium or osmotic laxatives, lactose sensitivity, magnesium antacids, sorbitol and mannitol (artificial sweeteners), excessive vitamin C intake, microbial infections, bacterial overgrowth, surgery, bile salt and fat malabsorption, cancer and tumours.
- Food sensitivities, nervous diarrhoea, diverticulitis, Coeliac's disease, pancreas disease, hyperthyroidism, malnutrition, Crohn's disease, ulcerative colitis, irritable bowel syndrome, food poisoning, drugs and excessive intake of some fruits, alcohol or coffee.

Complications
Those who experience severe acute diarrhoea, with signs of dehydration (dry mouth, strong body odour or sunken eyes), blood in stools and excessive diarrhoea, and children who experience diarrhoea, should be monitored by a physician immediately. Dehydration can lead to life-threatening complications.

Signs and symptoms
- Explosive elimination of stools and/or blood, pus or mucus in stools.
- Increased urge to defecate and abdominal cramps.
- Watery, malformed stools and undigested food in stools.
- Overpowering odour from stool matter.
- Bloating, stomach rumbling and poor appetite with increased thirst.

Naturopathic recommendations

Lifestyle hints
Identify the cause of diarrhoea for corrective treatment.

Food Hygiene
- Food hygiene must be adhered to as a prevention against opportunistic infections and as a tool for supporting a healthy immune system.
- Keep cooked foods and ready-to-eat foods separate from raw and unprocessed foods to avoid cross contamination.
- Eat freshly cooked foods as soon as possible after cooking.
- Use cooked or prepared food that has been stored in the fridge within two days.
- Reheat cooked food thoroughly so that it is 'piping hot', i.e. above 70°C (158°F). Take special care to heat thoroughly when using microwave ovens.
- Wash raw fruit and vegetables thoroughly to remove infectious organisms.
- Wash your hands, chopping boards and utensils before using for a different food, to avoid cross contamination. Use different cutting boards for raw and cooked foods.
- Boil drinking water for 1–5 minutes to avoid cryptosporidiosis and other pathogens.
- Thaw raw meat in the refrigerator rather than the open air, keeping the refrigerator temperature at 4.5°C (40°F) or lower.
- Cook meat thoroughly. Avoid pink meat, including rare steaks and burgers, and uncooked meat, including sushi. Diseases such as salmonella, toxoplasmosis and parasites are found in raw and uncooked chicken, pork, beef and fish.

Unsafe foods for people at risk
- Chilled, precooked or uncooked fish or seafood products
- Pâté
- Cold precooked chicken
- Ham and other chilled, precooked meat products
- Stored salads and coleslaws
- Raw, unpasteurised milk
- Avoid eating fresh vegetables and salads at restaurants or anywhere else where you can't be certain that the products are washed adequately to meet your needs.
- Avoid eating raw food containing raw eggs or partially cooked eggs, i.e. Caesar salad, sauces and salad dressings.

Nutrition

- Drink electrolyte drinks, herbal teas, flat lemonade, ice blocks, salted vegetable broths and diluted fruit juices to help replace lost water and electrolytes.
- Avoid dairy products, high-sugar foods, fatty foods and hard solid foods. The enzyme lactase that digests milk may be reduced so substitute milk for soy or rice milk.
- Eat acidophilus yoghurt, cooked fruits, soups, grated apples and include carob powder in your diet. Carob drinks sweetened with stevia actually help reduce diarrhoea symptoms. Mix 2 heaped tsp with a cup of heated soy milk.
- Discover any possible food or medication sensitivities, especially for those who suffer from chronic diarrhoea.

Supplements

Acidophilus Replaces beneficial bacteria that may be lost due to diarrhoea. It is especially important to take it after a bout of diarrhoea because beneficial bacteria gets flushed out of the digestive tract, leaving it vulnerable to new infections. Repopulate beneficial bacteria with Bifidus and Acidophilus species, including *Lactobacillus acidophilus, L. bulgaricus, Bifidobacterium bifidum* and *B. longum*. Take 1–10 billion per day.

Digestive enzymes Help with digestive enzyme deficiencies. Problems digesting fat, wheat, cellulose, protein and milk can often lead to diarrhoea. See your local health supplement retailer for a digestive enzyme formula.

Fibre Has a balancing effect for diarrhoea and constipation, taking up extra water from a loose stool, relieving diarrhoea, and adding lubrication to soften the stool when dry.

Flaxseeds, Pectin, Psyllium or **Slippery Elm** increase dietary fibre, absorb the toxins and aid the balance of beneficial gut bacteria or microflora. Take 1 tsp–3 tsp of these fibres, singly or in combination, with plenty of fluid daily.

Multi vitamin and **mineral** formula   The body finds it hard to absorb vitamins and minerals when you have diarrhoea, so it is good to supplement with a Multi. Take as directed.

Charcoal tablets Absorb toxins in the bloodstream and colon. Take 4 tablets every hour until diarrhoea subsides. Do not take at the same time as other supplements. Don't confuse these tablets with charcoal in food, which is carcinogenic.

Garlic Kills bacteria and enhances immunity. Take 2 capsules 3 times daily.

Colostrum Has immunoglobulin factors that are effective against pathogens, such as bacteria, viruses, fungi and parasites, that cause diarrhoea, and can aid regeneration and healing of the damaged gastrointestinal (G.I.) tract mucosa. Take 4g daily.

Lugol's (aqueous) Iodine Take 9 drops mixed with 1 tsp of apple cider vinegar and 1 tsp of manuka honey. Can be taken with digestive enzymes and parasite-cleansing herbs for *E. coli, Salmonella, Campylobacter, Helicobacter pylori, Shigella, Giardia, Blastocystis hominis* and *Cryptosporidium* infections. Take this drink once daily for a maximum of 5 days. Avoid if you have hyperthyroidism, are taking thyroid medication or if you are allergic to Iodine. If your nose becomes watery, discontinue Iodine dose.

Herbs

Meadowsweet One of the best gentle natural astringents helping to tone up the digestive membranes. Safe for adults and children. Take 2g–6g daily.

Parasite-cleansing herbs Take two 3-week courses of **Cloves** (1800mg daily) combined with **Wormwood** (2000mg daily) and **Black Walnut** (2000mg daily) to help eradicate parasites.

Goldenseal (0.5g–1g daily), **Wild Indigo** (2ml–5ml daily), **Olive Leaf extract** (270mg 3 times daily) and **Echinacea** (1200mg–6g daily)   Take for 10–30 days for signs of viral, bacterial or fungal infection within the gastrointestinal tract.

Slippery Elm (5g 3 times daily) and **Marshmallow Root** (2g–5g with cold water daily) Soothes inflamed mucous membranes in the lining of the digestive tract.

Chamomile, Fennel Seeds and **Aniseed**   Help to relieve gas and bloating associated with diarrhoea. Place 1 tsp of crushed Aniseed, Fennel Seeds and Chamomile flowers in a cup of hot water. Cover and steep for 15 minutes. Strain away the herbs and drink the herbal tea mixture 3 times a day or when discomfort occurs. Avoid during pregnancy.

Diverticulosis

Diverticula are frequently found in the sigmoid colon and occur in 50% of patients over the age of 50 years. They vary in diameter from 3mm to 3cm and are small formed pouches that herniate through weakened muscular areas of the colon.

Causes
- Diverticular disease seems to be related to the low-fibre diet eaten in western societies.
- A decrease in physical activity.
- Neglecting the urge to eliminate stools.
- Weakness of connective tissue or muscular tissue of the colon.

Complications
Diverticulitis is a complication of diverticulosis and occurs when faeces obstruct the neck of the diverticulum causing stagnation and allowing bacteria to multiply and produce inflammation. This can then lead to bowel perforation (peridiverticulitis), abscess formation, fistula (an abnormal passageway between two organs, e.g. the colon and the bladder) formation, or generalised peritonitis. There are several complications of acute diverticulitis. This is a medic alert. Hospital attention is essential.

Signs and symptoms
- Pain and tenderness (lower left quadrant) associated with constipation that alternates with diarrhoea. There may be fistula formation. Fever, nausea, rectal bleeding and vomiting may occur for several days. For the cause to be established, a barium enema with X-ray, colonoscopy and sometimes angiography may need to be undertaken.

Naturopathic recommendations

Lifestyle hints
- Do any treatment gradually because diverticular disease may be very painful for some. In acute stage seek medical advice and hospital attention immediately.
- Take warm baths with 1 handful of Epsom salts added and stay in the bath for a maximum of 15 minutes. The Epsom salts are absorbed through the skin and, the magnesium relaxes cramping and muscle spasms.
- Use appropriate aromatherapy oils for calming and relaxing, e.g. lavender. For colicky abdominal pains take 1 drop of cinnamon oil or peppermint oil on a little brown sugar 3 times a day between meals. Rub abdomen with peppermint oil, cinnamon and clary sage in a base of olive or almond oil. Gently massage abdomen in a clockwise direction if you have constipation and anti-clockwise for diarrhoea.
- Reflexology. Massage the whole foot working on tender areas to increase healing rate.

Massage left foot especially around sole and side of foot for diverticular disease.
- Lymphatic drainage clears out congested toxins. This is a massage technique mainly on lymphatic areas and lymph ducts. See a qualified naturopath.

Exercise
- Regular exercise is important. Exercise 3–4 times a week.

Nutrition
- Rest and fasting are indicated to help clear out toxins. Rest the bowel to stop further decomposition. Attempt fasting only under naturopathic supervision to avoid complications. Address the diet, eating habits and possible stress. The aim is to prevent constipation and the development of the disease by increasing the bulk of motions, which in turn increases the diameter of the colon and thereby reduces the pressure inside it. Psyllium may be too harsh to use. Eat vegetables, fruit and flax or slippery elm fibre. The mucosa of the colon may have atrophied or become weakened. Use cell salts to address this issue.
- Increase green leafy vegetables, water-filled fruits, prunes loaded in fibre, apples, etc., in the diet.
- Use berries as a form of antioxidant protection from a build-up of free radicals causing damage to cells.
- Drink 2 litres of pure, filtered water throughout the day, every day. As you increase your fibre intake, water intake must be increased to avoid constipation. It is known that a diet high in fibre (traditionally from vegetables, grains, gums, etc.) can produce some benefits to general health. These particular fibres work by absorbing water and remain undigested as they pass through the body, improving stool transit time and bulk.
- Eat healthy wholesome foods, more vegetables, especially green leafy varieties, fruit, lean meats and fewer processed foods, junk foods, fatty products and foods, alcohol and coffee. Lifestyle changes may include exercise, quitting smoking (or as my friend says, having a long break) and counselling.

Supplements
Multi vitamin and **mineral formula**   To supply high potency minerals and vitamins. Take as directed.
Vitamin C   Is thought to be particularly important in the prevention of fistula formation. It is also shown that patients with fistulas have lower Ascorbic acid levels than patients without fistulas. Vitamin C is also useful in maintaining the integrity and strength of veins, including haemorrhoids, and may provide resistance to infections. Take 1g daily.
Spirulina tablets   A highly nutritious food, easy to assimilate and absorb. Of the entire antioxidant spectrum, this is one of the richest wholefood sources and includes B complex vitamins, minerals, Gamma Linolenic acid (GLA), enzymes and cofactors. Take 3g daily.
Fibre   Necessary for intestine and colon health. It feeds and maintains a healthy intestinal flora made up of friendly little bacteria and yeasts that make some of our vitamins and protect us from 'unfriendly bugs'. A healthy colon minimises release of toxins back into our blood. It also reduces intestinal toxicity and pathogenic bacterial and yeast overgrowth. Mucilage, a soft, water-soluble fibre, soothes and protects the delicate stomach and intestinal lining, prevents irritation, and keeps contents moving smoothly along, pushing waste material past the diverticula and helping to prevent diverticula blockage. Take **Flax fibre** or **Slippery Elm** with plenty of fluid, because its mucilage absorbs 5 times the seeds' weight in water. Use 1 Tbsp per day. It can absorb water and swells to about 20 times its dry volume (therefore 5 times the volume of Flax being eaten, as fluid should accompany its consumption). Stools don't become hard and dry. It has no side effects.

Herbs

German Chamomile Eases spasms and inflammation, especially when associated with stress and anxiety. Drink the herb tea or take 2g–4g of dried flowers daily.
Aloe Vera juice Can speed up the healing time of the digestive tract, and increase absorption and digestion of nutrients from food. Take 50ml with every meal.
Liquorice Soothes as it coats the digestive tract, works on the adrenal glands and is excellent for healing the digestive system. Do not take this without naturopathic supervision if you have hypertension or extreme water retention. Take 1g–5g of Liquorice Root daily.
Wild Yam Reduces internal digestive inflammation. Take the equivalent of 2ml–4ml of a liquid extract daily.
Parasite-cleansing herbs To help eradicate hidden parasites, take two 3-week courses of **Cloves** (1800mg daily) combined with **Wormwood** (2000mg daily) and **Black Walnut** (2000mg daily).
Peppermint Carminative and antispasmodic. Take 0.2ml–0.4ml enteric coated Peppermint oil capsules between meals.
Goldenseal Heals mucous membrane and is antimicrobial. Take 2g–4g daily.
Echinacea Antimicrobial for infection. Take 1200mg–3000mg daily.
Slippery Elm or **Marshmallow Root** Drink, or take the capsules, between meals to soothe inflammation in the bowel. See label for dose recommendations.
Drink **Peppermint** and **Chamomile** teas.

Schuessler Tissue Salts

Calc Fluor Tones relaxed tissues. Addresses atrophied conditions of the bowel and body. Take a minimum of 1 tablet 4 times daily.
Calc Sulph Cleans out the accumulation of non-functional, organic matter in the tissues and causes infiltrated parts to discharge their contents, throwing off decaying organic matter so that it doesn't lie dormant or slowly decay and thus injure the surrounding tissues. Take a minimum of 1 tablet 4 times daily.
Ferr Phos For the first stage of inflammation or congestion, inflammatory pain, high temperature, quickened pulse, and/or bleeding. Take a minimum of 1 tablet 4 times daily.
Mag Phos For spasmodic conditions, such as muscular cramping, stomach cramps and flatulence. Mag Phos is indicated for symptoms aggravated by cold and relieved by heat. Take a minimum of 1 tablet 4 times daily.
Silica Acts upon organic substances of the body wherever there is pus formation or threatened suppuration, e.g. abscesses, etc. Take a minimum of 1 tablet 4 times daily.

Bach™ flower remedies

Choose a single remedy or a combination recommended by a health professional. This is an important part of the treatment to help with emotional factors. There are 38 remedies to choose from. Take 4 times daily or as recommended.
Agrimony If you are putting on a brave face, despite being tormented inside.
Aspen For anxiety about unknown things or situations that cause fear.
Holly For anger.
Star of Bethlehem For shock.

Ear Infection

Middle ear (otitis media) infection is very common among children and occurs when infection from the nose or throat travels towards the middle ear section causing inflammation and pain. Infections and food sensitivities, leading to a build-up of fluid or wax in the ear, should be determined by a health professional for a correct diagnosis. My father, a natural therapist, always reminds me that more happiness and less arguing helps earache. Perhaps he's right.

Causes
- Bacterial infection
- Food or environmental allergies
- Environmental aggravation from smoke
- Weakened immunity
- Frequent use of antibiotics
- Frequent exposure to colds and flu, for example at daycare centres
- Children who have not been breast-fed have increased incidence of otitis media.

Signs and symptoms
- Earache — a dull ache that may sometimes become a stabbing pain
- Ear discharge
- Diminished hearing
- Mild fever or a general feeling of malaise.

Naturopathic recommendations

Lifestyle hints
Avoid chemical irritants, inhalants and smoke from woodburning fires or tobacco to reduce external irritation.

Nutrition
- Common allergy foods include artificial colours and preservatives, dairy products, wheat, eggs, peanuts, soy, corn, tomatoes, chicken and apples (in this order). Reduce dietary intake of refined sugar, including confectionery and soft drinks.
- Encourage a diet high in vegetables and fruit. On a plate add ½ a banana, a slice of wheat-free bread spread with hummus or avocado, a small handful of rice crisps, a carrot, rolled ham or chicken or perhaps some tofu cubes, lentils or chickpeas as a vegetarian option to help with fussy eaters. I call these 'fairy plates' to appeal to kids' imaginations — they're a godsend!
- Drink plenty of pure water and carrot juice to increase fluid in the diet.

Supplements
Vitamin A   Take 20,000IU daily for adults or 1 **Cod liver oil** capsule mixed with honey or apple-free stewed fruit sauce for children under the age of six. Cod liver oil is rich in Vitamin A and helps soothe and heal the inflamed mucous membranes that line the ear canals.
Vitamin B complex   Helps strengthen the immune system for adults. Take as directed.
Liquid multi vitamin and **mineral formula**   Children may be given a liquid Multi to help with any nutrient deficiencies and to aid immunity. Take as directed.
Vitamin C   Take 1500mg daily or 500mg of **Ascorbic acid** dissolved in water and 1 tsp of Manuka honey daily for children under 6 years of age.
Zinc   Helps heal damaged tissue and aids the immune system. Adults take 45mg daily. Other dosages are dependent on the age of the individual. To establish the correct daily dosage multiply the child's age by 2.5mg, e.g. a 3 year old should take 7.5mg (3 x 2.5mg) daily. Take a maximum of 15mg daily.

Herbs

Wild Indigo (2ml–5ml daily), **Olive Leaf extract** (270mg 3 times daily) and **Echinacea** (1200mg–6g daily) Take for 10–30 days for signs of viral, bacterial or fungal infection within the gastrointestinal tract.

Goldenrod Reduces inflammation and mucous congestion in the upper respiratory tract region. Take 450mg 3 times daily.

Goldenseal Has antibiotic and soothing, toning actions on mucous membranes that line the ear canals. Take 0.5g–1g of dried rhizome and root daily.

Eyebright (875mg 3 times daily) Effective against mucus and inflammation of the eye, ear, nose and throat areas.

Doses of herbs for children 2–6 years old Herbal liquids mixed in Manuka honey are best. **Wild Indigo** (500ml daily), **Olive Leaf extract** (500mg daily), **Echinacea** (250mg–500mg daily), **Goldenrod** (450mg daily), **Goldenseal** (100mg daily) and **Eyebright** (450mg daily).

Mullein Ear drops, which help relieve pain and inflammation, are available from health shops. Warm the drops and place in the ear.

Eczema

Skin problems such as eczema are more difficult to treat than most people realise. I've often seen eczema in adults who are bartenders, chefs and hairdressers. Eczema is normally diagnosed by a health professional and can also be called dermatitis. The skin is normally overly dry and becomes itchy and patchy, and sometimes small blisters form, then dry and become crusty. Detergents can cause the skin to become too dry and cause cracking and fissuring of the skin. A form of eczema called atopic eczema can be found in joint flexures on the ankles, behind the knee, inside of elbows, front of wrists, neck and face. It's also associated with a hereditary predisposition to hayfever and asthma, as there is normally an allergic component to eczema.

Causes
- Allergies to plants, animals, dustmites, chemicals, shampoo, cosmetics, perfume, detergents, soap, nickel, foods, certain drugs, and certain physical disorders (Herpes simplex, hypothyroidism) or psychological disorders (such as emotional stress).
- Even humidity, heat, the drying of skin and contact with woollen clothing can cause flare-ups.
- Mast cells are specialised cells that sit within the respiratory lining and underneath the skin. Dietary allergens or environmental allergens stimulate the mast cells to release chemicals, e.g. histamine, in the body that cause inflammation and, as a result, itchiness.
- The bacteria *Staphylococcus aureus* appearing more abundantly on the skin and in nasal secretions than normal. This may cause the eczema to become infected.
- Nutrient vitamin or mineral deficiencies, including zinc, essential fatty acids (such as Omega 3 and 6) and hydrochloric stomach acid
- Leaky gut, hypothyroidism and overgrowth of candida have also been associated with eczema.

Signs and symptoms
- Itching, dry and red skin, blisters, crusts, swelling, oozing and scaly skin.
- The skin may become thickened, which is made worse by itching.

- Chronic inflamed skin can turn into a 'wet type' of eczema as it is rubbed raw and not given a chance to heal. Scratching increases the risk of bacterial infection.

Naturopathic recommendations

Lifestyle hints
- Discovering the foods you are allergic to and avoiding them is important. Following nutritional guidelines and using herbs as needed may help reduce swelling and allergic reactions.
- Eczema may be associated with stress and anxiety, so mind-body techniques, such as meditation, tai chi, yoga, and stress management, may help prevent it.
- Starch or oatmeal added to a bath may temporarily relieve the symptoms.
- Stay away from the things that irritate your skin, and avoid alcohol and tobacco.
- Wear natural fibres to prevent sweating and irritation.
- Wash soap, shampoo and conditioner thoroughly from the scalp and skin to prevent chemical irritation.

Nutrition
- Avoid foods you are allergic to and start eliminating all common allergenic food as these may account for a total of 81% of all eczema cases. Common allergenic foods include dairy products, especially milk, (if eliminating dairy products, take a calcium supplement or eat fortified food), citrus, peanuts, wheat, eggs, corn and tomatoes. Soy and fish very rarely cause eczema, but may be a factor.
- To avoid calcium deficiencies seek health professional recommendations and take calcium supplementation or eat fortified foods.
- Eat fewer foods that cause inflammation, such as saturated fats (meats, especially poultry, and dairy), refined foods and sugar. Reduce sugar in the diet, if you can't totally omit it, and avoid all food colouring and artificial preservatives.
- Eat fish at least four times per week. Don't be afraid to buy canned fish, but try to obtain fresh when you can. If you are not allergic to fish, substitute for meat with salmon, mackerel, snapper, herring and tuna to increase Omega 3 in the diet.
- Increase intake of fresh vegetables, whole grains, and essential fatty acids (cold-water fish, nuts and seeds).
- A rotation diet, in which the same food is not eaten more than once every four days, may be helpful in treating chronic eczema.
- Eat Ghee (small amount), goat's milk and yoghurt, white cheese, such as feta, quark, cottage cheese or ricotta, and nut milks. Check food allergies first.

How to make nut milk
Soak ½ cup of nuts (cashew) overnight in ½ litre of water and add a small vanilla pod. Blend and add ½ tsp of cold pressed oil (Flax oil, Apricot Kernel oil, Safflower oil).

Supplements
See a health professional for appropriate children's doses.
Calendula oil, Chamomile oil and **Zinc oxide**   Can be mixed with Vitamin E oil capsules or aqueous cream to soothe itchiness and aid healing of the skin.
Essential Fatty Acids (EFAs)   'Good', polyunsaturated oils that are also termed Omega 3 and 6. Abundant in **Flax**, **Borage**, **Evening Primrose Seeds** and fish, these oils help reduce EFA deficiencies, reduce inflammation and heal leaky gut syndrome associated with eczema. Take Flaxseed (1 tsp–1 Tbsp 3 times daily), Borage oil (1500mg 2 times daily), or

Evening Primrose oil (3000mg 2 times daily) to reduce swelling. Children can be supplemented with **Cod Liver oil** (½ tsp–1 tsp daily), or any of the above oils, 500mg 2 times daily. Evening Primrose oil and Flax oil may also be added to a bath or applied to affected parts.
Beta Carotene (25,000IU–100,000IU daily), **Zinc** (10mg–30mg daily) and **Vitamin E** (100IU–400IU daily)   Strengthen the immune system and help skin heal. Lower doses appropriately for children
Vitamin C (250mg–1000mg 2–4 times daily)   Reduces the body's response to substances that cause allergies. Vitamin C from rose hips or palmitate is citrus-free and hypoallergenic.
Bioflavonoids   Compounds found in dark berries and some plants, which help reduce swelling, strengthen connective tissue and help reduce allergic reactions. Eat more bioflavonoid foods to reduce inflammation. Take 400mg of **Quercetin** 3 times daily or 1000mg of mixed Bioflavonoids daily.
Leaky gut syndrome   Linked to eczema. Heal the gut lining with **Colostrum** (4g daily) combined with **Acidophilus** (1 billion daily), **Bifidus** (1 billion daily), **Flax oil** (2 Tbsp daily), **Vitamin A** (5000IU daily), **Zinc** (45mg daily) and **Folic acid** (300mcg daily).

Herbs
Milk Thistle (9g–10g of seed daily), **Dandelion Root** (3g–5g of dried root daily), **Yellow Dock** (2ml–4ml daily), **Cleavers** (2g–4g daily), **Sarsaparilla** (2g–4g of dried root 3 times daily), **Liquorice** (2g–4g daily or as prescribed), **Burdock** (2g–6g of dried root daily) and **Red Clover** (2g–4g daily)   Herbs that help heal the skin and increase lymphatic drainage, purify the blood and cleanse the liver are useful for relieving eczema, as they gently work to heal the skin from the inside out.
Marshmallow Root tea   May soothe and promote healing of gastrointestinal inflammation that is often found with eczema. Soak 1 heaped Tbsp of Marshmallow Root in 1 litre of cold water overnight. Strain and drink throughout the day. Also, apply Marshmallow Root to the skin to help reduce itchiness and inflammation. Alternate with a cold compress if inflammation and burning is severe
Perilla (900mg–3g daily) and **Boswellia** (3g daily)   Reduce the histamine allergy reaction, helpful in eczema, asthma and psoriasis.

Following up
Dietary guidelines should eventually become part of your lifestyle to help overcome allergy reactions and dietary deficiencies.

Special considerations
Starting an infant gradually and conservatively on solid foods may help prevent the food sensitivities that can cause eczema. Potato is a great example of a food sensitivity. Because potato is considered bland and easy to mash, it's often used as a weaning food. A small study involving eight children with eczema showed that elimination of cooked potato from the diet resulted in a 50% improvement in eczema symptoms, vomiting and wheezing. Eventually seven of the eight children outgrew the allergy by the age of six years. Visit a naturopath for weaning recommendations and substitutes for certain foods.[46]

Emphysema
The first time I encountered a man with emphysema, I was in my teens working as a naturopath apprentice to my dad. I noticed his chest heaved and stuck straight out like a puffed-up chicken, he had a very pink face and he gave me a tissue full of sticky sputum to examine. He was literally a 'Pink Puffer' (see below).

Emphysema

Emphysema is a condition in which there is inflammation, over-inflation and damaged tissue around the airways of the lungs (respiratory bronchioles) and/or the air sacs (alveoli). Chronic inflammation often leads to lung fibrosis and loss of lung elasticity.

Late in the disease process, as people with emphysema exhale, airflow is limited and air becomes trapped as the airways collapse. The loss of the lungs' elastic recoil causes decreased gas transfer, resulting in breathlessness, decreased oxygen and an increase in carbon dioxide.

Often individuals experience emphysema and chronic bronchitis together. This is known as chronic obstructive pulmonary disease (COPD).

Causes
- The number one cause is smoking; however, asbestos inhalation, environmental pollution or chemical inhalation can cause emphysema and lung damage.
- Bacterial infections and viral infections.
- A rare form of an inherited blood protein (α_1-antitrypsin) deficiency.

Signs and symptoms
- Early symptoms of emphysema include shortness of breath, wheezing and coughing. Although the names 'Pink Puffer' and 'Blue Bloater' sound like exotic fish, they actually describe two categories into which people with emphysema can fall.
- Pink Puffers have laboured breathing and hyperinflation of the lungs which causes a barrel chest, but they are not cyanotic (blue), being able to maintain a normal gas exchange until their disease progresses.
- Blue bloaters are cyanosed (rendered blue) and have excessive peripheral oedema and sputum as the emphysema worsens. They find it extremely difficult to breathe, which can make even simple tasks, such as eating or mild exercise, taxing. The lips are pursed on expiration to aid breathing, and they have a bounding pulse, a flapping tremor of their outstretched hands and progressive drowsiness.

Naturopathic recommendations

Lifestyle hints
As far as I'm aware emphysema damage is irreversible; however, that doesn't mean we can't achieve anything. The aim is to make the rest of your health improve, to increase the standard of comfort and well-being.
- Avoid exposure to smoke, including cigarette smoke and even second-hand smoke. Believe it or not, stopping smoking makes a big difference. It also helps reduce mucus production, and aids excretion.
- Avoid exposure to anyone with a respiratory tract infection or gatherings of people in small areas (especially in the winter season).
- Buteyko breathing techniques may be beneficial for those with emphysema. (See the section on Asthma.)
- Cold weather can trigger bronchial spasm making it more difficult to breathe, so cold weather masks or even a simple scarf lifted to the mouth to breathe through may be helpful.

Exercise
- Appropriate exercise can be beneficial if a programme is developed by a health profes-

sional who has experience in the field of lung rehabilitation. Exercise, such as the stationary bicycle, gentle yoga exercises and treadmill walking, increases oxygen and overall heart conditioning.

Nutrition

- Add garlic, ginger, horseradish and onions to your diet to help decrease mucous production and to reduce the risk of bacterial and viral infections.
- Eat small, frequent, nutritious meals, increase whole foods, legumes, sprouts, green leafy vegetables, fruit, and complex carbohydrates, such as root vegetables and whole grains, to improve overall balance in the diet.
- Drink plenty of water with pure lemon juice and honey to help loosen mucous secretions.
- Avoid dairy products and bananas as they increase mucus build-up. Use soy or rice milk products, and take calcium supplements to avoid calcium deficiencies. Other foods to avoid include peanuts and gluten. A reduction in simple carbohydrates, processed foods and meat protein may help improve breathing.

Supplements

Vitamin A Helps heal any damage to the lining of the airways. Take 5000IU–8000IU.

Vitamin B complex For adrenal exhaustion and stress, and to help the immune system reduce the risk of viral and bacterial infection. Take as directed.

Selenium (50mcg–100mcg daily) and **Vitamin E** (400IU daily) Help to preserve tissue elasticity, act as antioxidants and may help with internal scarring.

Magnesium Helps to relax the smooth muscles that constrict the air passages (bronchials). Take 200mg–450mg 2 times daily.

Bromelain An enzyme from pineapple that helps break down mucus and reduce inflammation and mucus production. Take 200mg–450mg 3 times daily.

Coenzyme Q10 May help with lowered energy levels and exercise as it plays a role in energy production, protects the heart and acts as an antioxidant against oxidative free radical damage. Take 75mg 2 times daily.

Flax oil, Fish oil, Borage oil, and **Evening Primrose oil** These oils act as natural anti-inflammatories. Take 1 Tbsp of Flax oil and 3000mg of Evening Primrose oil, Fish oil or Borage oil daily.

Herbs

Liquorice Soothing to the airways, reduces mucous congestion and reduces inflammation in the airways. Liquorice also has a mild action against viral infection, such as colds and flu. Take 1g–5g of Liquorice Root daily. (See Appendices for more information.)

Lobelia Stimulates release of mucus, calms down bronchial spasm and acts as a respiratory stimulant. Take 50mg–200mg of Lobelia dried herb 3 times daily. Start at the lower dose first and build up. High doses can cause vomiting.

Marshmallow Root (2g–5g daily) and the dried flowers or leaves of **Mullein** (2g–5g daily) Have soothing actions on the bronchi, reducing inflammation of the airways and decreasing the stickiness of mucus while helping the body to expel the mucus from the lungs.

Elecampane A warming expectorant (mucus clearer) that also stimulates the cilia hairs of the bronchi to eliminate mucous congestion from the lungs. Take 1g–4g of dried root daily

Olive Leaf extract (270mg 3 times daily) and **Echinacea** (1200mg–6g daily) Take for 10–30 days for signs of viral, bacterial or fungal infection. They also help to improve the body's immune system.

Bugleweed Helps release excess accumulation of fluid within the body caused by a weak heart, and tones the nervous system. An important aspect when dealing with chronic illness. Take 1ml–2ml of tincture 3 times daily or as prescribed by your herbalist or naturopath.
Hawthorn A wonderful antioxidant herb that protects against the extra stress that is put on the heart. Can be used in conjunction with aspirin and beta-blockers. Take 1.5g–3g of dried flower, leaf or berry daily.
Gotu Kola Helps reduce scar tissue damage when combined with Vitamin E. Take 30mg of Gotu Kola extract (Triterpenes) 3 times daily.

Aromatherapy
Essential oils including **Eucalyptus**, **Thyme**, **Rosemary** and **Lavender** can help to relax the bronchials and release sticky mucus. Put 3 drops of each in a bath or basin filled with hot water and inhale.

Schuessler tissue salts
Calc Fluor and Silica May help improve elasticity of the lungs. It may take at least 6 months of using tissue salts to get long-term results. Used with **Nat Mur** for chronic cases and **Ferr Phos** for inflammatory conditions, this combination of tissue salts works on a deeper level by providing homoeopathically-prepared mineral building blocks to the body.

Endometriosis

I can't tell you how many of my girlfriends have terrible endometriosis, but there are a lot. I must confess that I was also diagnosed with endometriosis. I believe with the right herbs and treatment, along with the right lifestyle and dietary choices, I have resolved my endometriosis and encouraged other women to do so, which gives me hope that you can beat yours too. It's a very common condition experienced by western women. Women experience a wide and varied range of signs, symptoms and pain. Some are not even aware they have it; for others, it can rule their life.

Endometriosis occurs when fragments of functional endometrium tissue from within the uterus are found outside the uterus. Common sites include the ovaries, broad ligaments, pelvis, vagina, vulva, perineum, intestines or bladder. This tissue bleeds every month, responding to hormonal stimulation, causing painful formation of tissue cysts, scar tissue, adhesions and inflammation.

Causes
There are many theories (some are listed below) although the causes remain largely unknown.
- During embryonic development, dormant cells of endometrium may be misplaced and may mature during adulthood, causing inflammation and pain.
- Retrograde menstruation. During menstruation particles of endometriumflow back towards the fallopian tubes, out into the peritoneal cavity and lodge on common sites around the uterus and cavity. Some suggest the use of tampons, the western style of living and daily inactivity may increase retrograde menstruation, although studies show women from many different ethnic groups may suffer from endometriosis.
- Infection. I know this may sound off-putting, but if you have had pinworms there could be a possibility that they are the cause. Parasitic pinworms may crawl from the anus to the vaginal opening, causing endometriosis.
- Imbalance of hormones oestrogen and progesterone.

Endometriosis

Signs and symptoms

- Chocolate cysts, or endometriomas, are small pockets of old blood that look like chocolate syrup. These cysts can rupture, leading to adhesions and inflammation in the surrounding area.
- Smaller lesions of endometrial tissue clusters may look black, bluish, opaque, clear, or red. Some are not visible to the naked eye.
- Scar and fibrous tissue may build up causing obstruction within the affected area and/or adhesions.
- PMS, fatigue, pain in the stomach region, breast tenderness, weight gain and bloating.
- Pain during sexual intercourse and menstruation, and infertility, are common indicators of endometriosis.
- Pain during urination, and constipation, diarrhoea or discomfort while defecating.

Naturopathic recommendations

Lifestyle hints

Lymphatic and deep tissue massage can help decrease pain and water retention (such as bloating), breast tenderness and sore legs.

Exercise

- Don't underestimate exercise when it comes to having a healthy hormonal balance and a reduction in endometriosis pain symptoms.
- Exercise moderately four times a week, for 30 minutes to an hour each session. For example, try power-walking, weights, gentle jogging, yoga and aerobics. My friends swear by belly and Tahitian dancing — great for blood circulation.

Nutrition

- Eat more fresh (organic) vegetables and fruit. Try 3 pieces of fruit and 2–4 cups of vegetables daily. Eat fish, such as salmon, tuna and sardines daily to help reduce pain and inflammation.
- Eat 3 meals daily and include two healthy snack meals in between. Eat small amounts of protein regularly at meals. Mix defatted meats with grains (rice, chickpea, couscous) or beans to reduce meat intake, as animal fats can increase pain and inflammation. If you are iron-deficient, add liver to your diet, or an iron supplement.
- Common food sensitivities, including chicken, eggs, wheat, citrus and dairy products, may promote inflammation. If a food doesn't agree with you, avoid it and substitute for it with another. For instance, only eat dairy foods in moderation if suitable, if not try calcium fortified soy milk. Try wheat- or gluten-free breads, pasta or rice. Eat certified organic, natural, sugar-free acidophilus yoghurt daily (avoid if allergic.)
- Eat soy foods and plant oestrogens to help keep oestradiol (the body's own oestrogen) levels lower. Plant oestrogens are estimated to be thousands of times weaker than oestradiol, and they can bind onto oestrogen receptors having a protective effect against oestradiol. Eat soya textured vegetable protein (TVP) as a mince substitute, tempeh, soy flour and flakes, soya vegetarian sausages, tofu, soy milk (sugar-free), linseed (fresh seeds), buckwheat, millet, sesame seeds, sunflower seeds, legumes, mung beans, sprouts and sprouted beans.
- Eat fibre or take fibre supplements, including flax, slippery elm and psyllium, to bind onto excess oestrogens. Include fresh fruit (pectins) and organic vegetables.
- If constipated with endometriosis take 1 tsp of Epsom salts with 1 tsp of sweetened powdered fruit drink for flavour, mix with warm water and drink. Do this for no more than

3 days or see your health professional if symptoms persist. Painkillers with codeine may aggravate constipation. For diarrhoea associated with endometriosis take fibre to help bind up the stool and provide bulk. Incidentally, fibre may help constipation by providing bulk and regular bowel movements.

- Avoid synthetic fats, such as margarine, and heated fats, such as vegetable shortenings. Use butter (sparingly), olive oil for stir fries and flax oil for salad and vegetable dressings. Cut back on the junkfood (fast food), salt, chocolate and caffeine.
- Avoid synthetic oestrogens as excess oestrogens have been implicated in endometriosis although more scientific research needs to be done to confirm this suggestion. Do not use plastic containers or plastic foodwrap to heat food in the microwave as plastics contain unwanted, potentially harmful oestrogens that can leach into the food and contribute to oestrogen overload. Use glass or porcelain instead.
- Absolutely avoid instant coffee (as instant coffee may increase pain), reduce caffeine, stop smoking and cut down on alcohol. Drink up to 2 litres of pure, fresh water daily.

Supplements

Magnesium   Has anti-spasmodic properties, helping to relieve the symptoms of muscle cramps. Take 200mg–450mg 2 times daily.

Vitamin B complex   Help the liver break down excess oestrogen. Take as directed.

Fish (2mg–4mg daily), **Borage** (2mg–4mg daily), **Evening Primrose** (2mg–4mg daily) or **Flax oil** (1 Tbsp–2 Tbsp daily)   Increase essential fatty acids to help reduce pain, inflammation and to promote excellent levels of essential fatty acids. These health oils also improve blood flow and regulate the synthesis of reproductive hormones. (2000mg–4000mg daily).

Vitamin E   Take 400IU daily to help with internal scarring and adhesions.

Herbs

First, cleanse the body to give it a good chance of responding to the healing process.

Parasite-cleansing herbs   To help eradicate the hidden parasites, take two 3-week courses of **Cloves** (1800mg daily) combined with **Wormwood** (2000mg daily) and **Black Walnut** (2000mg daily). Follow up with a complete body detox. (See Detoxing on page 131.)

Hormone balancing herbs   Take these herbs for a minimum of 3 months and up to 6 months before revision. If any unusual changes occur, please consult a naturopath or health professional. Do not take if pregnant or breastfeeding, and discontinue use if you experience nausea, gastric upset or vomiting.

    Chaste Tree   Has a normalising effect on hormonal imbalances (e.g. the oestrogen-progesterone balance). It may also help reduce PMS, heavy bleeding and pain. Take 750mg 2 times daily.

    Liquorice   Glycyrrhetinic acids found in Liquorice Root are reported to inhibit the development of ovarian cysts. This wonderful herb is anti-inflammatory and helps with adrenal balance to reduce stress. Take 300mg–500mg 2 times daily. Use for 3–4 weeks then lessen dose to 100mg–300mg daily. Liquorice can increase water retention. If you notice an increase in water retention or blood pressure, discontinue and use only under herbalist or naturopathic supervision.

    False Unicorn Root   Effective in reducing ovarian pain and an important medicinal herb for maintaining healthy hormonal levels. Take 500mg 2 times daily. Although False Unicorn Root produces great results, it may not suit all people with endometriosis.

    Raspberry Leaf   Perhaps the best known and widely recommended medicinal herb for female conditions, this acts as a uterine tonic and is effective for maintaining healthy uterine muscle function. Drink 1 teabag 3 times daily or take 500mg 2 times daily.

Scar Tissue and Adhesions   Take 30mg of **Gotu Kola** extract (Triterpenes) 3 times daily and 3g–5g of **Dan Shen** daily. These may help to break down adhesions and scar tissue.

Pain **Corydalis** (400mg 2 times daily) and **Jamaica Dogwood** (2g daily) provide effective relief for uterine pain. **Black Haw** (400mg 2 times daily) has potent anti-spasmodic properties. **Ginger** (100mg 2–4 times daily) encourages circulation to the pelvic area, reduces blood clotting and also helps to reduce inflammation.

Extra considerations
Bowel toxaemia   Lack of **Acidophilus** and **Bifidus** bacterium, and a low fibre diet contribute to excessive toxins within the bowel. Elimination of toxins and the introduction of good bowel bacteria increases bowel health. Dietary fibre is important because it absorbs the toxins excreted by the liver, including hormone products. Acidophilus and Bifidus are good bacteria that help to keep the digestive system healthy. Take 1 billion of the Acidophilus and Bifidus species in capsule form daily on an empty stomach to repopulate your digestive system.

Liver-cleansing herbs   Important for supporting the liver's enzymatic processes and helping to excrete excessive hormone products. **Dandelion** (3g–5g of dried root daily) and **Milk Thistle** (9g–10g of seed daily) enhance bile flow and detoxify the liver. **Burdock** (2g–6g of dried root daily) helps to cleanse the blood.

Excessive bleeding   Requires haemostatic formulas including herbs such as **Shepherd's Purse, American Cranesbill, Lady's Mantle** and **Yarrow** to reduce the bleeding. See a herbalist or naturopath to obtain these formulas, and if bleeding is excessive see a medical professional to help prevent further complications. Endometriosis can be associated with fibroids.

Immune-enhancing herbs   **Pokeroot** (as directed), **Astragalus** (500mg–10g daily), **Olive Leaf extract** (270mg 3 times daily), **Echinacea** (1200mg daily) and **Thuja** (see a herbalist) may help to resolve cysts and possible association of immune function imbalance. The active ingredients in Pokeroot may help dissolve cyst tissue. Pokeroot is a potent immune stimulant and its properties make it important for maintaining a healthy lymphatic system. Pokeroot can be dangerous and toxic in large doses. See your naturopath or herbalist for prescription.

Eye Care

Poor day or night vision, eye strain and eye fatigue may arise from prolonged computer use, reading, UV light exposure, smoking, cardiovascular disease (atherosclerosis, arteriosclerosis, hypertension) and low dietary intake of pigmented antioxidants found in green, orange and red vegetables and fruits. Research shows that with many of these conditions, the correct eye nutrients and dietary habits can preserve our eyesight so we can look forward to a bright, all-seeing future. Maintaining the condition of your eyes is just as important as exercising regularly and eating right.

Naturopathic recommendations

Lifestyle hints
General eye health recommendations
- Rest your eyes every 15 minutes, if you work on a computer, use a VDU screen, play video games or watch television. Focus your eyes on a very distant object and then relax your eyes.

- Blink frequently to help lubricate the eye naturally.
- Wear protective sunglasses or eyewear when exposed to UV light or sunlight to protect your eyes from sun glare and sun damage. Many sportspeople in the constant glare of the sun, such as cricketers, experience cataracts early on in their life.
- Get plenty of rest. Stress and lack of sleep cause eye strain.

Nutrition

- As we age an increase in the right kind of fruits, protein and vegetables supports optimum eye health and good vision. Increasing dietary intake of corn, kale, spinach, tomatoes and citrus fruits helps to provide precious plant pigments and vitamin C, essential for maintaining healthy vision. Increase green, red and yellow fruits and vegetables in your diet. They contain colourful pigments rich in antioxidants critical to protecting and supporting healthy vision.
- Increase consumption of legumes (high in sulphur-containing amino acids), yellow vegetables (for carotenes) and foods rich in vitamins E and C (fresh fruits and vegetables). Cherries, especially black cherries, blueberries, bilberries, raspberries and blackberries are great for the eyes as they contain flavonoids which support the blood vessels and contain blue and red pigments which help to protect the eyes.
- Drink at least 2 litres of pure water per day.
- Reduce saturated fat and high salt intake, and avoid smoking to reduce free radical damage to you eyes. Smoking, drinking excessive alcohol, high-fat diets, and excessive salt in the diet will affect precious eyesight and blood vessels.
- Avoid eating heated oils and other sources of free radicals, such as any preservatives, emulsifiers, colourings and additives.

Supplements

Vitamin A and **Carotenoids**   Very important for the eyes, keeping the mucous membranes of the eye healthy and supporting night vision. **Beta Carotene**, a Vitamin A precursor, converts to Vitamin A in the liver and then travels to the retina where it is converted into rhodopsin, the night-vision chemical. Intense sunlight exposure can bleach rhodopsin from the night-vision cells (called rods), causing poor vision at night. Take 5000IU–9000IU of retinal Vitamin A or 30,000IU–100,000IU of Beta Carotene per day. (Do not take the retinal source of Vitamin A if you have had or have liver problems or if you are pregnant).

Vitamin C   Deficiency can lead to eye conditions, including bloodshot eyes, allergies and blood vessel damage. Take 1500mg daily.

Vitamin E   Deficiencies can affect eye health and lead to diseases, such as arteriosclerosis, which reduces blood circulation to the eye. Vitamin E supplementation can help prevent fatty degeneration and act as an antioxidant. Take 400IU daily. (Do not take if on heart or blood medication, due to blood-thinning effects.)

Antioxidant formula   Minerals Selenium, Zinc, Chromium, Copper, Vitamins C and E, and Lipoic acid help the body make antioxidant enzymes which reduce the damaging effects of aging. Excess sunlight exposure causes cataracts, but the damage is greater when a Vitamin C deficiency is present. Other helpful antioxidants include bioflavonoids and carotenoids, Lutein and Zeaxanthin. A study showed that those taking Lutein and Zeaxanthin were 18% less likely to develop cataracts.[47] Deficiencies of Selenium can cause up to a 2500% increase in free radical-inducing hydrogen peroxide (H_2O_2) in the lens. Take a combined antioxidant formula as recommended.

Glucosamine   Helps keep the tear ducts clear, important to help prevent glaucoma, and supports the structures of the eye. Take 1500mg daily.

Bioflavonoids These include **Quercetin, Rutin** and **Hesperidin**, which help to keep the blood vessels of the eye healthy. Take 400mg of Quercetin 3 times daily, or 1000mg of mixed Bioflavonoids daily.

Omega 3 and **6 oils** Essential fatty acids from **Fish oil, Flax oil, Borage oil** and **Evening Primrose oil** help with eye lubrication and protect the delicate membranes of the eye if taken internally. Take 3000mg daily or 1 Tbsp–2 Tbsp of Flax oil.

Herbs

Key minerals, herbs, vitamins and antioxidants include ProenOthera®, Lutein, Zeaxanthin and Bilberry. These potent nutrients help to support the eyes' defences against free radical damage to the lens and act like sunglass filters to protect the retina and macula, the parts of the eye responsible for fine vision, colour, day and night vision.

ProenOthera® (Evening Primrose Seed Husk) Has antioxidants which help the blood vessels in the eye. It also reduces damage to eye cells, swelling, puffiness and eye fatigue, and improves circulation. Take 400mg–1g daily.

Lutein and **Zeaxanthin** (extracted from Marigold flowers) These nutrients improve visual function preventing ocular diseases, such as age-related macular degeneration (AMD) and cataracts. There are more than 400 known carotenoids, but in the past couple of years, research has singled out Lutein — found in dark green leafy vegetables — as a critical nutrient for good vision. Lutein and Zeaxanthin, a similar carotene produced by the body from Lutein, are concentrated in the macula and retina and act like filters, preventing photochemical damage and oxidation leading to AMD and cataracts. Take 5mg–6mg of Lutein and Zeaxanthin daily for prevention of degenerative eye conditions.

Bilberry Extracts reinforce the collagen structures of the retina and prevent free radical damage. Used for a wide range of eye conditions including poor day and night vision, glaucoma, diabetic retinopathy and macular degeneration. Take 3ml–6ml of 1:1 liquid extract daily or tablets providing 50mg–120mg of anthocyanins daily.

Ginkgo Has been shown in studies to provide significant improvement in the blood supply to the eyes in elderly patients.[48] Another study showed that Ginkgo also caused significant long-term improvement in patients with senile macular degeneration and severe retinal circulatory disturbances or glaucoma.[49] Take 4g–8g of whole leaf or 24mg–30mg of standardised extract of Ginkgo flavone glycosides daily. Avoid with the prescribed medication warfarin, as Ginkgo in large amounts may magnify the drug's blood-thinning effect.

Eyebright Helpful for mucous membranes of the eye and inflammation of the eye and internal catarrh. Take 2g–4g of dried herb 3 times daily.

Other eye condition recommendations

Blood vessel damage

Schuessler Tissue Salt Calc Fluor is a homeopathically prepared mineral to help tone broken blood vessels and is great for quick absorption and mineral function. Take 1 tablet 8 times regularly throughout the day.

Anti-haemorrhage herbs Witch Hazel and **Shepherd's Purse** can stem bleeding within the body. See a herbalist or naturopath for a consultation and prescription of the herbs and use internally, short-term only. You may also opt for a Witch Hazel eye lotion.

Vitamin C, Bioflavonoids, Ginkgo and **Bilberry** Strengthen leaky, damaged eye capillaries. See above for recommended doses.

Cataracts

See page 107.

Droopy eyelids
Vitamin B1   Droopy eyelids may be exacerbated by a deficiency of Vitamin B1. Take 100mg of Vitamin B1 with a B complex daily.
Marine Collagen and **Lyophilised Marine Protein**   Lack of dietary collagen or poor collagen repair may cause eyelids to become droopy. Take 400mg of Lyophilised Marine Protein and 100mg of Marine Collagen 2–3 times daily.

Dry eye
Oils help to maintain good flexibility of eye tissue, especially for damaged or aging eyes, as they tend to lose elasticity and flexibility within the cell membrane. Remember to blink frequently to help lubricate the eye.
Flax oil   This essential oil provides Omega 3, 6 and 9. It helps with the fluid behind the eye and assists with cell wall flexibility of all cells within the body. Take 1 Tbsp 3 times daily.
Evening Primrose oil   Rich in Omega 6, it also assists with cell wall flexibility of all cells within the body. Take 3 1000mg capsules daily.
Castor oil BP   I've had a lot of success using this oil as a topical eye conditioner to lubricate the eye and draw waste from tear ducts and eyelash follicles. Obtain Castor oil BP from the chemist and fill up a 20ml or 30ml glass bottle (with a 1ml glass dropper attached to lid) with the oil. Apply 1 drop to the eyeball without touching the dropper onto any surface to prevent contamination. Use 1–3 drops daily or before bed. Your eye will feel oily, almost stinging, for approximately 30 seconds and then as you roll your eye around you will feel it become soothing. Carefully wipe excess oil from the eye with a sterile tissue. Use every night until the bottle is finished. Place 1 drop in the eye for first 3 nights and then after that you may use the drops twice a day if you wish. If contaminated by touching a surface (eyeball, eyelashes, skin, etc.) sterilise the dropper or buy another one. To sterilise the dropper pop it in a pan of boiling water (take off rubber) and let it dry thoroughly or dry with a sterile cloth or tissue. Use only with medical or naturopathic supervision and do not use if you suspect any eye infection or allergies. Do not use on young children.

Eye allergies
- Remove any food sensitivities, avoid tobacco, exposure to allergic substances or environments, and potential environmental toxin exposure.
- Include adequate water intake and essential fatty acids.
- Take supplementary **Flax** or **Fish oil** for an anti-inflammatory effect against allergies.

Eyebright   Soothes irritated, red conjunctiva and the whites of the eye. Take 2g–4g daily.
Perilla   Reduces allergic reactions. Take 1g–2g daily.
Quercetin or **Rutin**   Strengthen the capillaries in the eye and reduce mast cell degranulation which sets up an allergy reaction. Take 200mg–450mg 2 times daily.
Schuessler Tissue Salts   Homeopathically prepared minerals. Take every ½ hour when infection is cleared or symptoms are removed or take more frequently, every 5 minutes for a faster working action.
  Combination H (hayfever)   Use for allergic conditions causing inflammation in the eyes, nose and upper respiratory tract. Can be used as a preventative for spring allergies, if taken 2–6 weeks prior to expected attack, by taking 4 tablets daily. When hayfever is severe, take every 1/2 hour or for super-quick relief take every 5 minutes.
  Ferr Phos   Use for the first stage of eye inflammation: redness, general pain from overstraining the eyes, burning sensations, granulated eyelids and bloodshot eyes.
  Nat Mur   Use for eye infections, when there is a discharge of watery mucus or tears. Discharges can cause soreness of skin or eruption of small blisters.
Tea bags   Cold applications are soothing to the eyes.

Eye floaters

Check with an eye specialist for a diagnosis as eye floaters may indicate a serious condition, or may be benign. These recommendations are for general floaters within the eye that do not pose a serious threat to eye vision.

Heavy Metal Detox   Floaters may be caused by heavy metal toxicity. Follow Detoxing recommendations on page 131.

Vitamin B complex   Deficiency of B Vitamins from stress or dietary lack may lead to floaters. Take a B complex daily.

Bioflavonoids and **Vitamin A**   See general eye health (above) for dosage recommendations. Have an adequate amount of protein in your diet and avoid or reduce alcohol to a minimum. Increase water intake to 8–9 glasses per day or more if you are exercising and perspiring frequently.

Eye infections (mild)

When treating infections of the eyes such as conjunctivitis, blepharitis (inflammation of the eyelids) or styes, focus on the immune system to treat the condition inside and out. The eyes are very delicate and you may require antibiotic therapy to assist with any bacterial infection. See your doctor and naturopath for professional supervision, consultation and advice.

Internally:

Goldenseal   For eye infections and to improve mucus membranes. Use short-term unless specified by a naturopath or herbalist. Take 0.5g–1g of dried rhizome and root daily.

Eyebright   Effective against mucous and inflammation for the eye, ear, nose and throat areas. Take 875mg 3 times daily.

Goldenrod   Useful for excessive eye mucus and it can also help treat eye infections, such as conjunctivitis and blepharitis. Take 2ml–4ml of Goldenrod tincture 3 times daily.

Schuessler Tissue Salts   Homeopathically prepared minerals. Take every ½ hour until infection is cleared or symptoms are removed or take more frequently, every 5 minutes, for a faster working action.

> **Kali Mur**   Use for the second stage of inflammation: a whitish, grey discharge, sore eyes with specks of white matter on lids and granulated eyelids with a feeling of sand in the eyes. Alternate with **Ferr Phos**.
>
> **Nat Phos**   Use for inflammation, golden-yellow creamy discharge, eyelids stuck together in the morning or a creamy coated tongue.
>
> **Silica**   Use for inflammation, with thick yellow discharges, styes, boils and indurations (hardening) around eyelids.

Other helpful herbs for long-term infections that won't budge include **Cleavers** (2g–4g daily), **Pokeroot** (use under herbalist supervision only), **Echinacea** (1200mg daily) and **Olive Leaf extract** (270mg 3 times daily).

Topically:

Depending on the intensity and the type of infection, herbalists can make an eyewash or compress of **Marigold, Goldenseal** and **Eyebright** to soothe the eye and work topically on the infections

Yellow sclera (white part of the eyes)

Yellowing may be caused by diets high in saturated fats, poor liver function, and may be exacerbated by overexposure to sun glare.

Cleanse the liver   See Detoxing page 131.

Use antioxidants   See General eye health recommendations (above) for dosages.

Protect the eyes from sun glare   See general eye health recommendations (above).

Fibroids

Uterine fibroids are benign (non-cancerous) tumours. They consist of a mass of thickened, hard muscular tissue that grows on the uterus. They can protrude into the uterus or be found under the outer lining of the uterus below the endometrial lining. Some fibroids are harmless and do not affect other organs due to their position or size. Other fibroids can cause many signs and symptoms that affect quality of life. Twenty percent of women over the age of 35 may be affected.

Causes

The cause of fibroids is generally unknown; however, a few factors may be associated with fibroid development.
- Poor oestrogen-progesterone balance. Although oestrogen may appear to be at a normal range, oestrogen receptors are found in greater than normal numbers on the fibroid tissue.
- Excess oestrogen, possibly from oral contraceptive or hormone therapies, pregnancy, the liver's inability to break down excess oestrogen, and elevated levels of synthetic oestrogens in our environment and our diet.
- Lack of essential fatty acids (omega 3 and 6) as this may affect growth hormone levels.
- Lack of beneficial bacteria in the digestive system. Healthy plant oestrogens that may block harmful oestrogens need to be converted in the digestive tract by beneficial bacteria.
- Lack of isoflavones or plant oestrogens within the diet.
- Hypoglycaemia (low blood sugar) must be addressed, as one theory suggests that sugar imbalance has an effect on growth hormone levels that may trigger fibroid growth.
- Other factors associated with fibroids are family history, poor diet, endometriosis, toxins (e.g. DDT — dichlorodiphenyltrichloroethane), hypothyroidism (underactive thyroid gland), whether or not a woman has had a child, and race. Black women are 3 times more likely to suffer from fibroids than Caucasian, Asian or Latino women.
- According to Ayurvedic medicine the following general types of imbalances are at the source of most chronic conditions including fibroids and endometriosis:
    toxins accumulating in tissues and blocking circulation;
    poor nutrition;
    poor digestion;
    imbalance of the nervous system;
    accumulation of physical and mental stress;
    lowering of natural resistance and immunity; and
    disruption of natural biological rhythms.

Signs and symptoms

- One of the main symptoms is heavy menstrual bleeding which occurs because the fibroid muscle mass is unable to contract, leading to anaemia and anaemic symptoms. Normally the uterus contracts during menstrual bleeding. In the USA, 33% of hysterectomy operations are due to fibroids.
- Some women have small fibroids for many years without signs or symptoms (asymptomatic). This is likely to be due to the positioning of the fibroids.
- A congested dragging feeling in the abdomen.
- If the fibroids enlarge in size they may cause pressure, bloating, pain, excessive urination, constipation, bleeding between periods, and excessive bleeding during periods.
- Infertility or problems with egg implantation.
- Obstruction due to the fibroid's enlargement or its position within the uterus.
- Immediate surgery may be required if a fibroid twists or obstructs other organs.

Naturopathic recommendations

Lifestyle hints

Please continue to see your GP for regular checks and examinations to prevent further complications. If you are over 35 years old and infertility or miscarriage is a concern, you may need to consider any recommended surgical removal of the fibroid if it is large (5cm or above). As you get older your chances of fertility are lowered and it may take too long waiting on dietary and herbal measures to dissolve the fibroid — and these measures may not be successful on large fibroids. Conversely, you may be asked to wait for 6 months post-operation before attempting to conceive.

- Relax; take time out for yourself doing something you enjoy, such as aromatherapy oil baths, reading, stretching or meditation.

Exercise

- Exercise 3–6 times weekly for 20–40 minutes per session to encourage circulation and stress release.
- Yoga, belly dancing, Hawaiian or Tahitian style dancing are great for the pelvis, abdominal area and circulation.

Nutrition

- Sip a few drops of Swedish bitters mixed with soda before meals to aid digestion and mineral absorption, or alternatively sip 50ml of Aloe Vera juice.
- Eat more fresh (organic) vegetables and fruit. Try 3 pieces of fruit and 2–4 cups of vegetables daily.
- Eat small amounts of protein regularly at meals. Mix defatted meats with grains (rice, chickpea, couscous) or beans to reduce meat intake, as animal fats can increase pain and inflammation. If you are iron deficient you may add more liver (try organic chicken pâté) to your diet, or an iron supplement. Eat steamed or grilled fish (e.g. salmon, tuna and sardines) daily to help reduce pain and inflammation. Reduce intake of non-organic chicken and eggs, or avoid completely until you are tested free from poultry sensitivity by a naturopath or herbalist.
- If a food doesn't agree with you, substitute another. For example, try substituting for milk with calcium fortified soy milk, or wheat/gluten with gluten-free breads, pasta or rice. Eat dairy foods in moderation if suitable.
- Eat 3 meals daily and include two healthy snack meals in between.
- For 10 days prior to bleeding, eat smaller meals more often (6 times daily) to reduce tendency to hypoglycaemia.
- Eat certified organic, natural, low-sugar acidophilus yoghurt daily. Avoid if allergic to dairy and take acidophilus and bifidus supplements instead.
- Eat soy foods and plant oestrogens to help keep oestradiol (the body's own oestrogen) levels lower. Plant oestrogens are estimated to be thousands of times weaker than oestradiol, and they can bind onto oestrogen receptors to give a protective effect against oestradiol. Eat soya textured vegetable protein (TVP) as a mince substitute, tempeh, soy flour and flakes, soya vegetarian sausages, tofu, soy milk (sugar-free), linseed (fresh seeds), buckwheat, millet, sesame seeds, sunflower seeds, legumes, mung beans, sprouts, sprouted beans. Oestrogen therapy may increase excess oestrogens, which have been implicated in endometriosis and fibroids, although more scientific research is needed to confirm this suggestion.
- Eat more dietary fibre (vegetables, fruit, supplementary fibres, flaxseed fibre or sprinkled ground flaxseed on breakfast cereal) to bind onto excess oestrogens.

- Try seaweed broth as it is a source of micronutrients, including iodine, and a hormonal balancer. There has been an association between hypothyroidism and fibroid growth. Even women who tested normal on their thyroid panel shown benefit from the iodine.
- Eat a low-fat diet. Once again, we need to focus on improving the function of the liver. Avoid synthetic fats, such as margarine, and heated fats, such as vegetable shortenings. Use butter (sparingly) or flaxseed oil.
- Do not use plastic containers or plastic food wrap to heat food in the microwave as plastics contain unwanted, potentially harmful, oestrogens that can leach into the food and contribute to oestrogen overload. Use glass or porcelain instead.
- Absolutely avoid instant coffee (as instant coffee may increase pain). Eliminate methylxanthines from the diet, i.e. caffeine in all forms (coffee, caffeinated soda drinks, black and green tea, and chocolate). Caffeine may increase fibroid development. Avoid drinking black tea and red wine as they contains tannins that have an ability to inhibit iron absorption. Also avoid aspirin use and ask your doctor about certain drugs, e.g. cholestyramine and tetracycline, that also inhibit iron absorption.
- Avoid sugar and highly-processed foods, such as sweets, dried fruits, undiluted fruit juices, cakes and biscuits. Eat more complex carbohydrates including whole grain breads, rice and oats (if you are tested free of grain sensitivity).

Supplements

Vitamin E (200IU daily) and the herb **Gotu Kola** (40mg of extract 3 times daily)   May help internal fibroids and scarring.

Anaemia   See page 73 for iron supplementation recommendations.

To deal with excess oestrogen take:

Fibre   Increase dietary fibre by using the above nutritional recommendations or by adding supplementary fibre, such as **Flax fibre**, into your diet to bind to and absorb excess oestrogen. Take 1 Tbsp–3 Tbsp of Flax fibre daily.

Vitamin B complex   Aids adrenal stress and helps the liver with excessive oestrogen metabolism. Take 1 tablet daily.

Diindolylmethane (DIM)   Has been shown to significantly influence oestrogen metabolites and healthy hormonal balance. Take 40mg 2 times daily.

Flax oil, Fish oil and **Evening Primrose oil**   Help reduce inflammation in adults and promote good levels of essential fatty acids to assist hormone balance. Take 3000mg of Even-ing Primrose oil or Fish oil daily, or 1 Tbsp–2 Tbsp (13,000mg–26,000mg) of Flax oil daily.

Herbs

If you have had the fibroids surgically removed, you have removed the symptoms but not dealt with the cause. Like endometriosis, you may need to follow dietary and herbal recommendations to prevent the further development of fibroids. Discontinue supplements and herbs prior to conception, unless otherwise prescribed by a naturopath or herbalist.

Parasite-cleansing herbs   Use these herbs first. Parasites may be implicated in the stimulation of fibroid growth. I almost always advise using a parasite cleanse when it comes to male and female reproductive conditions as it seem to increase the success of the treatment. Take two 3-week courses of **Cloves** (1800mg daily) combined with **Wormwood** (2000mg daily) and **Black Walnut** (2000mg daily) to help eradicate parasites. After completing the parasite cleanse, detox your body following the recommendations on page 131.

Liver-cleansing herbs   **Dandelion** (1g of dried root daily) and **Milk Thistle** (2g of seed daily) enhance bile flow and encourage the enzymatic processing of toxins and oestrogen by the liver.

Herbs that help the reproductive system

Raspberry Leaf   Used to help tone the uterus and maintain healthy uterus tissue. Take 1g daily.

Chaste Tree   Helps to balance reproductive hormones, e.g. the progesterone, oestrogen ratio. Take 1g–1.5g daily.

Corydalis (800mg–1g daily) and **Black Haw** (800mg–1g daily)   Help muscle spasms, cramping and dragging pain.

Ginger   Reduces inflammation, bloating, digestion and congestion, and increases circulation. Take 1g–1.5g with food daily over several months.

Liquorice   Helps any associated ovarian cyst development. Also exerts a balancing effect on male hormones, androgens, and helps the body adapt to stress. Take 500mg daily for 3–6 months. Non-deglycyrrhizinised Liquorice can increase blood pressure and water retention symptoms. Monitor your blood pressure and water retention symptoms, and reduce or stop taking Liquorice if they increase.

Pokeroot   Improves weak immune systems, which can be linked to female reproductive conditions. I suggest that you ask a naturopath or herbalist for advice before using this herb because, although effective in large doses, it can be very toxic.

Other herbs recommended to reduce fibroids are **Calendula** and **Thuja**. I have also had success including 500mg–1g of **False Unicorn Root** into daily herbal recommendations to help balance hormone levels, increase conception chances and decrease the risk of miscarriage, but it may not be suitable for all women as one theory suggests it may enhance fibroid growth in some women.

Herbs that prevent excessive bleeding

These include **Yarrow** and **Shepherd's Purse**. Please see a herbalist or naturopath for a formula which will be specifically designed for you and supervised throughout your treatment. I normally recommend adding 2 handfuls of dried Yarrow leaves, flowers and stalks to 1 litre of near-boiling water. Cover and steep for 4 hours. If bleeding heavily, drink 3 cups per day until bleeding has stopped. Do not drink for more than 1 week unless prescribed by a professional naturopath. Seek your doctor's advice if bleeding continues or if you feel weak or dizzy.

Externally

Castor oil packs   These have been known to help with pain during bleeding and testimonials suggest that they may help to dissolve fibroids. Use with dietary and herbal recommendations.

> *How to make a Castor oil pack*
>
> You will need: Castor oil (obtained from the chemist), a soft, clean cotton cloth, plastic wrap, a plastic container to store the oil-laden cloth, and a hot water bottle. Directions: Soak the cloth in Castor oil. Place the folded cloth over the stomach or lower abdomen area where the fibroid is approximately located. Cover the cloth completely with plastic wrap both to avoid staining your clothes and to keep in the warmth. Place a towel over the plastic and put a hot water bottle on it. Leave it on overnight. Repeat this five nights in a row and then rest for two nights. Do this for three weeks.

Fibromyalgia

Over the years I've tended a direct naturopathic hotline. The people who seek naturopathic advice for fibromyalgia almost always start by telling me they are relieved to have a diagnosis of their collection of symptoms, although most have been told at some time through their diagnostic search, 'It's all in your mind'. Fibromyalgia is a chronic condition that involves widespread muscle pain, fatigue and weakness. Naturopathy has so much to offer in the treatment of fibromyalgia. A healthy change of lifestyle and a new look at dealing with stresses can make a world of difference to the majority of fibromyalgic individuals and, indeed, to sufferers from most chronic diseases.

Causes
- Several conditions are linked with fibromyalgia: irritable bowel syndrome, severe migraine or non-migraine headaches, Raynaud's disease or Sicca (Sjögren) syndrome, chronic fatigue syndrome, osteoarthritis and rheumatoid arthritis.
- Some theories suggest that viral, fungal or bacterial infections may be the cause or autoimmune involvement where the body attacks itself.
- Other possible factors involved in fibromyalgia are an overload of toxins, heavy metals, electrical sensitivity, food sensitivities, immune system abnormalities, leaky gut syndrome, candida, low serotonin levels and nutrient deficiencies.
- Silicone breast implants and substance abuse are also implicated.

Signs and symptoms
- All-over muscle pain is the main symptom. The muscles ache or are stiff, especially in the morning before movement restores circulation. Cold or humid weather can make this worse.
- Joint swelling, numbness and tingling sensations.
- There are 18 certain pressure points on the body. If on examination by a health professional over 11 of these points are tender, and there is a fair history of widespread pain in the body, the diagnosis is likely to be fibromyalgia.
- Depression, anxiety or insomnia (disturbed sleeping patterns) may occur.

Naturopathic recommendations

Lifestyle hints
- Remove mercury fillings.
- Seek therapeutic massage once a week and use cold compresses for acute pain, or hot compresses with the anti-inflammatory essential oils chamomile and lavender to reduce inflammation.
- Soak in a hot to warm bath for 15 minutes with a handful of magnesium salts (Epsom Salts) added to the water to assist muscle relaxation.

Exercise
- Try to increase muscular circulation and encourage a deeper sleep by exercising for 20–30 minutes every day. Hard-impact exercise is not really suitable and over-exercising can often cause a relapse in symptoms and pain. Instead opt for gentle exercise, such as gentle forms of yoga, bicycling, water aerobics or swimming. Initially exercise for only 3–5 minutes until you feel you can increase the time.

Nutrition

- Identify any food sensitivities. See a naturopath for guidance and ask for the Elimination Diet to help discover your food sensitivities. Common food allergies that may trigger fibromyalgia symptoms include citrus fruits, nuts, gluten found in rye, oats, barley and wheat products, and dairy products. Rice and rice milk are an acceptable substitute for grains and dairy.
- Avoid all refined carbohydrates, caffeine, potatoes, tomatoes, eggplant (aubergine), tobacco and peppers, all members of the nightshade family. Reduce red meat intake as these foods may increase pain.
- Avoid toxins from tobacco, alcohol, artificial sugars, monosodium glutamate (MSG), artificial food preservatives, additives and colourings.
- Do not drink carbonated beverages. Instead opt for plenty of fresh water, weak black tea, green tea, herbal teas, diluted fruit juices and fresh vegetable juices.
- Eat more deep-sea fish for the anti-inflammatory omega 3 oils they possess and if you eat shellfish, reduce consumption to a minimum and do not eat at the same time as drinking alcohol to help avoid gouty build-up and inflammation in the joints.
- Increase antioxidant, anti-inflammatory foods, including evening primrose oil, flax oil, ginger, garlic, vitamin E, colourful berries, cherries, fruit (except citrus), legumes and vegetables, especially dark, leafy greens.

Supplements

Leaky gut syndrome   Linked to fibromyalgia. Heal the gut lining with **Colostrum** (4g daily) combined with **Acidophilus** (1 billion daily), **Bifidus** (1 billion daily), **Flax oil** (2 Tbsp daily), **Vitamin A** (5000IU daily), **Zinc** (45mg daily) and **Folic acid** (300mcg daily).

Flax oil, Fish oil and **Evening Primrose oil**   To help reduce inflammation take, 3000mg daily of Evening Primrose oil or Fish oil, or 1 Tbsp–2 Tbsp (13,000mg–26,000mg) of Flax oil daily.

MSM (methyl sulphonyl methane)   This natural sulphur compound is helpful for relieving muscular pain. Take 2g daily.

Betaine or **Hydrochloric acid supplements**   Lack of stomach acid may contribute to rheumatoid arthritis. Take 100mg–200mg 3 times daily with meals, or opt for **Bromelain**, an enzyme from pineapple that reduces inflammation and bruising, increases good protein digestion, and aids healing. Dosage equates to 2000mg (1200mcu–1800mcu 'milk clotting units') per day divided into five doses taken on an empty stomach or 250mg–750mg 2 times daily.

5-Hydroxy tryptophan (5HTP)   A safe, natural substance derived from protein or directly from the *Griffonia simplicifolia* herb that can help balance serotonin levels within the brain. Migraine headaches and fibromyalgia share a common feature: both are low serotonin syndromes. 5HTP can largely improve the symptoms of pain, anxiety, sleeplessness and mild depression associated with low serotonin levels. Take 100mg–300mg daily.

Magnesium, Calcium and **Zinc**   Common deficiencies associated with fibromyalgia and muscle pain. Take a high-dose mineral supplement daily.

Herbs

Parasite-cleansing herbs   Use these herbs first. Parasites can inflame, irritate and perforate the intestinal lining, resulting in 'leaky gut'. This can lead to undigested food particles entering the bloodstream creating food allergies and inflammation. Parasites can settle in the joints and muscles, form cysts, and create inflammation. Take two 3-week courses of **Cloves** (1800mg daily) combined with **Wormwood** (2000mg daily) and **Black Walnut** (2000mg daily) to help eradicate parasites. After completing the parasite cleanse, detox your body following the recommendations on page 131.

Olive Leaf extract   Helps immunity against a deluge of microbes, including viruses, bacteria and fungi, and maintains an anti-parasitic environment after completing the parasite cleanse. Microbial infection is often thought to be a trigger of fibromyalgia and viruses may lay dormant for many years without noticeable skeletal or muscular symptoms or pain. Take 270mg 3 times daily.

Liver-cleansing herbs   **Dandelion** (1g of dried root daily) and **Milk Thistle** (2g of seed daily) enhance bile flow and help detoxify the liver. **Bupleurum** helps to modulate the immune system and protect the liver. Take 3g–12g of dried root daily. After completing a detox you need to take these herbs daily, to encourage and support the enzymatic processing of toxins by the liver.

Ginger   Not only a good treatment for nausea and motion sickness, but also has a natural anti-inflammatory effect in fibromyalgia. Take 1g–2g daily with food over several months.

Black Cohosh   Has traditionally been used for menopause, pain, muscular spasms, and muscular and uterine inflammatory processes. It is also useful for fibromyalgia and other musculoskeletal inflammatory processes. Take 1g–3g daily.

White Willow Bark (1g–2g daily), **Feverfew** (50mg–200mg daily), **Wild Yam** (2g–4g daily), **Devil's Claw** (500mg of dried root daily) and **Yarrow** (2g–4g 3 times daily) may also be helpful, natural anti-inflammatory agents. **Liquorice Root** (2g–4g daily or as prescribed), **Valerian** (1g–3g daily) and homeopathics have also been successful in fibromyalgia treatment.

Food Allergies and Sensitivities

Rather than describe true food allergies that cause anaphylaxis or toxic shock, e.g. peanuts, I want to explain other food sensitivities, intolerances or allergies that are commonly experienced every day by the unsuspecting individual. There are two types of food allergies:

A fixed allergy causes a predictable reaction after you consume a particular food, e.g. shellfish or strawberries. It's normally pretty quick and can happen within 24 hours. The immune system mistakes a particular food for a harmful substance and reacts by sending inflammatory chemicals through the bloodstream, which sets off reactions that may include a skin rash, shortness of breath and vomiting.

A non-fixed allergy, or an addictive allergy, is when the body craves for a food or substance to prevent addictive withdrawal, such as tobacco, alcohol, wheat, sugar or caffeine.

Another non-fixed allergy, which is the most common type that naturopaths deal with, is a cyclic, or masked, allergy. A person may consume an allergy food or substance but they may not appear to have any symptoms or signs relating to that allergy until 3–5 days later. A cyclic allergy is an overload of a particular food substance, developed by repetitive eating of that same substance. On avoidance of that allergen over a period of about 4 months the symptoms disappear until the allergen is eaten or consumed again. If it's not picked up it becomes a masked allergy as the symptoms are so ongoing they are unnoticed or are thought to be not related to the food substance. The time it takes for the body to digest and assimilate the substance accounts for the delay in the reaction. The table below gives a graphic idea of a food allergy reaction. Allergy reaction symptoms or signs occur once they rise over the allergic threshold.

As you can see, the graph on the right indicates what can happen when you eat a food or substance that causes a masked reaction. The following is an example of an allergic reaction to wheat. In the morning 2 pieces of toast or wheat biscuits are eaten. At lunch you might have sandwiches and then finally pasta for dinner. You may experience cramps in the stomach, moodiness or a headache that comes and goes throughout the day and blame it on fatigue, but it could actually be a food allergy to wheat.

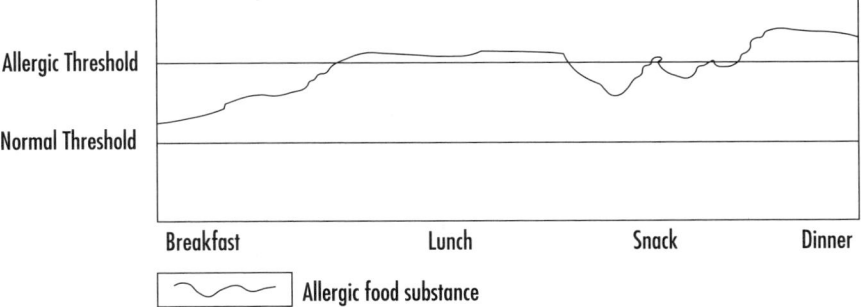

Often people will have an ongoing sensitivity or intolerance to a food that they don't notice because they've eaten it all their lives. It may be iceberg lettuce, oranges, tomatoes, apples or bread. With elimination of identified food allergies, chronic symptoms can disappear quite quickly. If you experiment and try the allergen food you'll notice that your symptoms can come back two-fold…yikes.

Causes

- Common allergen substances include gluten (wheat, oats, rye and barley), corn, soy, sugar, yeast, chicken, beef, eggs, fish, milk, oranges (often all of the citrus group), potatoes, bananas, tomatoes, apples, iceberg lettuce, carrots, peas, green beans, food additives, peanuts, tea, tobacco, alcohol, coffee and chocolate. Wheat may even be found in different foodstuffs, including alcoholic beverages, condiments and sauces.
- Leaky gut syndrome.
- Early or improper weaning of babies and lack of beneficial digestive bacteria. Soy is often introduced too early to babies as it believed to be a non-allergic food.
- Exposure to toxins, chemicals and medicines either environmentally or intrinsically.
- Dust mites, animal fur, plants, spores, pollens, fungi and chemicals, including shampoo, conditioner and make-up.
- Hereditary or genetic predisposition.
- Eating foods out of season or without a break. Allergies to food may be created when individuals eat too much of the same food, too often or too young.
- Manipulation of foods, irradiation, genetic modification and excessive consumption of processed foods.
- Naturally occurring food chemicals may trigger reactions in some people. These include salicylates, phenylethylamine, tryptamine, histamine, tyramine and caffeine.
- Hypochlorhydria (insufficient production of hydrochloric acid) in the stomach can be the underlying cause of allergies.
- Hypothyroidism.
- Dehydration.

Signs and symptoms

- Swelling in different parts of the body.
- Heavy sweating unrelated to anxiety or exercise.
- Fatigue and sleepiness that is not helped by rest, and chronic fatigue syndrome (CFS) symptoms. Normally grains, in particular wheat (especially when there is bloating as well), are the culprits.

- Increased pulse rate unrelated to exertion or anxiety.
- Longitudinal ridges on nails, itchy throat and creased eyelids.
- A dry, raspy cough that never seems to go, and swollen glands
- The skin surrounding the eye appears red or blue as capillaries constrict.
- White or yellowish line around the lips after consuming allergen.
- Prickly, dry little bumps or itchiness, especially on upper arm (e.g. wheat allergy).
- Weight gain or weight loss. Increased hunger may indicate allergy to grains.
- Acne, asthma, eczema, hayfever, arthritis, candida, high blood pressure, skin rashes, skin peeling, hives, ear inflammation, headache or migraines (often in the morning), inflammatory conditions, difficulty breathing, muscle or joints that ache, increased mucus, addiction, mouth ulcers, bad breath, unusual tastes in mouth, interstitial cystitis, bloating, digestive problems, digestive ulcers, reflux, attention deficit disorder (ADD), attention deficit hyperactivity disorder (ADHD), mood swings, violence and depression.
- Allergic line across the nose that is caused by a constant, unconscious rubbing with the back of the hand.

Naturopathic recommendations

Lifestyle hints
- If a person is allergic to wheat they most likely will be allergic to rye and, if they are true Coeliac sufferers, also lactose from milk products.
- Asians (90%–95%), Polynesians (54%–64%) and Europeans from the Mediterranean and Southern Europe (56%) are most allergic to lactose found in dairy products.
- An addictive allergy may be present if there is a strong need for a particular food or if there is a food that you eat often. With addictive allergies associated with withdrawal symptoms, you may often feel better when you eat the allergen.
- Eliminate all substances that cause food reactions and sensitivities.
- Eat food when it is in season and choose organic.
- There are plenty of food substitutes to choose from these days. If you are unsure of your food substitute possibilities see a naturopath.

Testing for sensitivities
Hair testing is one of the most accurate ways of testing for food or substance sensitivities. Muscle testing applied by an experienced practitioner is one of my favourite forms of testing. Although there is little scientific evidence and few clinical studies to prove this style of diagnosis, I've witnessed tremendous success with clients and family members over the years.

How to test for a food allergy
For three weeks eat only (organic if possible):
- Meat: lamb, turkey, rabbit, and all game.
- Fish: except smoked fish or shellfish.
- All vegetables: except canned or bottled vegetables or juice, iceberg lettuce, potatoes, eggplant, tomatoes, onions and corn.
- All fruits: except citrus, dried fruit, canned or bottled fruit or juice, raw apples and strawberries.
- Legumes: chickpeas.
- Oils: flax, evening primrose, olive, safflower, almond or grape seed oils.
- Grains: millet, buckwheat and rice in any form, except glutinous rice.
- Sweeteners: raw or manuka honey is best.
- Natural flavourings: herbs, spices (except for paprika), carob and sea salt.

- Beverages: bottled water, herbal teas, dandelion or chicory coffee, vegetable and fruit juices, except those indicated above

During the three weeks write down a list of everything you eat and any adverse reactions (see signs and symptoms list). This may identify any possible allergen foods that are on the above list. Discontinue those foods that are recommended to be eaten in the three week period if they cause major reactions. If you do not like a food, avoid it. Discontinue the diet if you do not see a major improvement after three weeks, and see a naturopath for a professional consultation. If you have any serious health conditions consult with your health practitioner before self-testing for an allergy. Certain drugs may upset results. These include the use of corticosteroids (prednisone), tobacco and painkillers.

After three weeks start reintroducing other foods and beverages into your diet one day at a time. Reintroduce one item at one time every day. Wait for 24 hours and if there are no symptoms add this item to your list. An example of these foods may be pork, beef, processed meat, shellfish or smoked fish, nuts and seeds, soy, tofu, eggs, strawberries, raw apples and citrus fruits. Wheat, corn, and all grains, milk and milk products, tap water, tea, coffee, cocoa, alcohol, canned or bottled fruit or vegetable juices are also suitable. All processed foods, refined carbohydrates, including cakes, biscuits and ice cream, should be added last, as should any other foods you suspect you may be allergic to. Always keep the diary and record any signs and symptoms.

What if I find an allergy food? You most likely will experience a dramatic reaction when the food is reintroduced into your diet and your symptoms may be more dramatic and pronounced than before. Clear the allergy by drinking 1 litre of water with an added teaspoon of baking soda and eliminate that substance from your diet for at least 6 months.

Anaphylactic reactions Just to be on the safe side, if you experience shortness of breath, extreme skin rash, swollen throat, lips or tongue, do not eat more of that substance, and see a doctor as soon as possible as your next reaction to exposure to that substance is likely to be more severe and possibly life-threatening.

Nutrition

The Elimination diet is a gentle cleanse designed to expose allergens, avoid developing allergies and to control existing allergies. It is slightly more complex than the above diet recommended for three weeks to determine a food allergy. See a naturopath to help you with the elimination diet, and to help monitor your progress and discuss food substitutes.

- If you discover a masked allergen it's best to avoid the food for at least 6 months to 1 year. Then if you do want to reintroduce it into your diet only eat the substance 1 day in 4.
- If you experience headaches, moodiness, dizziness, sleepiness you may be experiencing a withdrawal symptom.
- Avoid empty calories in alcohol, high-sugar or junk foods. Eat wholesome food that can help put the nutrition back into your body.
- For those addicted to wheat, eating a meal made out of one-third millet and two-thirds rice can help them get over their hunger while avoiding all wheat in their diet.
- Alternatives to milk may be nut, rice, goat's or soy milk. Rotate these milks over a 4 day period.
- Cut down on saturated animal fats, the fat found on meat.
- Gluten is a protein within wheat, rye, barley and oats. You may be asked to avoid the following foods due to their gluten content: wheat, found in most breads (wholemeal, wholewheat and wheatmeal flour), wheat bran, barley, rye, rye flour, pasta, noodles and semolina. All baked foods made from wheat, rye, semolina, barley and pearl barley flour, glutinous rice, oats, spelt, couscous, polenta and pasta that isn't labelled gluten-free, sponge pudding, pastry, pies and wafers. Barley-based drinks, barley fruit drinks, malted

drinks and beer. Beware of gluten in other products, please check labels, e.g. soy sauce (wheat protein), stocks, etc. Some substitutes include:
>   Wheat flour — Soy, chickpea, buckwheat, corn, rice, pea, potato, tapioca and millet flour. Use rice flour, cornflour or arrowroot for thickening.
>   Breads and bread products — All gluten-free breads usually made out of soy or rice flour.
>   Porridge — Rice porridge.
>   Corn — Tacos, breads and pasta.

- Dairy products, such as milk, cream, cheese, ice cream, yoghurt and, to a lesser degree, butter. You may be asked to avoid these also. Some substitutes include:
>   Milk — Rice, soy, nut or goat's milk.
>   Spreads — Nut butters.
>   Yoghurt and ice cream — Soy varieties.

Supplements

Flaxseed oil (2 Tbsp daily) **Evening Primrose oil** (3g daily) and **Colostrum** (4g daily) May help reduce leaky gut syndrome and inflammation associated with allergies. See also Leaky gut recommendations on page 218.

Antioxidant formula   Enhance healing of the digestive system's walls to prevent leaky gut syndrome and to deal with toxic and free radical overload. Antioxidant formulas (full spectrum) include ProenOthera® from Evening Primrose Seed husk, Green tea, Grape Seed, Pine Bark, Beta Carotene, Vitamins E, A and C, oligomeric proanthocyanidins, flavonoids and adjunctive minerals (Zinc, Selenium, Manganese and Iron). Take as professionally advised or as supplement labels suggest.

Acidophilus and **Bifidus**   Beneficial bacteria that help to keep the digestive system healthy. Take 1 billion of the Acidophilus and Bifidus species in capsule form daily on an empty stomach to repopulate your digestive system.

Vitamin C (500mg–1g daily), **Calcium** (1g–1.5g daily) and **Magnesium** (450mg daily) Help build up tolerance to allergies.

Celloids or **Schuessler Tissue Salts**   **Silica**, **Calc Fluor** and **Mag Phos** tissue salts aid healing of the digestive system and reduce susceptibility to allergies. Take as directed.

Herbs

Parasite-cleansing herbs   Use these herbs first. Parasites can inflame, irritate and perforate the intestinal lining, resulting in 'leaky gut'. This can lead to undigested food particles entering the bloodstream and create food allergies and inflammation. Take two 3-week courses of **Cloves** (1800mg daily) combined with **Wormwood** (2000mg daily) and **Black Walnut** (2000mg daily) to help eradicate parasites.

After completing the parasite cleanse   Detox your body. Follow recommendations on page 131.

Liver-cleansing herbs   **Dandelion** (1g of dried root daily) and **Milk Thistle** (2g of seed daily) enhance bile flow and help detoxify the liver. **Bupleurum** (3g–12g of dried root daily) helps to modulate immune system and protect liver.

Adrenal glands   Always affected by allergies. Take 500mg of **Liquorice** daily for 3–6 months. Non-deglycyrrhizinised Liquorice can increase blood pressure and water retention symptoms. Monitor blood pressure and water retention symptoms, and reduce or stop takng Liquorice if they increase.

Perilla   Reduces the histamine allergy reaction and is helpful in eczema and asthma. Take 900mg daily. The longer you take Perilla the more effective it is, and it's also effective for hayfever symptoms, rheumatism (muscle pain) and psoriasis.

Increase good digestive juices   Sip a few drops of Swedish bitters mixed with soda or

50ml of **Aloe Vera** juice before meals to aid digestion and mineral absorption. Alternatively choose digestive enzyme formulas as lack of stomach acid may contribute to allergies. Take 100mg–200mg of **Betaine** 3 times daily with meals or drink **Gentian**, a bitter herb, with meals daily to help increase stomach acid.

Homeopathic remedies May be developed or matched against specific allergy characteristics. See an experienced homeopath for details.

Fungal Infection

The superficial fungal infections also known as dermatophytosis include ringworm, tinea and yeast infections, such as candida and pityrosporum. Ringworm, athlete's foot, jock itch and fungal nail infections are not life threatening, but still need to be dealt with to stop progression, unsightly pigmentation or nail deformation, and spreading. Sometimes the fungal infections may spread into the lower or deeper skin tissues and, like the tip of an iceberg, they may actually have an insidious, deeper involvement in immune-suppressed individuals.

The fungi feed on the keratin cell layers or dead skin cells that produce the surface of the skin, nails and hair, leading to deformities in these structures, including nail ridges, broken hair, scaling skin or affected melanin pigmentation.

Causes
- Antibiotic use reduces the number of helpful bacteria that live in the body, which gives fungal infections a chance to colonise.
- Corticosteroid use reduces the response of the immune system and therefore inflammation. However, it also gives opportunistic infections, including fungi, a chance to grow.
- Medical conditions, including diabetes, HIV, AIDS and some cancers, such as leukaemia, increase susceptibility to fungal infections. Immune suppressive drugs or a compromised immune system also have the same effect.
- Environmental factors. Warm moist areas provide perfect breeding grounds for fungal infections. These include communal showers, changing rooms, damp used towels, sweaty clothing or shoes, and warm, sweaty or moist areas on the body, including the mouth, vagina, anus, penis, skin fold creases between toes, under breasts, the groin and buttock crease.
- Genetic predisposition. We all have weaknesses, and some people may find fungal infection (which may also run through the family) is one of them.
- Fungal infections can be passed by contact from person to person or from objects and surfaces to a person.

Signs and symptoms
- White patches on the skin that may turn to salmon pink, dull red or dark brown. The patches may not tan. Often seen on the face, arms and back.
- Red patches on the skin. Pustular scaly round patches may be found on scalp. Ring worm (not a worm infection) is characteristically red and round with a central clearing in the middle.
- Men often carry the chicken-skin look around their necks, normally attributed to shaving or age.
- Athlete's foot or foot tinea varies from a mild scaling lesion to cracking of skin that can be painful, odorous and very itchy.

Fungal Infection

- Itchiness or a mild burning sensation that may increase in the wet, hot summer months and tend to be less symptomatic during the cooler, dryer months.
- Irritability, moodiness and brain fog.
- Well-defined, red, rash-like patches that are moist or dry may appear on the breast, groin, anus, toes, finger webs and trunk of the body.
- The nails can look red and sore around the nail bed and while initially the nail looks opaque, it can start to deform, look yellow and fall off. This may spread to other nails.
- Hair loss or raised capillaries on the face.
- A blister, which may be surrounded by a redness of the skin, on the palm, back of hand or fingers.
- Fungi can trigger an allergic or immune response. They also release exotoxins that may affect deeper layers.
- Diagnosis is performed by taking a swab of the possible infected area and growing the fungi on a Petri dish and/or by focusing ultraviolet light on the skin for identification.

Naturopathic recommendations

Lifestyle hints

I know some purists might view it as sacrilege to recommend chemical drugs along with herbs. However, I have found the most successful treatment of skin fungal infections is to combine these two modalities. Use Pevaryl® foaming cream if it's recommended by the pharmacist for your type of fungal infection. Follow the directions and use the naturopathic recommendations below. If you have skin patches that do not tan and have used two treatments of Pevaryl® along with naturopathic recommendations, it may take 9 months or longer for your melanin skin cells to become normal again.

- Avoid antibiotics and steroids unless absolutely necessary. Also avoid applying chemicals, such as bubble baths, deodorant, tampons or pads and scented toilet paper, near or on candida areas.
- Avoid nylon and tight pantyhose or underwear.
- Sterilise all towels and socks that contact fungal areas after each use in extremely hot water with Dettol or Napisan to avoid cross contamination. Do not use the same towel to dry your affected and non-affected parts. I've seen a lot of fungal infections transferred from one place to another by doing this. Those who work out at the gym are more likely to be at risk of fungal infection. If you have a chronic fungal infection, wipe benches down with supplied cleaners and paper towels and use your own towel. Change your clothing regularly so you do not become infected with fungi left on warm moist benches or flooring at the gyms. Remember to wash the towel and your gym clothes before wearing or using them again.
- Try not to get over-paranoid about 'catching' fungal infections. You just need to strengthen your immunity and get your acid skin barrier back into balance. Apply diluted apple cider vinegar (ACV) to the fungal infection to balance your acid skin barrier, because using soaps can make the skin too alkaline.
- Scrupulously clean and dry fungal areas twice daily. If you have chronic fungal infection and do not do this properly the other treatments may not work.
- Change socks daily if affected with fungi on the feet.

Nutrition — For very chronic situations

- Fungi can be devilish to get rid of. If this is the case you may need to try the anti-fungal diet to accompany your external fungal treatment. Follow the candida diet and recommendations on page 102 for 3–6 months.

Supplements

Apple cider vinegar (ACV) Wash affected area with ACV. If the lesion is not tender, raw or the skin is not broken, gently wash it with a cotton bud saturated with ACV. I normally rub quite hard on olive skinned people; however, for those with fair skin, ACV can seem to burn the face and sometimes the body. Just experiment gently to see what suits your skin type. The idea is to remove natural oily barriers of the skin, to make the skin acidic rather than alkaline, which creates a barrier against fungal infection and prepares the skin for the Lugol's Iodine. I prefer Lugol's Iodine to BP Iodine tincture.

Iodine (Do not use if allergic to Iodine). There are 2 types of Iodine that you can obtain from a health shop or pharmacy.

1. **Lugol's (aqueous) Iodine** For internal and external use. Do not take iodine without medical supervision if you have thyroid problems, are taking thyroid medication or have a history of thyroid problems.
   External use: Place 6 drops of Lugol's Iodine in ¼ cup of boiled water. Wash all affected areas on your body and external surfaces with this solution.
   Internal use: Take 6 drops of Lugol's Iodine in 1 cup of hot water with 1 tsp of manuka honey and 1 capful of ACV (for flavour), 4 times daily for 7 days.
2. **Iodine BP tincture** Do not take this iodine internally.

Colloidal silver cream Apply as directed to affected areas after thoroughly washing skin with ACV and Lugol's Iodine.

Herbs

Internally

Antifungal and **alterative (blood cleansing) herbs** To prevent or treat fungal infections include **Garlic** (400mg–1200mg daily), **Ginger** (1g–2g daily), **Liquorice** (2g–4g daily or as prescribed), **Chamomile** (3g daily), **Echinacea** (1200mg daily), **Olive Leaf extract** (270mg 3 times daily), **Sarsaparilla** (2g–4g 3 times daily) and **Goldenseal** (500mg–1g daily).

External applications

Thuja Has strong anti-fungal properties. Use a tincture or alcoholic preparation on affected areas twice daily.

Echinacea Has antimicrobial and antifungal properties. Use in place of Thuja or before the Thuja application, and wait until it has dried. Apply liquid alcohol tincture to affected areas twice daily.

Tea Tree oil Apply to affected area twice daily. It may also be added to shampoo and conditioner for scalp infections and dandruff. If it is too strong for the skin, dilute with oil (olive or almond) or water.

Myrrh Make a paste of Myrrh by opening a capsule and mixing it with hot water. Brush affected area when paste is cooled with a clean pastry brush or cotton bud. Also take internally as directed on the bottle.

Nail fungus This takes several months to resolve and applications 2–4 times daily may seem like a bother, but you must persevere. Wash affected nail in warm water and Tea Tree oil. Dry thoroughly. Apply Tea Tree oil or a combination of it and **Lavender oil** on the affected area 2–3 times a day. If the Tea Tree oil burns, just wash nail 4 times daily as directed in water and Tea Tree oil, and apply Thuja cream. If necessary you may need to do the internal candida cleanse by taking appropriate herbs and by doing the candida diet.

Oregano oil Also very effective for hard nail fungus that is difficult to eradicate. Apply 2 drops onto fungi twice daily or as directed.

Gallstones

When you vomit you might taste bile, that horrible substance that makes your vomit take on a green or yellow tinge. Bile helps with the digestion process of fat and excretes other unwanted materials from the body. It's formed by the liver, but is concentrated and stored in a sump, called the gall bladder, until we eat a meal containing fat or oil.

Gallstones are smallish, hard collections that form into a solid irregular stone and are normally located in the gall bladder. However, they may travel from the gall bladder through the gall bladder ducts. Gallstones can be serious if they lodge in the ducts or create obstruction. If a duct becomes blocked (partially or totally) the bile may build up behind the stone and cause the lining of the ducts to inflame, leading to pain. Smaller gallstones can pass through the digestive tract and are often confused with kidney stones (that are passed through the urethra). If they are too large to pass through the ducts, or symptoms are recurring, surgical intervention may be necessary to avoid further complications, including peritonitis, pancreatitis and increased risk of gall bladder cancer.

Gallstones are characterised into the folowing types:
Pure cholesterol Due to either an increase in cholesterol or a decrease in bile acids, lecithin or water (extremely rare).
Pure calcium bilirubinate pigment (Extremely rare).
Mixed Composed of cholesterol, bile salts, bile pigments, inorganic salts of calcium.
Stones Composed entirely of minerals: calcium, silicon, aluminium oxides.

Causes
- Lack of fibre or fluid.
- excess saturated dietary fat, poor diet or a highly refined diet.
- Obesity.
- Parasite infection.
- Family history.
- Certain drugs.
- Age.
- Certain diseases such as Crohn's disease and cystic fibrosis.

Signs and symptoms
(Some people may have gallstones without symptoms.)
- Gall bladder inflammation.
- Uncomfortable sensation in abdomen.
- Pain that may feel cramp-like and build in intensity, and that may also shoot back toward the right shoulder blade or be felt under the ribs and sternum.
- Nausea and vomiting are common along with bloating, gas and indigestion.
- The skin may take on a slight yellowish hue and may be itchy if the stone blocks the gall bladder duct. This may be accompanied by clay-like stools and dark urine.
- Eating a fatty or oily meal may precipitate the pain. This happens as the gall bladder contracts to release bile to emulsify the fat from the diet. A formed stone may dislodge from the gall bladder and be released into the duct, causing bile build-up and obstruction.

Naturopathic recommendations

Lifestyle hints
Exercise
- Reduces obesity, insulin resistance and blood levels of triglycerides (fats) linked to gallstones, and may lessen the risk of gallstone production by up to 30%.
- Exercise 4–5 times weekly, e.g. power-walking, jogging, swimming, dancing or going to the gym. If you are not mobile bounce on a trampoline and seek assistance if needed.

Nutrition
Gall Bladder Flush Fast
The Gall Bladder Flush takes three days and is designed to encourage the stones to become more soluble, smaller in size and to reduce gall bladder inflammation. It is not for the fainthearted as you have to fast on apple juice for two and a half days to complete it successfully. Do not attempt to drive or do any strenuous activity while on the third day of the gall bladder flush as it may cause cramps, pain and dizziness. I know this from personal experience. It is recommended you consult with a health professional or check with your doctor before attempting the fast.

Day One: Drink 1 cup of pure, organic apple juice every hour after waking. Apple juice contains malic acid, which may help dissolve stones. At night drink 1 Tbsp of dissolved Epsom Salts with ½ a cup of warm water and flavour it with ½ a cup of apple or orange juice. Epsom salts help to dilate the gall bladder duct by releasing muscle contraction.

Day Two: Follow directions above.

Day Three: Follow directions above until the evening, then whip up one cup of pure fat cream and eat the cream with a small bowel of fruit salad. After 15 minutes drink the Epsom salts mixture. The cream will make the gall bladder contract and the Epsom salts makes the duct relax for stones to go through. Immediately go to bed and either lie at a 45° angle or lie on your right side with your knees drawn up for the first 30 minutes or until you go to the toilet or go to sleep.

What will happen?
As the gall bladder releases the gallstones by contracting in response to the cream, you should excrete stools and gallstones. Some green jelly lumps will be evident and can be mistaken for stones but that's just the cream and bile mixing together.

Do not resume eating your normal meals until the fourth day. If you have any serious medical conditions that may be affected by this diet please see a naturopath who may assist you with advice before embarking on the three-day programme. Do not stop taking any prescribed medication.

- Food sensitivities to the following foods can lead to inflammation and immune system reactions. Eliminating foods, including eggs, pork, onions, milk, coffee, oranges, corn, beans and nuts, has been shown to reduce symptoms dramatically. See page 164 for food sensitivity testing to identify your possible food allergies.
- Reduce saturated fats, including all animal fats, dairy produce and margarine, as they are implicated in the manifestation of gallstones. Eat lean meat and more fish daily. Animal fats aggravate the gall bladder more than saturated vegetable fats like coconut milk. Poly- and monounsaturated fats help fat metabolism and reduce inflammation, so substitute animal fats for these beneficial fats and oils, e.g. olive oil, canola, oil, flaxseed oil and evening primrose oil.
- High-sugar and refined carbohydrate intake increases cholesterol production and blood triglyceride levels of the liver, triggered by a pancreas response to the sugar. Reduce sugar

intake to prevent cholesterol metabolism problems involved with gallstones. Reduce sugary foods (cakes, biscuits and fatty sugary crackers) to a minimum.
- Eat plenty of fibre from fruit, grains (bran, ground flaxseed, oat bran and pectin) and vegetables.
- Drink 8–9 glasses of fresh water daily to prevent dehydration.

Supplements

Lecithin Helps to keep cholesterol soluble and acts as a fat emulsifier, helping the digestion and breakdown of fats. Take 1000mg–5000mg daily. Or, if you are not food sensitive to eggs, eat 1–2 eggs (free range only) 3–4 times per week.

Antioxidant formulas Those that include Vitamin E, the amino acid Protein Methionine and the mineral Manganese are beneficial, as deficiencies in antioxidants (particularly these ones) are thought to contribute to gall bladder disease and gallstone formation. Take a broad spectrum antioxidant formula as directed.

Magnesium Helps to relax the gall bladder sphincter, which helps release gallstones. Take 450mg daily.

Herbs

Fibre Helps to bind onto excess dietary cholesterol for excretion. Take 1–3 tsp of **Flaxseed fibre**, **Psyllium Husk** or other fibre products.

Liver-cleansing herbs Take 420mg of **Milk Thistle** (standardised silymarin content) daily, or 1.5g–4g of dried **Globe Artichoke Leaf** daily. These promote the flow and discharge of bile.

Gall bladder herbs **Dandelion Root** (3g–5g of dried root daily), **Burdock Root** (2g–6g of dried root daily) and **Peppermint** (enteric coated peppermint capsules normally recommended for upset stomachs) may dissolve stones and prevent the formation of cholesterol crystals involved in the production of gallstones.

Goldenseal A choleretic, for infection due to inflammation and waste matter build-up in the gall bladder or ducts. Take 500mg–1g daily.

Externally

Castor oil packs Apply to the right under the rib cage to reduce pain and inflammation.

> *How to make a Castor oil pack*
>
> You will need: Castor oil (obtained from the chemist), a soft clean cotton cloth, plastic wrap, a plastic container to store the oil-laden cloth, and a hot water bottle. Directions: Soak the cloth in Castor oil. Place the folded cloth just under the right rib area. Cover the cloth completely with plastic wrap both to avoid staining your clothes and to keep in the warmth. Place a towel over the plastic and put a hot water bottle on it. Leave it on overnight. Repeat this five nights in a row and rest for two nights. Do this for three weeks.

Glandular Fever (Infectious mononucleosis)

Glandular fever is a viral infection that has a couple of less favourable names: infectious mononucleosis (due to affected monocyte cells); and the kissing disease, as the main mode of transference is saliva. The virus spreads through the bloodstream, lymphatic system and into the glands causing them to enlarge as well as causing a fever, hence the name glandular fever.

Glandular Fever (Infectious mononucleosis)

Cause
- Epstein-Barr virus (EBV), a member of the herpes virus family.

Signs and symptoms
- Flu-like symptoms
- Fever and sore throat
- Swollen, enlarged, tender glands in the neck, groin and armpit
- Extreme tiredness, mild depression and fatigue
- Depending on the severity of the viral infection, rash and jaundice may manifest although this is rare.

The major symptoms usually disappear within 2 or 3 weeks, but for a further period of at least 2 weeks you may feel weak, lacking in energy and depressed. Occasionally the lethargy can last for months on end and may even develop into chronic fatigue syndrome if not treated properly with rest, good nutrition and strengthening of the immune system.

When children contract EBV, it is generally mistaken for the flu. Young adults (15–25 years old) often contract EBV and show symptoms of glandular fever, especially after stress or trauma in their lives. Let's face it, if you're a teenager when aren't you go through stress and the angst of growing up?

Naturopathic recommendations

Lifestyle hints
- Reduce the amount of exposure to chemicals, toxins, pollutants and additives to reduce the potential overload of toxins in the body. Avoid exposure to hairspray, hair dye, pesticides, cleaning chemicals, food additives and perfumes. Take a good look around your home and if you don't need it, don't use it. At this time it is important to raise the immune system and avoid lifestyles and thought patterns harmful to the body.

Rest
- The neglect of convalescence may be one of our biggest mistakes ever. With the discovery of new medical drugs, we often have the idea that we can cure problems directly. We carry on with our fast-paced lives and we forget to convalesce. There are very few people who take a week off after the flu, or 3 months off for glandular fever. Rest and seek time out to heal. If you don't get your rest requirements now, you may be forced to have them later as your relapses become worse. You need plenty of rest and routine. Get to bed early.

Exercise
- Do light to moderate exercise, such as Tai Chi, yoga, stretches, walking, swimming and reflexology.
- Exercise may sound like a contradiction when you don't have the energy to move. But it's essential to clear adrenal overactivity. Exercise for 5–15 minutes, or if you feel the need and are fit, 30 minutes. A gentle stroll is good enough; however, if you have the energy, power walking or low impact aerobics is fine. Just get the circulation pumping and the heart rate increased.
- Only in extreme cases should exercise be avoided altogether.

Nutrition
- Eliminate food sensitivities (e.g. dairy), alcohol, tobacco and caffeine. Drink herbal teas, water and diluted juices instead.

- Drink 8–9 glasses of pure, fresh water daily.
- Drink green juices or vegetable juices daily. Try spirulina, chlorella, barley or wheatgrass drinks. Other varieties are freshly juiced carrots, apple, silverbeet and beetroot juices.
- Eat three small meals and three snack-sized meals daily to assist metabolism, digestion and blood sugar levels. Oscillating blood sugar levels will make you tired and fatigued.
- Avoid refined carbohydrates, excessive consumption of sugar, saturated fats or fried foods including fast foods. 50g of sugar (regardless of its source, including fruit juice, milk [lactose], hidden sugars in food, etc.) lowers the immune system. Choose whole fruits over concentrated fruit juices, dried fruit or excess stewed fruit.
- Eat organic fruits, vegetables and meats. Pesticides, herbicides and food stabilisers are likely to put more stress on the body.
- Eat whole foods that are prepared from scratch rather than heavily refined and processed foods. Try the nourishing foods that you feel inclined to eat, such as hot meals, stew, and all cooked and raw vegetables.
- Consume adequate amounts of protein either from meat or vegetable protein. Obviously a combination of both is beneficial, for instance add chickpeas to a tuna casserole or dhal (legumes) to a chicken meal for interesting, tasty dishes.

Supplements
Vitamin C Enhances white blood cell activity and immune support. Take 200mg–1500mg daily.
Zinc Requirements are increased during poor immunity. Take 45mg daily. Zinc gluconate lozenges (5mg–10mg) taken every 2 hours help to coat the throat and mouth, improving zinc levels and helping to inhibit viral replication.

Herbs
Olive Leaf extract Has several antiviral properties that help to boost the immune system and may also help to eradicate viruses. Research shows that Olive Leaf extract with oleuropein can destroy the protein coating of the EBV helping to reduce symptoms and ongoing infection. Take 540mg of Olive Leaf extract 3 times daily. Take for 1 month then stop for 1 week. At this time you may feel your symptoms coming back, including a sore throat. When these symptoms arrive take another course of Olive Leaf extract for 1 month then reduce to a maintenance dose of 540mg daily. Take the Olive Leaf extract with Astragalus and Pau D'Arco and then follow the detoxing recommendations on page 131 to complete the programme. If symptoms do not reappear take the maintenance dose for 3–6 months.
Astragalus The antiviral action of Astragalus is mainly due to increased immunity and interferon production. Take 500mg–10g daily.
Pau D'Arco Effective against viral activity (including herpes virus families, EBV and influenza). Take 1.5g–3.5g daily.
If you have suffered from jaundice or hepatitis Support and protect the liver against inflammation and toxins with 420mg of **Milk Thistle** (standardised silymarin content) daily or 1.5g–4g of dried **Globe Artichoke Leaf** daily.

Schuessler tissue salts
Calc Phos and **Kali Phos** help the body following infection and lowered vitality and weariness by aiding the nervous system.

Bach™ flower remedies
Take **Rescue Remedy** or choose a single remedy or a combination recommended by a health professional. Take 4 times daily or as recommended. Learn how to meditate every morning if stress and emotions trigger off a feeling of illness or fatigue.

Gout

The word gout evokes the classic image of a middle-aged, overweight man writhing in pain with sweat dripping down his forehead, clutching at his big toe, after a night out on the town drinking alcohol and enjoying platters of seafood and tender fillets of beef. Gout is classified as a type of arthritis or pain in the joints caused by a build-up of uric acid crystals in the joints, blood, kidneys and soft tissue.

Causes

Gout has a hereditary nature. It's caused by hyperuricemia, an over-production of uric acid (monosodium urate crystals), or reduced excretion of uric acid by the kidney. 10–20% of uric acid is produced from foods that contain purines — these include meat, yeast and seafood. Normally the kidney excretes two thirds of the uric acid produced daily and the digestive tract the other third. Individuals with gout have improper urate metabolism and they cannot clear the urate properly. The uric acid crystals can form in peripheral areas of the body due to poor circulation and cooling of the body temperature. The crystallisation attracts inflammation and the chemical pain response of the body.

Other causes include:
- Kidney damage, psoriasis, surgery, chemotherapy drugs and cancer.
- Excessive purine intake.
- Analgesic doses of aspirin, salicylate- and oxalate-containing foods, high intakes of vitamin C (more than 3g daily) and vitamin B3 (50mg of niacin daily), some diuretics (thiazides), excessive exercise, dieting, poor diets, and alcohol intake interfere with excretion and accumulation of uric acid in some people.
- Purine metabolism dysfunction.
- Lead toxicity.

Signs and symptoms
- Gouty pain usually occurs at night and is often preceded by an excess of alcohol, seafood or meat.
- Acute pain with redness and swelling. The pain may last for days or weeks.
- The big toe is the most common site for pain, but other areas affected include feet, elbows, insteps, ankles, fingers and knees.
- Inflammation, fever and chills may occur if attack progresses.
- Tophi are large, hard irregular nodules from a build-up of uric acid that are commonly found on the cartilage of the upper ear and Achilles tendon.
- With long-term gout, joint deformities and changes may occur.

Naturopathic recommendations

Lifestyle hints
Exercise
Exercise 4 times weekly, e.g. power-walking, jogging, swimming, dancing or going to the gym. If you are not mobile, bounce on a trampoline or seek advice from a professional trainer.

Reflexology
Massage the soles of the feet with your knuckle concentrating on tender spots to increase healing mechanisms within the body. Do not linger on a tender spot for more than 5 minutes at a time. Massage at least 3 times a week.

Obesity

Body weight should be kept within a healthy range. Obesity is linked to gout as is the excessive consumption of calories, saturated fat and refined carbohydrates. See page 50 for weight management.

Nutrition

- Increase water and herbal tea intake to 2–3 litres daily to help dilute uric acid deposits.
- Eat plenty of canned or fresh cherries or berries (250g daily) to help reduce uric acid levels.
- Eat a healthy diet that contains plenty of complex carbohydrates and vegetables with moderate levels of protein and oils (essential fatty acids, omega 3 and 6).
- Avoid purines in foods such as organ meats, meat, shellfish, sardines, mackerel, anchovies and yeast. Poultry, cooked dried legumes, fish, mushrooms and asparagus contain moderate levels of purines.
- Avoid spinach, silverbeet and rhubarb due to their high oxalic acid content.
- Avoid alcohol to reduce uric acid levels and prevent gout attacks.
- Reduce sugar, simple sugars (corn syrup, fructose, honey, refined sugar, etc.), caffeine, refined carbohydrates (which increase uric acid production), and saturated fats (which decrease uric acid excretion).
- Avoid excessive salicylate intake from aspirin, apples (gala, granny smiths), dried fruits, apricots, grapes, citrus fruits, pineapples, plums, rockmelon, capsicum, olives, radish, tomatoes, zucchini, black tea, peppermint tea, soft drinks, vinegar, almonds, chestnuts, Vegemite, Marmite, Promite, mustard, curries and mint.

Supplements

Aloe Vera juice Can be used to help prevent gouty attacks of pain. Sip 20ml–50ml up to 3 times daily before meals and to maintain drink 20ml daily.

Fish oil Containing EPA and DHA, Fish oil helps to reduce inflammation, tissue damage and pain. Take 3000mg daily.

Vitamin E Like Fish oil, Vitamin E reduces inflammation and can also act as an antioxidant. Take 400IU daily.

Antioxidant formula Those that are rich in oligomeric proanthocyanidins (antioxidant plant compounds) reduce uric acid levels and inflammation. Like in cherries and berries the oligomeric proanthocyanidins are rich in Evening Primrose Seed Husk, Bilberries, Grape Seed and Pine Bark extracts. Take as professionally advised or as supplement labels suggest.

Herbs

Ginger and **Turmeric** Increase circulation and reduce inflammation. Add a pinch of Ginger or Turmeric to your foods or take as a supplement. Ginger tea is great as a beverage. Mix ¼ teaspoon of Ginger powder with 1 teaspoon of honey and 1 Tbsp of powdered skim milk in a mug. Fill with hot water and stir.

Devil's Claw Paints a vivid picture of pain, clawed fingers or the grip of some unseen malignancy. Aptly named, this herb assists with arthritis signs and symptoms. It is a remarkable herb that relieves joint pain and inflammation. Take 0.5g–2g daily with meals.

Celery Seed Has over twenty-four anti-inflammatory compounds and has been used to relieve gouty attacks throughout the centuries. It also acts as a diuretic and reduces mild swelling associated with a gouty attack. Take 0.5g–2g 3 times daily.

Gum Disease

Inflammation of the gums happens to most adults in their lifetime. It's generally due to a build-up of bacteria in the plaque that builds up around the neck of the tooth.

Causes
- Vitamin A, C, B5 and coenzyme Q10 deficiencies.
- Microbial infections including bacterial and fungal overgrowth (e.g. candida).
- Poor dental hygiene and a build-up of plaque around the gums.
- Constant oral irritation from trauma, smoking or toxins.
- Severely compromised immune systems, e.g. AIDS or cancer.
- Bleeding disorders (only in rare cases).
- Chronic gum swelling can be triggered by pregnancy, and as a side effect of medication.

Signs and symptoms
- Red inflamed gums and bad breath.
- Tender gums, and/or the gums can bleed when brushed or flossed.

Naturopathic recommendations

Lifestyle hints
- Floss and brush teeth gently twice daily especially after meals.
- Avoid smoking and gum irritants.

Nutrition
- Eat plenty of vitamin-loaded fruits and vegetables including green leafy vegetables, carrots, pumpkin, corn and citrus fruits.
- Drink plenty of fresh water and vegetable juices daily.

Supplements
Apple Cider Vinegar (ACV)   This may sound unpleasant but you may come to enjoy it. Brush teeth with ACV, using this as your mouth rinse and follow with a brushing of gums using toothpaste to rid yourself of the taste. This normally stops bleeding gums within days.
Bioflavonoids   Tone and strengthen the gums and blood capillaries. Take 50mg–500mg daily.
Nutrient deficiencies   Cause gum disease. Take **Vitamin A** (5000IU–10,000IU daily), **Coenzyme Q10** (take 75mg daily and also apply directly on gums twice daily), **Vitamin C** (2g–5g daily) and **B5** (50mg–100mg daily) accompanied by a **Vitamin B complex**.

Herbs
Myrrh or **Bee Propolis tincture**   Brush the tincture directly onto the gums, gargle and take internal amount as directed on the bottle. It will not taste very nice, but due to its antiseptic and astringent qualities Myrrh is very effective against gum disease.
Sage tea   Very astringent; helps to tone the gums. Add 1 tsp of Sage leaves (fresh or dried) to a cup of boiling hot water. Cover cup with a saucer to lock in oils of the herb and steep for 15 minutes. Drink 3 times daily.
Olive Leaf extract (270mg 3 times daily) and **Echinacea** (1200mg–6g)   Take daily for 10–30 days for signs of viral, bacterial or fungal infection. These herbs boost immunity and help eradicate mild gum infection.

Haemorrhoids (Piles)

As the naturopath guest on an hour-long radio show, would you believe that one of the most common calls I receive for naturopathic advice is for haemorrhoids, otherwise known as piles? A haemorrhoid is a swollen blood vessel in the rectal area that appears as a baggy swelling. The mention of piles often sends the radio host (who shall remain nameless) into peals of laughter and hiccups. It surprises me that even though at least 80% of adults develop haemorrhoids, we are still embarrassed to talk about the basics of body functions and conditions.

Causes
- Genetic weakness, relaxation or lack of tone of the veins or venous valves
- Excessive venous pressure due to an increase in straining during defecation
- Constipation
- Long periods of standing and/or heavy lifting
- Damage to the veins or venous valves from trauma
- Pregnancy or increased pelvic congestion or pressure
- High sugar or refined carbohydrate diets
- Low fibre intake
- Alcohol consumption.

Signs and symptoms
- Internal haemorrhoids occur above the anus sphincter but can be large enough to prolapse or appear below the anus sphincter.
- External haemorrhoids appear below the anus sphincter, increasing the need for personal hygiene after defecation.
- Bright red blood before, during or after defecation may be found on toilet paper, in toilet bowl or around the stool.
- Itchiness around haemorrhoid due to irritation or from toilet paper usage.
- Inflammation and burning around haemorrhoid.

Naturopathic recommendations

Lifestyle hints
The haemorrhoid will need medical attention if it is uncomfortably large, has become infected, has become twisted or thrombotic (blood clot) or is causing excessive bleeding leading to anaemia. Often corrective surgery is recommended. This may remove the haemorrhoid, but the focus after surgery is corrective nutrition, increasing fibre in the diet and using herbs to strengthen weak connective tissue, thus avoiding development of future haemorrhoids.
- Wash anal area gently with luke-warm to cold water after defecating.
- Avoid G-string underwear or any type of tight underwear that may cause irritation to external haemorrhoids.
- Try changing position as you defecate. Bring your feet closer to your chest by bending your knees and planting feet on the seat as you sit, for a more natural position. If you are not supple enough to try this, just lean back a little on the toilet.
- Massage stomach clockwise (as you look down) if it is difficult to pass the stool matter. This should help to aid removal of hard stools that cause obstruction and therefore straining.

Exercise
- To avoid a sedentary lifestyle, exercise 3–4 times weekly.

Nutrition
- In contrast to Western countries, haemorrhoids are rarely seen in parts of the world where high-fibre, unrefined diets are consumed. A diet low in fibre and high in refined foods contributes greatly to the development of haemorrhoids.
- Eat foods that provide dietary fibre, bioflavonoids and vitamin C. These include whole grains, dark leafy green vegetables, salads, celery, carrots, beans and legumes, and fruits that are high in fibre including berries, citrus, kiwifruit, prunes and apples. Increase fibre intake with water-soluble fibres such as oat bran, flax fibre, apple pectin, slippery elm and psyllium supplements.
- To increase fibre add 1 tsp–1 Tbsp of freshly crushed linseed to your daily diet by sprinkling on cereal or porridge in the morning or salads for lunch and dinner.
- Eat more natural antioxidants found in vegetables (leafy greens, yellow and red), cherries and berries.
- Drink 2 litres of pure, fresh water daily as a natural stool lubricant and include a cup or two of antioxidant green tea daily to enhance healing.
- Avoid refined carbohydrates including white bread or flour products and glutinous rice. If you eat a lot of white rice daily, limit your intake to ½ cup of cooked white rice mixed with ½ cup of cooked brown rice. White rice can be obstructive to the bowel causing straining during defecation.
- Avoid high levels of saturated fats including fatty animal meats, fried foods and excessive cheese or butter, and replace with flax oil, olive oil or lean meat. Boost meat meals with legumes, beans or chickpeas and eat more fish.
- Avoid binge drinking.

Supplements
Calc Fluor   Calcium fluoride is a homeopathic Schuessler Tissue Salt mineral that provides strength to the relaxed, weakened veins that cause haemorrhoids. Dissolve 1 tablet in mouth every ½ hour until the haemorrhoid is reduced. Then take 4 tablets daily to maintain.
Vitamin C (500mg–3g daily) and **Bioflavonoids** (50mg–2g daily)   Support weakened veins by strengthening and shrinking relaxed haemorrhoidal walls.
Glucosamine and **Chondroitin**   Supply the connective layer of veins and haemorrhoids with ingredients to strengthen and shrink relaxed veins that cause haemorrhoids. Additionally these ingredients enhance cartilage repair and regeneration for arthritis or sports injuries affecting the joints, protect against glaucoma and may assist with cystitis and cellulite. Take 500mg of Glucosamine daily and 1200mg of Chondroitin daily.
Fibre supplements   Help to soften the stool to reduce straining during defecation. As you increase your fibre intake the water intake must be increased to avoid constipation. It is known that a diet high in fibre (traditionally from vegetables, grains, gums, etc.) can be beneficial for digestion and general health. These particular fibres work by absorbing water, and remain undigested as they pass through the body improving stool transit time and bulk. Take 1 tsp–2 tsp of **Flax fibre** or **Psyllium** daily.

Herbs
Gotu Kola extract   Shows positive strengthening effects on damaged connective tissue and relaxed veins that cause haemorrhoids. Take 30mg of Gotu Kola extract (Triterpenes) 3 times daily.
Grape Seed extract   Contains bioflavonoids and powerful antioxidants that protect cells and blood vessels from damage, and tone damaged haemorrhoidal veins. Take 500mg–10g daily.

Horse Chestnut extract Has anti-inflammatory and anti-oedema properties. The unique actions of Horse Chestnut are on the vessels of the circulatory system. It increases the strength and tone of the veins in particular. It may be used for varicose veins, unsightly capillaries, inflammation in the veins and haemorrhoids. Take 10mg–20mg of **Aescin** (standardised Horse Chestnut extract) 3 times daily.

Other herbs and **nutrients** that may be helpful include **Butchers Broom**, **Bilberry** and **Bromelain**, an enzyme from pineapple.

External applications

Some creams will only provide relief. **Pure Witch hazel** cream is often used as a soothing astringent cream to shrink the haemorrhoids and provide relief from itching and pain. Witch hazel tonic can also be dabbed onto washed external haemorrhoids with a cotton ball.

Hayfever

While many of us look forward to the spring and summer seasons after the cold dreary winter, those who suffer from hayfever shrink from the thought of gorgeous, colourful blooms and freshly mowed lawns. When spring arrives, many find themselves reaching for the tissue box, rubbing their eyes and enduring bouts of sneezing.

The following are common types of hayfever:
- **Spring seasonal** hayfever is usually due to tree pollens.
- **Summer seasonal** hayfever is usually due to summer grass and weeds.
- **Perennial allergic rhinitis** is when hayfever symptoms last all year round. This form of hayfever may or may not be due to pollens.

Causes
- Allergies are caused by an overreaction of the immune system to foreign materials, such as pollen or mould spores, causing tissue inflammation, mucus production, sinus congestion, itchy and watery eyes and nose, and fatigue. The head feels blocked and 'post nasal drip' occurs at night resulting in coughs and, at its worst, chestiness.
- Allergies to dust mites, cat fur or cat saliva.
- Pollens, mould and grasses. Pollen exposure accounts for up to 75% of hayfever cases. Privet and pine pollen is an absolute nuisance to those with hayfever, as are grasses and some tree pollens.
- Food allergies (including wine and beer preservatives) and intolerance may trigger hayfever reactions

Signs and symptoms
- Fatigue and constant irritation
- Headache
- Watery, itchy eyes
- Sore, red eyes
- Mucous congestion in the sinuses, nasal passages and airways
- Sore throat
- Streaming nose
- Itchy skin
- Cough
- Sneezing.

Hayfever

Naturopathic recommendations

Lifestyle hints
I know it's hard to avoid all that pollen floating around, but follow these handy hints, which may help lessen exposure to pollen.
- Avoid outdoor activities between 5 a.m. and 10 a.m. when pollen production is at its highest. Also, keep home and car windows closed during these hours.
- Because pollen from the air can collect on your hair and clothing, it's a good idea to change your clothes and take a quick shower after being outdoors.
- Wash your hands frequently, especially before touching your eyes.
- Don't hang laundry outdoors. Pollen flying through the air will settle on it.

Nutrition
Avoid reaching your allergy symptoms threshold by reducing intake of any food sensitivities that may increase your allergy reactions. See page 164 for food allergies and sensitivities.

Supplements
Nutrients may help the body's response to pollen allergies. For example, **Histidine** and **Quercetin** (a bioflavonoid) aid the system's stabilisation of the cells' membranes that release allergy chemicals into the body and trigger allergic symptoms. Take 450mg of Histidine or Quercetin daily.

Herbs
Perilla Regulates the immune system and relieves allergic symptoms. Japanese studies showed that over a 2–3 month period, the use of Perilla improved allergic symptoms including seasonal pollinosis, allergic rhinitis, recurrent sneezing, watery and itchy nose and eyes, and facial itching.[50] Take 150mg–200mg of the extract daily initially for 2 weeks, then 100mg daily.
Boswellia Exhibits anti-inflammatory properties, effectively shrinking inflamed tissues without side effects, and inhibits leukotriene formation, which is involved with inflammatory processes associated with sinus. Take 200mg of Boswellia Gum extract (standardised to 70% Boswellic acid) 3 times daily.
Elder Rich in natural flavonoids, Elder (berry) is a natural anti-inflammatory helpful for reducing inflamed bronchial, sinus and mucous membranes, and is useful for catarrhal (mucous) build-up, helping blocked noses and catarrhal deafness. Take 400mg 3 times daily.
Eyebright An anti-inflammatory herb indicated for eye irritation, redness, nasal catarrh and profuse watery flow, sinusitis, chronic sneezing, hayfever, middle ear conditions and sore throats. Take 1.5g daily.
Fenugreek A warming expectorant that helps move out chesty phlegm and coughs. It helps bronchitis and sore throats, and aids the body in expelling mucus from the sinuses and upper/lower respiratory areas. Take 300mg 3 times daily.
Skullcap Chinese Skullcap also effectively fights inflammation without causing serious side effects. Experts believe its bioflavonoids stop the body from making biochemicals that inflame tissues. Aside from restricting inflammation, these bioflavonoids also act as antioxidants. Use for all allergy reactions, asthma, sinus, eczema and hayfever. Take 400mg 3 times daily.

To treat hayfever successfully avoid allergens as much as possible and take herbs every day. To start you may have to wait 4–7 days for the herbs to reduce the hayfever reaction and its symptoms.

Headaches and Migraines

Headaches and migraines appear to have a strong genetic component, commonly occuring among family members. The typical migraine lasts from 1–72 hours. Some 10%–20% of people who suffer migraines see shimmering lights, feel pins and needles, or have difficulty thinking and speaking before the pain hits. There are many triggers of headaches and migraines, as listed below.

Causes
- Women aged 25–44 suffer the most from hormonal-related migraines. Migraines that affect women generally occur during or just before ovulation, or during or right after a menstrual period. One factor in hormonal headaches is when the oestrogen levels are low, typically around menstruation and/or peri-menopause, menopause and post menopause, which leads to lower serotonin (a brain chemical) levels.
- Tension in the neck and shoulder can cause cluster headaches and migraines. This is often preceded by stress, worry, fumes, noise, eye strain and depression.
- Serotonin and nutrient deficiencies. Low serotonin levels can lead to insomnia, anxiety and migraines. B vitamin, coenzyme Q10, magnesium and calcium deficiencies may also lead to migraine attacks.
- Low blood sugar. Stress hormones and irregular eating habits trigger blood sugar fluctuations which can induce attacks of migraines and headaches.
- Food intolerance. See a naturopath to identify food intolerances that trigger the pain or read the nutrition suggestions below.
- Heat, dehydration, bright light and glare.
- Hangovers.
- Withdrawal from caffeine, nicotine and certain drugs.
- Freezer burn from eating cold slushies (frozen ice) or ice cream.
- Sinus or viral/bacterial headache.
- Toxic build-up in colon and constipation.
- Relaxation can cause headaches or migraines after a heavy period of stress. This is common during holidays, causing frustration as the pain increases as you relax.
- Other causes may include head injury, external pressure, brain abscesses and cancerous tumours, nerve excitation or damage, structural trauma (cervical spondylosis, cerebral haemorrhage), stroke, high blood pressure, excessive exercise, and meningitis.

If headaches or migraines persist, it is important to see your doctor for a consultation.

Signs and symptoms
- The main feature is pain in the head area.
- Cluster headaches create an area of pain which is centred behind one eye.
- Tension headaches create a tight band around the head, behind the shoulder blade and neck. Pressure is felt behind the eyes, and there may be throbbing and bursting pain.
- Tenderness and inflammatory pain in the sinuses, eyes, cheek bones, temples and scalp.
- Tingling or numbness in limbs
- Migraines can sometimes cause temporary blindness or sensory flashes; nausea; vomiting; odd sense of smells that are not truly there; splitting headaches that worsen throughout the attack if not treated; irritation; aversion to bright lights; better for pressure and coolness on painful areas.

Naturopathic recommendations

Lifestyle hints
Exercise
Physical exercise may also help promote deeper quality of sleep. Exercise 3–6 times weekly for 20–40 minutes per session to encourage circulation and stress release.

Relaxation
Regularly perform relaxation exercises (deep breathing, meditation, prayer, visualisation, etc.) for 10–15 minutes each day. Have a weekly massage and use reflexology to help with tension headaches.

Freezer burn headaches
Plant your tongue firmly on the soft palate part of the roof of your mouth to warm the frozen area. The pain should subside within a minute or two.

Nutrition
Studies show migraine sufferers have a high incidence of food allergies. Allergy foods are foods that are constantly consumed, and it's not so much the food itself but what's in it that is the problem. For instance, cured meats, such as hot dogs, salami, bacon and ham, contain sodium nitrates that are known to trigger reactions in some headache or migraine sufferers. Other studies have found foods rich in tyramine and phenylalanine may constrict blood vessels and inhibit blood flow. Avoid foods that are rich in tyramine and phenylalanine. Have food sensitivity tests (see page 164) or avoid the following:

- Tyramine-rich foods include fermented products, such as wine and beer, and pickled products. Tyramine is also found in cereals and grains including wheat, wheat germ (also contains phenylalanine), soy and corn. Some beans and vegetables have smaller amounts of tyramine.
- Yeast and proteins, such as beef, turkey, wild game, and eggs, contain phenylalanine and tyramine. Also cured meats, including pork, shellfish and hot dogs.
- Fruit, such as large amounts of oranges, bananas, figs, prunes, pineapples and raisins, contain tyramine.
- Fats, such as cheese (tyramine), ricotta (phenylalanine), ice cream, chocolate, nuts and milk.
- Beverages, such as wine, beer, whiskey, tea, cola, coffee and heavy metal-contaminated tap water.
- Excess sugar, alcohol and processed junk food.
- Artificial synthetic foods, including preservatives, additives and flavourings, pesticides, sodium nitrate, MSG and artificial sweeteners.
- Drink 8 glasses of water a day and more if you drink coffee or alcohol.

Supplements
Magnesium   In a 1996 German study of 81 migraine patients published in the headache journal *Cephalalgia*, 41.6% of subjects taking oral Magnesium reduced both the duration and intensity of migraine attacks. They also reduced their reliance on medications to control their migraines.[51] Take 450mg daily.

Calcium   Deficiencies of Calcium are common and may lead to headaches, migraines, muscle cramps, anxiety and depression. Take 1500mg at night after a meal for better absorption.

Vitamin B complex   Required for adrenal function. Vitamin B deficiencies may trigger headaches and migraines. Take as directed.

5-Hydroxy tryptophan (5HTP)   A serotonin precursor made naturally by the body and also sourced from the plant *Griffonia simplicifolia*. 5HTP helps boost serotonin levels, relieving migraines and headaches. Improvement may be over the course of months. Take 150mg–300mg daily.

MSM (methyl sulphonyl methane)   A naturally occurring compound of bioavailable plant sulphur. MSM has been clinically shown to be an anti-inflammatory agent. Pain can be influenced by weather and humidity, as the outside pressure drops, cells swell and press on nerves, contributing to pain symptoms. MSM helps to equalise this pressure, reducing pain symptoms. Take 3g daily.

DIM (diindolylmethane)   Has a protective effect on hormone-sensitive tissues. Take these compounds if you suffer from migraines, have come off HRT (hormone replacement therapy) or have a family history of oestrogenic and breast cancers. Take 60mg–100mg of DIM 2 times daily. See your practitioner for product details.

Coenzyme Q10   Taking a 150mg dose every day for 30 days has shown a reduction in the symptoms and frequency of migraines.

Herbs

White Willow   Reduces the pain and inflammation of mild headaches due to the natural salicin in the Willow Bark. It is the natural forerunner of aspirin, reducing pain by inhibiting inflammatory chemicals (prostaglandins). Take 500mg–2g daily.

Feverfew   A recent survey found that 70 migraine sufferers (out of a group of 270) who had eaten Feverfew daily for prolonged periods claimed the herb decreased the frequency and/or intensity of their attacks. Many had been unresponsive to orthodox medicine.[52] Feverfew must be taken every day to have an effect. Add 1–2 bitter washed leaves in a sandwich or take 50mg–200mg daily.

Hormonal headaches and **migraines**   Take **Chaste Tree** (750mg 2 times daily), **False Unicorn Root** (500mg 2 times daily), **Dong Quai** (1g–2g daily), **Wild Yam** (2g–4g daily) and **Black Cohosh** (40mg–200mg daily). Combine with 5HTP to help balance serotonin levels. If you are on an oral contraceptive, talk to your doctor about the possible trigger effects of the drug.

Low blood sugar triggered migraines and **headaches**   May be helped by eating 6 small, healthy, well-balanced meals daily. Herbs and nutrients that may help are **Gymnema** (200mg 2 times daily), **Bitter Melon** (2g daily) and **Chromium** (200mcg–400mcg) and remember your **Vitamin B complex**.

Sinus or **viral/bacterial headache**   Take **Olive Leaf extract** (270mg 3 times daily) and **Echinacea** (1200mg–6g daily) for 10–30 days for signs of viral, bacterial or fungal infection. Another herb, **Goldenrod** helps to reduce inflammation and mucous congestion in the upper respiratory tract region. Take 450mg 3 times daily. **Goldenseal** has an antibiotic and soothing, toning action on mucous membranes that line the sinuses. Take 0.5g–1g of dried rhizome and root daily.

Toxic build-up in colon   If you feel toxic, see your local health store or pharmacy for a total body cleanse herbal formula and **Acidophilus**. See Detoxing on page 131 or Constipation on page 122.

External applications

Apply cool packs onto neck and pain area. Use ice packs, frozen peas or beans in bags, chilly bin ice packs or bean bags obtained from chemist or health shop that can be refrigerated. Essential oils of **Lavender, Rosemary** and **Peppermint** are useful for headaches and migraines. Use a few drops in steam and inhale, or massage a drop into the temple or scalp area, taking care to avoid the eyes, or add a few drops to a cotton ball and place under the pillow covers.

Hiatus Hernia

To understand a hiatus hernia we need to picture the muscle called the diaphragm that separates the lungs from the abdomen. It contains a small hole on the left side through which the liquid and food tube (oesophagus) passes from the chest area in the upper abdominal area to join the stomach. Normally this hole, called a hiatus, is small and fits snugly around the oesophagus. A hernia is when the upper part of the stomach gets pulled into the chest or lung area as the hiatus becomes weakened or enlarges.

Causes
- Hereditary
- Obesity
- Exercises such as incorrect weightlifting
- Straining at defecation
- Common after age 60
- Poor digestion, causing gases to accumulate in the stomach, which increase pressure on the diaphragm.

Signs and symptoms
- In most patients hiatus hernias cause no symptoms.
- Heartburn and regurgitation, when stomach acid refluxes back into the oesophagus.
- Chronic reflux of acid into the oesophagus, which may cause injury and bleeding, is quite rare but if it does occur it may lead to anaemia.
- Chronic inflammation of the lower oesophagus may produce scarring and make swallowing difficult as food cannot pass easily into the stomach.
- Pain and discomfort in the lower chest that can mimic heart pain, particularly after eating or on bending over or lying down.

Naturopathic recommendations

Lifestyle hints
The major cause leans to weakness in the hiatus wall from a possible deficiency of minerals and protein. The main aims of naturopathic treatment are to reduce the need for antacid medication, increase minerals and protein for repair, soothe inflamed digestive tissue, reduce stress, and encourage eating small meals and chewing well.
- Avoid bending, stooping, incorrect abdominal exercises, tight belts and girdles, all of which increase abdominal pressure and promote reflux.
- If overweight, lose weight. Obesity also increases abdominal pressure.
- Elevate the head of the bed 20–25cm (8–10 inches) by putting pillows or a wedge under the upper part of the mattress. Gravity then helps keep stomach acid out of the oesophagus while sleeping.
- Check with your doctor to see if any prescription medications have reflux as a side effect. Certain drugs, such as intestinal antispasmodics, calcium channel blockers and some antidepressants, weaken the muscle strength of the lower oesophagus.
- If reflux or burning pain occurs after eating, quickly drink 2 large glasses of water and jump up and down 5–7 times. Sounds crazy, doesn't it? But the water weighs the stomach down and the jumping pulls the stomach back underneath the diaphragm. Water also helps to flush the oesophagus of reflux acid that may have been trapped above the diaphragm.

- Reduce stress levels.
- Avoid smoking.

Nutrition

- Eat smaller, more frequent meals and do not eat within 2–3 hours of bedtime.
- Drink 30ml–50ml of aloe vera juice with or before meals, to aid healing and digestion.
- Avoid refined carbohydrates and any foods that produce an allergy or sensitivity response (reflux), especially caffeine, fatty and spicy foods, alcohol, tea and coffee.
- Avoid milk when you have a reflux attack. Milk actually increases gastric acid output. Instead drink aloe vera juice, marshmallow root or slippery elm fibre to help soothe the stomach and oesophagus lining.
- If roughage such as bran irritates and leads to reflux burn and indigestion, avoid roughage for a few months while undertaking naturopathic recommendations.

Supplements

Protein Take full spectrum protein supplements including **Glutamine** to heal and strengthen weakened digestive structures. Many protein powder drinks already have full spectrum proteins with added Glutamine. Mix with water, skim milk, or rice or soy milk. Other digestive healing proteins include **Colostrum** supplements.

Minerals Schuessler Tissue Salts **Silica** and **Calc Fluor** help to normalise and strengthen hiatus walls. Other homeopathically prepared minerals that may be helpful include **Nat Phos** for excessive reflux and heartburn, which acts as a digestive buffer and removes metabolic wastes, or **Kali Mur** and **Ferr Phos** for pain and inflammation. Take 1 tablet every 5 minutes for severe symptoms until symptoms decrease. For maintenance take 4 tablets throughout the day.

Heal the digestive tract lining Take **Vitamin E** (200IU daily), **Vitamin A** (5000IU–10,000IU daily), **Zinc** (15mg–45mg daily) and **Evening Primrose oil** (3g daily).

Herbs

Meadowsweet Protects and soothes mucous membranes in digestive tract, balances acidity and eases nausea. Take 2g–4g daily.

Chamomile Helps the digestive tract recover from inflammation processes in the stomach and mucous membranes. Take 2g–4g daily.

Flaxseed fibre, Marshmallow Root or **Slippery Elm** Heal inflamed gastric membranes by coating the digestive tract, allowing the mucous membranes to heal. Mix 1 tsp of each in a glass of water and drink quickly.

Agrimony Tones damaged stomach and gastric membranes. Take 1ml–3ml of tincture 3 times daily.

Goldenseal Promotes healing of mucous membranes. Take 0.5g–1g for 2–3 weeks.

High Blood Pressure (Hypertension)

Are we to blame for our own increase in blood pressure? High blood pressure is a condition that is predominant in modern Western cultures. Those cultures that are remote, car-less and have traditional diets have very little incidence of high blood pressure, even with advancing age. This news is exciting as it promises that through diet, lifestyle and intelligent preventative measures we may be able to improve the heart and blood condition, and take control of our health.

High Blood Pressure (Hypertension)

Causes

- More than 90% of people with high blood pressure have primary or essential hypertension, meaning no apparent disorder or disease process can account for their elevated blood pressure. In this circumstance, natural therapies, particularly lifestyle and dietary modifications, can result in significant improvements.
- Kidney failure or disease is the main cause of secondary hypertension although many other known causes may include adrenal involvement, pregnancy and drug-induced hypertension.
- Age, race and genetics.
- Lifestyle factors, such as stress, high salt, caffeine, alcohol or fat intake, lack of exercise, obesity, heavy metal poisoning and smoking or inhaling second-hand smoke.
- Drugs, such as oral contraceptives or hormone replacement, steroids, some prescribed medications and high doses of liquorice.
- Deficiencies in calcium, magnesium, potassium, coenzyme Q10, vitamin C and essential fatty acids (omega 3 and 6).
- Early manifestation of high cholesterol, end organ damage, kidney disease, diabetes, hormonal (adrenal or endocrine) dysfunction.

Signs and symptoms

- Headaches and shortness of breath
- Ringing in ears
- Fatigue and irritability
- Blurred vision, nausea and vomiting
- Sometimes signs and symptoms may be absent as the body is remarkable at adapting, although long term this too may have negative repercussions
- Abnormal heart sounds
- A high blood pressure measurement is over 140/90 — 140 (systolic) and 90 (diastolic).

Naturopathic recommendations

Lifestyle hints

If your blood pressure is over 160/115 please continue to see your doctor for supervision. You can still employ the naturopathic recommendations but you will have to stay on hypertensive medication for at least 3–6 months to achieve initial blood pressure control. Once under a satisfactory level, reduction of your medication can be employed under your doctor's supervision to reduce possible negative complications.

- Reduce weight if necessary.

Exercise

- Exercise must start off lightly and be gradual if it is not a regular habit by now.
- Walking 3–4 times weekly is a good start. Increase your speed if it becomes too easy. You should walk for 40 minutes to 1 hour. Intensity of speed or exercise can decrease the length of time you need to exercise down to 20–30 minutes.
- If you have bone, joint or muscle injuries consult a professional personal trainer for advice on an adaptive exercise programme.
- Cardio and weight-bearing exercise is excellent for blood circulation, bone health, muscle tone and strength, and increases a sense of well-being and relaxation.

High Blood Pressure (Hypertension)

Relaxation
- Important to help relieve stress, both mentally and physically. Stress exacerbates angina, poor fat metabolism and high blood pressure.
- Balance exercise with relaxation four times a week. Enjoy a good book or take bubble baths.
- Learn to relax by using yoga, meditation, or other relaxing techniques to suit your needs.

Eliminate smoking
- This is an absolute must. It damages the blood vessels and causes constriction and atherosclerosis. If you do choose to continue, supplement with vitamin C and a multi containing vitamins and minerals.

Nutrition
- Eat fewer animal products, by opting for a more vegetarian diet with lowered cheese or dairy product intake. Increase fresh fruits, nuts, seeds and vegetables in the diet to assist with calcium levels.
- Reduce total fat intake and favour vegetable oils over saturated animal fats. Non-heated polyunsaturated, or monounsaturated fats found in vegetable oils (olive oil or avocado) can lower blood pressure. Use omega 3 and 6 essential fatty acids or 'good fats' including flax oil or small amounts of olive oil and avocado as a substitute for butter and margarine. Use small amounts of olive oil or avocado to stir-fry foods.
- Avoid alcohol (especially bingeing) as this increases cholesterol triglycerides. If you choose to drink, never binge and limit yourself to 5 servings a week (1 serving equals 300ml beer, 60ml of sherry, martini or port, 30ml of spirits or 100ml of wine, preferably red).
- Reduce or eliminate coffee, caffeine, salt and soft drink intake.
- Reduce refined carbohydrates, such as white flour, white rice, croissants, toasted muesli, cakes, biscuits, pastries, pies, breadcrumbs and soft drinks.
- Consume complex carbohydrates. Halve the amount you normally have or eat 3 servings the size of your fist daily. Include dense grainy breads, lots of whole grains, oat bran and textured wholemeal or white sourdough, long grain white rice, basmati or brown rice, kumara, taro, yam, pasta, noodles, barley and bulgur wheat, porridge, untoasted muesli, Special K and All-Bran. Choose low-fat low-sugar biscuits made with oats.
- Use sugars sparingly, even those in honey, fruit juices, dried fruits and maple syrup. Avoid artificial sweetener or processed sugar.
- Eat more fibrous carbohydrates like salads, celery, onions, garlic, asparagus, and beans and legumes rather than starchy carbohydrates like potatoes, corn, rice, pasta and breads. Increasing fibre intake with water-soluble fibres such as oat bran, flax fibre, apple pectin and psyllium may lower both cholesterol and blood pressure. Add 1 tsp of freshly crushed linseeds to your porridge or salads daily.
- Eat more natural antioxidants found in vegetables (leafy greens, yellow and red), cherries and berries.
- Eat six small meals daily to help balance sugar levels, which may have a positive effect on fat metabolism.
- Eat at least 3 fish meals weekly. Sardines, tuna and salmon are great sources of omega 3 oils. Tinned fish may be an affordable option but grilled or steamed fresh fish is preferable.
- Consume copious amounts of turmeric, ginger, garlic and onions with meals to help break down fibrous deposits (fibrinogen) on the arteries and thin the blood. Eat soy products, oat bran, whole grain cereals, legumes, alfalfa and sprouts, nuts and linseeds to help reduce cholesterol levels.
- Drink 2 litres of pure, fresh water daily and include a cup or two of green tea daily. Low

High Blood Pressure (Hypertension)

in caffeine and rich in catechin antioxidants, green tea helps lower cholesterol and improve fat metabolism.

Supplements

Vitamin C   Helps to reduce the risk of blood clot formation, relaxes arterial walls and therefore blood pressure. Take an antioxidant formula that combines 500mg of Vitamin C daily with other antioxidants that help to reduce free radical damage of heart and blood vessels.

Vitamin B complex   Lack of B vitamins especially Folic acid (folate), B3 and B6 may lead to heart complications and high blood pressure. The B vitamins reduce the risk of cardiovascular disease by helping to convert homocysteine into a harmless amino acid preventing homocysteine damaging the heart. Any regular Vitamin B complex product will be suitable.

Coenzyme Q10 (Co Q10)   Levels are low in individuals with high blood pressure. As an antioxidant specific for the heart, many people have found Co Q10 to prevent the negative progression of high blood pressure. It can be used with beta-blockers, statins and flurozine — well-known high blood pressure, diuretic and cholesterol drugs. Incredibly, these drugs reduce Co Q10 levels and deficiency of Co Q10 may lead to high blood pressure. Take 150mg–300mg daily.

L-carnitine   A nonessential amino acid that may benefit people with cardiovascular diseases.[53] Patients taking L-carnitine in addition to their regular medication decreased the need for the drugs while improving cardiac function.[54] Take 900mg–4g daily.

Minerals   Magnesium (450mg daily), **Potassium** (50mg–300mg daily) and **Calcium** (1500mg daily) supplementation helps to reduce these important mineral deficiencies that lead to hypertension. Take Potassium and Magnesium in the morning and Calcium at night with meals.

Vitamin E and **Fish oil**   A combination of these two with garlic helps to reduce high blood pressure. Take 200IU–400IU of Vitamin E daily and 3g of Fish oil daily.

Herbs

Hawthorn   Beneficial for high cholesterol and blood pressure and angina. Acts as an antioxidant and is therefore protective with atherosclerotic conditions. Can be used in conjunction with aspirin and beta-blockers. Take 1.5g–3g of dried flower, leaf or berry daily.

Garlic   A hypotensive agent that is able to break down fibrous material and improve elasticity of blood vessel walls. In addition to using fresh Garlic in your cooking, you can also take a therapeutic dose of Garlic in supplement form. One clove of fresh Garlic a day or 400mg of Garlic extract, is suggested to reduce high blood pressure. Look for Garlic supplements with standardised Allicin. Avoid taking with the prescribed medication warfarin, as Garlic in large amounts may magnify the drug's blood-thinning effect, although adding to food in natural form should be fine.

Ginger   Helps circulation and breaks down fibrous deposits on blood vessels and arteries. Take 500mg 2–4 times daily, and add Ginger to foods and teas. Avoid taking with the prescribed medication warfarin, as Ginger in large supplement or herbal extract amounts may magnify the drug's blood-thinning effect. Ginger tea and adding to food should be fine.

Passionflower (4g–8g of dried herb daily), **Lime Flower** (1ml–2ml of tincture 3 times daily) and **Valerian** (1g–3g daily)   Have muscle relaxant and anti-anxiety effects, helping to reduce stress symptoms.

Ginkgo Biloba   Helps reduce risk of stroke, heart attack and intermittent claudication. Has a relaxing effect, serving to dilate vessels and reduces blood pressure. Take 4g–8g of whole leaf or 24mg–30mg of standardised extract of Ginkgo flavone glycosides daily. Avoid with the prescribed medication warfarin, as Ginkgo in large amounts may magnify the drug's blood-thinning effect.

Bugleweed Aids a weak heart accompanied by fluid accumulation and congestion of body tissues (congestive heart failure). Take under medical advice and see a naturopath for supervision and dose.

High Cholesterol

The word cholesterol often conjures up images of a 'fry-up' breakfast with bacon, fried eggs and toast dripping with butter. However, cholesterol is an important wax-like substance that our body uses to make hormones, vitamin D, and our cell walls stronger and more flexible. It synthesises bile and even provides a protective coating around the nerves in our body. Unfortunately high blood cholesterol levels are linked with heart attacks and strokes. Keeping a balance in life is one of the keys to staying healthy and this means making sure your cholesterol levels are at a normal level. Cutting back on the 'fry-up' for breakfast and choosing healthy alternatives, including stopping smoking, reducing caffeine and alcohol intake, increasing exercise and using anti-cholesterol supplements and antioxidants, are important tools to normalising your cholesterol and increasing your longevity.

Familial high cholesterol is an inherited high cholesterol condition that may be manifested in one out of every 500 people. It's not caused by eating too much cholesterol. There is a problem with a receptor on the low-density lipoproteins (LDL) that normally tells the liver to stop making cholesterol, thus cholesterol levels are increased.

Cholesterol is transported in the blood by lipoproteins, a mixture of fats (including triglycerides), cholesterol and protein. The important lipoproteins to remember are:

- High-density lipoproteins (HDL) act like sponges, absorbing excess fat or cholesterol from the body's cells to transport it back to the liver. Evidence suggests that a high concentration of HDLs may reduce cholesterol deposits within arterial walls, reducing the risk factor of atherosclerosis or cholesterol build-up on the blood vessel walls.
- Low-density lipoproteins (LDL) and very low density lipoproteins (VLDL) transport fats and cholesterol from the liver to the body cells for regeneration, repair and hormone synthesis. People with small LDL particles compared to those with larger LDLs are at greater risk of atherosclerotic lesions.

In layman's terms, LDLs are said to contain 'bad cholesterol' whereas the HDLs contain 'good cholesterol', although in truth both are essential to our survival. LDL plasma excess and a low concentration of HDLs increase the risk of cardiovascular disease.

Within the lipoproteins are smaller lipoproteins (a) that have a major role in cholesterol metabolism.

Lipoprotein (a) is a cofactor protein, involved in the transport of fats and cholesterol. High levels of lipoprotein (a) can make the VLDL and LDL stick to the walls of the artery like glue, increasing the risk of heart disease to ten times greater than just having levels of LDL and VLDL elevated above the normal range. To put it simply, naturopaths use antioxidants to reduce the oxidation or 'stickiness' of the adhesive protein (lipoproteins [a]) and fats so that even if LDL and VLDL cholesterol proteins are elevated in number they are decreased in stickiness and are more likely to pass the walls harmlessly.

Causes

- Peri-menopause and menopause, a family history of high cholesterol, high blood pressure (above 140/90), smoking and low HDLs are risk-factor indicators for high cholesterol.

- Men over 45 and women over 55 years old are at increased risk of high cholesterol.
- Excessive dietary intake of calories, cholesterol, saturated animal fats and trans fatty acids from margarines, heated oils or lard. Fried foods, hydrogenated oils, excessive intake of coffee, alcohol, sugar, refined carbohydrates and a diet low in fibre may lead to high cholesterol.
- Increased sensitivity to dietary cholesterol and lack of LDL receptors.
- High cholesterol is linked to high blood pressure, obesity, stroke and heart attacks.
- Familial high cholesterol, hypothyroidism, pregnancy and diabetes.
- Pancreatic, kidney, liver and adrenal dysfunction.
- Gall bladder and bile pathway obstruction.
- Nutrient deficiency of vitamin C, fibre, calcium, coenzyme Q10, chromium, copper, magnesium and dietary antioxidants.
- Smoking and toxins damage the blood vessel walls triggering a domino effect where fibrous tissue, white blood cells and inflammation cause further damage to blood vessel walls.

Signs and symptoms
- Diagnostic readings: a total cholesterol reading is usually within the following ranges:
  5.0 mmol/L or less than 200mg/dl = normal
  5.0–6.5 mmol/L or 200mg/dl–239mg/dl = increased risk
  Above 6.5mmol/L or above 240mg/dl = high risk
  HDL less than 35mg/dl increased risk
- High levels of total blood cholesterol especially triglycerides, LDL and VLDL accompanied by low levels of HDL.
- Symptoms are often apparent.
- Fatty deposits in the whites of the eye or sitting around the eyelid. The pupil may take on a hazy blue rim around the outside.
- The liver area may become painful if high levels of fat penetrate the liver's cells.

Naturopathic recommendations

Lifestyle hints
The ideal overall cholesterol picture would include low plasma triglycerides and LDL cholesterol, high HDL cholesterol, and large LDLs with reduced lipoprotein (a). We can help achieve this through diet, using vitamin B3, antioxidants and other supplementation, exercise and healthy lifestyle choices.
- Lose excess weight if necessary.

Exercise
- Exercise must start off lightly and be gradual if it is not a regular habit by now.
- Walking 3–4 times weekly is a good start. Increase your speed if it becomes too easy. You should walk for 40 minutes to 1 hour. Intensity of speed or exercise can decrease the length of time you need to exercise down to 20–30 minutes.
- If you have bone, joint or muscle injuries consult a professional personal trainer for advice on an adaptive exercise programme. Cardio and weight-bearing exercise is excellent for blood circulation, bone health, muscle tone and strength, and increases a sense of well-being and relaxation.

Eliminate smoking
- This is an absolute must. It damages the blood vessels, increases the risk of high cholesterol and causes constriction and atherosclerosis (build-up in the arteries).

High Cholesterol

- If you do choose to continue, supplement with vitamin C and a multi containing vitamins, beta carotene and minerals.

Relaxation

- Stress exacerbates angina and poor fat metabolism, leading to high cholesterol and high blood pressure.
- Learn to relax by using yoga or meditation, or other relaxing techniques to suit your needs.

Nutrition

Dramatic results can be experienced by individuals who switch to a healthier lifestyle and diet, although those with familial high cholesterol will have to do a lot more than just watching their diets. The LDL receptors decrease in number if there is an overload in dietary cholesterol, so reducing the overall cholesterol in the diet is still beneficial for those with familial high cholesterol.

Saturated fats containing cholesterol from animal and coconut oil products appear to interfere with the LDL receptors' ability to clear LDLs from the bloodstream. These types of foods increase LDLs and triglycerides, and lower HDLs, increasing cardiovascular disease risk factors.

For those with high cholesterol, studies show that to help maintain healthier levels of cholesterol, a reduction of dietary saturated fat and trans fatty acids (e.g. margarine) and heated fat intake along with an increase of polyunsaturated fats (from vegetable oil) and monounsaturated (e.g. olive oil) fats may reduce plasma LDL cholesterol levels. However, a more aggressive approach with the inclusion of herbal treatment and supplements will make more of a difference in lowering the cholesterol than diet alone.

- Avoid excessive intake of cholesterol. Cholesterol is an odourless, white waxy substance found in all animal foods, fish, offal, seafood and eggs. The type of fat you eat can affect your blood cholesterol level even more than does the amount of fat. Eating a lot of foods that are high in saturated or trans fatty acids, such as butter, cream, coconut cream, squid, prawns, palm oil, takeaway foods, fatty meats or fried foods, can raise your blood cholesterol. Limit eggs to 2 egg yolks per week and choose mostly white meat, fish and organic poultry. Cholesterol is not present in fruits or vegetables.
- Avoid excessive intake of saturated fats and trans fatty acids (TFAs). Saturated fats are fats that go hard at room temperature, such as lard, animal fats, dripping, butter, coconut and palm oil. Reduce saturated fat intake by removing visible fats and skin from meat, choosing grilling, steaming, baking or microwaving over frying and roasting. TFAs should also be avoided. TFAs are contained in margarine, shortenings, shortening oils and some salad oils and heated meats or fats.
- On the other hand, non-heated polyunsaturated or monounsaturated fats found in vegetable oils (olive oil or canola) can actually lower cholesterol. Use omega 3 and 6 essential fatty acids or 'good fats' including flax oil or small amounts of olive oil and avocado as a substitute for butter and margarine. Use small amounts of olive or avocado oil to stir-fry foods.
- Reduce refined carbohydrates, such as white flour, white rice, croissants, toasted muesli, cakes, biscuits, pastries, pies, breadcrumbs and soft drinks.
- Eat complex carbohydrates. Halve the amount you normally have or eat 3 servings the size of your fist daily. Include dense grainy breads, lots of whole grains, oat bran and textured wholemeal or white sourdough, long grain white rice, basmati or brown rice, kumara, taro, yam, pasta, noodles, barley and bulgur wheat, porridge, untoasted muesli, Special K and All-Bran. Choose low-fat, low-sugar biscuits made with oats.

- Use sugars sparingly, even those in honey, fruit juices, dried fruits and maple syrup. Avoid artificial sweeteners or processed sugar.
- Eat more fibrous carbohydrates like salads, celery, onions, garlic, asparagus, and beans and legumes, rather than starchy carbohydrates like potatoes, corn, rice, pasta and breads. Eat more dietary fibre and natural antioxidants found in vegetables (leafy greens, yellow and red), cherries and berries. Fibre binds onto excess dietary cholesterol and removes it. Grind flaxseeds and eat 2 Tbsp–4 Tbsp of Flaxseed fibre daily; this will provide fibre and omega 3 and 6. Add to salads or cereals. Other excellent sources of fibre incude oatbran, psyllium and pectin or apple fibre.
- Eat six small meals daily to help balance sugar levels which may have a positive effect on fat metabolism.
- Avoid alcohol (especially bingeing) as this increases cholesterol triglycerides. If you do choose to drink, never binge and limit yourself to 5 servings a week (1 serving equals 300ml of beer, 60ml of sherry, martini or port, 30ml of spirits or 100ml of wine, preferably red).
- Reduce or eliminate coffee, caffeine, salt and soft drink intake.

Other dietary hints

- Increase non-sweetened yoghurt intake and choose low-fat, skim dairy products, such as low-fat yoghurt, cottage and ricotta cheese, quark or feta. Acidophilus yoghurt may actually help reduce cholesterol. A study by G Hepner showed an average reduction in cholesterol from 252mg/dl–230mg/dl by the end of the first week of the experiment. It stayed at 230 for the remainder of the study.[55]
- Eat at least 3 fish meals weekly. Sardines, tuna and salmon are great sources of omega 3 oils. Tinned fish may be an affordable option but grilled or steamed fresh fish is preferable.
- Consume copious amounts of ginger, garlic and onions with meals to help break down fibrous deposits (fibrinogen) on the arteries and thin the blood, and eat soy products, oat bran, whole grain cereals, legumes, alfalfa and sprouts, nuts and linseeds to help reduce cholesterol levels.
- Drink 2 litres of pure, fresh water daily and include a cup or two of green tea daily. Low in caffeine and rich in catechin antioxidants, green tea helps lower cholesterol and improve fat metabolism.

Supplements

Inositol hexaniacinate   A type of non-flushing **Vitamin B3** (**Niacin**). It lowers the cholesterol especially LDL, lipoprotein (a), triglycerides and fibrinogen (a fibrous material that can cause clotting and atherosclerosis).[56] Inositol hexaniacinate works better than standard cholesterol medication if taken as directed, and is the only cholesterol-lowering agent that actually reduces mortality. Take 500mg 3 times daily with meals for 2 weeks then increase dosage to 1000mg 3 times daily with meals. Check cholesterol levels and liver enzyme levels every 3 months. If liver enzyme levels are increased, reduce the dose to 250mg 3 times daily with meals.

Antioxidant formulas (full spectrum)   Include ProenOthera® from Evening Primrose Seed Husk, Green tea, Grape Seed, Pine Bark, Beta Carotene, Vitamins E, A and C, oligomeric proanthocyanidins, flavonoids and adjunctive minerals (Zinc, Selenium, Manganese and Iron). These are essential to help prevent oxidation and stickiness of LDL and to reduce inflammation and atherosclerotic formation within the blood vessels. One of my number one choices for heart and cholesterol conditions. Take as professionally advised or as supplement labels suggest.

Lecithin   Helps emulsify and break down dietary fat. Take 3000mg daily or 3 tsp of granules on breakfast cereal daily.

Omega 3 oils   Help to thin the blood and improve cholesterol levels and poor heart function. Take 3000mg of **Fish oil** daily or 2 Tbsp of **Flax oil** daily. Avoid with the prescribed medication warfarin, as these oils in large amounts may have a blood-thinning effect.

Vitamin C   Lowers triglycerides and LDLs, and increases HDLs. Take 500mg 3 times daily.

Pantethine   A component of Vitamin B5, or Pantothenic acid, that supports healthy HDL, LDL, and triglyceride levels. Take 300mg 3 times daily.

Multi vitamin and **mineral formula**   Take a Multi containing Calcium, Magnesium, Chromium and Copper along with other full spectrum minerals as an excellent deterrent to heart disease and high cholesterol. Take as directed.

Policosanol   Derived from a waxy substance found in sugar cane, Policosanol reduces total cholesterol and LDL cholesterol levels. Take 5mg–10mg daily.

Herbs

Garlic   Reduces triglycerides and LDL cholesterol, and prevents LDL oxidation, while raising HDLs. In addition to using fresh garlic in your cooking, you can also take a therapeutic dose of Garlic in supplement form. One clove of fresh Garlic, or 400mg of Garlic extract, a day is suggested to reduce cholesterol. Look for Garlic supplements with standardised allicin. Avoid with the prescribed medication warfarin, as Garlic in large amounts or standardised form may magnify the drug's blood-thinning effect, although adding to food in natural form should be fine.

Milk Thistle (210mg–630mg, 80% silymarin daily), **Artichoke** (500mg, 15% cynarin daily) and **Curcumin** also from Turmeric (900mg daily)   The specific antioxidant herbs to help the liver metabolise fats.

Guggul   The refined extract of this resinous herb native to India is called Gugulipid. It has been shown to decrease both LDL cholesterol and triglycerides. Take Guggul standardised to contain 25mg of guggulsterones 3 times daily.

Ginger   Helps circulation and breaks down fibrous deposits on blood vessels and arteries. Take 500mg 2–4 times daily, and add Ginger to foods and teas. Avoid with the prescribed medication warfarin, as Ginger in large supplement or herbal extract amounts may magnify the drug's blood-thinning effect. Ginger tea and adding to food should be fine.

Hyperpigmentation of the Skin

Hyperpigmentation is also referred to as melasma or chloasma. It is most commonly seen following sun exposure but may also follow inflammatory changes in the skin. It is often more evident in those races whose skins are heavily pigmented.

Causes

- Haemochromatosis (a genetic predisposition to iron build-up) may often lead to liver damage and liver disease, causing hyperpigmentation. The sun exposed areas of the skin may look grey or black. People with primary bilary cirrhosis (liver disease) also often suffer from hyperpigmentation.
- Low folic acid levels caused by pregnancy and the contraceptive pill may lead to skin pigmentation.
- Topical agents (applications that go onto the skin). The application of perfumes (e.g. those containing bergaptine and citrus) sulphonamides and antimicrobial agents (e.g. halogenated salicylanilides) may produce sunlight-sensitive reactions which may cause pigmentation.

Hyperpigmentation of the Skin

- Addison's disease.
- Hyperthyroidism.
- Cushing's syndrome.
- Kidney failure.
- Systemic sclerosis.
- Chemical exposure, e.g. those who process silver and those exposed to mercury.
- Drugs, such as chloroquine and chlorpromazine.
- Fungal infections.
- Exposure or overloading of free radicals causing accelerated aging of skin.

Signs and symptoms

- The skin will change from a normal skin tone to having darker patches on the body or face.
- Most people notice skin changes appearing in their late twenties as the skin's response to the sun increases hyperpigmentation and the skin on the face becomes darkened with irregular patches.
- Most commonly affects brown or olive skinned people.

Naturopathic recommendations

Lifestyle hints

- Do not overexpose skin to the sun. If exposing skin to sun, wear 30+ sun block, clothing and a hat.
- Do not wear perfumes and rinse all skin cleansers (soap, etc.) off thoroughly. Bergamot, an essential oil, can cause the skin to pigment if exposed to the sun.
- Get sufficient rest. The face reflects the first signs of fatigue.
- Exercise to improve circulation and enzymatic activity of the skin.
- If you smoke, quit, and avoid alcohol.
- If it is a fungal infection, see a naturopath or medical doctor for antifungal topical applications to eradicate it. See page 169 for fungal infection recommendations.
- Avoid exposure to free radical sources, such as smoking and radiation, which can cause damage to the skin, accelerating aging. Other sources of radiation include excess sun exposure, tanning and sun-beds, microwave radiation, TV, VDU computer screens, X-rays, radiation therapy and mobile phones.
- Other external sources of free radicals may include air pollutants, smog, exhaust fumes (traffic-jam fumes), acid rain, industry pollutants and waste burn-off. Reduce exposure to pesticides, drugs, hydrocarbons, aerosol sprays, petroleum-based products and solvents like formaldehyde, toluene and benzene.

Nutrition

Avoid

- Foods that increase free radical load include fried, smoked, barbecued and cured foods. Added chemicals in food colouring, preservatives, emulsifiers, antibiotics, nitrates, food enhancers, some sweeteners and any sort of synthetic additive to food and drink also increase free radicals.
- Beverages like alcohol, coffee, carbonated soft drinks, drinks with artificial flavours and sweeteners. Copper or lead piping supplying drinking water may contaminate and pollute the water. Drink only fresh, filtered or purified water, 1–2 litres daily. Add chlorophyll (optional) for oxygenation and gentle detoxing.

- Using heavy metals like aluminium pots, foil and utensils, and products with aluminium in them, such as deodorants. Switch mercury fillings in teeth to healthier filling substitutes. A lot of these free radical sources may be difficult to avoid. To help reduce free radicals within our bodies, follow the lifestyle, dietary suggestions and supplement recommendations.
- Saturated fats, excessive fat from dairy products, processed foods, pork, beef and especially altered, unnatural fat derivatives in margarines and shortenings. Avoid or cut down on cheeses, butter, animal fats, coconut cream and fried foods.
- Refined foods and beverages are not very nutritious compared to 'whole foods', or foods prepared from scratch. Whole foods provide a good range of nutrients and the body does not have to detox synthetic food chemicals or fats (trans fatty acids). Good nutrition helps rebuild and maintain beautiful skin.
- Cut down on cakes, biscuits, white breads, lollies, sugary foods and soft drinks.

Eat plenty of
- Vitamin C foods. Rich sources include kiwifruit, citrus fruits such as oranges, lemons, tangerines and grapefruit, cranberries, blackcurrants, strawberries, cherries, tomatoes, papaya, capsicums and green leafy vegetables. Antioxidants called carotenoids are found in yellow, orange, red and green fruits and vegetables. Include spirulina, carrots, squash, yams, sweet potatoes, apricots and raw carrot juice in your diet.
- Cruciferous vegetables such as cabbage, broccoli, brussels sprouts and cauliflower.
- The onion family, including garlic, onions, shallots, spring onions and leeks.
- Food rich in selenium such as the onion family, seafood and fish, meats, brewer's yeast, wheat germ and bran, whole grains and sesame seeds; zinc, such as pumpkin, sunflower seeds, oysters, seafood and meats; manganese, such as whole grains, green leafy vegetables, legumes, nuts, pineapples and egg yolks; Methionine and cysteine, such as beans, fish, liver, eggs, brewer's yeast and nuts.
- Antioxidant condiments and herbs. Use garlic, turmeric, onions, ginger and rosemary.
- Cherries and bilberries (blueberries) and other dark red-blue berries are rich sources of anthocyanidins and oligomeric proanthocyanidins. These compounds are antioxidants (flavonoid molecules), which gives them their deep red-blue colour. These flavonoids are remarkable in their ability to enhance collagen matrix integrity and structure. Liberal consumption of these collagen-stabilising flavonoids is encouraged.
- Enzymes, such as those in aloe vera juice, avocados, papayas, pineapples, bananas, mangoes and bean sprouts help with the skin's regeneration processes.

Supplements
Folic acid   If the melasma pigmentation is due to oral contraceptive pill use or pregnancy, take 300mcg 2 times daily with a **Vitamin B complex** formula.
Evening Primrose oil   Helps the healing processes within skin cells. Take 3000mg daily.
Antioxidant formula (full spectrum)   Include ProenOthera® from Evening Primrose Seed Husk, Green tea, Grape Seed, Pine Bark, Beta Carotene, Vitamins E, A and C, oligomeric proanthocyanidins, flavonoids and adjunctive minerals (Zinc, Selenium, Manganese and Iron). Antioxidants protect the skin against the UV damage caused by excessive exposure to the sun. Take as professionally advised or as supplement labels suggest.

Herbs
Liver-cleansing herbs   Important for supporting the liver's enzymatic processes. **Dandelion** (3g–5g of dried root daily) and **Milk Thistle** (9g–10g of seed daily) enhance bile flow and detoxify the liver. **Burdock** (2g–6g of dried root daily) helps to cleanse the blood and is a specific herb indicated for skin problems.

Sarsaparilla   Traditionally used to clear skin discolouration and conditions. Take 2g–4g daily.
Black Cohosh   Can reduce skin blemishes if used over a long period of time at a low dose. Take 40mg of dried rhizome and root daily.

External applications
Scrub   Use **Papaya** mixed with **Oatmeal** as a skin scrub. Papaya enzymes exfoliate old, dead skin cells and help to regenerate new cells. Then apply **Aloe Vera** gel to skin as it increases the skin's healing ability 9-fold. The gel is a brilliant pre-moisturiser as you can wear it underneath sun block or moisturiser. Another option is to wipe Aloe Vera onto skin as a skin cleanser.
Creams   Those that contain **Vitamins C, E, A**, and plant extracts of **Liquorice, Bearberry** and **Grapefruit** assist with skin whitening, reducing sun spots, blemishes and freckles. Use twice daily on moisturised skin. Apply a sun block after application.

Hyperthyroidism

A condition caused by excessive secretion of the thyroid hormones from the thyroid gland, which increases the basal metabolic rate (the amount of calories your body uses to run normal cellular processes) and alters body functions.

Causes
- Graves' disease (thyrotoxicosis).
- Autoimmune system makes antibodies that attack the thyroid receptors causing malfunction and stimulating them to produce too much thyroid hormone.
- Multi-nodular goitre (90% are non-cancerous tumour nodules).
- Adenoma of the thyroid.
- Tumours may form on the thyroid causing stimulation of thyroid hormone output.
- Infection or inflammation of the thyroid.
- Excessive intake of iodine, kelp or seaweed.
- Excessive intake of thyroid hormone.

Signs and symptoms
- Exophthalmia (protruding eyes)
- Goitre (swollen area around neck)
- Altered bowel activity
- Insomnia and light sensitivity
- Weakness
- Hair loss and separation, flaking and splitting of the nails
- Weight loss despite a large appetite
- Nervousness, restlessness, irritability and fatigue
- Heart palpitations and high blood pressure
- Shortness of breath, Parkinson signs and symptoms
- Excessive sweating and muscle cramps
- Heat sensitivity
- Fine muscle tremors
- Frequent blinking
- Thin hair and skin appearance
- Osteoporosis (bone loss)
- Changes in menstruation.

Hyperthyroidism

Naturopathic recommendations

Lifestyle hints
Rather than try to treat this condition, naturopaths try to support the thyroid gland and the symptoms (e.g. heart stress and nervousness) while working with the medical treatment recommendations.

Exercise
- Although the metabolic rate is increased, gentle exercise including yoga or Pilates will help with nervousness, stress and insomnia related to hyperthyroidism symptoms.

Nutrition
- Check for food allergies and sensitivities, see page 164.
- Avoid kelp, seaweeds and iodised salt in the diet.
- Avoid/minimise saturated fats (cooking oils, nut butters, margarine and butter), sugar and salt.
- Eat all foods high in thiourea (these reduce thyroid function). These include Brussels sprouts, cabbage, kale, mustard greens, peaches, peanuts, pears, rutabaga, spinach, strawberries, walnuts, almonds, apples, soy and turnips. Some of these are classified as goitrogenic foods. Cooking deactivates the thiourea (which we don't want), so eat the food raw when you can.
- Avoid stimulants, alcohol, coffee, tea, nicotine and soft drinks. Smoking nicotine increases toxic substances in your body.
- Avoid highly chlorinated water. Drink filtered or distilled water.

Supplements
Antioxidant formulas (full spectrum)   Include ProenOthera® from Evening Primrose Seed Husk, Green tea, Grape Seed, Pine Bark, Beta Carotene, Vitamins E, A and C, oligomeric proanthocyanidins, flavonoids and adjunctive minerals (Zinc, Selenium, Manganese and Iron). Antioxidants provide protection against the free radicals that cause excessive tissue damage, inflammation and overload of oxidative stress associated with hyperthyroidism. Take as professionally advised or as supplement labels suggest.

Calcium   The hydroxyapatite form combined in mineral formulas helps to increase bone density and prevent bone loss caused by hyperthyroidism. Take 1500mg at night after a meal for better Calcium absorption or as professionally advised.

Coenzyme Q10 (Co Q10)   Can be protective as hyperthyroidism can lead to extra stress on the cardiovascular system leading to heart conditions. Take 150mg–300mg daily.

Herbs
Lemon balm   Helps support hyperthyroid medical treatment. Lemon balm has the added advantage of assisting with PMS symptoms, agitation, insomnia and indigestion due to anxiety. See your herbalist or naturopath for herb prescription and dose, as Lemon balm in large doses is known to block the action of thyroid hormones and must be taken under careful supervision.

Motherwort   May relieve heart palpitations, reduce nervous tension and act as a tonic for the heart. Take 2g–4g of dried herb daily.

Hawthorn   Beneficial for high cholesterol, blood pressure and angina and acts as an antioxidant, therefore is protective with heart conditions linked with hyperthyroidism. Take 1.5g–3g of dried flower, leaf or berry daily.

Passionflower (4g–8g of dried herb) and **Valerian** (1g–3g daily)   Have muscle relaxant

and anti-anxiety effects, helping to reduce stress symptoms.
Sarsaparilla   Helps break the cycle of cellular damage. Take 2g–4g daily.
Milk Thistle   Improves metabolism of thyroid hormones and medication while assisting liver detoxification and protects the liver from damage with natural antioxidants. Take 9g–10g of dried seed daily.
Chinese Foxglove   Supports the adrenal glands. Overactive adrenals can cause weight loss (avoid in high doses if you have high blood pressure). Take 20g–30g of uncured root daily prescribed by a naturopath or herbalist.
Gentian   Used to increase the appetite for those who just don't feel like eating. Take 600mg–2g in a herbal tea infusion one hour before meals to stimulate appetite.
Bugleweed   A traditional herb that helps inactivate thyroid antibodies, affecting iodine metabolism and that also inhibits the conversion of thyroid hormones (T4–T3) in peripheral tissues. See a naturopath or herbalist for a prescription if recommended after a consultation.
Toxic nodular goitre   An enlarged thyroid gland with nodules may benefit from herbs such as **Pokeroot**, **Calendula** and **Red Clover**. See a naturopath or herbalist for a prescription if recommended after a consultation.

Hypothyroidism

Hypothyroidism is a term that refers to low thyroid gland function and a decrease in metabolic rate, increasing oedema and swelling within the intercellular spaces, leading to characteristic puffiness. This butterfly-shaped gland is situated just below the voice box. The role of the thyroid gland has been understood for some time now. Although conventional medicine places emphasis on its contribution to regulating the body's metabolism, growth and development in children, an equally important role is its contribution to the immunological health of the body.

Causes

- Congenital (a defect in the thyroid hormones, receptors or gland at birth). This is treated by hormone replacement.
- Iodine deficiency or defective metabolism. Interestingly, excessive iodine intake from iodine preparations or kelp can cause autoimmune thyroid disease, leading to hypothyroidism.
- Surgical removal of the thyroid gland or certain drugs including antithyroid drugs and lithium (used for mental illnesses).
- Thyroid gland treated with radiotherapy.
- Excessive intake of goitrogenic foods (foods that block iodine use). Halogens, such as lithium, fluoride, chlorine and bromide found in treated water, can displace the halogen iodine, leading to deficiency.
- Family history of thyroid problems increases the risk of developing hypothyroidism.
- Autoimmune disease (Hashimoto's thyroiditis).
- Heavy metal toxicity or overexposure to environmental toxins.
- Viruses.
- Nutritional deficiencies of vitamins, minerals, tyrosine, iodine and EFAs (omega 3 and 6) can lead to elderly individuals developing mild hypothyroidism.
- Overexposure to oestrogen.
- Chronic long-term stress may weaken the thyroid.

Hypothyroidism

Signs and symptoms
- Goitre
- Depression
- Sluggishness, lethargy and lack of motivation to exercise
- Hoarse or gravelly voice
- Puffy, swollen face and eye area
- Joint pain
- Problems conceiving
- Weight gain and inability to lose weight through correct diet and exercise
- Decreased appetite and constipation
- Dry skin, nails and hair, or hair loss. The skin can become rough and pale yellow. The hairs at the end third of the eyebrow may fall out.
- Headaches
- High cholesterol
- PMS-type symptoms
- Low immunity with chronic infections
- Feel the cold
- Tiredness and fatigue
- Throat constriction.

Naturopathic recommendations

Lifestyle hints
The naturopathic aim is to support the thyroid gland with nutrients and correct diet. Non-medical low thyroid conditions may be assisted by the supplements and herbs recommended below. Medically diagnosed hypothyroidism should not be treated without naturopathic and medical supervision as, in extreme cases, it can be a life-threatening condition.

- Check your basal metabolic rate:
  Procedure: Men and postmenopausal women may perform the test at any time. Menstruating women must perform this test on the second, third and fourth days of menstruating.
  1. Shake down your thermometer to below 35°C (95°F) and place it by your bed before going to sleep at night.
  2. On waking, place the thermometer under your armpit for a full ten minutes. It is important to move as little as possible; lying and resting with your eyes closed is best. Do not get up until the ten minute test is completed.
  3. After ten minutes, read and record the temperature and date.
  4. Record the temperature for at least three mornings (at the same time of the day).

  Interpretation: Your basal temperature should be between 36.4°C–36.8°C (97.6°F–98.2°F). If the average temperature of the recordings is below 36.4°C, the thyroid is underactive. Low basal temperatures are common and may reflect hypothyroidism, which in turn may lead to weight gain.
- Do not use an electric blanket or water bed as body metabolism will be raised slightly if the body is forced to generate its own heat to keep warm.
- Take a cool shower morning (and evening if you can) to stimulate metabolism.
- Alternate hot and cold compresses on the thyroid gland. Mould a hot compress to the neck and upper chest and maintain for 5 minutes. Alternate with an ice-cold compress for 30 seconds. Repeat 3–5 times. Do this every morning and evening for one week and then mornings only for 30 days.

- Discontinue smoking, caffeine and alcohol use.
- Keep warm by wearing clothes in layers.

Exercise
- To stimulate thyroid gland secretion and metabolism exercise 3–4 times weekly for 20–40 minutes with a mixture of cardiovascular exercise (walking, running) and resistance (yoga, lunges, weights).

Nutrition
- Check for food allergies and sensitivities, see page 164.
- Add kelp and seaweeds to the diet.
- Avoid/minimise saturated fats (cooking oils, nut butters, margarine and butter), sugar and salt.
- Avoid all foods high in thiourea (these reduce thyroid function). These include Brussels sprouts, cabbage, kale, mustard greens, peaches, peanuts, pears, rutabaga, spinach, strawberries, walnuts, almonds, apples, soy and turnips or, if you eat them, make sure that they've gone through a cooking process to inactivate their inhibiting nature on iodine. These are classified as goitrogenic foods.
- Avoid highly chlorinated water. Drink filtered or distilled water.

Supplements
Multi vitamin and **mineral formula** Supports the manufacture of thyroid hormones and the thyroid gland. Take a multi vitamin and mineral formula daily that includes Vitamin A (5000IU), Vitamin C (1g–4g), Vitamin E (400IU), Vitamin B2 (15mg), Vitamin B3 (25mg–50mg), Vitamin B6 (25mg–50mg), Zinc (30mg–40mg) and Copper (2mg–4mg).
Tyrosine An amino acid that along with iodine helps to make thyroid hormones. Take 250mg daily.
Thyroid Glandular Dessicated, natural thyroid gland sold in health stores may be helpful for mild forms of hypothyroidism. See your local health store for details.
Lugol's (aqueous) Iodine Paint on the sole of the feet daily until they will not absorb the iodine and remain deep gold for 48 hours. If the colour fades within this time the body is absorbing the amount of iodine it requires. If you are in doubt at any time, see your health professional and do not take internally unless prescribed. Lugol's is my favourite supplement to use for hypothyroidism. However, there is the concern that in rare cases, if the body becomes overloaded with iodine, hypothyroidism may actually result. Work with a naturopath and a doctor to make sure you are iodine deficient before using iodine as a supplement.

Herbs
Milk Thistle Stimulates thyroid function and improves thyroid hormone conversion. Take 210mg–630mg (80% silymarin) daily.
See a naturopath or herbalist for a prescription of the following herbs if recommended after a consultation.
Bladderwrack Contains iodine that can help with iodine deficiency and stimulates thyroid function.
Coleus Stimulates the release of thyroid hormone.
Guggul Contains guggulsterones that exhibit thyroid-stimulating activity.

Indigestion

Most people tend to suffer from indigestion on Christmas Day or other days of celebration when too much good food has been consumed and groans of satisfaction are replaced by groans of discomfort caused by pain in the upper abdomen. Some individuals may experience indigestion on a daily basis, and others know that if they overindulge in a particular beverage or food (e.g. pastries) they can expect to suffer. Some people describe indigestion as heartburn, a burning pain felt behind the breastbone area.

Causes
- Excessive activity after eating.
- Pregnancy.
- Infections, such as *Helicobacter pylori* (stomach ulcers), candida and parasites.
- Low or high output of stomach juices.
- Food sensitivities and allergies.
- Eating too quickly.
- Digestive conditions, for example irritable bowel syndrome, candida, Crohn's disease, intestinal obstruction, lack of bowel bacteria, malabsorption, Coeliac disease, lactose intolerance, ulcers and digestive enzyme deficiencies.
- Overindulgence in alcohol, fatty or spicy foods, caffeine (coffee) or aspirin use.
- Drugs, such as pain killers and non-steroidal anti-inflammatories.
- Disorders of the liver, gall bladder or pancreas.
- Inflammation of the stomach lining.
- Leaky gut syndrome.
- Smoking, stress or swallowing excessive amounts of air while eating.
- Tight, restrictive clothing around the abdomen or obesity.
- Phytate-containing foods, including beans, legumes, grains, nuts and seeds.
- Sulpherous vegetables, including cabbage, broccoli, Brussels sprouts and cauliflower can cause a build-up of gas, leading to indigestion.
- Uncooked starches (bread) can cause indigestion in some individuals. Starch in bread is rendered more edible when toasted.

Signs and symptoms
- Burping and gas
- Reflux or burning after eating
- Bloating
- Nausea
- Pain in upper abdomen
- Retching or even vomiting after eating.

Naturopathic recommendations

Lifestyle hints
- If stress sets off indigestion, use calming techniques such as exercise or meditation to help release the tension.
- Lose weight if necessary.
- Wear loose, unrestrictive clothing around the abdomen.

- Avoid bending down or lying flat after meals.
- Eat your evening meal well before going to bed so that it has time to digest.
- Raise the head of the bed 15–20cm (6–8 inches) on blocks to prevent reflux or stomach acid discomfort.

Nutrition

- Enjoy eating and drinking in moderation and avoid foods or beverages that you know will cause indigestion.
- Avoid smoking and overindulging in alcohol, coffee, fatty or spicy foods, especially when you are stressed or fatigued.
- Eat 6 small meals daily in a relaxed state and chew food thoroughly.
- Enjoy a bitter aperitif, such as vermouth or soda, lime and bitters, before dinner to encourage digestive juices.

Supplements

Flaxseed oil (2 Tbsp daily) and **Colostrum** (4g daily)   May help reduce leaky gut syndrome and inflammation associated with indigestion.
Aloe Vera juice   Can speed up the healing time of the stomach lining, and increase absorption and digestion of nutrients from food. Take 50ml with every meal.
Hydrochloric acid or **digestive enzyme formulas**   Increase digestive juices and break down foods properly. Take as recommended.
Acidophilus and **Bifidus**   Lack of bacterium can cause indigestion and may lead to an overgrowth of candida in the digestive tract. Take 1 billion of the Acidophilus and Bifidus species in capsule form daily on an empty stomach to repopulate your digestive system.

Herbs

Slippery Elm   Acts as a gentle, nutritious coating to the digestive system allowing healing to take place. Mix 1 tsp (3g) in a glass of water and drink quickly to heal inflamed gastric membranes. This should be taken separately from the other herbs.
Chamomile   Assists recovery from inflammation processes in the stomach and mucous membranes, and is soothing to the nerves. Drink the herb tea or take 2g–4g of dried flowers daily.
Meadowsweet   Used in cases of over-acidity, easing nausea and soothing an inflamed digestive tract lining. Take 1 tsp (2g–6g) of dried leaf and steep in a cup of hot water for 15 minutes before drinking. Drink 3 cups daily.
Peppermint tea and **Fennel tea**   Useful when there is flatulence associated with the indigestion. Drink Peppermint tea to help relieve gas and bloating or try Fennel tea. Crush 1 tsp of Fennel Seeds and add to 1 cup of hot water. Cover the top of the cup with a saucer and steep seeds in water for 15 minutes. Remove saucer and sip tea.

Infertility

It's not fair. Millions of men and women use contraceptives to avoid pregnancy and, meanwhile, an estimated 10–15% of people want to conceive a child, but can't.

Natural fertility management methods practised by qualified naturopaths offer alternative and complementary treatments to ongoing orthodox in-vitro fertilisation (IVF) treatment, and many couples are jumping at the opportunity for their second chance.

Female infertility

Infertility is defined as failure to conceive after a year of unprotected intercourse. About 40% of infertility is caused by sperm problems, 20% by ovulatory dysfunction, 20% by abnormal tubal function, 5% by cervical factors and 15% by unidentified factors.

Causes
- Damage to the uterus from infection or fibroids
- Retroversion of the uterus
- Structural abnormalities of the uterus or fallopian tubes
- Abnormally thick mucus or mucousal antibodies that attack the sperm
- Absence of menstruation or imbalanced menstruation
- Blocked fallopian tubes
- Failure to produce or balance reproductive hormones
- Immature eggs not fully developing into mature eggs
- Stress, trauma or chronic ill health
- Obesity or being underweight
- Endometriosis or polycystic ovary syndrome
- Micronutrient deficiencies of vitamins B and E, magnesium, zinc, potassium and essential fatty acids.

Lifestyle hints
- Avoid smoking.

Enhancing female fertility
Hormonal abnormalities leading to infertility should be ruled out with blood tests. Uterine fibroids, endometriosis, ovarian cysts and infections that may impair fertility must be diagnosed by a doctor. Treat all infections (see your GP) and also consider taking a herbal parasite cleanse.

Lunaception
Women's ovulation is naturally ruled by cycles of the moon. Natural fertility experts are using lunaception as part of their recommendations for enhancing fertility. Ovulation may be helped by light. Leave your light on for 3 nights midway through the menstrual cycle and your room in full darkness all other nights. Ovulation may be stimulated when the light is on. Intercourse should occur especially during the 3 'light nights' to help conception. See a naturopath who has trained in natural fertility to analyse your lunar cycle.

Nutrition
- Avoid alcohol as too much alcohol, especially beer, causes an increase in prolactin which is known to contribute to infertility. Even moderate consumption of 2 glasses daily reduces conception chances by 25%.[57, 58]
- Drinking 2–3 cups of coffee and other drinks containing caffeine, including tea, colas and chocolate, can reduce your chances of conception by 25%.[59, 60, 61]
- Eat adequate protein. You may like to include spirulina in your diet to enhance protein intake.
- Avoid foods containing MSG (monosodium glutamate).

Supplements
Vitamin B6 Take 50mg daily. It's best to look out for supplements that include a full complement **Vitamin B complex** with 50mg of B6 already added.

Folic acid, Vitamin B12, Magnesium and **Zinc**   Also contribute to conception nutrition. Take a Women's Multi daily to ensure a balance of nutrients with a good balanced diet.
Vitamin E   May help to improve fertility. Take 400IU daily.
Fish oil, Flax oil, Borage oil and **Evening Primrose oil** (EPO)   Help to increase essential fatty acids ('good fats'), which are necessary to help promote hormone production and balance. Take 2 Tbsp of Flax oil and 2–3 capsules each of Fish oil, EPO or Borage oil daily.

Herbs

Detox   Complete a gentle detox herbal programme and a parasite-cleansing programme to balance the internal body organs before trying to get pregnant. Detox herbs should include **Burdock** (2g–6g of dried root daily), **Cleavers** (2g–4g daily) and **Red Clover** (2g–4g daily), which help to cleanse the blood and clear the lymphatics. **Dandelion** (3g–5g of dried root daily) and **Milk Thistle** (9–10g of seed daily) enhance bile flow and detoxify the liver.

Parasite-cleansing herbs   Take two 3-week courses of **Cloves** (1800mg daily) combined with **Wormwood** (2000mg daily) and **Black Walnut** (2000mg daily) to help eradicate parasites.

Herbs to help improve female fertility include **Chaste Tree, Liquorice, Dong Quai, Red Clover** and **Siberian Ginseng**.

    Chaste Tree (1g–1.5g daily) and **Liquorice** (500mg daily)   Helpful for women who are not ovulating regularly or with irregular periods. Chaste Tree is also good for women who have been on birth control pills and have yet to establish a normal cycle. Normalising hormonal cycles is important to improve fertilisation

    Dong Quai   Removes blockages in the reproductive system and can help women become pregnant by regulating cycles, although it should not be used during pregnancy. Take 1g–3g of dried root boiled decoction daily or 1g–2g in tablet or capsule form daily.

    Red Clover   Helpful in situations where there is oestrogen deficiency. Take 2g–4g 3 times daily.

    Siberian Ginseng   Useful for poor contraception due to stress. Take 1g–4g daily.

False Unicorn Root   Wonderful for women who have a predisposition to miscarriages or pelvic congestion as it helps to tone the uterus. Take 500mg 2 times daily.

Red Raspberry Leaf tea   Very gentle on the uterus and is therefore recommended for uterus health. Take 2g–4g 3 times daily.

Other herbs considered helpful for fertility include **Tansy, Yarrow** or **Feverfew** which help regulate menstruation. Do not use if pregnant as these may cause spontaneous abortion if used in a specific dose. Consult a naturopath for doses.

Caution: There are many more herbs to recommend. However, you must not use them if you are pregnant because of their regulating nature. So the dilemma is…you want to get pregnant, but need the herbs to help improve your chances. The best idea is to take these herbs for a programme of 3–6 months while using a form of contraception, such as condoms, and then discontinue the herbs and contraception and attempt to conceive again.

Increase sexual activity

Take herbs if your libido is low including **Damiana** (2g 3 times daily), **Horny Goat Weed** (1g–2g daily) and **False Unicorn Root** (500mg–1g daily).

Male infertility

Couples trying to conceive can relate to the saying 'It takes two, baby'. For optimum conception success, both partners should identify their fertile health issues by seeing a doctor or fertility specialist. It may sound simple but many couples also forget to ensure healthy optimum nutrition levels and, as everyone knows, oysters are great for guys, as they are rich in zinc, important for male fertility.

Male infertility is responsible for 40%–50% of failure to conceive and the key to male fertility is large numbers of healthy sperm. A medical analysis to determine sperm health for quantity, form and motility is essential.

The specific cause of infertility should always be diagnosed by a physician before considering possible solutions. See your GP to check infections or if you need to consider surgery to restore fertility.

Causes

- Low sperm count, sperm agglutination, impotence and ejaculatory disorders are the major causes of infertility where nutritional intervention has a role.
- Decreased sperm motility (power of spontaneous movement). There are multiple possible underlying causes of a decrease in the number, quality or motility of sperm. Some of the causes of infertility readily respond to natural medicine, while others do not.
- Anatomical problems, such as enlarged scrotal veins or fluid accumulation in scrotum (hydrocele).
- Chromosomal abnormalities and glandular disease, such as diabetes, thyroid problems or other hormonal malfunction.
- Mumps orchitis (if there was inflammation of the testes following the mumps).
- Nutritional deficiencies.
- Exposure to toxins — heavy metals, alcohol and marijuana.

Lifestyle hints

- Correct circulation to testes with exercise.
- Take cold and warm sitz baths. This is a procedure where you sit in a tub of either warm or cold water (depending on the temperature of the testes) with your buttocks and hips immersed. You should remain in a sitting position.
- Control testicular temperature. Wearing tight underwear will hold testes closer to the body and so keep them at a higher temperature, therefore decreasing spermatogenesis (production of sperm). Keep groin area cool by wearing loose clothing, such as boxers instead of tight underpants, and avoid heat exposure such as long soaks in a hot tub or bath.
- Evidence suggests that environmental pollutants can depress male fertility.
- Avoid recreational drugs and, where possible, pharmaceutical drugs.
- Avoid smoking, caffeine and alcohol.

Enhancing male fertility

Hormonal abnormalities leading to infertility should be ruled out with blood tests. Treat all infections (see your GP) and also consider taking a herbal parasite cleanse.

1. Begin programme at least 6 months prior to conception. A minimum of 4 months' corrective treatment with supplements and digestive aids is required before couples with nutritional deficiencies can be advised to attempt conception. Try digestive enzymes, aloe vera juice and spirulina.
2. Follow a herbal 7-day detoxification programme to reduce chemical toxic burden. Blood cleansing is very important to ensure healthy sperm production.
3. If low sperm count is a problem, increase ejaculation frequency to aid sperm transport.
4. Organic foods: In a study of Danish greenhouse workers, an unexpectedly high sperm count was found among organic farmers, who grew their products without the use of pesticides or chemical fertilisers.[62]

Nutrition

- Sperm is released from the tubules after 70 days. Fourteen days later it is motile (fertile). Therefore it is important to correct male dietary inadequacies about 3 months prior to conception. Pharmaceutical and recreational drugs will often contribute to male infertility.
- Avoid alcohol as too much is known to contribute to infertility. In a study of men with poor sperm quality, excessive alcohol consumption was associated with a decrease in the percentage of normal sperm.[63]
- Avoid coffee and drinks and food containing caffeine, such as tea, colas and chocolate.
- Eat adequate protein. You may like to include spirulina in your diet to enhance protein intake.
- Eat organic fruits and vegetables.
- Do not use plastic containers or plastic food wrap to heat food in the microwave as plastics contain unwanted, potentially harmful oestrogens that can leach into the food and contribute to infertility. Use glass or porcelain instead.

Supplements

Zinc Semen contains high concentrations of Zinc. Zinc is also recommended to help benign prostate enlargement. Oysters, pumpkin seeds, ham, beef, eggs and chicken are good sources of Zinc. Take 30mg–60mg daily.

Vitamin E Crucial for proper reproduction in both men and women. Did you know that the chemical name for Vitamin E, tocopherol, originates from the Greek words 'to bear offspring'? Take 400IU daily.

Amino acids **Arginine** and **Taurine** (2g–4g daily) have shown to raise sperm counts and sperm motility. Increase consumption of Arginine-rich foods, such as pheasant, duck, clams, scallops, shark, meat, nuts and cheese.

Herbs

Detox Complete a gentle detox herbal programme and a parasite-cleansing programme to balance the internal body organs and prepare for a healthy start. **Burdock** (2g–6g of dried root daily), **Cleavers** (2g–4g daily) and **Red Clover** (2g–4g daily) help to cleanse the blood and clear the lymphatics. **Dandelion** (3g–5g of dried root daily) and **Milk Thistle** (9g–10g of seed daily) enhance bile flow and detoxify the liver.

Parasite-cleansing herbs Take two 3-week courses of **Cloves** (1800mg daily) combined with **Wormwood** (2000mg daily) and **Black Walnut** (2000mg daily) to help eradicate parasites.

Pygeum This is an extract from the bark of an African tree that assists with enhancing fertility in men. Take 50mg–100mg of Pygeum extract (standardised to contain 14% triterpenes) 2 times daily.

Ginseng There are several types of Ginseng but Korean, or *Panax*, and Siberian Ginseng have great reputations for enhancing men's and women's fertility, stress adaption, stamina and health. Take 600mg–10g of dried Korean Ginseng root daily unless otherwise prescribed and 1g–4g of Siberian Ginseng daily to assist with spermatogenesis.

Saw Palmetto Tones and strengthens the male reproductive system, is used for prostate enlargement and also enhances endurance. The prostate gland is located below a man's bladder. It produces most of the fluid in semen. It also has a tube running through it, the urethra, which carries urine and semen out of the body. Saw Palmetto is also used for testicular atrophy and sexual dysfunction. Take 5g–6g of dried Saw Palmetto fruit daily.

Maca Increases seminal volume, libido, sperm count per ejaculation, motile sperm count and sperm motility. Take 1g–2g daily.

Increase sexual activity

Take herbs if your libido is low. Some herbs to choose from include **Damiana** (2g 3 times daily), **Tribulus** (500mg 3 times daily), **Oats** (0.6ml–2ml daily), **Horny Goat Weed** (1g–2g daily), **Nettle** (2g–6g 3 times daily). Drink Nettle tea and eat Oats every morning. The best time to try to conceive is the day before the woman ovulates. After following these recommendations, it's best to have your sperm count checked every 3–6 months or as professionally advised.

Insomnia

Insomnia can be the inability to fall asleep, restlessness while sleeping, or waking up earlier than desired and not being able to return to sleep. However it manifests, it is an unhealthy state. People who have chronic insomnia find the night more stressful than the day, and the sleep deprivation caused by insomnia makes their work and daytime activities less enjoyable, as well as inefficient and even dangerous to themselves and others.

Causes

- Chronic stress and tension, worry, fear, shift work and other anxieties are usually the root of insomnia.
- Dietary stimulants (caffeine), indigestion, overeating and pain.
- Blood-sugar imbalances can release stimulatory hormones that keep you awake.
- Serotonin or vitamin B6 deficiency. B6 assists in the formation of the neurotransmitter serotonin, which helps regulate sleep. The serotonin precursor 5-Hydroxy tryptophan (5HTP) has also been shown to help bring on sleep.
- Omega 3, magnesium and calcium deficiencies associated with muscle cramps may also lead to insomnia.

Signs and symptoms

The 3 main types of insomnia are
- Mild insomnia, which lasts for about 3 days and is normally due to too much excitement, stress, late nights, jetlag, relationship problems, etc.
- Short term insomnia, which lasts for periods of 2–3 weeks and can be the result of the death of a loved one, relationship or money stress, intense workload or illness.
- Long-term insomnia, which mothers and fathers with babies will recognise, lasts longer. Other causes can be from underlying physical, emotional or lifestyle issues which may need to be addressed by a health professional. Some people find it runs in their family.

Naturopathic recommendations

Lifestyle hints

- Learn to meditate and relax your mind and body. Talk to friends about your feelings or get support, whatever it takes. It is easy to isolate yourself and that is okay as long as you don't do it for too long.
- Go to bed early at the same time every night and get up at the same time every morning. Get plenty of sunlight and fresh air.
- Avoid caffeinated beverages in the hours before you go to bed. We all know about this

one, but remember caffeine lurks in hot chocolate and many soft drinks as well as tea and coffee.
- Don't watch television in your bedroom and try to make the room as restful as possible.

Exercise
- A period of more than half an hour of fairly intense exercise leaves your body requiring more 'deep' sleep and therefore you will have better sleep quality that night. But remember, don't exercise just before bed as you will still be on a 'high' when you go to bed.

Nutrition
- To boost the production of serotonin, eat carbohydrate-rich foods (pasta, starchy vegetables, potatoes, cereals, breads). Carbohydrates enhance the absorption of tryptophan, which is converted into serotonin in the brain. Within about thirty minutes of eating a carbohydrate snack you will feel more calm and relaxed. The effects will last several hours.
- Meals that are high in carbohydrates and low to medium in protein will help you relax in the evening and set you up for a good night's sleep. Try the following 'dinners for sleep':
Pasta with parmesan cheese; scrambled eggs and cheese; tofu stir-fry; hummus with whole wheat pita bread; seafood, pasta, and cottage cheese; meats and poultry with veggies; tuna salad sandwich; chilli with beans (not spicy); and sesame seeds (rich in tryptophan) sprinkled on salad with tuna chunks and whole wheat crackers.

Supplements
5-Hydroxy tryptophan (5HTP) From the herb *Griffonia simplicifolia*, 5HTP gives the body the ingredients to make the brain chemical serotonin. If serotonin is too low, feelings of unhappiness, depression and symptoms, such as insomnia, may be evident. Take 150mg–300mg daily. Take with Vitamin B6 to help convert 5HTP to serotonin.
Vitamin B6 Take 25mg–50mg daily with a Vitamin B complex to assist with exhausted adrenal function due to stress.
Calcium and **Magnesium** Deficiencies of these are common and may lead to muscle cramps, anxiety and depression. Take 1500mg of Calcium at night after a meal for better absorption and 450mg–900mg of Magnesium daily.
Melatonin Levels may be reduced with anxiety, leading to insomnia. Seek a prescription from your doctor and take 1mg–3mg at night before sleep. Not recommended for children as their levels are generally adequate.
Fish oil Known as a sleep-inducing fat. Take 3 capsules daily.

Herbs
Herbs can relieve the symptoms and treat the underlying causes of mild insomnia. Anyone suffering from insomnia must search deeply for the underlying cause. Once corrected, the person will have a greater momentum for living with optimal health, a prerequisite of which is enjoyable and nurturing sleep. Remember, herbs are not like drugs; they take time to work and, because this condition is heightened by anxiety, while waiting for the natural therapies to work, patience is needed.
Californian Poppy Has a relaxing effect on the mind and potential mood-elevating actions without addictive side effects. Take 900mg daily.
Valerian Widely used in herbal medicine, Valerian is one of the safest sedative plants. It has been shown to relieve insomnia by calming nerves, relieving nervous tension, improving the quality of sleep and reducing the time it takes to fall asleep. The active constituents

of Valerian are not known. It appears from clinical anecdotes that Valerian relaxes the nervous system with tranquilising, antispasmodic and pain-relieving properties. The root is used in a decoction for anxiety and insomnia. Some individuals experience alertness with Valerian. Sleeping formulas without Valerian are available. Take 1g–3g daily.

Skullcap (750mg 3–5 times daily), **Jamaican Dogwood** (4g daily) and **Passionflower** (4g–8g of dried herb daily; action magnified when combined with **5HTP**)   These herbs are sedative, analgesic and hypnotic. Widely used to calm the nervous system and promote sleep.

Chamomile flowers   Said to be a gift from the gods. Chamomile has been used to calm an excited mind and relax a nervous stomach. A tea made from the flower is used as an anti-inflammatory, antispasmodic and sedative. Try the good old remedies like having Chamomile tea at night. Incidentally this is very good for indigestion. Take 1 teabag of Chamomile tea and steep in hot water with a saucer lidded over the cup for 15 minutes, then drink.

Lavender oil   An aromatherapy oil which, placed in an oil burner or directly onto cotton wool and placed under a pillow, may be helpful.

Irritable Bowel Syndrome

Irritable bowel syndrome (IBS) is a functional disorder involving the gastro-intestinal (GI) tract. In other words, even though there are no anatomic structural problems or underlying measurable causes, the GI tract just doesn't seem to work properly.

Although IBS is not colitis, and certainly not limited to the colon, the terms mucous colitis, nervous colon, spastic colon and irritable colon have been used to describe this disorder.

Constipation-predominant IBS

Bowel movements are variable. Most patients have pain over one or more areas of the colon associated with periodic constipation or diarrhoea. Symptoms commonly include bloating, flatulence, nausea, headache, fatigue, anxiety and difficulty in concentration. Stools may be frequent and of small volume, ribbon-like, rabbit pellet-like, lumpy or narrow in appearance, leaving the patient with a feeling of incomplete emptying of the rectum. Defecation or wind may relieve symptoms.

Caution: Beware of dehydration caused by constant diarrhoea.

Causes

- Although no pathological or anatomical causes can be found we do know that certain things may trigger IBS symptoms. These include emotional factors or stress, food sensitivities, drugs or hormones.
- Stool examinations have revealed imbalances in beneficial bacteria (acidophilus and bifidus), undigested food and the presence of some parasites (not 'considered' to be disease-causing).
- Diets low in fibre, high in sugar and fats, and including known bowel irritants, such as coffee and alcohol, may also trigger IBS.
- Leaky gut syndrome.

Signs and symptoms

These symptoms nearly always occur when awake.
- Abdominal pain or discomfort (the pain is either colicky, coming in bouts or a dull ache) over the area of the sigmoid colon. Pain is generally relieved by defecation.

- Diarrhoea and/or constipation.
- Uncomfortable distension or abdominal bloating after eating.
- Stools become more frequent and looser as abdominal pain increases.
- The rectal area can be tender.
- Headache, nausea, heartburn, belching, gas, mucous stools, frequent urination and fatigue may accompany the condition.
- Women with IBS often also suffer painful menstrual periods, prompting researchers to consider a hormonal connection.

Naturopathic recommendations

Lifestyle hints

Fundamentally the naturopathic treatment focuses on the elimination of allergen (intolerant) foods, controlling and treating the emotional triggers and nervous system, increasing dietary fibre and using herbs and supplements for a more holistic approach.

Stress reduction

- Routine time-out is a must to help reduce stress. Getting absorbed in a book, taking bubble baths and meditating can help put causes of stress into perspective. It's very important for IBS individuals to acknowledge and identify their stress and find a way to deal with it, such as getting counselling rather than just bottling things up.
- If you have IBS you will have to work on your emotional stress level, but I can assure you that you will reap the rewards with improved well-being and health.

Exercise

- An increase in exercise has shown to be beneficial for IBS sufferers. Exercise relieves stress, which can dramatically reduce the symptoms and triggers associated with IBS.
- Exercise 4–6 times weekly choosing a mixture of cardiovascular training (walking, running, swimming) and resistance training (lunges, weights, yoga).
- Daily leisurely walks for a minimum of 10–15 minutes are beneficial, not just for the body but for the mind and spirit as well.

Nutrition

- Food sensitivities have long been understood to contribute to IBS. Common well-known offenders are wheat and dairy. Anyone treating IBS patients should also consider the possible irritant effects of corn, coffee, tea and citrus fruits (in order of importance). Lactose (milk sugar) and gluten intolerance (oats, wheat, rye, barley) is common especially in Asians and people from eastern Mediterranean countries. See the section on food allergies and sensitivites for more information.
- Laxative abuse, drinking excess tea and coffee, eggs, spicy food intolerance, carbonated drinks and alcohol can affect gastric motility and function and can trigger IBS symptoms.
- Reduce fried and fatty foods, refined carbohydrates, excess sugar, unnatural synthetic foods including colouring, flavouring and food additives. One theory suggests that a diet high in sugar and refined carbohydrates is the leading cause of IBS as it slows down the normal contractions of the GI tract.
- Increased dietary fibre improves the colon structure and tone. Fibre is the main supplement that is recommended for IBS individuals as it works on both constipation and diarrhoea, as well as motility of the digestive system. Psyllium seed is more readily tolerated as a protective bowel bulking agent than wheat bran for those sensitive to wheat.

In a study of 80 IBS patients with constipation and/or diarrhoea symptoms, 82% generally improved following psyllium treatment compared to 53% on a placebo.[64] Bran as a fibre often worsens the complaint, as it is irritating to the bowel; however, increasing the intake of natural fibres other than cereals, especially non-allergen vegetables and fruits that include flaxseed fibre, apple pectins, guar gum and legumes, can be more beneficial to those who suffer from grain allergies and lack dietary fibre. As a general rule I prefer flaxseed fibre because it seems to be better tolerated and also contains beneficial essential fatty acids (EFA), and lignans, which are cancer protective.

- Eat more fibrous carbohydrates, like salads, celery, onions, garlic, asparagus, and beans and legumes, than starchy carbohydrates, like potatoes, corn, rice, pasta and breads. Eat more dietary fibre and natural antioxidants found in vegetables (leafy greens, yellow and red), cherries and berries.
- Use sugars sparingly, even those in honey, fruit juices, dried fruits and maple syrup. Avoid artificial sweetener or processed sugar.
- Eat six small meals daily to help balance blood sugar levels which may have a positive effect on digestion.
- Drink plenty of fresh water every day. Beneficial herb teas may include peppermint, liquorice and chamomile.

Supplements

Digestive enzymes Problems digesting fat, wheat, cellulose, protein and milk can often lead to diarrhoea. See your local health supplement retailer for a digestive enzyme formula.

Flaxseed oil (2 Tbsp daily) and **Colostrum** (4g daily) May help reduce leaky gut syndrome and inflammation associated with candida and possibly IBS.

Flaxseed fibre Reduces intestinal toxicity and pathogenic bacterial and yeast overgrowth. Improves bowel functioning and transit time and protects against haemorrhoids, bowel cancer and varicose veins. Softer more gentle types of fibre are more beneficial to the intestinal tract. Flaxseed fibre can soften and lubricate the stool in a non-irritating way and has a balancing effect for diarrhoea and constipation by taking up water from loose stools (relieving diarrhoea) and adding bulk to soften the stool when dry. Take 1–2 servings per day. Shake together 1 Tbsp of fibre in a glass of fruit juice or add 1 Tbsp on food (e.g. porridge). Liquid intake should always be increased with fibre products because of their water-absorbing nature and to prevent dry impacted constipation. Other supplementary fibres that are beneficial include psyllium and apple pectins. Fibre does not suit all IBS sufferers, so start with a low dose of Flax fibre or Pectin first.

Acidophilus and **Bifidus** Beneficial bacteria that help to keep the digestive system healthy. Take 1 billion of the Acidophilus and Bifidus species in capsule form daily on an empty stomach to repopulate your digestive system.

Vitamin B complex Helps reduce adrenal stimulation and involvement of nervous system and regenerates exhausted adrenals to help stress. As stress is a major trigger for IBS symptoms, nutrients including B vitamins assist with rebalancing the nervous system and therefore reducing this trigger. Take as directed.

Multi vitamin and **mineral formula** IBS individuals require basic vitamins and minerals due to improper digestion of food. Take a Multi vitamin and mineral formula or 1 tsp of **Spirulina** daily.

Nutrient Shake A favourite nutrient shake of mine for IBS includes **Spirulina** (1 tsp), **Flaxseed fibre** (2 tsp), **Acidophilus** and **Bifidus** (either from yoghurt or an opened capsule), **Flaxseed oil** (2 tsp), 1 cup of fruit juice, 1 opened **Vitamin E** oil capsule blended with papaya (contains natural enzymes to help digestion) or a banana and 5 ice cubes. Great for breakfast and as a snack, and loaded with nutrients. Yummy.

Herbs

Parasite-cleansing herbs Whether or not parasites have a pathological effect on the digestive system is debatable. A parasite is an organism that lives off a host, obtaining nourishment, but is of no benefit to the host. Eradicate parasites by taking two 3-week courses of **Cloves** (1800mg daily) combined with **Wormwood** (2000mg daily) and **Black Walnut** (2000mg daily).

Peppermint oil Enteric-coated capsules prohibit the absorption of antispasmodic menthol into the stomach, allowing it instead to be delivered directly to the large intestine. The menthol relaxes the muscles in the small intestine. Take 0.2ml (1 capsule) 3 times daily between meals.

Ginger Helps to expel gas (as does charcoal for those who prefer methods other than Ginger) and many IBS suffers find the inclusion of this herb helpful. Mix ¼–½ tsp of Ginger with milk powder (if tolerant) and honey and drink after meals or when bloating occurs.

Peppermint tea and **Fennel tea** Useful for relieving flatulence or bloating associated with indigestion. Crush 1 tsp of Fennel seeds and add to one cup of hot water. Cover the top of the cup with a saucer and steep seeds for 15 minutes. Remove saucer and sip tea.

Aloe Vera juice Heals the digestive tract, and encourages and improves digestion and assimilation of nutrients. Besides supplementary fibre and **Peppermint oil**, this is my favourite remedy for IBS. Many people vow they can control IBS with Aloe juice alone. Take 20ml–50ml with every meal.

Chamomile (2g–4g 3 times daily as a herbal tea infusion) and **Cramp Bark** (4ml–8ml of tincture 3 times daily)   Used to reduce the cramping pain associated with IBS.

Sedative herbs **Valerian** (1g–3g daily) and **Skullcap** (750mg 3–5 times daily) have both relaxing and antispasmodic properties, and therefore are indicated for IBS patients who also suffer from insomnia and/or anxiety.

Bach™ flower remedies

Bach™ flowers can be indicated for emotional states. Choose a maximum of 6–7 remedies and mix 2 drops of each (4 drops for **Rescue Remedy**). Mix your chosen remedies in a 25ml or 30ml treatment bottle (with a dropper lid). Choose the ones appropriate to you today. Take a minimum of 4 drops 4 times a day for 3 weeks.

Mimulus For fear (of the known).

Agrimony For putting on a brave face while feeling great anxiety inside.

Reflexology

Massage sole of foot especially in tender areas for 5 minutes every day. The effectiveness of this simple method of home treatment is often underestimated.

Kidney Stones

Accumulation of minerals that form into kidney stones can become lodged anywhere in the urinary tract. They are mostly formed in the kidneys, but can also be made in the urinary tract or bladder. Kidney stone attacks are twice as common in men than in women. Nearly 10% of all men will experience an attack during their lifetime, usually after the age of 30.

The are four main types of stones, around 75% of which are composed mainly of calcium (oxalate and phosphate). The other stones can be composed from crystal that doesn't contain calcium, struvite stones (containing magnesium ammonium phosphate), uric acid stones and cystine stones.

Calcium stones are the most common kidney stones. Tests show an increased concentration of calcium and oxalates (a salt of oxalic acid) in the urine and the blood as the they both precipitate out of solution. This can occur when a person has too much oxalate in their system, not enough water to keep oxalate in solution, or both.

Struvite stones form in the presence of bacteria and only in alkaline urine. Magnesium is naturally found in the urine and because the urine is alkaline the phosphate levels increase. A bacterial enzyme causes the urea in the urine to form into an ammonium ion and when the magnesium, ammonium and phosphate are combined they form these staghorned shaped stones.

Uric acid stones show elevated uric acid in the blood and urine and are associated with acidic conditions such as gout.

Cystine stones are rare. They contain the amino acid (protein) cysteine and are caused by a congenital defect.

In acute cases medical intervention may be necessary to remove the stones through surgery or use of sound waves.

Causes
- A diet high in sugar or refined carbohydrate and low in fibre.
- High intake of oxalates, phosphates, alcohol, animal protein and fat.
- Excessive intake of calcium and vitamin D-fortified milk products, coupled with low magnesium levels, can lead to kidney stones. It's the magnesium-calcium balance that is the main cause, not the intake of calcium alone.
- Dehydration is a factor in kidney stone production. In fact during Ramadan (a Muslim religious fasting tradition) some Muslims in hot countries experience kidney stone problems as they become dehydrated due to a lack of daytime fluids and constant perspiration. Causes of dehydration include lack of fluid intake, use of diuretics, overheating, exercise and overuse of hot, dry saunas.
- Excessive use of antacids.
- Chronic diseases, such as hyperparathyroidism, bowel disease, calcium excretion defects, sarcoidosis, obesity and Cushing's syndrome.
- Urinary tract infections can cause struvite stones from the bacteria found in the urine.
- Cystinuria, or increased levels of the amino acid cysteine in the urine.
- Elevated concentration of urine.
- A familial history normally increases the risk.

Signs and symptoms
- Kidney stones may not cause any symptoms until the stone is dislodged.
- If a 1mm–5mm stone is caught in the ureters (the tubes that run from the kidney to the bladder) leading to an obstruction in the flow of urine, excruciating pain is experienced in the lower back region. Sometimes the pain is felt in the lower abdomen, bladder area, perineum (space between anus and penis or vagina) and the scrotum.
- Other symptoms include vomiting, nausea and abdominal bloating.
- In the presence of urinary infection, lower abdominal pain, cold clammy skin, chills and fever, and increased desire to pass urine may be experienced.

Naturopathic recommendations

Lifestyle hints
- Avoid antacids containing aluminium.
- Lose excess weight if necessary.

Kidney Stones

- For struvite stones, eliminate infection. See the section on cystitis.
- For urea stones, avoid purine rich foods including organ meats, meat, shellfish, sardines, mackerel, anchovies and yeast. Eat less poultry, dried legumes, fish, mushrooms and asparagus.
- For cystine stones, avoid excessive soy, wheat, dairy products, fish, meat, beans, mushrooms and nuts.

Nutrition

- Vegetarian diets decrease the risk and prevent the formation of kidney stones. Fibre is essential to the diet. Switch from white bread to whole wheat bread as this lowers calcium levels in the urine.
- Drink pure, fresh water to keep the urine from getting too concentrated and the body from becoming dehydrated. Drink at least 2 litres of water, herb teas and aloe vera juice daily. Drink 200ml–300ml of marshmallow tea daily. It will help strengthen the bladder, soothe the bladder and kidneys, and expel kidney stones.
- Eat garlic, parsley, watercress, celery, cucumbers and papaya. Also include barley, bran, corn, soy, oats, brown rice, millet, potato, banana and avocado because they have high magnesium:calcium ratios. Eat seeds, sprouts and green leafy vegetables. Increase fresh fruits and vegetable intake to lower the incidence of stone formation.
- Limit the intake of carbonated drinks and dairy products (except those that are soured such as yogurt, buttermilk and cottage cheese). Goat's milk is acceptable.
- Diets should be low in protein, obtaining protein from vegetable sources. Protein is broken down by the liver and kidneys. High-protein diets cause the body to lose calcium and when this is excreted it passes through the kidneys and can cause painful kidney stones. Accumulation of protein can result in uraemia, which is the toxic build-up of protein waste (such as urea) in the bloodstream.

Avoid

- Phosphates that are found in abundance in meat, bread, cereals and pasta. These can form into phosphate crystals, leading to kidney stones.
- Oxalates are found in spinach, beet tops, rhubarb, silver beet, Swiss chard, black tea, cocoa and chocolate. Excess oxalic acid may lead to kidney stones. Carbonated soft drinks can lead to calcium leaching or imbalance. Avoid these types of beverages as well.
- Sugar increases calcium oxalate excretion and aggravates those with recurrent kidney stone problems. Reduce simple sugars and refined carbohydrates.
- Salt and potassium chloride (salt substitute). Use moderate amounts of sea salt or Celtic sea salt.

Supplements

Vitamin B6 (250mg daily with a **Vitamin B complex** formula) and **Magnesium oxide** or **magnesium citrate** (300mg daily)   Help to stop the stones forming, but only if you stop drinking tea. Magnesium increases the solubility of calcium oxalate crystals, and supplemental Magnesium has been shown to effectively prevent recurrences of kidney stones. Reduce Vitamin B6 to 25mg–50mg as a maintenance dose.

Calcium   Increasing Calcium and **Citrate** (citric acid) intake reduces oxalate absorption and increases oxalate urinary excretion. Take 300mg of Calcium Citrate to reduce stone formation.

Herbs

Professor Hulda Clark (M.A., Ph.D. Physiology), based at the Century Nutrition Clinic in Mexico, one of my favourite natural therapists, recommends the following herbs combined together to be used as a kidney stone dissolver.

> *How to prepare herbs for dissolving kidney stones*
>
> **Gravel Root, Marshmallow** and dried **Hydrangea Root**   Soak ¼ cup of each of the herbs in 10 cups of water for 4 hours (in a bucket), then bring the mixture to a boil and simmer for 30 minutes. Strain then cool and store the liquid. When cool drink ¼ cup. Throw away after 4 days.
> **Parsley**   Boil 4 bunches of rinsed, organic parsley in 750ml of water and then strain, store and cool liquid. When cool drink ¼ cup. Throw away after 4 days. Each morning thereafter mix ¾ cup of Root mixture and ½ cup of Parsley water with 2 Tbsp of **Black Cherry** concentrate, 20 drops of **Goldenrod** tincture and 1 Tbsp of **Glycerin**. Drink this mixture in 4 divided doses throughout the day. It will give you a stomachache if you drink it all at once. Complete this programme a total of 3 times in sucession. Take **Ginger**, **Bearberry** (Uva Ursi), **Vitamin B6**, a **Vitamin B complex** and **Magnesium** at the same time.

Ginger   Reduces inflammation, bloating, digestion and congestion, and increases circulation. Take 1g–1.5g daily with food over several months.

Bearberry (Uva Ursi)   Has a marked antiseptic and astringent effect on the membranes of the urinary system, soothing, toning and strengthening them. Take 250mg–500mg of powdered solid extract (10% arbutin) daily or 1.5g–4g of dried leaves as a tea.

Leaky Gut Syndrome

This condition is more common than you think. Sometimes the symptoms are so unobtrusive it may go undetected until it leads to chronic illnesses. Often these illnesses become the main focus of treatment and leaky gut syndrome may not be diagnosed or linked to these conditions. The lining of the intestine leaks like a sieve as it is more permeable (has larger spaces or holes) than normal. The tight junctions of the cells become destroyed in some cases, and gaps appear. This allows microbes, toxins, partially digested foods and waste material entry into the bloodstream, into which they would not normally cross. The immune system recognises these substances as harmful and creates antibody soldiers to mount an immune response, leading to a list of possible inflammatory conditions. Leaky gut syndrome puts stress on the liver as well.

Causes

- Inflammation of the intestine.
- Damaged gut lining or mucosa from alcohol, drugs, antibiotics, microbial infections, gastritis, smoking, stress and possible familial tendency.
- Immune hypersensitivity.
- Junk food.

Signs and symptoms

- Fibromyalgia, psoriasis, rheumatoid arthritis or sore joints and muscles.
- Lupus and chronic fatigue syndrome.
- Bloating, gas, abdominal pain, food sensitivities and allergies.
- Mineral deficiencies.
- Diarrhoea alternating with constipation and cramps, leading to irritable bowel syndrome.
- Fatigue, irritability, poor concentration and brain fog.

- Candida.
- Mouth ulcers, anal fissure, malnutrition due to poor absorption.
- Allergies.
- Inflammatory digestive conditions. This results in malabsorption of nutrients in food, leading to vitamin and mineral deficiencies, anaemia and thin bones (osteoporosis).

Naturopathic recommendations

Nutrition

- People with compromised digestive systems have found relief from eliminating certain foods from their diet. Studies show that removing certain common foods, such as dairy, wheat, corn, yeast, eggs, pork, chicken, lamb, shellfish and beef, can bring blessed relief from pain and inflammation, while their return can cause a flare-up. The improvement that follows an elimination diet appears to be long-lasting. To try an elimination diet, see a qualified naturopath.
- Alcohol, painkillers (e.g. aspirin) and non-steroidal, anti inflammatory drugs increase the permeability of the gut, leading to leaky gut syndrome. Saturated animal fats, red meat, dairy products and coffee increase the inflammatory response by stimulating the production of inflammatory prostaglandins and leukotrienes. Eliminate nightshade foods (e.g. potatoes, tomatoes, peppers and eggplant) to help relieve muscle pain. The majority of cases can benefit from a diet that eliminates dairy and all grains except rice, all refined carbohydrates, MSG, soda drinks, artificial foods, and sugars and processed foods.
- Eat more cold-water fish such as salmon, trout, mackerel, sardines, swordfish, shark, cod and halibut as an alternative way of obtaining anti-inflammatory essential fatty acids (EFA). These fish contain high concentrations of omega 3 fatty acids which have also been documented as inhibiting the inflammatory or allergic response. If fish is either unpalatable or not readily available in certain inland areas, supplementation of 9g–12g daily with fish oil capsules is an alternative.
- Drink 8 glasses daily of chamomile, lemon balm, St John's Wort, verbena and other herb teas, and fresh water.
- Add flax oil to salads and vegetables as a salad dressing. For example, you can mix 1 Tbsp with lemon juice, salt and pepper and toss with salad.

Supplements

Evening Primrose oil (3000mg daily) and **Flaxseed oil** (2 Tbsp daily) or **Fish oil** (3000mg daily)   May help reduce leaky gut syndrome and inflammation. Flax oil contains EFA components of membranes that surround each cell. Lack of EFA causes cells to leak. Incompletely digested food molecules can be inappropriately absorbed into the systemic circulation. This can lead to various diseases and the development of food allergies.
Colostrum   Helps to heal the leaky gut and destroy microbes that can colonise the gut causing infections and releasing toxins into the blood stream, leading to inflammatory responses. Take 4g daily.
Other beneficial supplements include **Glutamine** (3g daily), **Glucosamine** (1500mg daily) and **Chondroitin** (1200mg daily) to help heal the leaky barrier of the gut; and a Multi vitamin and mineral formula that contains **Zinc** (15mg–45mg daily), **Vitamin A** (5000IU–8000IU daily), **Vitamin E** (200IU–400IU daily) and **Folic acid** (200mcg–400mcg daily) to heal cell membranes in the stomach wall. **Aloe Vera** (20ml 3 times daily), and **Acidophilus** and **Bifidus** (1 billion daily) are also complementary nutrients to aid digestion and heal the gut lining.

Herbs

Fenugreek Tea or tincture helps to tone the digestive system, soothe and coat the digestive tract, and relieve gas and bloating. Test to see if you can stomach this and make the tea very weak at first. Add ½ tsp of crushed Fenugreek to hot water, cover with a saucer and let it sit for 10 minutes. Add honey and drink before or after meals.

Slippery Elm Mix 1 tsp in a glass of water and drink quickly, to heal inflamed gastric membranes. This should be taken separately from the other herbs.

Marshmallow Works in a similar way to Slippery Elm. Marshmallow has a demulcent (protective) action and is rich in mucilage, soothing and protecting irritated or inflamed internal tissue. It also binds and eliminates toxins, allowing the body to cleanse itself. Take 1.5g before meals daily.

Chamomile Helps recovery from inflammatory processes in the stomach and mucous membranes. Take 2g–4g 3 times daily in a herbal tea infusion.

Liquorice Soothes and coats the lining of the stomach reducing inflammation, works on adrenals and is excellent for healing the digestive system. Take 1g–5g daily. Do not take this without naturopathic supervision if you have hypertension or extreme water retention. Other helpful herbs include **Wild Yam**, **Lemon Balm**, **St John's Wort** and **Verbena**. These herbs are wonderful for inflammation, nervousness, anxiety and mild depression that can also be linked to leaky gut syndrome.

Schuessler tissue salts

Homeopathically prepared minerals. Take 1 tablet every 30 minutes for 5 days to help reduce symptoms rapidly, then take at least 4 tablets daily to enhance healing of the gut lining. Talk to the health store or pharmacy stockist as you may find some of these tissue salts in one combined formula.

Nat phos (Sodium phosphate) Acts as a digestive buffer and removes metabolic wastes.

Calc phos (Calcium phosphate) and **Ferr phos** (Phosphate of Iron) For pain and inflammation

Mag phos (Magnesium phosphate) Helps rebuild the intestinal membrane and relieves cramping pains in the abdomen, bloating and gas.

Silica and **Calc fluor** (Calcium fluoride) Normalise tissue for cell integrity.

Lymphoedema

Lymphoedema is a swelling of the limb(s) caused by a blockage of lymph flow through the lymphatic system. The lymph system, or lymphatics as it's commonly called, may be perceived as a poor cousin to the blood and circulatory system. Most people are unaware that it even exists, yet it is no less important.

Impurities within the body are processed as waste matter from cells transported via lymph vessels to lymph nodes, and then released into the bloodstream to be excreted. The lymph system plays a vital role in waste elimination, as well as fluid distribution, immune function and metabolic regulation. Loss of proper lymphatic function can cause waste accumulation and fluid stagnation in the tissues, water retention, swollen lymph glands or nodes, and fibrocystic breasts.

Causes

- Lymphatic obstruction from microbial infection or parasitic blockages.
- Swollen glands seen in the neck, armpit or groin.

- Lymphangitis and cellulitis (inflammation of skin tissues due to bacterial infection).
- Tonsillitis, appendicitis and fibrocystic breast disease.
- Malignant disease.
- Lymphatic surgery.
- Abnormalities of lymphatic system (rare).
- Minor lymphatic obstruction may be caused by hormonal fluctuations resulting in swollen breasts, bloating in the stomach and minor weight gain.

Signs and symptoms
- The affected area is swollen and initially there is pitting (the skin becomes depressed when pressure is applied).
- In chronic lymphoedema the limb becomes hard and non-pitting, and the underlying tissue becomes thickened.
- Localised lymphoedema occurs transiently with any skin infection, causing minor or significant swelling of the lymph nodes and affected lymphatic channels. The skin may become hot, tender or swollen with red streaks near the enlarged lymph nodes.

Naturopathic recommendations

Lifestyle hints
- Wet and dry saunas promote perspiration and sweating, increasing circulation through the lymph and blood vessels, which assists elimination of toxins through the skin. Drink plenty of water to replace lost fluids.
- Baths and showers, lymphatic massage, reflexology, sports massage and deep tissue massage facilitate the removal of toxins from the skin and muscles. Self-massage before you shower, by gently scrubbing your body all over with a dry flannel. At the end of your warm shower have a blast of cold water to stimulate your body and the removal of toxins. A handful of Epsom salts (magnesium) or rock salt added to your bath for the last 15 minutes can aid removal of toxins and relax fatigued muscles.
- Lymphatic massage is one of my favourite types of massage because after the lymph blockages are cleared the massage normally ends with a gentle rolling/rocking motion of the entire body that sends you into a blissful state of peace. Lymphatic massage is a technique which includes a gentle clearing of lymphatic node areas and a pumping motion of the body to clear fluid build-up through the tissues. One of the best ways to promote circulation and support lymphatic flow is to stimulate the body through massage. See a naturopath to clear lymphatic blockages using this method. They will also show you how to maintain clear lymph flow through simple self-massage techniques that you can use 2–3 times daily. To give you a basic idea of how it is done, the lymph glands, stomach and chest area are massaged in a gentle pumping action followed by the lymph node areas found under the arms, neck, behind the knees and the groin. After these areas have been gently pumped by the therapist's hands, the surface of the skin is massaged to encourage lymph flow and the body is rocked side to side in a very slight pumping, rocking motion. This treatment is a major priority for lymphoedema sufferers and must be practised by qualified health professionals who are aware of the contraindications.

Exercise
- All types of exercise can improve both blood and lymphatic circulation because the motion helps to mechanically move lymph fluid through the lymph vessels.

Lymphoedema

- Bounce on a trampoline to improve lymphatic flow. This movement is similar to exercise and is especially recommended for the convalescent or infirm. If an individual is too weak to bounce on a trampoline, someone else can gently bounce on it at the same time to enhance the lymph flow.

Nutrition

- Reduce red meat intake, chicken and eggs (unless organic), sugar and refined carbohydrates.
- Avoid greasy, fatty foods, fried foods, saturated fats from animal products, dairy products, vinegar, pickles and alcohol. Also eliminate heavily processed meats (red or white meat, fish or poultry), carbonated drinks, coffee and black tea, artificial flavouring, colouring and preservatives.
- Eat fresh fruit and vegetables, lean white meat (especially fish or organic chicken).
- Drink plenty of fresh water, herb teas and diluted vegetable juices. Lymphatic cleansing herbs, such as Clivers (also known as Cleavers) and Chickweed, can be juiced and added to vegetable and fruit juices (e.g. apple, carrot and beetroot).

Supplements

Bioflavonoids and **Quercetin**   Reduce blood vessel fragility, in turn reducing excess flow of fluid into the lymph system. Take 450mg of mixed Bioflavonoids or Quercetin daily.

Herbs

Lymphatic cleansing herbs   The lymphatic system often goes unnoticed but is an essential factor in detoxification, immunity and for removal of fluid from tissues.

Parasite-cleansing herbs   Parasites can cause obstruction in the lymphatics system. Use a combination of anti-parasitic herbs first to eliminate parasites and their inflammatory waste products. Take two 3-week courses of **Cloves** (1800mg daily) combined with **Wormwood** (2000mg daily) and **Black Walnut** (2000mg daily).

Sweet Clover   Used to reduce congestion or pitting because it improves lymph flow by breaking down accumulated protein associated with lymphatic oedema. Take 10ml daily of Sweet Clover (1:2 extract) in divided doses throughout the day.

Cleavers   Helps the lymphatic system clear congestion and accumulated fluids. Take 2g–4g daily.

Horse Chestnut extract   Improves venous return and thereby reduces lymphatic congestion. Clinical studies show **Aescin** (standardised Horse Chestnut extract) has positive strengthening effects on damaged connective tissue and the reduction of excess fluid pooling in the legs.[65,66,67] Take 10mg–20mg of Aescin 3 times daily.

Pokeroot   This herb is especially recommended for congestion of watery fluid and glandular tissues, specifically when the enlarged lymph node or organ is firm and hard, and is beneficial for mastitis, breast lumps and lymphatic engorgement. Caution: large doses are emetic, causing vomiting. See your herbalist or naturopath for prescription and dose.

Calendula   Enhances circulatory and lymphatic flow assisting removal of waste from tissues, thereby reducing the risk of many infectious, inflammatory, cystic and glandular pathologies. Take 1ml–4ml of tincture daily.

Echinacea   Has long been used for infections and as a detoxifying herb to reduce disease-producing waste material in the system. Take 1200mg daily.

Self Heal   This herb has wonderful lymphatic properties which assist with conditions such as lymphadenopathies and similar swellings, glandular fever, mumps and mastitis. Take 2g 3 times daily.

Schuessler tissue salts

Homeopathically prepared minerals. Take 1 tablet every 30 minutes for 5 days to help reduce symptoms rapidly, then take at least 4 tablets of each mineral for 3–6 months. Talk to the health store or pharmacy stockist as you may find some of these tissue salts in one combined formula.

Kali mur (Potassium chloride)   For sluggish conditions and enlarged glands.
Nat mur (Sodium chloride)   A fluid distributor.
Nat sulph (Sodium sulphate)   A fluid eliminator.

Memory Problems

At some stage in life we will all feel that we suffer from memory problems. Educational videos and nutritional tonics to help enhance memory and brain function are popular with the baby boomers, who are looking to enhance their prompt memory recall, cognition (the faculty of apprehension, awareness, comprehension, perception, reasoning and understanding) and to deter fatty brain degeneration due to age-related diseases.

Causes

- Poor blood flow to the brain.
- Lack of dietary vitamins, minerals, antioxidants, omega 3 (docosahexaenoic acid, DHA, and eicosapentaenoic acid, EPA) and phosphatidylserine (PS).
- Toxin exposure from drugs, carbon monoxides and heavy metals.
- Candida.
- Menopause.
- Head trauma or brain dysfunction.
- Dementia.
- Alzheimer's disease.
- Hypothyroidism and hypoparathyroidism.
- Pellagra, a vitamin B3 deficiency.
- Alcoholism.
- Huntington's chorea and multiple sclerosis.
- Stress.
- Dehydration.

Signs and symptoms

- Brain fog
- Forgetting where you put an item such as car keys
- Confusion and forgetfulness
- Poor recall
- Poor short-term memory
- Poor cognition and comprehension associated with poor memory.

Naturopathic recommendations

Lifestyle hints

Have you ever thought about what makes up your brain? If your brain became deficient in its vital elements, how would that eventually affect your brain function? This happens with other diseases like arthritis, for example, where joint cartilage nutrients become deficient causing osteoarthritis.

The brain is about 60% fat. Brain neurons that transmit information and signals are rich in PS and polyunsaturated fatty acids (PUFAs) especially DHA and arachidonic acid (AA) from fish.

Scientific evidence links PUFA deficiency to poor memory, attention deficit disorder (ADD) and hyperactivity disorders, dyslexia, senile dementia, Alzheimer's disease, clinical depression, bipolar disorder and even schizophrenia. There are two major reasons for a deficiency in PUFAs. First, the reduction in dietary intake of shellfish, fish, organ meats and wild game supplying PUFAs, and second, problems converting linoleic acid (LA) and alpha-linolenic acid (LNA) into brain fats. Direct intake of AA and DHA into the brain tissue is 10 times greater than dietary intake of LA and LNA (e.g. from flax oil)

- Brain exercises, such as crossword puzzles, bingo, reading to keep up vocabulary, studying, memory videos (learned techniques) and recall memory games are all fun exercises to keep your brain active.
- If you're getting frustrated with forgetting, relax and let your intuition take over.
- Avoid smoking as it reduces blood flow to the brain by constricting blood vessels and increasing toxicity within the body.

Exercise

- Exercise 4 times weekly, e.g. power-walking, jogging, swimming, dancing or going to the gym.
- If you are not mobile bounce on a trampoline and seek assistance if needed.
- Exercise increases circulation to the brain.

Nutrition

- Enjoy a bitter aperitif, such as vermouth or soda, lime and bitters, before dinner to encourage digestive juices. Alternatively take 50ml of aloe vera juice with every meal to increase absorption and digestion of nutrients from food.
- Do not cook in or with aluminium utensils, foils or pots and pans, as aluminium is linked with Alzheimer's.
- Include ginger in your diet to increase the circulation of nutrients around the body.
- Eat fish at least 3–4 times weekly as it is rich in omega 3 oil. Good sources include tuna, salmon, sardines, and other types of oily deep-sea fish.
- Drink plenty of fresh water, herb teas and diluted vegetable juices. Dehydration is known to cause poor memory. Avoid diuretics, antihistamines, tea, caffeine, coffee and alcohol.
- Eat 3 meals daily and include two healthy snack meals in between.

Supplements

Antioxidant formulas   Reduce the free radical damage to brain fats and nerves, and encourage the body to make antioxidant enzymes which mop up thousands of free radicals. Antioxidants include ProenOthera® from Evening Primrose Seed Husk, Green tea, Grape Seed, Pine Bark, Beta Carotene, Vitamins E, A and C, amino acids Methionine and Cysteine, oligomeric proanthocyanidins, Flavonoids and adjunctive minerals (Zinc, Selenium, Manganese). Take a complex antioxidant as directed.

Phosphatidylserine (PS)   Derived from **Lecithin**, PS is a vital fatty lipid found in abundance in the brain and is important for brain functioning, nerve cell health and other neurological functions. One of the most extensively researched brain nutrients, PS is shown to reduce stress hormone levels and increase brain waves in healthy young men.[68] It also showed consistent memory in PS-supplemented elderly women and a marked improvement

in PS-supplemented senile dementia patients.[69,70,71] PS dramatically improves cognitive functioning in older adults. Take 150mg daily.
Vitamin E Vitamin E is fat-soluble and therefore acts in cell membranes and other fat-containing tissues. Functioning as an antioxidant, it protects other fat-soluble vitamins and nutrients, and strengthens cell membranes. Vitamin E is important especially for the elderly as they eat and absorb fewer fat-protecting antioxidants. In the elderly the fats in the brain tend to oxidise, leading to reduced cognition and increased risk of dementia. Take 400IU daily.
Fish oil Provides DHA and EPA. DHA is one of the major building blocks for the brain, nervous system and eyes, and is essential for their development. It is most abundant in the grey matter of the brain (25%) and the retina of the eye. The brain nerves need high concentrations of DHA to send messages. DHA enhances memory and helps concentration. Take 3g daily.
Evening Primrose oil Provides GLA (gamma-linolenic acid), vital for brain and eye function. Supplementation is essential due to decreased dietary sources in the average western diet. GLA is important for normal transmission of messages along nerves and for the development of memory. Take 3g daily.
Multi vitamin and **mineral formula** Vitamins and minerals encourage the formation of antioxidants and also play a role in brain function. For instance, Vitamin B3 is used to increase blood flow and circulation, lower harmful blood lipids, namely cholesterol, triglycerides, and lipoproteins and to raise HDL (good cholesterol). Vitamin B5 is a key brain vitamin used in the manufacture of red blood cells, hormones, and acetylcholine. Acetylcholine is a neurotransmitter responsible for carrying signals between nerve cells in the brain. Folic acid and Vitamin B12 deficiency results in impaired nerve function that can cause impaired mental function. Vitamin B12 and Folic acid deficiency is common in the elderly and may be a contributing factor in depression. Left untreated, these deficiencies may lead to impaired neurological and cognitive function. Take a Multi vitamin and mineral formula as directed.
DMAE (2-dimethylaminoethanol) An acetylcholine precursor. Studies indicate that DMAE can reduce lipofuscin (cellular garbage) in brain cells, and is thought to increase levels of the brain neurotransmitter acetylcholine.[72] In general, DMAE is associated with mental focus, memory, and mood enhancement.[73,74,75,76] DMAE is non-toxic and there have been no reported side effects with doses of less than 1600mg daily.
Tyrosine A nonessential amino acid, Tyrosine is a protein building block that is important to the structure of almost all proteins in the body. It is also a precursor of several neurotransmitters including epinephrine, norepinephrine, dopamine, and L-dopamine. Studies indicate that Tyrosine, along with other amino acids, is beneficial for people affected by dementia, including Alzheimer's disease.[77,78,79] Take 50mg daily.

Herbs
Heavy metal toxin build-up Try gentle herbal body cleanses with **St Mary's Thistle**, **Dandelion Root**, **Red Clover** and fibre supplements that include **Vitamin C** and **Pectin** (from apples) to chelate or bind to toxins to help excrete them from the body. See page 131 for Detoxing recommendations.
Ginkgo The most popular herb for memory, as it increases circulation to the brain, increases brain function, normalises acetylcholine brain receptors and increases brain transmissions. Take 4g–8g of whole leaf or 24mg–30mg of standardised extract of Ginkgo flavone glycosides daily. Avoid with the prescribed medication warfarin, as Ginkgo in large amounts may magnify the drug's blood-thinning effect.
Rosemary Stimulates circulation and memory. Take 50mg 2 times daily or add 2 drops of essential Rosemary oil to hot water and inhale.

Bacopa   A traditional Indian Ayurvedic herb, well known for stimulating memory. Take 2g–3g daily.

Gotu Kola   Has been an important herb in the medicinal systems of Asia for centuries. In Sri Lanka it was purported to prolong life, increase energy, and boost mental processes. Recent studies have shown that Gotu Kola has memory enhancing properties. Gotu Kola is also used to keep veins strong, and reduce symptoms of connective tissue diseases. Take 30mg of Gotu Kola extract (Triterpenes) 3 times daily.

Senile dementia and Alzheimer's disease

Fish oil, Vitamin E and **Evening Primrose oil**   Reports suggest that deficiencies in GLA and DHA could be a key factor in aging.[80,81,82] Reduced levels of PUFAs in blood have been recorded from Alzheimer's and senile dementia patients. DHA is especially used for brain signals and depletion results in reduced cognition. Higher levels of fish consumption are also correlated to a lower incidence of dementia. Excessive oxidation of PUFAs in neural cell membranes may also cause dementia. Studies show that higher blood levels of antioxidants, such as Vitamin E, improve cognition: 633 Americans 65+ were observed; 91 of them in a 4.3-year follow-up developed Alzheimer's. None of the 50 persons supplementing with Vitamin E were among the 91 that developed Alzheimer's.[83] Prevention and treatment for dementia may be enhanced by supplementation with antioxidants and PUFAs.

Menopause

In some parts of Asia a female is not considered a 'full woman' until she reaches menopause. Postmenopausal women are revered and deeply respected by all. Their wisdom, knowledge and passion are in high demand. Many herbs are taken to ensure that skin remains healthy and energy levels high. Asian women have a very high intake of soy products like tofu and tempeh, instead of high-fat foods and meat. It is well known that these women suffer fewer menopausal symptoms than women on Western diets.

Most women reach the peak of their reproductive abilities in their late 20s. After that, ovarian function declines gradually. As oestrogen production declines, many ovarian cycles become anovulatory (not producing or releasing eggs), and menstrual periods become erratic and shorter in length. Eventually ovulation and periods cease entirely; this normally occurs between the ages of 46 and 55 years and is called menopause. Menopause is considered to have occurred when a whole year has passed without menstruation. Some women feel this is a time when they can relax and enjoy a full life without the worries of contraception and the monthly use of tampons and pads. Although ovarian oestrogen production continues for a while after menopause, the ovaries finally become nonfunctional as endocrine organs.

Causes

- Menopause occurs when the ovaries stop producing oestrogen and progesterone, as in natural menopause, or from surgical removal of both ovaries, called surgical menopause.
- Surgical ovarian removal or damaged reproductive organs can bring on early menopause.
- Genetics, tubal ligation and stress can influence menopausal symptoms.
- Women who tend to be underweight and lack body fat (which normally has a beneficial effect on oestrogen balance) can experience menopausal symptoms too. Ovarian oestrogen production decreases dramatically at menopause, but does not stop completely. Additionally, another weaker kind of oestrogen (estrone) is produced in fat tissue.

Production of this form of oestrogen increases with age and increases with the amount of fat tissue. Some studies indicate that women with more fat tissue experience less severe menopausal symptoms.
- Smoking can exacerbate menopausal symptoms and is linked to early menopause.
- Stress often exacerbates menopausal symptoms.

Signs and symptoms
- Flushing is caused by oestrogen decline, resulting in small bursts (approximately every hour) of the luteinising hormone that cause the blood vessels near the skin to dilate. Although a hot flush can be an alien and irritating feeling, it's a natural occurrence in response to menopause and as many as three-quarters of all menopausal women experience some form of hot flushing. We don't know exactly why hot flushes start when oestrogen levels fall, nor do we know why some women have them and others don't. But we do know that they seem to be a part of the body's adjustment to lower oestrogen levels.
- Insomnia, headaches, poor memory, low libido and anxiety.
- When oestrogen starts to reduce, the reproductive organs and breasts may start to atrophy. The vagina may become dry, thin and lose muscle tone, and intercourse may become painful (particularly if infrequent) for some women. Vaginal infections may become increasingly common as vaginal mucus is reduced, changing the normal protective pH of the vagina.
- Breast size and firmness change, hair becomes thinner and the skin can lose its firmness, leading to wrinkles.
- Cessation of oestrogen release can also lead to irritability and other mood changes, gradual thinning of the skin, infertility, loss of bone mass, and slowly rising blood cholesterol levels and blood pressure.
- Interestingly, some recent studies suggest there is no link between menopause and depression. Menopausal women were not found to be more susceptible to depression than menstruating women.[84]
- Menopausal symptoms may last from 1–25 years. Some women may experience hot flushing well into their 70s and 80s.

Naturopathic recommendations

Lifestyle hints
Recently the media highlighted the increased health risks and dangers of Hormone Replacement Therapy (HRT) again. We already know that researchers reported an increased risk of breast cancer associated with taking HRT (oestrogen combined with progesterone) but this time the media also pointed out the increased risk of heart disease, stroke, dementia and blood clots in the lungs.[85]

It concerns me that supporters of HRT claim the risk is very small and they will continue to recommend HRT. Why play Russian roulette with your health — it's not worth it! Plenty of research dollars are being poured into safe alternatives to HRT, including herbal and nutrient formulas.
- Wear layers of clothing so that when you feel hot, you can peel the layers off to help you cool down. Natural fibres, such as cotton, tend to breathe a lot better than most synthetic materials.
- Learn how to relax by trying yoga, receiving a massage, or learning meditation or breathing techniques.

- Get plenty of restful sleep. Make sure the room is completely dark to help ensure sleep.
- Sexual intercourse helps to increase circulation and keep the vagina lubricated and toned. Use a water-based lubricant to avoid irritating the vaginal walls.

Exercise
- Exercise 4 times weekly, e.g. power-walking, jogging, swimming, dancing or going to the gym.
- If you are not mobile bounce on a trampoline and seek assistance if needed.

Nutrition
- Avoid caffeine (including coffee, cola drinks, chocolate, black and green tea), tobacco (smoking) and recreational drugs. Smoking is associated with the risk of osteoporosis, coronary heart disease and lung cancer.
- Do not use plastic containers or plastic food wrap to heat food in the microwave as plastics contain unwanted, potentially harmful oestrogens that can leach into the food and contribute to oestrogen overload. Use glass or porcelain instead.
- Eliminate excessive saturated animal fats and synthetic fats, such as margarine, and heated fats, such as vegetable shortenings. Use small amounts of butter or flaxseed oil.
- Reduce intake of sugary foods, refined carbohydrates and processed foods.
- Reduce alcohol intake and have at least 4 alcohol-free days a week.
- Be aware of food sensitivities. If a food doesn't agree with you, substitute it with another. For example, try substituting for milk with calcium fortified soy milk, and for wheat and gluten with gluten-free breads, pasta or rice. Avoid spicy foods that increase circulation and may trigger hot flushes.
- Eat more fresh (organic) vegetables and fruit, especially citrus fruits that supply vitamin C and bioflavonoids. Try 3 pieces of fruit and 2–4 cups of vegetables daily.
- To help increase omega 3 levels eat fish 3–4 times weekly including salmon, tuna and sardines.
- Eat small amounts of protein regularly at meals. Mix defatted or lean meats with grains (rice, chickpea, couscous) or beans to reduce meat. If you're iron deficient add liver to the diet or an iron supplement.
- Certified organic, natural sugar-free acidophilus yoghurt eaten daily (avoid if allergic) can be beneficial to help convert plant oestrogens into usable oestrogen and progesterone in your body. Eat dairy foods in moderation if you are not sensitive to them.
- Plant isoflavones from soy foods and plant oestrogens help keep endogenous oestrogen levels lower. Soya textured vegetable protein (TVP), a mince substitute, tempeh, soy flour and flakes, soya vegetarian sausages, tofu, soy milk (sugar-free), flaxseed (fresh), buckwheat, millet, parsley, fennel, celery, sesame seeds, sunflower seeds, legumes, mung beans, sprouts and sprouted beans are rich in plant oestrogens. As plant oestrogens are estimated to be hundreds of times weaker than the body-made oestrogen (oestradiol), they can bind onto oestrogen receptors, having a protective effect.
- Indole-3-carbinol and sulphoraphane are found in plants including broccoli, cauliflower, cabbage, Brussels sprouts and kale. Indoles activate detoxification enzymes in the intestinal tract, bind to chemical carcinogens, rendering them inactive, and improve oestrogen balance, reducing the risk of breast cancer. Indole-3-carbinol helps break down oestrogen into 'good' metabolites and leaves less of the 'bad' oestrogen metabolites.
- Eat 3 meals daily and include two healthy snack meals in between.
- Enjoy a bitter aperitif, such as vermouth or soda, lime and bitters, before dinner to encourage digestive juices. Alternatively take 50ml of aloe vera juice with every meal to increase absorption and digestion of nutrients from food. Most women over the age of 55 have reduced stomach acid, which reduces the digestion of tablets and certain foods

and minerals (calcium).
- Drink plenty (at least 1–2 litres) of fresh water, herb teas and diluted vegetable juices. Drink sage tea for hot flushes and night sweats. Add 1 tsp of sage leaves, fresh or dried, to a cup of boiling hot water. Cover cup with a saucer to lock in the oils of the herb and steep for 15 minutes. Drink 3 times daily.

Supplements

Vitamin B complex   A complex with B1, B2, B3, B5, B12 and Folic acid helps the adrenals adapt to hormonal changes. The body relies on oestrogen manufacture from fat cells and adrenal influence after menopause. B complex vitamins also assist liver detoxification of excessive and potentially harmful HRT oestrogen residue, and replace any deficiencies that may exacerbate menopausal symptoms. Take a B complex as directed.

Vitamin C (1200mg daily), **Bioflavonoids** (Hesperidin 900mg daily) and **Vitamin E** (400IU daily)   They may improve high blood pressure and vaginal atrophy and have a protective effect on cholesterol. Deficiencies have been linked to menopausal hot flushing. Take until symptoms improve.

DIM (Diindolylmethane) and **Rosemary (Rosmarinic acid)**   Have a protective effect on hormone-sensitive tissues against carcinogenesis (development of cancer). Take these compounds if you suffer from migraines, have come off HRT or have a family history of oestrogenic and breast cancers. Take 100mg of DIM 2 times daily and 50mg of Rosemary 2 times daily. See your practitioner for product details.

Calcium   Deficiencies of Calcium and low oestrogen levels may lead to thinning of the bones. Calcium is recommended for the treatment of osteoporosis and maintaining optimal bone health. Calcium hydroxyapatite and Calcium citrate are the two most absorbable forms of Calcium. Take a **combined formula** of Calcium, Magnesium, Zinc, Manganese and Boron for ultimate absorption and bone protection. Take 1500mg–3000mg of Calcium at night after a meal for better absorption.

Flaxseed oil (2 Tbsp daily) and **Flaxseed fibre** (1 tsp daily)   Contain Omega 3, 6 and 9 oils and lignans. These are said to provide essential fatty acids (EFA) important for preventing EFA deficiencies and menopausal symptoms. Lignans protect the body from oestrogen-dominant cancers. Grind Flaxseeds in a coffee grinder and sprinkle 1 tsp over your food (cereals or salads) every day.

Acidophilus and **Bifidus**   Assist the body's conversion of phyto-oestrogens which have beneficial effects on menopausal symptoms. Take 1 billion of the Acidophilus and Bifidus species in capsule form daily on an empty stomach to repopulate your digestive system.

Herbs

Give herbs time to work their beneficial effects.

Wild Yam, Soy, Red Clover, Dong Quai and **Kudzu**   Herbs that contain plant oestrogenic substances also known as isoflavones or phyto-oestrogens. They are also found in many other herbs and food sources (see above). Although their activity compared to oestrogen is only 1:400, phyto-oestrogens are capable of exerting oestrogenic effects and counteracting extreme oestrogen levels by binding onto oestrogen receptor sites found on cells.

With regard to menopause, phyto-oestrogens have some oestrogenic activity, causing an increase in oestrogen effect if oestrogen levels are low. Similarly if oestrogen levels are high, phyto-oestrogens bind to receptor sites, competing with oestrogen and decreasing oestrogen effects. For best results use a combination of phyto-oestrogenic herbs such as **Soy**, **Red Clover** and **Kudzu** mixed with **Black Cohosh**. This works far better for hot flushes and menopausal symptoms than using a single phyto-oestrogenic herb. Take up to 60mg of isolated plant isoflavones daily from a combination of isoflavone herbs or as professionally directed.

Wild Yam Take 2g–4g of dried root 3 times daily.
Soy Take 25mg–50mg of isolated plant isoflavones daily.
Red Clover Take 2g–4g daily.
Kudzu Traditional Chinese herbalists use Kudzu for menopausal symptoms including hypertension, headache, dizziness, heating in the body (hot flushes) and stiff or tight upper back and neck. Take 500mg 2 times daily.
Dong Quai Used in combination with other herbs, Dong Quai produces a reduction in the severity of hot flushes, insomnia, mood changes and vaginal dryness. It exerts an action on androgenic and oestrogenic receptors found on cells. Take 1g–2g daily.
Sage Decreases sweating and hot flushes. For best results combine with the herb **Passionflower** for night-time sweats and insomnia. Take 1.5g–2g daily.
Black Cohosh The natural health community chooses Black Cohosh as the specific or main herb for hot flushes. Black Cohosh may reduce hot flushes relating to menopause by acting on temperature regulation, rather than through its oestrogen-like effects as originally thought. As a woman in my thirties and a health professional, I for one look forward to new safe alternatives (not just HRT substitutes) to the many common conventional medications that carry unwanted side effects. Take 1g daily.
Motherwort May relieve heart palpitations, reduce nervous tension and act as a tonic for the heart. Take 2g–4g of dried herb daily.
Chaste Tree This herb may be beneficial for some women's menopausal symptoms as it has an effect on the luteinising hormone associated with hot flushes and may assist with irregular periods and PMT during perimenopause. Take 1g–2g daily.
Nerve-restoring herbs Take **Valerian** (1g–3g daily), **Kava** (1.5g–3g of dried root daily), **Passionflower** (4g–8g of dried herb daily), *Griffonia simplicifolia* (providing 150mg–300mg of 5-Hydroxy tryptophan), **Siberian Ginseng** (adrenals) (1g–4g daily) and **St John's Wort** (2g–5g of dried herb daily) for mild depression, insomnia, night sweats and anxiety. **Ginkgo Biloba** is an excellent herb to assist with memory or concentration problems. Take 4g–8g of whole leaf or 24mg–30mg of standardised extract of Ginkgo flavone glycosides daily. Avoid with the prescribed medication warfarin, as Ginkgo in large amounts may magnify the drug's blood-thinning effect.
Vaginal irritation and dryness Mix 10g of **Manuka honey** with 100g of aqueous cream obtained from the pharmacy and 400IU of **Vitamin E**. Avoid antihistamines, alcohol and diuretics as these tend to dry up mucous membranes and the walls of the vagina. Apply to vagina to help lubrication. For external use only.
Perimenopause The stage just before menopause. Women may experience hot flushes but still have their periods at irregular times throughout the years before menopause is complete. The herb **False Unicorn Root** is beneficial during these stages to balance hormones and sporadic menstrual periods. Take 500mg 2 times daily. Also see above for Chaste Tree.
Breast Cancer If you have cancer or a history of familial cancer (breast, colon or oestrogenic-sensitive cancers) it is recommended you see a naturopath before taking phyto-oestrogenic herbs to assess your oestrogen metabolism by means of a Great Smokies Diagnostic test. There are different ways that the body can metabolise oestrogens, including phyto-oestrogens. A blocking action may be beneficial for some individuals with cancer or cancer risk. However, in rare cases some men and women may metabolise phyto-oestrogens in a way that actually increases oestrogenic-sensitive growth, thus increasing the risk of cancer. See a health professional who uses Great Smokies Diagnostic Laboratories to test whether certain herbs and supplements are suitable for you.

Multiple Sclerosis

Multiple sclerosis (MS) is a chronic progressive inflammatory demyelinating disease of the central nervous system (CNS). Demyelination occurs when the protective sheath (myelin) around nerve fibres becomes damaged, preventing nerve transmission and revealing the sensitive nerve fibres underneath. The white brain matter, spinal cord and optic nerves eventually become destroyed and demyelinated patches (i.e. sclerosis, lesions or plaques) can occur.

Causes

- The cause of MS is unknown although it is suspected to be an autoimmune condition where the body's own immune system attacks the fatty nerve sheaths, exposing the nerves.
- Another theory is that the demyelination is caused by a viral infection.
- Other factors thought to exacerbate MS include food sensitivities (gluten and milk products), high intake of saturated animal fats, heredity, sinus infection and chemical poisoning.
- MS is more common in women aged 20–40 years and in those living in temperate climates.

Signs and symptoms

Four categories describe the course and progression of symptoms.

Benign: 20% of MS cases are benign. There are long asymptomatic periods with mild or completely remitting attacks.

Relapsing: 25% of MS cases are relapsing. Acute onset of transient symptoms is followed by partial or complete recovery as the myelin is replaced. Some demyelinated fibres regenerate causing the symptoms to disappear.

Relapsing progressive: 40% of MS cases are relapsing progressive. Slow deterioration in function is highlighted by exacerbations with modest recovery and significant residual impairment.

Chronic progressive: 15% of MS cases are chronic progressive. Deterioration of function is continuous over months to years with an increased risk from life-threatening complications. Scar tissue replaces myelin, leaving permanent scarring and therefore inhibited nerve transmission, causing permanent disability.

- Demyelinisation interrupts, inhibits or slows nerve transmission and conduction mainly in the brain and spinal column.
- Depending on the duration or location of the lesions, the manifesting signs and symptoms may include disturbances in the visual field, speech and swallowing, muscle strength, gait and coordination, balance, eye function, and position and vibratory sensation. Optic neuritis (i.e. visual clouding, loss of vision and pain on movement of the globe), diplopia or gaze paralysis may also occur.
- Paraesthesia symptoms include numbness, tingling, burning sensations or pressure on the face or involved extremities. Neck flexion may produce Lhermitte's sign and 80% of MS persons experience pain, e.g. from spasticity. Speech disturbance, fatigue, nystagmus (involuntary movement of the eye), vertigo, abnormal gait and sexual dysfunction are other common symptoms.
- Psychological manifestations include depression, euphoria, inattentiveness, apathy and loss of memory.
- Neurologic deficits may worsen as small increases in body temperature affect and block impulse conduction in demyelinated nerve fibres.

Naturopathic recommendations

Lifestyle hints
- Check for candida and food sensitivities with a naturopath.
- Avoid smoking as it reduces blood flow to the brain by constricting blood vessels and increasing toxicity within the body.

Nutrition
- Avoid a high intake of saturated fats (animal fats), deep fried foods and heated oils, trans fatty acids (margarine and lard), artificial sugars, processed foods and refined carbohydrates. Also eliminate coffee, tea, cola, alcohol, solvents, smoking and exposure to toxins.
- Gluten and dairy free diets are beneficial for some MS individuals. Test for food sensitivites (see page 164) and avoid if allergic.
- Do not cook in or with aluminium utensils, foils or pots and pans, as aluminium is linked with Alzheimer's disease, although this is not yet fully established.
- Enjoy a bitter aperitif, such as vermouth or soda, lime and bitters, before dinner to encourage digestive juices. Alternatively take 50ml of aloe vera juice with every meal to increase absorption and digestion of nutrients from food.
- Include ginger in your diet to increase the circulation of nutrients around the body.
- Eat fish at least 3–4 times weekly as it's rich in omega 3 oil. Good sources include tuna, sardines, and other types of oily, deep-sea fish.
- Drink plenty of fresh water, herb teas and diluted vegetable juices. Avoid diuretics, antihistamines, tea, caffeine, coffee and alcohol.
- Consume 3 meals daily and include two healthy snack meals in between. Add cherries, berries and red grape skins and seeds to improve antioxidant intake, which helps protect myelin sheaths from free radical (oxidising) damage. Eat fresh, organic produce.

Supplements
Vitamin B complex   The main vitamin and mineral deficiencies linked to MS are **Vitamins B12** and **D**, **Calcium** and **Magnesium**. Take a high potency Multi vitamin and mineral formula as directed and a combined Calcium, Vitamin D and Magnesium formula as directed.

5-Hydroxy tryptophan (5HTP)   Serotonin levels have been found to be deficient in those with MS. This can affect mood, appetite and motivation. Take 50mg of 5HTP 3 times daily, derived naturally fom the *Griffonia simplicifolia* plant.

Antioxidant formula, bioflavonoids and **anthocyanidins**   These reduce the free radical damage to brain fats and nerves, and encourage the body to make antioxidant enzymes which mop up thousands of free radicals. Antioxidants include ProenOthera® from Evening Primrose Seed Husk, Green tea, Grape Seed, Pine Bark, Beta Carotene, Vitamins E, A and C, amino acids Methionine and Cysteine, oligomeric proanthocyanidins, flavonoids and adjunctive minerals (Zinc, Selenium, Manganese). Take a complex antioxidant as directed.

The myelin nerve sheaths   The protective covering of the nerves is mainly composed of fats. Take Phosphatidylserine, Flaxseed oil, Fish oil and Evening Primrose oil, which assist with normal myelin sheath composition by improving myelination and reducing inflammation.

> **Phosphatidylserine (PS)**   Derived from **Lecithin**, PS is a vital fatty lipid found in abundance in the brain and is important for brain functioning, nerve cell health and other neurological functions. Take 150mg daily.
>
> **Vitamin E**   Vitamin E is fat-soluble and therefore acts in cell membranes and other fat-containing tissues. Functioning as an antioxidant, it protects other fat-soluble vitamins and nutrients, and strengthens cell membranes. Take 400IU daily.

Fish oil Provides DHA (Docosahexaenoic acid) and EPA (Eicosapentaenoic acid). DHA is one of the major building blocks for the brain, nervous system and eyes, and is essential for development. It is most abundant in the grey matter of the brain (25%) and the retina of the eye. The brain nerves need high concentrations of DHA to send messages. DHA enhances memory and helps concentration. Take 3g–6g daily.

Evening Primrose Oil Provides GLA (Gamma-linolenic acid), vital for brain and eye function. Supplementation is essential due to decreased dietary sources in the average western diet. GLA is important for normal transmission of messages along nerves. Take 3g–6g daily.

Herbs

Parasite-cleansing herbs Parasites can cause inflammation in the body and may be a factor relating to the trigger of MS. Use a combination of anti-parasitic herbs to eliminate parasites and their inflamatory waste products. Take two 3-week courses of **Cloves** (1800mg daily) combined with **Wormwood** (2000mg daily) and **Black Walnut** (2000mg daily) to help eradicate parasites.

Detox Complete a gentle detox herbal programme and a parasite-cleansing programme to balance the internal body organs and prepare for a healthy start. **Burdock** (2g–6g of dried root daily), **Cleavers** (2g–4g daily) and **Red Clover** (2g–4g daily) help cleanse the blood and clear the lymphatics. **Dandelion** (3g–5g of dried root daily) and **Milk Thistle** (9g–10g of seed daily) enhance bile flow and detoxify the liver. Fibre supplements mop up heavy metals and toxins. Take 1 tsp–2 tsp of **Flaxseed fibre** daily while detoxing or to help with constipation.

Olive Leaf extract (270mg 6 times daily) and **Echinacea** (1200mg daily) Help to purify the blood and eradicate viral infections.

Skullcap Relaxes nervous tension, helps soothe the nervous system and combines well with the herb Valerian. Take 750mg 3–5 times daily.

Valerian Has anti-anxiety effects. Take 1g–3g daily.

Nerve Pain

What a nerve! Nerve pain has the audacity to come and go at will, not to mention destroying the comfort of our lives and psyches. Whatever the cause, nerve pain is hard to ignore and can manifest itself in so many ways.

Causes

- Viral infections, e.g. shingles (herpes zoster), post herpetic neuralgia.
- Obstruction, inflammation or pinching of nerves.
- Trauma or damage to nerves.
- Deterioration of nerves associated with metabolic disorders and degenerative illness including diabetes, gout and leukaemia.
- Nutritional deficiencies of B complex vitamins, omega 3 and 6 essential fatty acids (EFA) and 5HTP (5-Hydroxy tryptophan).
- Toxicity from medications, chemicals, heavy metals and alcohol.

Signs and symptoms

- Pain
- Tingling and 'pins and needles'
- Pain with alternating numbness or loss of sensation

- Muscle weakness and fatigue
- Burning sensation
- Paralysis
- Swelling and redness
- Depression and anxiety.

Naturopathic recommendations

Lifestyle hints
- Ring a counselling service, or if appropriate, seek spiritual or health professional guidance or communicate with helpful friends or family. As the emotions are affected through anxiety and fear, counselling can help with the mental aspects of pain.
- Learn how to relax by trying yoga, receiving a massage, or learning meditation or breathing techniques.
- Get plenty of restful sleep. Make sure the room is completely dark to help ensure sleep.

Exercise
- Exercise 4 times weekly, e.g. power-walking, jogging, swimming, dancing or going to the gym.
- If you are not mobile bounce on a trampoline and seek assistance if needed.

Nutrition
- Avoid red meats and coffee (especially instant). These increase pain and inflammation. Alcohol, tobacco and recreational drugs should be avoided.
- Eat 6 small meals frequently throughout the day.
- Drink 1–2 litres of fresh water daily.
- Identify any possible food allergies and avoid to reduce nerve sensitivity, inflammation and pain. See page 164 for details.
- Ginger, berries, cherries and grapes (flavonoids). Turmeric and cayenne (capsaicin) are remarkable condiment herbs that inhibit pain pathways, reducing the sensation of pain and inflammation. Use liberally on food.

Supplements
Vitamin B complex   Deficiencies of B vitamins can lead to deterioration of nerves and even paralysis. Supplement with a high potency Vitamin B complex to cover any deficiencies. For example, burning feet respond well to **Vitamins B1** and **B5** and **Choline**. Take as directed.

Vitamin C   Reduces inflammation and is necessary for proper nerve transmission. Take 1500mg daily.

Calcium and **Magnesium**   Deficiencies of these lead to abnormal nerve response and muscle contraction. Deficiencies are also related to anxiety, muscle cramps and depression. Take 1500mg of Calcium at night after a meal for better absorption and 450mg–900mg of Magnesium daily.

5-Hydroxy tryptophan (5HTP)   A serotonin precursor made naturally by the body and also sourced from the plant *Griffonia simplicifolia*, 5HTP helps boost serotonin levels reducing the sensitivity to pain, aiding anxiety and insomnia. Take 150mg–300mg daily.

MSM (methyl sulphonyl methane)   This natural sulphur compound is helpful for relieving muscular pain. Take 2g daily.

Antioxidant formula, bioflavonoids and **anthocyanidins**   These reduce free radical damage to nerves, reducing the sensitivity of nerve pain, and aid healing to damaged nerves.

Antioxidants include ProenOthera® from Evening Primrose Seed Husk, Green tea, Grape Seed, Pine Bark, Beta Carotene, Vitamins E, A and C, amino acids Methionine and Cysteine, oligomeric proanthocyanidins, flavonoids and adjunctive minerals (Zinc, Selenium, Manganese). Take an antioxidant formula as directed.

Nerve damage The protective covering of the nerves is mainly composed of fats. If this becomes damaged the nerves are exposed, like stripping the plastic off a copper wire. Take Phosphatidylserine, Flaxseed oil, Fish oil and Evening Primrose oil, which assist with normal myelin sheath composition by improving myelination and reducing inflammation.

> **Phosphatidylserine (PS)** Derived from **Lecithin**, PS is a vital fatty lipid found in abundance in the brain and is important for brain functioning, nerve cell health and other neurological functions. Take 150mg daily.
>
> **Vitamin E** Vitamin E is fat-soluble and therefore acts in cell membranes and other fat-containing tissues. Functioning as an antioxidant, it protects other fat-soluble vitamins and nutrients, and strengthens cell membranes. Take 400IU daily.
>
> **Fish oil** and **Flaxseed oil** Provide Omega 3, DHA (Docosahexaenoic acid) and EPA (Eicosapentaenoic acid). Flax oil works in a similar way providing a blend of Omega 3 and 6 (EFA). These EFA reduce inflammation and help protect the nerve sheaths. Take 3g daily.

Herbs

Detox Complete a gentle detox herbal programme to balance the internal body organs and clear heavy metals and toxins that may be causing nerve pain and inflammation. **Burdock** (2g–6g of dried root daily), **Cleavers** (2g–4g daily) and **Red Clover** (2g–4g daily) help cleanse the blood and clear the lymphatics. **Dandelion** (3g–5g of dried root daily) and **Milk Thistle** (9g–10g of seed daily) enhance bile flow and detoxify the liver. Fibre supplements mop up heavy metals and toxins. Take 1 tsp–2 tsp of **Flaxseed fibre** daily.

St John's Wort Acts as a mild sedative, reducing pain, and is beneficial for mild depression, anxiety and nervousness associated with chronic pain. Take 2g–5g of dried herb or use topically (on the skin) as a tincture poultice, cream or oil on nerve pain sites.

Corydalis Has analgesic effects and relaxes smooth muscle contraction, especially in the abdominal region. Take 800mg–1g daily.

Cailfornian Poppy Has mild analgesic and sedative properties. It also exhibits a relaxing effect on the mind and potential mood elevating actions without addictive side effects. Take 900mg daily.

Jamaican Dogwood Used for neuralgia, migraines and insomnia due to its anti-inflammatory and sedative effects. Take 2g–4g of dried root bark up to 3 times daily.

Capsaicin Capsaicin, derived from **Cayenne**, desensitises nerves. Capsiacin cream is used for postherpetic pain from shingles, phantom limb pain, cluster headaches, neuropathies, osteoarthritis and pain from skin conditions including psoriasis and pruritus.[86,87] In one study patients suffering from postherpetic neuralgia found that a topical application of Capsaicin cream (0.025%v capsaicin) on painful areas was beneficial.[88]

Cloves The oil from this age-old spice is used by dentists to desensitise exposed nerves in the mouth during tooth extraction. Use the Clove oil externally by placing a few drops on a cotton ball and putting it on the area of pain in the mouth. Overuse of this oil may cause nausea, so use a small amount first.

Feverfew Reduces inflammatory processes which may exacerbate pain sensation. Feverfew must be taken every day to have an effect. Add 1–2 leaves to a sandwich or take 50mg–200mg daily.

Kava Has sedating and analgesic effects to aid nerve pain and associated anxiety symptoms. Take 1.5g–3g of dried root daily.

Other therapies

Fasting and detoxing are helpful to remove inflammatory response to toxins and food sensitvities. Try the Gall Bladder Flush Fast, see page 173.

Massage, acupuncture, osteopathy, craniopathy and **reflexology** are superb treatments on their own or in combination with herbs and supplements. They work on a physical and emotional level to help control pain, increase circulation, clear blockages and balance the body. See your health professional for details.

Castor oil packs have been known to help with pain when used in combination with dietary and herbal recommendations.

> *How to make a Castor oil pack*
> You will need: Castor oil (obtained from the chemist), a soft clean cotton cloth, plastic wrap, a plastic container to store the oil-laden cloth, and a hot water bottle. Directions: Soak the cloth in castor oil. Place the folded cloth over affected area. Cover the cloth completely with plastic wrap, both to avoid staining your clothes and to keep in the warmth. Place a towel over the plastic and put a hot water bottle on it. Leave it on overnight. Repeat this five nights in a row and then rest for two nights. Do this for three weeks.

Epsom salts baths or baths with **Valerian** or **Skullcap** extracts are helpful for aches and injuries.

Poultices

Herbs can be applied topically to soothe pain, reduce swelling and promote healing.

Cool or warm compresses Saturate a cloth in a strong herbal tea made from essential oils or dried herbs. See above herbs for details.

Poultices Combine warm, moist herbs, such as **Chamomile**, **White Willow**, **Peppermint**, **Skullcap**, **Meadowsweet** or **Valerian**, in a binder of powdered **Oatmeal**, **Slippery Elm** or **Flaxseed**, and apply to injury site.

Semi-poultices Use a cloth compress filled with ground herbs for poultice benefits without the mess. Try **St John's Wort** for nerve pain.

Osteoporosis

This condition causes a progressive loss of calcium from the bones producing a corresponding loss of bone mass. This leads to a weakening of bone matrix and collagenous fibres, leading to bone fragility, and fractures are therefore more likely to occur.

This condition is more common in postmenopausal women and generally worsens as people age.

Causes

- Lack of oestrogen results in a loss of bone mineralisation.
- Nutrient deficiencies, including calcium, magnesium, boron, manganese, silica, zinc, copper, vitamins A, C, D and K, prevent good bone formation and lead to a weaker bone structure.
- Aging, menopause, early menopause and postmenopause.
- Genetics; some people are more prone to osteoporosis than others due to family history.
- This condition affects approx 1 in 4 women but only 1 in 40 men.

- Those with a larger and denser bone mass are less likely to suffer as much. A lean, short-statured person with small bone structure has a higher risk.
- Inactivity can lead to weaker bones. Weight-bearing exercise stimulates an increase in bone density.
- Lack of hydrochloric acid (stomach acid juices).
- A very acidic diet (lots of meat and no fruit and vegetables), and a high intake of sugar, promotes bone loss as does a diet low in minerals and trace nutrients.
- A history of eating disorders can deplete important bone nutrients and cause low oestrogen levels, leading to reduced bone density.
- Excess caffeine, carbonated drinks, cola, excessive phosphate intake, alcohol and smoking all deplete bone density.
- Hormonal disorders, such as hyperthyroidism, Cushing's syndrome or adrenal deficiency and low oestrogen levels, can all affect bone density.
- Steroid medication can also lower bone density.

Signs and symptoms
- Bone mass reaches its peak at 30–35 years of age in women and then declines as they age. Hormonal factors (mainly reduced oestrogen in postmenopausal women) can increase the likelihood of osteoporosis. Because this process is gradual no signs or symptoms may be evident.
- Over time there can be a gradual loss of height due to vertebral body compressions in the spine. A forward stoop can develop due to rounding in the mid-spine.
- The most common symptom is sudden back pain in the middle to lower regions.
- Fractures in the upper femur, hipbone, and lower arm and wrist may occur with relatively minor trauma.
- Bone scans and X-rays may reveal fractures.

Naturopathic recommendations

Lifestyle hints
Preventative exercise
- Regular weight-bearing and weight-training exercise (4–5 times weekly) combined with walking or running can boost bone density.
- Women with osteoporosis should consult with a doctor to establish an exercise programme.

Nutrition
- Increase your intake of calcium by including more dried fruit, seeds and nuts, green leafy vegetables and fish in your diet. Increase boron-rich foods as boron reduces calcium excretion. Molasses, honey and rosehip tea are all good sources.
- Avoid fizzy drinks which are high in phosphorus and cause calcium depletion. If your diet is high in protein make sure you eat lots of fruit and vegetables to balance the acids in the protein. Keep sugar to a minimum. Avoid caffeine-containing drinks (coffee, cola and black tea) and carbonated drinks. Drink a range of herbal teas instead. Avoid alcohol and cigarettes.
- Reduce salt, refined carbohydrates and sugar intake.
- Cod liver oil is a good source of vitamins A and D.
- Kelp is rich in minerals to boost bone mineralisation.
- Eat foods containing phyto-oestrogens to boost oestrogen levels. These include lentils, soy foods, chickpeas, red clover tea and flaxseeds.

- Enjoy a bitter aperitif, such as vermouth or soda, lime and bitters, before dinner to encourage digestive juices. Alternatively take 50ml of aloe vera juice with every meal to increase absorption and digestion of nutrients from food.

Supplements

Hydrochloric acid or **digestive enzyme formulas**   Increase digestive juices and calcium absorption. Take as recommended.

Calcium Hydroxyapatite   This is a freeze-dried (cold processed) source of concentrated Calcium obtained from New Zealand. This special Calcium contains a 2:1 ratio of Calcium to Phosphorus. It also contains trace minerals, matrix proteins and glycosaminoglycans. Hydroxyapatite supplies Calcium in the form it occurs in the body. As such, it can be rapidly absorbed. Take 1500mg at night after a meal for better absorption.

In one study a group of postmenopausal women receiving Calcium Hydroxyapatite was compared with a control group (not receiving any minerals) and another group receiving Calcium Gluconate over a period of 14 months. During this time there was a significant loss of cortical bone in the control group and a significant increase in cortical bone thickness in the Calcium Hydroxyapatite group. Patients receiving Calcium Hydroxyapatite had a net cortical bone gain of 11.6%. The group receiving Calcium Gluconate showed only a net gain of 7%. The difference between 7% and 11.6% represents a gain of over 60%. The control group had cortical bone loss. Calcium Hydroxyapatite promotes positive cortical bone balance and prevents bone thinning.[89]

Vitamin D   Vitamin D is necessary to enhance calcium absorption. Vitamin D works with the parathyroid hormone (PTH) to regulate the amount of calcium in the blood. It also stimulates the production of calcium binding proteins in the intestinal wall which helps absorption. Take 400IU daily.

Magnesium   Also important for maximum Calcium absorption. It is thought to be just as important for the bones as Calcium. The absorption and metabolism of Calcium and Magnesium is one of mutual dependence, and therefore, the balance between these two minerals is especially important. If Calcium consumption is high, Magnesium intake needs to be high also. Take 450mg daily.

Silica and **Manganese**   Silica is important for bone hardening and Manganese assists with calcium utilisation. Take 1mg of each daily.

Boron   In one trial, 12 menopausal women who had been eating a diet low in Boron (devoid of fruits and vegetables) received a 3mg/day Boron supplement for 119 days. The women showed a dramatic increase in blood oestradiol (the most potent of the naturally produced oestrogens), a reduction in calcium excretion, and a significant increase in blood levels of testosterone.[90] These changes are consistent with the prevention of bone demineralisation. Take 3mg daily.

Ipriflavone   Ipriflavone is a synthetic flavonoid (isoflavone) derived from the soy compound daidzein. Ipriflavone promotes the incorporation of calcium into bone. It also inhibits bone breakdown. Many clinical studies, including numerous double-blind studies, have clearly shown that long-term treatment with Ipriflavone along with supplemental **Calcium**, is both safe and effective in halting bone loss in postmenopausal women or in women who have had their ovaries removed.[91] Ipriflavone has also been found to improve bone density in cases of osteoporosis. Take 300mg 2 times daily in conjunction with a Calcium supplement.

Vitamin B complex   **Vitamin B6, B12** and **Folic acid** may become deficient in the elderly and are linked to osteoporosis. High potency B complex supplements that contain B6, B12 and Folic acid assist bone synthesis. Take a high potency B complex as directed.

Schuessler Tissue Salts Combination U   A homeopathically prepared tissue salt mineral combination that helps the body to utilise calcium properly. Take 2 tablets daily.

Polycystic Ovary Syndrome

Polycystic ovary syndrome (PCOS) is a hormonal disorder characterised by multiple cystic ovarian follicles. Also termed Stein-Leventhal syndrome or polycystic ovarian disease, PCOS is normally accompanied by menstruation and ovulation irregularities and excess androgen (male) hormone production, mainly from the ovaries and possibly the adrenal glands. Most women tend to focus on PCOS when they want to start a family or become concerned about weight gain or skin condition — these are fairly normal concerns for women in their twenties or thirties. Then they discover they have PCOS, either by having an ultrasound scan or blood tests, which leads to their search for natural therapies instead of hormonal medications. Natural therapies benefit many women with reproduction conditions, including PCOS, and in some severe cases can be combined with medication under health professional supervision.

Causes

- It is believed to be an inherited disorder as the condition tends to run in families.
- It is unknown whether PCOS causes obesity and insulin resistance, or if excessive weight gain leads to insulin resistance causing PCOS.
- Excess androgens, male hormones made by the ovaries, are the cause of acne and hirsutism (excessive hair growth).

Signs and symptoms

Women with PCOS have varying degrees of signs and symptoms and may present with one or more of the listings below.

- Multiple follicular cysts are seen during an ovarian ultrasound. Follicles are tiny sack-like structures within the ovary that hold tiny immature eggs called oocytes for reproduction. Normally, once the follicle matures every month the oocyte (egg) is ejected from the follicle into the fallopian tube (ovulation) and the ruptured follicle transforms into a corpus luteum that eventually disintegrates. Cysts are created if the follicle fails to release the oocyte and it continues to grow or if the follicle fails to disintegrate. PCOS cysts are normally fairly small and are frequently reabsorbed without need for surgical intervention.
- Irregular, erratic menstrual cycles (with or without periods) occur in 90% of all PCOS individuals.
- No ovulation or erratic ovulation.
- Infertility and/or miscarriage occurs in 75% of all PCOS individuals. Menstruation may not necessarily indicate ovulation (release of egg into fallopian tube).
- Hirsutism (excessive hair growth) occurs in 60% of all PCOS individuals and is often seen on the face (beard, moustache, etc.). It is often referred to as male patterned hair growth.
- Acne may increase due to a raise in androgen hormone levels.
- Excessive weight gain (occurs in 40% of all PCOS individuals) can occur with increased fat distribution around the waist and in the upper abdominal region, although many women with PCOS are of normal weight.
- Insulin resistance (occurs in 50% of all PCOS individuals) can lead to type 2 diabetes and heart disease, including high blood pressure and high cholesterol levels.
- Raised levels of androgens, testosterone, dehydroepiandrosterone sulphate or adrostenedione due to overproduction from the ovaries or adrenals with possible pituitary involvement.
- Raised luteinising hormone (LH) levels with normal oestrogen and follicle stimulating

hormone (FSH) production. Instead of the ratio being 1:1 the LH level is substantially higher, putting the ratio out of balance.
- Decreased sex hormone-binding globulin (SHBG) levels.
- Hypothyroidism, or low thyroid function.
- Mild hyperprolactinaemia (increased prolactin levels).
- Androgenic alopecia (male pattern hair loss or baldness).
- Depression.
- Pelvic pain.
- PMS.

Naturopathic recommendations

Lifestyle hints
The naturopathic aim is to improve insulin sensitivity and ovulation, to regulate the menstrual cycle, to reduce the risk of high cholesterol and diabetes, and to lower raised androgen levels. A healthy weight is necessary to improve PCOS symptoms. See Weight loss on page 50.

Exercise
- Exercise stimulates thyroid gland secretion, regulates insulin levels and metabolism.
- Exercise 3–4 times weekly for 20–40 minutes with a mixture of cardiovascular exercise (walking, running) and resistance exercise (yoga, lunges, weights).

Nutrition
- Consume low-glycaemic index (GI) foods. The GI is a method of classifying foods according to their potential to increase blood sugar levels. Eating high-GI foods results in higher and more rapid increases in blood glucose levels compared to eating low-GI foods. Switch from a high sugar and refined carbohydrate intake to a low-fat, complex carbohydrate, low-GI diet to reduce insulin resistance and normalise hormonal imbalances, assisting with fertility.
- Rapid increases in blood glucose cause the pancreas to increase insulin secretion, leading to insulin resistance and ultimately to the loss of the insulin-secreting function of the pancreas, which triggers diabetes, obesity and heart disease.
- By comparison, the consumption of low-GI foods results in lower and more sustained increases in blood glucose, and lower insulin secretions by the pancreas.
- Eat more of the following low-GI foods:
  Breads   Multigrain, wholemeal or whole grain, sour dough and rye. Avoid light white breads, cookies, cakes and crackers.
  Cereals and grains   Wholemeal grains, basmati rice, long grain rice, rice bran, bulgur wheat, buckwheat, corn (avoid cornflakes and puffed corn), oats, oat bran, muesli (unsweetened and untoasted) and pearl barley.
  Other   Beans, legumes, tofu (and soy products), nuts, seeds, pasta and noodles (avoid corn and rice pasta), vegetables (avoid potatoes), all fresh fruits, skim milk, yoghurt and soy milk.
- Avoid high-GI foods including sugars (sugar, glucose, maltose, fructose, honey and sucrose); white bread, white rice, puffed rice, short grain rice and jasmine rice; potatoes (most varieties), pumpkin and beetroot; most breakfast cereals, most biscuits and crackers; tropical fruit (mango, pineapple) and some dried fruits (raisins).
- Eat 3 meals daily and include two healthy snack meals in between.
- Plant isoflavones and lignans from soy foods, flaxseed and plant oestrogens help to nor-

malise blood sugar levels, reduce androgens and stimulate the liver to produce SHBG, which is low in individuals with PCOS. Include soya textured vegetable protein (TVP) as a mince substitute or mixed with mince, soy tempeh, soy flour and flakes, soya vegetarian sausages, tofu, soy milk (sugar free), flaxseed (fresh seeds) or flaxseed fibre, buckwheat, millet, parsley, fennel, celery, sesame seeds, sunflower seeds, legumes, mung beans, sprouts and sprouted beans.

- Eat small amounts of protein regularly with each snack or meal. Good sources include eggs, lean meat, whey protein, fish, tofu, nuts, seeds, beans and lentils. Mix defatted or lean meats with grains (rice, chickpea, couscous), beans, legumes and mushrooms to reduce meat intake. If you're iron deficient add liver to the diet or an iron supplement. To help increase omega 3 essential fatty acids levels, eat fish 3–4 times weekly including salmon, tuna and sardines.
- Eat more fresh (organic) green leafy vegetables and fruit. Try 3 pieces of fruit and 2–4 cups of vegetables daily.
- Avoid caffeine (coffee, cola drinks, chocolate, black and green tea), tobacco (smoking) and recreational drugs. Smoking is associated with the risk of osteoporosis, coronary heart disease and lung cancer.
- Do not use plastic containers or plastic food wrap to heat food in the microwave as plastics contain unwanted, potentially harmful oestrogens that can leach into the food and contribute to oestrogen overload. Use glass or porcelain instead.
- Eliminate excessive saturated animal fats and synthetic fats, such as margarine, and heated fats, such as vegetable shortenings. Use small amounts of butter, olive oil, vegetable oil or unheated flaxseed oil.
- Reduce sugary foods, refined carbohydrates and processed foods.
- Reduce alcohol intake and have at least 4 alcohol-free days a week. Drink at least 1–2 litres of pure, fresh water daily.
- If a food doesn't agree with you, substitute it with another. Common food sensitivities include diary products, chicken, eggs, wheat, fatty meat and citrus fruits (mainly oranges). Try replacing milk with calcium fortified soy milk or wheat and gluten with gluten-free breads, pasta or rice.

Supplements
Insulin resistance
Chromium (**Chromium Picolinate**)   This essential trace element is required for normal insulin functioning. Chromium stimulates the activity of enzymes involved in the metabolism of glucose for energy and the synthesis of fatty acids and cholesterol. Adequate amounts of Chromium can significantly reduce insulin requirements and play a physiological role in promoting insulin tissue sensitivity. Various lines of evidence suggest that good Chromium nutrition may protect cardiovascular health. Take 300mcg–400mcg daily.
Magnesium (200mg–450mg 2 times daily) and **Zinc** (55mg daily)   Improve insulin resistance.
Fibre   **Flaxseed**, **Guar Gum**, **Pysllium**, **Pectin** and **Slippery Elm** should be taken to increase fibre and chelate onto heavy metals and cholesterol. Fibre improves glucose tolerance, causing food to be released slowly into the intestine, allowing blood glucose to rise gradually. Take 1 tsp–3 tsp daily.

Adrenal protection
Vitamin B complex   Recommended to help normalise adrenals partly responsible for androgen production and to protect against rising stress levels and cortisol production, which has a major impact on the pancreas and insulin resistance. Take 1 tablet daily

Omega 3 and 6 and lignans
Flaxseed oil (2 Tbsp daily) and **Flaxseed fibre** (1 tsp daily) These contain Omega 3, 6 and 9 oils and lignans. Essential fatty acids (EFA) reduce the risk of heart disease and diabetes by normalising blood sugar levels, reduce androgens and stimulate the liver to produce SHBG. Grind Flaxseeds in a coffee grinder and sprinkle one tsp over your food (cereals or salads) every day. Add Flaxseed oil to salad, protein shakes, yoghurt, mayonnaise or vegetable dressings.
Fish, Borage or **Evening Primrose oil** Take these to increase EFA and promote healthy fat metabolism. These healthy oils also improve blood flow and regulate the synthesis of reproductive hormones. Take 2000mg–4000mg daily.

Mild hyperprolactinaemia
High prolactin levels can cause slight discharges from the nipples. Avoid hops and beer as they may raise prolactin levels.[92]
Vitamin B6 and **Chaste Tree** Take 250mg of Vitamin B6 in divided doses daily with 750mg of Chaste Tree 2 times daily. Take a Vitamin B complex supplement as well. If you have an excess of Vitamin B6 you will feel a tingling or numbness in your upper lip or fingertips that is easily reversed by discontinuing Vitamin B6. The Vitamin B complex should still be suitable to take.

Herbs
First, cleanse the body to give it a good chance of responding to the healing process.
Parasite-cleansing herbs Microscopic parasites are sometimes implicated in POCS, fibroids and endometriosis. This will ensure a complete body cleanse and also aid the liver and digestion function of the body. To help eradicate the hidden parasites take two 3-week courses of **Cloves** (1800mg daily) combined with **Wormwood** (2000mg daily) and **Black Walnut** (2000mg daily). Then follow up with a total body detox. See Detoxing on page 131.

Hormone Balancing
Take these herbs for a minimum of 3 months and up to 6 months before revision. If any unusual changes occur, consult a naturopath or health professional. Do not take if pregnant or breastfeeding or if you have mild prolactinaemia, and discontinue use if you experience nausea, nipple discharge, gastric upset or vomiting.
Leutinising Hormone (LH) reduction **Hops** (1g–3g daily before sleeping) and **Black Cohosh** (1g–2g daily) suppress LH and may also reduce androgens.

Androgen hormone reduction
Peony and **Saw Palmetto** These reduce androgen production, are beneficial for acne and PCOS, and improve progesterone levels by normalising ovarian function. Take 2g–4g of dried Saw Palmetto berries daily and 3.5ml of Peony (1:2 fluid extract) 2 times daily.
Liquorice Glycyrrhetinic acids found in Liquorice Root are reported to inhibit the development of ovarian cysts. This wonderful herb has the added action of an anti-inflammatory and helps with adrenal balance from stress. Take 300mg–500mg 2 times daily, standardised to 50mg–100mg of glycyrrhizin. Use for 3–4 weeks then lessen dose to 100mg–300mg daily.

Warning: When taken continuously for several weeks, Liquorice can cause sodium and water retention as well as potassium loss, resulting in elevated blood pressure. Therefore use small doses over a long period of time. I still recommend Liquorice, but you should eat a diet high in potassium and low in salt (sodium), and monitor your blood pressure every three weeks. Good sources of potassium include fresh vegetables, such as dandelion leaves, watercress, endive, cabbage, celery, parsley, courgettes, radishes, pumpkin, mushrooms, cauliflower, asparagus, avocado, raw carrots, corn, cooked lima beans, spinach, potatoes and raw tomatoes; fresh fruits, such as apples, dried apricots, bananas, oranges, peaches, plums and strawberries; seaweed; brewer's yeast; and unprocessed cooked fish and meats, such as flounder, salmon, drained tuna, chicken (the white meat), pork, roast lamb and beef.

Improve ovulation and regulate the menstrual cycle
Dong Quai (1g–2g daily) and **Black Cohosh** (1g–2g daily)   Help to regulate the menstrual cycle.
Yarrow   Helps bring on menstruation. Take 2g–4g 3 times daily. Do not take during pregnancy.

Increase fertility
Chaste Tree (750mg 2 times daily) and **False Unicorn Root** (500mg 2 times daily)   Although False Unicorn Root and Chaste Tree produce great results they may not always suit some people with PCOS. Use these herbs under naturopathic or herbalist supervision. Other herbs that are helpful include **Tribulus** (500mg 3 times daily), **Wild Yam** (2g–4g of dried root 3 times daily) and **Damiana** (2g 3 times daily).

Weight management
Achieve a healthy body mass index (BMI) reading. See Weight loss on page 50. A low carbohydrate, high fibre diet has been beneficial to many women with PCOS. Controversial diets, including the Syndrome X diet and the Atkins diet, have produced great results for those who follow the guidelines properly.

Reduce hirsutism and acne
Include **Saw Palmetto, Peony, Black Cohosh, Liquorice** and **Hops** (dosages as above), and **Damiana** (2g 3 times daily) and **Sarsaparilla** (2g–4g 3 times daily).

Premenstrual Syndrome

Premenstrual syndrome, or PMS, used to be referred to as premenstrual tension (PMT). It is the most common of all female hormone-related disorders. Isn't it amazing that hormones can create so much havoc? In my teens, I used to think women complaining about PMS or 'getting emotional' were making it up so they could vent their frustration on everyone else. Now I know better! PMS is the term used to describe the emotional and physical symptoms that may occur between one and 14 days before menstruation begins.

Although more than 150 individual PMS symptoms have been noted, the most common have been put into five different categories. Women may experience a combination of these.

PMS-A (Anxiety)
This type of PMS is thought to be caused by a relative excess of oestrogen and a deficiency of progesterone. The cause of this imbalance is possibly related to poor liver clearance of oestrogens or deficient progesterone production, perhaps due to anovulatory cycles or progesterone receptors that are malfunctioning.

Symptoms include irritability, nervous tension, mood swings, insomnia and anxiety.

PMS-C (Cravings)
This type of PMS rarely exists by itself and often accompanies PMS-A. It is associated with low blood sugars (functional hypoglycaemia), prostaglandin imbalance (decreased), magnesium deficiency, poor carbohydrate metabolism and poor digestion.

Symptoms include a craving for sweets and carbohydrates, increased appetite, low blood sugar, fatigue, dizziness or fainting, headaches and heart palpitations.

PMS-D (Depression)
Depression and withdrawal characterise this form of PMS which is thought to be associated with relative oestrogen deficiency, increased progesterone during the luteal phase, or decreased serotonin levels.

Symptoms include depression, forgetfulness, crying, confusion, insomnia and withdrawal.

PMS-H (Hyper-hydration)
This is related to fluid retention caused by an increase in aldosterone levels. Aldosterone elevation can be caused by deficient progesterone, elevated oestrogen, magnesium deficiency, serotonin or dopamine imbalances, stress, or potassium imbalance. Prolactin is thought to be a factor if there is breast tenderness and swelling.

Symptoms include breast tenderness, abdominal bloating, weight gain and water retention.

PMS-P (Pain)
PMS-P reflects an increased sensitivity to pain and is believed to be associated with prostaglandin imbalance. Possible causes are elevated oestrogen and excessive animal fat intake, believed to increase production of inflammatory series 2 prostaglandins.

Symptoms include aches and pains, reduced pain threshold, dysmenorrhoea (cramping), and headaches.

Naturopathic recommendations

Lifestyle hints
- Check for food sensitivities and thyroid gland dysfunction.
- Lymphatic and deep tissue massage can help decrease pain and water retention, including bloating, breast tenderness and sore legs.
- Learn how to relax by trying yoga, receiving a massage, or learning meditation or breathing techniques.
- Get plenty of restful sleep. Make sure the room is completely dark to help ensure sleep.
- Sexual intercourse helps to increase the 'feel good' hormones oxytocin and dopamine. It can also increase circulation and relieve abdominal cramps.
- If you are taking oral contraceptives (OC), check with your doctor that they are suited to you and not causing any PMS symptoms.

Exercise
- Exercise 3–4 times weekly for 20–40 minutes with a mixture of cardiovascular exercise (walking, gentle jogging, running) and resistance exercise (yoga, lunges, weights).
- Don't underestimate exercise when it comes to maintaining a healthy hormonal balance and a reduction in endometriosis pain symptoms.
- My friends swear by belly and Tahitian dancing — great for the libido, and blood circulation.

Nutrition

- Reduce salt and sugar intake. When sugar and caffeine are combined, PMS symptoms can worsen. Salt increases water retention.
- Eat fibre or take fibre supplements including flax fibre, slippery elm and psyllium to bind onto excess oestrogens. Include fresh, organic fruit (pectins) and vegetables.
- Eat certified organic, natural, sugar-free acidophilus yoghurt daily. Avoid if allergic to dairy and take acidophilus and bifidus supplements instead. Yoghurt can be beneficial for helping convert plant oestrogens into usable forms in your body. Eat dairy foods in moderation if you are not sensitive to dairy products.
- Consume 3 meals daily and include two healthy snack meals in between. For 10 days prior to bleeding eat smaller meals more often (6 times daily) to reduce the possibility of hypoglycaemia.
- Plant isoflavones and lignans from soy foods, flaxseed and plant oestrogens help keep endogenous oestrogen levels lower and normalise blood sugar levels. Eat soya textured vegetable protein (TVP) as a mince substitute, tempeh, soy flour and flakes, soya vegetarian sausages, tofu, soy milk (sugar-free), flaxseed (fresh seeds), buckwheat, millet, parsley, fennel, celery, sesame seeds, sunflower seeds, legumes, mung beans, sprouts and sprouted beans. Plant oestrogens are estimated to be thousands of times weaker than the body made oestrogen, oestradiol, and can bind onto oestrogen receptors, having a protective effect.
- Indole-3-carbinol and sulphoraphane are found in plants, such as broccoli, cauliflower, cabbage, Brussels sprouts and kale. Indoles activate detoxification enzymes in the intestinal tract, bind to chemical carcinogens, rendering them inactive, and improve oestrogen balance, reducing the risk of breast cancer. Indole-3-carbinol helps break down oestrogen into 'good' metabolites and leaves less of the 'bad' oestrogen metabolites.
- Eat small amounts of protein regularly at meals. Good sources include whey protein, fish, tofu, nuts, seeds, beans and lentils. Mix defatted or lean meats with grains (rice, chickpea, couscous) or beans, legumes and mushrooms to reduce meat intake. Eat protein with each meal. If you're iron deficient add liver to the diet, or an iron supplement.
- Eat more fresh, organic, green leafy vegetables and fruit. Try 3 pieces of fruit and 2–4 cups of vegetables daily. To help increase omega 3 levels eat fish 3–4 times weekly including salmon, tuna and sardines.
- Avoid caffeine (coffee, cola drinks, chocolate, black and green tea), tobacco (smoking) and recreational drugs. Smoking is associated with the risk of osteoporosis, coronary heart disease and lung cancer.
- Do not use plastic containers or plastic food wrap to heat food in the microwave as plastics contain unwanted, potentially harmful oestrogens that can leach into the food and contribute to oestrogen overload. Use glass or porcelain instead.
- Eliminate excessive saturated animal fats and synthetic fats, such as margarine, and heated fats, such as vegetable shortenings. Use small amounts of butter or flaxseed oil.
- Reduce sugary foods, refined carbohydrates and processed foods. Reduce alcohol intake and have at least 4 alcohol-free days a week.
- Drink at least 1–2 litres of pure, fresh water daily and herbal teas, including St John's Wort, ginseng, ginger, chamomile and peppermint.
- Enjoy a bitter aperitif, such as vermouth or a soda, lime and bitters, before dinner to encourage digestive juices and help the liver metabolise oestrogens. Alternatively take 50ml of aloe vera juice with every meal to increase absorption and digestion of nutrients from food.

Supplements

Progesterone Deficiencies of progesterone can lead to postnatal depression, breast tenderness, depression, endometriosis, lethargy, irregular menstrual cycles, facial hair and darkening under the eyes, menopausal symptoms, PMS, weight fluctuations, fluid retention, vaginal dryness, headaches and migraines, insomnia, irritability, acne, libido loss, panic, weepiness and fibroids. Progesterone cream can be prescribed to balance progesterone deficiency. See your health practitioner for details.

Vitamin B complex A Vitamin B complex with B1, B2, B3, B5, B12 and Folic acid will help the adrenals adapt to hormonal changes. B complex vitamins also assist liver detoxification of excessive and potentially harmful oestrogen residue, and replace any deficiencies that may exacerbate PMS symptoms. Take a Vitamin B complex as directed.

Flaxseed oil (2 Tbsp daily) and **Flaxseed fibre** (1 tsp daily) These contain Omega 3, 6 and 9 oils and lignans, which are said to provide essential fatty acids (EFA) important for preventing EFA deficiencies and PMS symptoms. Lignans protect the body from oestrogen-dominant cancers and hormone imbalances. Grind Flaxseeds in a coffee grinder and sprinkle 1 tsp over your food (cereals or salads) every day.

Herbs

Detox Complete a gentle detox herbal programme and a parasite-cleansing programme to balance the internal body organs and prepare for a healthy start. Detox herbs should include **Burdock** (2g–6g of dried root daily), **Cleavers** (2g–4g daily) and **Red Clover** (2g–4g daily) to help to cleanse the blood and clear the lymphatics. **Dandelion** (3g–5g of dried root daily) and **Milk Thistle** (9g–10g of seed daily) enhance bile flow and detoxify the liver.

Parasite-cleansing herbs Take two 3-week courses of **Cloves** (1800mg daily) combined with **Wormwood** (2000mg daily) and **Black Walnut** (2000mg daily) to help eradicate parasites. Parasites are implicated in PMS symptomatology.

PMS-A (Anxiety)

Vegetarian diets are beneficial as they enable you to clear more oestrogen. A diet low in sugar and dairy products reduces PMS-A symptoms.

Detoxing will help clear oestrogen excess, see above for details.

Vitmin B complex Take a high potency Vitamin B complex containing 50mg of **B6** 2 times daily, for 14 days leading up to menstruation.

Progesterone deficiency Natural Progesterone or Synthetic Progesterone cream is normally prescribed to balance progesterone deficiency. See your health practitioner for details.

Vitamin C (1200mg daily), **Bioflavonoids** (900mg of Hesperidin daily) and **Vitamin E** (400IU daily) Deficiencies have been linked to PMS-A. Take until symptoms improve.

DIM (Diindolylmethane) Helps the liver to metabolise oestrogens properly and has a protective effect on hormone-sensitive tissues against carcinogenesis. Take these compounds if you suffer from migraines, have come off oral contraception, have PMS-A or have a family history of oestrogenic and breast cancers. Take 100mg of DIM 2 times daily. See your practitioner for product details.

Bach™ Flower remedies Choose a single remedy or a combination recommended by a health professional. **Beech** and **Impatiens** are good for intolerance of others and impatience. Take 2 drops in a 1 litre bottle of spring water daily.

PMS-C (Cravings)

Fibre Flax, Guar Gum, Pysllium, Pectin and **Slippery Elm** should be taken to increase fibre and chelate onto heavy metals and cholesterol. Fibre improves glucose toler-

ance causing food to be released slowly into the intestine allowing blood glucose to rise gradually. Take 1 tsp–3 tsp of these fibres, singly or in combination, daily.
Chromium (Chromium Picolinate)   This essential trace element is required for normal insulin functioning. Chromium stimulates the activity of enzymes involved in the metabolism of glucose for energy and the synthesis of fatty acids and cholesterol. Adequate amounts of Chromium can significantly reduce insulin requirements and plays a physiological role in promoting insulin tissue sensitivity, and various lines of evidence suggest that good Chromium nutrition may protect cardiovascular health. Take 300mcg–400mcg daily.
Magnesium   To compensate for any deficiency take 450mg–900mg daily.
Other beneficial supplements to help balance prostaglandins include **Vitamin E** (400IU daily) and essential fatty acids, such as **Fish oil** (3g daily), **Flaxseed oil** (2 Tbsp daily), **Evening Primrose oil** (6g daily) and **Borage Seed** oil (3g daily).
Gymnema   The leaf is well known for its ability to remove the taste of and cravings for sugars when chewed. Clinical studies have shown remarkable results in a reduction of insulin and glucose levels.[93,94] Gymnema (25% Gymnemic acids) is thought to increase insulin production by stimulating the pancreas and may repair the Islet of Langerhans in the pancreas. It also increases the activities of the enzymes, which facilitate the use of glucose by insulin-dependent pathways, and increases intake of glycogen by liver and muscles. Take 200mg 2 times daily.
American Ginseng   New findings support this herb's effectiveness as a blood glucose modulator. Take 1g–3g 3 times daily.

PMS-D (Depression)
Magnesium   To compensate for any deficiency take 450mg–900mg daily.
Borage oil and **Fish oil**   Gamma-linolenic acid (GLA) from Borage or **Starflower oil** and Omega 3 from Fish oil may help reduce tearfulness and emotional upset. Take 3g of each daily.
5-Hydroxy tryptophan (5HTP)   A serotonin precursor made naturally by the body and also sourced from the plant *Griffonia simplicifolia*, 5HTP helps boost serotonin levels reducing anxiety and insomnia. Take 150mg–300mg daily.
Detox   Toxins and heavy metals (lead) have been implicated with PMS-D. See page 131 for detoxing recommendations.
Nerve-restoring herbs   Include **Valerian** (1g–3g daily), **Kava** (1.5g–3g of dried root daily), **Passionflower** (4g–8g of dried herb daily), **Siberian Ginseng** (adrenals) (1g–4g daily) and **St John's Wort** (2g–5g of dried herb daily) for mild depression, insomnia and anxiety.

PMS-H (Hyper-hydration)
Eat potassium rich foods to avoid deficiencies. These include fresh vegetables, such as dandelion leaves, watercress, endive, cabbage, celery, parsley, courgettes, radishes, pumpkin, mushrooms, cauliflower, asparagus, avocado, raw carrots, corn, cooked lima beans, spinach, potatoes and raw tomatoes; fresh fruits, such as apples, dried apricots, bananas, oranges, peaches, plums and strawberries; seaweed; brewer's yeast; and unprocessed cooked fish and meats such as flounder, salmon, drained tuna, chicken (the white meat), pork, roast lamb and beef.
Reduce salt and carbohydrate (bread, rice, potatoes) intake. They increase water retention.
Magnesium   To compensate for any deficiency take 450mg–900mg daily.
5-Hydroxy tryptophan (5HTP)   A serotonin precursor made naturally by the body and also sourced from the plant *Griffonia simplicifolia*, 5HTP helps boost serotonin levels aiding anxiety and insomnia. Take 150mg–300mg daily.
Fluid retention   Diuretics that increase urination and reduce water retention include Parsely, Juniper Berry, Celery Seed, Dandelion Leaf and Yarrow. See your local health store for herbal diuretic teas or capsules.

> How to make diuretic parsley tea

Diuretic parsley tea involves boiling four bunches of rinsed organic fresh parsley. Strain parsley juice from parsley bunches, and cool and store liquid. When cool drink ¼ cup. Drink ½ cup of parsley water 3 times daily. May be flavoured with 2 tsp of black cherry concentrate. Throw away after 4 days.

Chaste Tree   Helps to balance progesterone and oestrogen ratio. Take 750mg 2 times daily.
Liquorice   Blocks the effects of aldosterone. Take Liquorice for 14 days leading up to menstruation. Take 1g–2g daily. Reduce dose to 100mg–200mg after 3 months.
Breast tenderness and **swelling**   Take **Evening Primrose oil** (6g daily) and **Vitamin E** (400IU daily) for 2–3 months. If breast tenderness is still evident take **Vitamin B6** and **Chaste Tree**. Take 250mg of Vitamin B6 in divided doses daily with 750mg 2 times daily of Chaste Tree. Take a **Vitamin B complex** supplement as well. If you have an excess of Vitamin B6 you will feel a tingling or numbness in your upper lip or fingertips that is easily reversed by discontinuing Vitamin B6. The B complex should still be suitable to take.

PMS-P (Pain)

Avoid saturated fats especially altered unnatural fat derivatives in margarines and shortenings as they can aggravate swelling and inflammation. Avoid or cut down on cheeses, butter, animal fats (e.g. from pork and beef), coconut cream, and trans fatty acids, including fried foods. Saturated fats in the diet may be an inflammatory and clogging factor, which depresses the immune system function thereby worsening premenstrual syndrome.
Avoid tea, chocolate, caffeine-containing products and coffee, as the methyl-xanthines contained in these compounds may make the body more receptive to pain by blocking natural painkillers that the body already produces. Restrict alcohol, tobacco use and salt intake. If needed use only unbleached celtic sea salt (see your health shop).
Essential fatty acids are good fats, such as **Fish oil** (3g daily), **Flaxseed oil** (2 Tbsp daily), **Evening Primrose oil** (6g) and **Borage Seed oil** (6g). These are easy to come by in supplement form. They reduce inflammatory pathways, balance hormones, and reduce pain and inflammation.
Anti-inflammatory foods   Bromelain is an enzyme found in pineapple. It works by blocking some of the pro-inflammatory metabolites that 'rev up' the inflammatory process. Fruits and vegetables that contain **Vitamin C** and bioflavonoids are also anti-inflammatory. Eat citrus fruits, fejoas, cranberries, blackcurrants, strawberries, cherries, tomatoes, papaya, capsicums and green leafy vegetables.
Turmeric and **Ginger**   The yellow pigment seen in curries and turmeric dishes is **Curcumin** (from Turmeric). It is known for its antioxidant and anti-inflammatory properties. Curcumin and another well known spice, Ginger, block leukotrienes pathways inhibiting the inflammation response.
Magnesium and **Vitamin E**   To compensate for any deficiency take 450mg–900mg of Magnesium and 400IU of Vitamin E daily.
Feverfew   Helps to reduce prostaglandin inflammatory reactions. Add 1–2 leaves in a sandwich or take 50mg–200mg daily.
Dong Quai and **Black Cohosh**   Help balance hormones and reduce pain during abdominal cramping. Take 1g–2g of each daily.

Prostate Enlargement

Most men I know shudder at the thought of having their prostate gland checked through the rectum. A hand slipped in to a surgical rubber glove, the finger lubricated with a big dollop of KY Jelly, is pretty common comic material that comedians employ in the movies, but the message is still clear that men over forty are recommended to have their prostate gland checked to ensure that it is a normal size and shape.

The word prostate is often confused with the word prostrate. The prostate is a walnut-sized gland that encircles a man's urethra like a donut, and is located beneath the bladder and in front of the rectum. Its normal function is to secrete a milky substance (seminal fluid) to nourish, transport and enhance sperm motility and lubricate the urethra to prevent infection. An enlarged prostate gland can obstruct the flow of urine giving rise to the symptoms of bladder outlet obstruction. It's an extremely common condition affecting 50%–60% of middle-aged men and this statistic increases to around 90% in men over 85 years of age.

Causes

The cause of benign prostatic hyperplasia (BHP) is unknown; however, it is associated with hormonal changes that occur as men age.

Testosterone is a hormone produced by the testes which is converted to dihydrotestosterone (DHT) and oestradiol (oestrogen) in certain tissues. Increased levels of DHT can cause the tissue of the prostate to grow. The cells multiply around the urethra squeezing it tighter or, in the case of middle-lobe prostate growth, the cells grow into the urethra and the bladder outlet area. This type of growth typically requires surgery.

How do the DHT levels increase?

Testosterone levels decrease around 50 years of age, but oestrogen, prolactin, luteinising hormone and follicle stimulating hormone levels increase, leading to:
- An increased activity of an enzyme (5-alpha-reductase) that converts testosterone to DHT.
- Elevated oestrogen levels which reduce the removal of DHT from the prostate gland.
- Raised prolactin levels which increase prostate uptake of testosterone.

All this contributes to an increased concentration of testosterone in the prostate gland.

Signs and symptoms

- Urgency to urinate
- Pushing or straining to begin urination
- Need to urinate often at night
- Reduced force or pressure of urine outflow
- Increased urinary frequency
- Inability to urinate or to void bladder completely
- Dribbling after voiding
- Hesitant, interrupted or weak urine flow
- Leakage of urine (incontinence).

In severe cases acute urinary retention causes severe pain and discomfort and catheterisation may be necessary to drain urine from the bladder and obtain relief. Enlarged prostate should not be self-diagnosed. Please see your doctor for a consultation.

Naturopathic recommendations

Lifestyle hints
- It is recommended that men over forty have regular prostate check-ups.
- Eliminate food sensitivities, see page 164.
- Cholesterol damaged by toxins can stimulate prostate cell formation. High cholesterol is also linked to enlargement of the prostate gland. Maintain healthy cholesterol levels. See the High cholesterol recommendations on page 192 and follow them (especially the antioxidant recommendations) to reduce toxicity levels.
- A PSA (prostate-specific antigen) test can differentiate an enlarged prostate gland (BHP) from prostate cancer. See your doctor for details.
- Avoid toxins, especially pesticides, herbicides, chemicals (household and environmental), cadmium (from cigarette smoke), food preservatives, artificial colourings, flavourings or sugars, and environmental toxins. Toxins, pesticides and chemicals increase enlargement of prostate glands and abnormal cell growth, and cadmium from cigarette smoke increases the activity of an enzyme (5-alpha-reductase) that converts testosterone to DHT.

Exercise
- Exercise helps to regulate hormonal levels, increase cardiovascular fitness and health, and reduce cholesterol levels.
- Exercise 3–4 times weekly for 20–40 minutes with a mixture of cardiovascular exercise (walking, gentle jogging, running) and resistance exercise (yoga, lunges, weights).

Nutrition
- Soy inhibits the activity of the enzyme (5-alpha-reductase) that converts testosterone to DHT. Soy also contains beta-sitosterol that studies show reduces cholesterol and improves the urine flow, decreasing the amount of urine left in the bladder. Eat soya textured vegetable protein (TVP) as a mince substitute, tempeh, soy flour and flakes, soya vegetarian sausages, tofu, soy milk (sugar-free), flaxseed (fresh seeds), buckwheat, millet, parsley, fennel, celery, legumes, mung beans, sprouts and sprouted beans. Plant oestrogens are estimated be thousands of times weaker than the body-made oestrogen, oestradiol, and can bind onto sensitive oestrogen receptors, having a protective effect against prostate cancer.
- Sunflower seeds, flaxseeds and pumpkin seeds provide excellent sources of essential fatty acids (omega 3 and 6) and omega 9 to reduce urinary symptoms. Eat ¼ cup of raw seeds daily. Grind flaxseed and sunflower seeds and add to cereal. Pumpkin seeds are slightly bitter and better eaten whole. Although toasted pumpkin seeds taste great the fragile beneficial pumpkin seed oil will become rancid during cooking.
- Lignans protect the body from oestrogen-dominant cancers and hormone imbalances. A rich source includes flaxseed. Grind flaxseeds in a coffee grinder and sprinkle 1 Tbsp over your food (cereals or salads) every day or alternatively buy flaxseed fibre and use as a fibre supplement.
- Consume half the amount of complex carbohydrates you normally have or eat 3 servings the size of your fist daily. Include dense, grainy breads, lots of whole grains, oat bran and textured wholemeal or white sourdough, long grain white, basmati and brown rice, kumara, taro, yam, pasta, noodles, barley and bulgur wheat, porridge, untoasted muesli, Special K, All-Bran. Choose low-fat, low-sugar biscuits made with oats.
- Use sugars sparingly, even those in honey, fruit juices, dried fruits and maple syrup. Avoid artificial sweeteners or processed sugar.

Prostate Enlargement

- Eat more fibrous carbohydrates, like salads, celery, onions, garlic, asparagus, and beans and legumes, than starchy carbohydrates, like potatoes, corn, rice, pasta and breads. Eat more dietary fibre and natural antioxidants found in vegetables (leafy greens, yellow and red), cherries and berries. Include vegetables such as broccoli, cauliflower, cabbage, Brussels sprouts and kale.
- Fibre binds onto excess dietary cholesterol and removes it. Grind 2 Tbsp–4 Tbsp of flaxseed fibre daily and add to cereal, porridge or salads — this will provide fibre and omega 3 and 6. Other excellent sources of fibre include oat bran, psyllium, and pectin or apple fibre.
- Drink 1–2 litres of pure, fresh water and herb teas, such as nettle and oat straw tea.
- Eliminate excessive saturated animal fats and synthetic fats, such as margarine, and heated fats, such as vegetable shortenings. Use small amounts of butter or flaxseed oil.
- Reduce intake of sugary foods, refined carbohydrates and processed foods.
- Eliminate alcohol because studies show that it (especially spirits and beer) is linked to prostate enlargement.[95, 96] The herb hops that is used during the beer-making process increases the hormone prolactin, consequently increasing the prostate uptake of testosterone.[97]
- Avoid coffee, caffeine, soft drinks and excessive salt intake.
- Reduce refined carbohydrates, such as white flour, white rice, croissants, toasted muesli, cakes, biscuits, pastries, pies, breadcrumbs and man-made carbohydrates.
- Avoid overexposure to hormones. Do not use plastic containers or plastic food wrap to heat food in the microwave as plastics contain unwanted, potentially harmful oestrogens that can leach into the food, decrease removal of DHT from the prostate gland and contribute to oestrogen overload. Use glass or porcelain instead.
- Indole-3-carbinol and sulphoraphane are found in plants such as broccoli, cauliflower, cabbage, Brussels sprouts and kale. Indoles activate detoxification enzymes in the liver, bind to chemical carcinogens, rendering them inactive, and improve oestrogen balance, reducing the risk of prostate cancer. Indole-3-carbinol helps break down oestrogen into 'good' metabolites and leaves less of the 'bad' oestrogen metabolites.

Supplements

Zinc   Reduces prostate enlargement by inhibiting prolactin, which decreases the uptake of DHT in the prostate gland, and by inhibiting the activity of an enzyme (5-alpha-reductase) that converts testosterone to DHT. Zinc also reduces many of the symptoms, increases fertility and immunity, and can also reduce impotence. Take 45mg–60mg daily.

Amino acids   **Glycine**, **Glutamic acid** and **Alanine** help to reduce the symptoms of urinary discomfort (full bladder feeling), urgency, frequency and the urge to urinate at night, which as a result improves sleep. Take 200mg of each Amino acid daily.

Cernilton   Cernilton is an extract of flower pollen that has been used in Europe for over 30 years to treat prostate enlargement, its signs and symptoms. It also inhibits growth of the prostate cells and can result in an improvement for 70% of those who try it.[98] Take 63mg–126mg 2–3 times daily.

Antioxidant formulas (full spectrum)   Include ProenOthera® from Evening Primrose Seed Husk, Green tea, Grape Seed, Pine Bark, Beta Carotene, Vitamins E, A and C, oligomeric proanthocyanidins, flavonoids and adjunctive minerals (Zinc, Selenium, Manganese and Iron). These are essential to help prevent oxidation and free radicals causing cholesterol to become toxic and carcinogenic to the prostate. Take as professionally advised or as supplement labels suggest.

Essential fatty acids   Studies show essential fatty acids may correct underlying deficiencies and reduce many urinary symptoms associated with prostate conditions.[99] Take **Evening Primrose Seed oil**, **Sunflower Seed oil**, **Flaxseed oil** and **Pumpkin Seed oil** unheated to prevent rancidity reducing their beneficial effects. Take 1 Tbsp–2 Tbsp of these oils combined daily.

Herbs

Detox Complete a gentle detox herbal programme and a parasite-cleansing programme to balance the internal body organs and prepare for a healthy start. Detox herbs should include **Burdock** (2g–6g of dried root daily), **Cleavers** (2g–4g daily) and **Red Clover** (2g–4g daily) help to cleanse the blood and clear the lymphatics. **Dandelion** (3g–5g of dried root daily) and **Milk Thistle** (9g–10g of seed daily) enhance bile flow and detoxify the liver.

Parasite-cleansing herbs Take two 3-week courses of **Cloves** (1800mg daily) combined with **Wormwood** (2000mg daily) and **Black Walnut** (2000mg daily) to help eradicate parasites. Parasites are implicated in prostate enlargement and symptomatology.

Saw Palmetto Improves urine flow, promotes emptying of the bladder, and reduces nocturia (night time urination), pain and discomfort all within 30 days. The plant sterols, mainly sitosterol, have hormonal effects on the gland, inhibit the conversion of testosterone to DHT in the prostate and help improve all symptoms of BPH. Take 320mg of standardised extract daily (all at once or in two doses). For best results take a standardised extract containing 85%–95% fatty acids and sterols.

Pygeum Reduces the signs and symptoms of prostate enlargement especially in early cases. Urine flow rate and residual urine symptoms improve dramatically. Combine with **Saw Palmetto**, **Cernilton** and **Nettle** for best results. Take 50mg–200mg of extract (standardised extract containing 14% triterpenes including beta-sitosterol 0.5%) 2 times daily.

Nettle Reduces the signs and symptoms of prostate enlargement. Take 300mg–600mg of Nettle extract daily.

Psoriasis

I had an amazing experience as an apprentice with a psoriasis patient. My father is also a natural therapist and uses Indonesian herbal therapy and psychosomatic counselling, a form of counselling which believes that thought or memories may manifest as disease in the body. A young lady my father was treating had the most terrible psoriasis I've ever seen, which almost completely covered her body from head to toe with thickened patches. I can't go into detail, but she had a moment of enlightenment from the counselling and all her psoriasis literally fell off. Her skin underneath was clear, brand-new looking and baby pink. I grumbled at having to vacuum the couch she sat on after she left, not realising the amazing miracle that had happened. I now always recommend counselling as a form of treatment for psoriasis in conjunction with herbs, supplements and a healthy lifestyle.

Psoriasis is a skin condition which can be found just about anywhere on the body, especially the scalp, elbows, knees, wrists and ankles. It's caused by skin cells that pile up by replicating too quickly — approximately 1000 times faster than normal. This causes the skin cells to accumulate, resulting in the 'silvery scale' appearance.

The skin can become hardened and reddish around these scaly patches, which vary in size, and, as the skin loses flexibility within these patches, they can split easily, causing painful sore areas.

Causes

- Cyclic adenosine monophosphate (cAMP) and cyclic guanosine monophosphate (cGMP) imbalance. These two important compounds within the body are responsible for skin growth and 'shedding' or breakdown. If the cGMP increases and cAMP decreases too much this creates an unbalanced ratio and the cells replicate too quickly, so maintaining a balanced ratio and normalising these internal compounds is the key to the treatment of psoriasis.

- Incomplete protein digestion leads to toxins which reduce the production of cAMP.
- Stress levels can cause excessive production of psoriasis patches. In one study 39% of psoriasis sufferers reported a stressful situation occurring one month prior to the worsening of psoriasis symptoms.[100]
- Skin trauma.
- Bowel toxaemia, from improper balance of gut bacteria and improper clearing out of toxins, causes cGMP to increase.
- Candida.
- Smoking.
- Liver toxicity and malfunction causes a build-up of toxic compounds, which have an impact on the balance of cAMP:cGMP.
- Alcohol and saturated fat consumption increases the gut's toxin absorption, reducing the liver's ability to detoxify.
- Genetics plays a role in the risk of developing psoriasis.
- Certain medications, such as heart medication, i.e. propranolol (ß-receptor antagonists) and lithium carbonate, may cause psoriasis as they inhibit adenylate cyclase activity.

Signs and symptoms

- Patches over the torso and limbs may follow (10–14 days) after a strep. throat infection.
- Appearance of very well defined, salmon-pink plaques or lesions on the skin.
- Scattered smaller patches on the limbs and the trunk of the body.
- Possible development of psoriatic arthritis and nail pitting.
- Silvery scaled patches of skin over the elbows, knees, body and scalp.
- Increased complications of skin infection if the patches become itchy and are scratched.
- Flexural psoriasis on the groin, genitals or perianal site.
- Pustular psoriasis normally on fingers, palms of hands or soles of feet, but can spread to the body.

Naturopathic recommendations

Lifestyle hints

- Identify and eliminate any food allergies or sensitivities. See page 164 for more details.
- Meditation, hypnosis and relaxation techniques reportedly reduce psoriasis outbreaks.
- Ultraviolet rays and bathing in mineral or sea water have been known to diminish psoriasis patches. Medical treatment involves taking the drug psoralen and using ultraviolet therapy, apparently without side effects. Ultrasound and heating to the affected area has also shown to be a helpful therapy.
- Counselling may be quite a powerful tool in the treatment of psoriasis, especially if stress exacerbates the condition.
- Candida increases toxins thereby increasing psoriasis lesions. See page 102 for candida treatment recommendations.

Exercise

- Exercise helps reduce stress.
- Exercise 3–4 times weekly for 20–40 minutes with a mixture of cardiovascular exercise (walking, gentle jogging, running) and resistance exercise (yoga, lunges, weights).

Nutrition

- Reduce intake of sugar, alcohol, meat and gluten foods. Increase fibre, fresh fruit, vegetables and fish.
- Reduce alcohol intake as it exacerbates psoriasis and puts too much stress on the detoxifying abilities of the liver.
- Decrease intake of saturated fats that contain arachidonic acid (AA), such as animal fats, animal meats and dairy products, to reduce the production of inflammatory chemicals that AA promotes.
- Good oils and fats include unheated avocado, fish oil (3g daily), flaxseed oil (1 Tbsp daily), olive oil and cold pressed vegetable oils.
- Eat a diet high in fish as this will help improve psoriasis by providing essential fatty acids (EFA) reducing EFA deficiencies and inflammation, and promtoing healing. Eat fish at least 3–4 times a week. This includes tuna, salmon, sardines and snapper. Sorry…this doesn't mean having fish and chips 4 times a week.
- Increase fibre to help lessen gut toxicity from partially digested proteins and heavy metals involved with psoriasis.
- People with psoriasis may improve on vegetarian and gluten-free diets. This may be due to production of fewer toxins and reduction of inflammation in the gut. See Food sensitivities on page 164 for gluten-free diet recommendations.
- Enjoy a bitter aperitif, such as vermouth or soda, lime and bitters, before dinner to encourage digestive juices. Alternatively take 50ml of aloe vera juice with every meal to increase absorption and digestion of nutrients from food.
- Drink 1–2 litres of pure, fresh water and herb teas, such as chamomile, peppermint, liquorice, echinacea and nerve relaxing teas.
- Eat 3 meals daily and include two healthy snack meals in between to help balance blood sugar levels.

Supplements

Flaxseed oil (2 Tbsp daily) and **Colostrum** (4g daily)   May help reduce leaky gut syndrome and inflammation associated with psoriasis.

Acidophilus   Help to repopulate the gut with beneficial bacteria and lessen bowel toxicity. Take 1–2 capsules daily that contain 1 billion of both *Bifidus* and *Lactobacillus acidophilus* strains.

Super polyunsaturated oils   **Fish oil** with high levels of EPA and DHA (10g daily), **Evening Primrose oil** (3000mg daily) and **Flax oil** (2 Tbsp daily) have been shown to help reduce psoriasis. Take for at least 3 months for this to be effective.

Hydrochloric acid or **digestive enzyme formulas**   Increase digestive juices and the digestion of protein. Incomplete protein digestion is associated with psoriasis because toxins from the protein cause an imbalance between the ratio of cGMP and cAMP. Take as recommended.

Vitamin B complex   Take a high potency complex as directed to help with stress, healing of skin and lesions, and immunity.

Antioxidant formulas (full spectrum)   Include ProenOthera® from Evening Primrose Seed Husk, Green tea, Grape Seed, Pine Bark, Beta Carotene, Vitamins E, A and C, oligomeric proanthocyanidins, flavonoids and adjunctive minerals (Zinc, Selenium, Manganese and Iron). These are essential to help prevent antioxidant deficiencies and reduce psoriasis symptoms. Take as professionally advised or as supplement labels suggest.

Bioflavonoids   Found in dark berries and some plants, Bioflavonoids help reduce swelling, strengthen connective tissue and help reduce psoriasis lesions. Take 200mg–450mg of **Rutin** or **Quercetin** daily.

Chromium (Chromium Picolinate) This essential trace element is required for normal insulin functioning as psoriasis individuals have an increase of blood insulin and glucose levels. Adequate amounts of Chromium can significantly reduce insulin requirements and play a physiological role in promoting insulin tissue sensitivity. Take 300mcg–400mcg daily.

Herbs

Detox Complete a gentle detox herbal programme and a parasite-cleansing programme to balance the internal body organs and prepare for a healthy start. Detox herbs should include **Burdock** (2g–6g of dried root daily), **Cleavers** (2g–4g daily) and **Red Clover** (2g–4g daily) to help cleanse the blood and clear the lymphatics. **Dandelion** (3g–5g of dried root daily) and **Milk Thistle** (9g–10g of seed daily) enhance bile flow and detoxify the liver.
Parasite-cleansing herbs Take two 3-week courses of **Cloves** (1800mg daily) combined with **Wormwood** (2000mg daily) and **Black Walnut** (2000mg daily) to help eradicate parasites. Parasites are implicated in psoriasis.
Bitter Melon Has an effect on cAMP:cGMP ratios by lowering cGMP. Blood sugar levels may be irregular in individuals with psoriasis. Bitter Melon in conjunction with **Chromium** (400mcg daily) has a balancing action on blood sugar levels. Take 1g 2 times daily.
Milk Thistle Also known as **St Mary's Thistle**, it helps to improve liver function, inhibit inflammation and reduce excessive cell proliferation. Take 9g–10g of seed or 70mg–210mg of silymarin 3 times daily.
Sarsaparilla A specific herb for treating psoriasis, especially the large scaly patches. Take 1g–4g daily.
Olive Leaf extract (270mg 3 times daily) and **Echinacea** (1200mg–6g daily) Take for 10–30 days for signs of viral, bacterial or fungal infection, and to purify blood.
Skullcap Relaxes nervous tension, helps soothe the nervous system and combines well with the herb **Valerian** (1g–3g daily). Take 750mg 3–5 times daily.

External applications

Creams that include **Aloe Vera, Comfrey, Liquorice, Capsaicin** (for itch and pain), **Calendula** and **Chamomile** help to soothe psoriasis patches.
Marshmallow Root May soothe and promote healing of gastrointestinal inflammation that is often found with psoriasis. Soak 1 heaped Tbsp of Marshmallow Root in 1 litre of cold water overnight. Strain, mash and apply pulp to psoriasis.
Add 1 Tbsp of **Flax oil** and 3 capsules of **Evening Primrose oil** to the bath to keep skin smooth and supple. Moisturise frequently after showering or bathing

Restless Leg Syndrome

Restless leg syndrome (RLS) often causes disturbed sleep. The legs seem to have a mind of their own as individuals feel an irresistible urge to move them. This is different from the small twitches in the legs and body that occur just before sleep.

Causes

- Blood glucose imbalance
- Caffeine
- Nutrient deficiencies of folic acid, vitamin E, iron, 5HTP (5-Hydroxy tryptophan), chromium and magnesium

- Uraemia: an increased concentration of urea or creatinine in the blood linked to kidney disease.

Signs and symptoms
- Uncomfortable sensations in the legs
- Unpleasant crawling or aching sensation in the lower legs
- Symptoms occur while resting, in the early evening or at night
- Spontaneous leg cramps.

Naturopathic recommendations

Lifestyle hints
This syndrome is difficult to treat if an iron deficiency is present. See page 73 for Anaemia and iron treatment recommendations.

Exercise
- Exercise improves the quality of sleep and reduces stress.
- Exercise 3–4 times weekly for 20–40 minutes with a mixture of cardiovascular exercise (walking, gentle jogging, running) and resistance exercise (yoga, lunges, weights).

Nutrition
- A sugar-free, high-protein diet dramatically reduces symptoms and studies show RLS patients have gone into complete remission following these diets.[101, 102]
- Consume 3 meals daily and include two healthy snack meals in between to help balance blood sugar levels. Frequent snacking has been known to put symptoms into remission.
- Late-night feeding helps to balance blood sugar levels. If RLS is keeping you awake get up and make a snack that contains carbohydrates and protein, such as a protein drink with a banana, or a tuna sandwich.
- Avoid caffeine cocoa, chocolate, coffee, cola, black and green tea. Caffeine has been shown to increase symptoms and imbalance blood sugar levels.
- Drink 1–2 litres of pure, fresh water and herb teas, including chamomile, kava and nerve-relaxing teas.

Supplements
Folic acid Deficiencies may lead to RLS and nerve problems. Take 5mg–30mg daily. Medical supervision is needed for testing and because high dose Folic acid supplementation can mask other anaemia-related deficiencies. Take Folic acid with a high potency **Vitamin B complex**.
Iron Succinate or fumarate are the preferred iron forms that are highly absorbable, do not appear to upset the stomach and do not cause constipation. Take 30mg 3 times daily with meals.
Magnesium Helps to relax the muscles and allay any Magnesium deficiencies associated with RLS. Take 450mg daily.
5-Hydroxy tryptophan (5HTP) Helps relax muscles by balancing serotonin levels with 5HTP, the serotonin regulation precursor. Take 50mg–300mg daily.
Vitamin E Deficiencies may lead to RLS and poor circulation. Take 400IU daily for at least 3 months for it to be effective.
Chromium (Chromium Picolinate) This essential trace element is required for normal insulin functioning. Adequate amounts of Chromium can significantly reduce insulin

requirements and play a physiological role in promoting insulin tissue sensitivity. Take 300mcg–400mcg daily.

Seasonal Affective Disorder

As winter approaches and the days get shorter, some people experience a form of depression that is not present during the spring and summer months. It is known as seasonal affective disorder (SAD). SAD is an extreme case of the 'winter blues'.

Causes

The exact cause of SAD is still unknown; however, we do know that people with SAD have a difficult time adjusting to the lack of bright light in the winter months. During the autumn and winter months, less light passes through our eyes, inhibiting the release of an important brain chemical, serotonin. When serotonin is not released in sufficient quantity, depressive symptoms begin to occur. Melatonin, another important brain chemical, is produced as we are exposed to darkness. The brain may release too much melatonin, also contributing to depressive symptoms.

Signs and symptoms

In all cases, people who think they may have SAD should discuss their symptoms with a (mental) healthcare professional.
- **Subsyndromal SAD** or 'winter blues' is a more mild form of SAD. Symptoms include mild depression or anxiety, irritability, low libido, fatigue and lethargy. Insomnia in the form of disturbed sleep or waking up too early and not feeling fully rested may also occur. Feelings of sleepiness throughout the day and cravings for carbohydrates (sugary, starchy foods) can lead to weight gain.
- **SAD** individuals have the same symptoms (as above), but much more severe and including a deep form of depression that can actually prevent them from functioning normally. SAD symptoms may disappear during spring, either suddenly, with a short period (e.g. four weeks) of hyperactivity, or gradually, depending on the intensity of sunlight in the spring and early summer.

Naturopathic recommendations

Lifestyle hints
- You don't need to wait for the spring months or move closer to the equator to experience more sunlight to overcome SAD. Traditionally SAD has been treated with psychotherapy and antidepressants. However, for mild symptoms, spending time outdoors during the day or arranging homes and workplaces to receive more sunlight may be helpful. Sit near a window and look outside for 15 minutes at a time, 3 times daily. An hour's walk in winter sunlight may be as effective as two and a half hours under bright, artificial light.
- Extend each day through artificial sunlight. Light therapy has shown great promise in treating those suffering from moderate to severe cases of SAD. Light therapy can include sitting near SAD light boxes for 1–2 hours daily, (at least 2500lux–10,000lux [lux is the technical measure of brightness] is needed). Specially designed light boxes can be positioned anywhere in the room. You don't have to sit too close for it to be effective. Most people take the time out to read, knit, work or watch TV.

- Increase your outdoor physical activity during winter months and surround yourself with friends, family members or co-workers to avoid isolation.
- Limit stimulants such as alcohol, nicotine and caffeine.

Supplements

5-Hydroxy tryptophan (5HTP)   People who suffer from SAD or depression have low serotonin levels. Serotonin is the 'feel good' neurotransmitter chemical in the brain. To help boost serotonin levels, I suggest a course of 5HTP, which is derived from the African plant *Griffonia simplicifolia*. 5HTP is a serotonin precursor and is often recommended as low serotonin levels may contribute to depression and are also linked with SAD. Take 150mg–300mg daily.

Immunity   There is also a link between SAD sufferers and a weakened immune system. Immune disorders including colds and flus, chronic fatigue syndrome and bacterial infections, such as sinusitis and bronchitis, further complicate depression. Taking herbs, vitamins and minerals may help boost your immune system. These include **Garlic** (400mg daily), **Echinacea** (1200mg–6g daily), **Vitamin C** (1500mg daily), **Zinc** (45mg) and **Olive Leaf extract** (1g–2g daily). Most sufferers show signs of a weakened immune system during winter, making them more vulnerable to infections and other illnesses.

Herbs

St John's Wort   For mild depression, anxiety and nervousness. Take 2g–5g of dried herb daily.

Nerve tonics   **Jamaican Dogwood** (2g–4g of dried root bark up to 3 times daily), **Californian Poppy** (900mg daily), **Skullcap** (750mg 3–5 times daily) and **Passionflower** (4g–8g daily) are useful for anxiety associated with depression and may also help relax muscles that are tight and knotty from nervous tension.

Seborrhoeic Dermatitis

Seborrhoeic dermatitis is a disorder of the sebaceous (oil secreting) glands which creates scaly patches of skin. It often appears on the scalp, chest and face, but can appear on other parts of the body as well. It is often mistaken for dandruff as the scalp can beome greasy and flaky. Seborrhoeic dermatitis can be triggered by trauma, illness, hormonal imbalances and improper carbohydrate and sugar consumption. Deficiencies of vitamins, essential fatty acids and selenium have also been linked.

Causes

- The cause is not known; however, nutritional deficiencies may be associated with the cause (i.e. biotin and vitamin A).
- Yeast *Pityrosporum ovale* may be a cause, and heredity and climate also play a role.
- Adult seborrhoea is often exacerbated by stress and anxiety.
- Other triggers may include psoriasis, Parkinson's disease, acne rosacea and AIDS.
- Infrequent shampooing, allergy to hair products, excessively oily skin or high-sugar or refined carbohydrate diets may also contribute to seborrhoeic dermatitis.
- Food allergies.

Signs and symptoms

- Skin can often become itchy.
- Seborrhoeic skin may be yellowish and greasy, or dry and flaky.

Seborrhoeic Dermatitis

- Smallish lumps that are slightly pink from itching and irritation may appear.
- The lumps can form together as irritated patchy skin.
- Common in infancy as cradle cap, or can occur at middle age.

Naturopathic recommendations

Lifestyle hints
- Identify food allergies and sensitivities, see page 164 for details.
- Dry skin thoroughly after bathing or showering.

Nutrition
- Eliminate dairy products, fried foods, sugar and flour. If avoiding dairy, substitute with calcium fortified soy or take supplements if choosing rice milk varieties.
- Do not eat raw egg whites as this inhibits biotin absorption.
- Consume low-glycaemic index (GI) foods. The GI is a method of classifying foods according to their potential to increase blood sugar levels. Eating high-GI foods results in higher and more rapid increases in blood glucose levels compared to eating low-GI foods. Switch from a high sugar and refined carbohydrate intake to a low-fat, complex carbohydrate, low-GI diet to reduce insulin resistance. High saturated fat and sugar intake consumption is linked to seborrhoeic dermatitis.
- Eat more of the following low-GI foods:
  Breads   Multigrain, wholemeal or whole grain, sour dough and rye. Avoid light white breads, cookies, cakes and crackers.
  Cereals and grains   Wholemeal grains, basmati rice, long grain rice, rice bran, bulgur wheat, buckwheat, corn (avoid cornflakes and puffed corn), oats, oat bran, muesli (unsweetened and untoasted) and pearl barley.
  Other   Beans, legumes, tofu (and soy products), nuts, seeds, pasta and noodles (avoid corn and rice pasta), vegetables (avoid potatoes), fresh fruits, skim milk, yoghurt and soy milk.
- Avoid saturated fats, especially altered unnatural fat derivatives in margarines and shortenings as they can aggravate inflammation. Avoid or cut down on cheeses, butter, animal fats (e.g. from pork and beef), coconut cream, and trans fatty acids, including fried foods.
- Restrict alcohol, tobacco use and salt intake. If needed only use unbleached Celtic sea salt (see your health shop).

Supplements
Zinc   The importance of Zinc for skin health is well recognised as it can improve and increase skin healing and health within 12 weeks. Take up to 45mg of Zinc amino acid chelate daily. Non-oily zinc cream is also known to be beneficial.
Selenium and **Chromium**   Assist with healing of the skin. Take 200mcg of Selenium and 300mcg of Chromium daily and combine with a **Vitamin B complex**.
Flax oil and **Evening Primrose oil**   These plant seeds supply Omega 6 oil (Linoleic acid) which is often deficient in the sebum and this may contribute to the disruption of healthy sebum secretion. Take 1 Tbsp of Flax oil (or 10 1000mg capsules) and 3000mg of Evening Primrose oil daily. Another way to include Flax oil in your diet is to mix 1 Tbsp–2 Tbsp of Flaxseed oil daily with the juice of ½–1 lemon, salt and pepper for a delicious salad dressing.
Vitamin B complex   Contains **Biotin** which has been shown to be deficient in seborrhoeic dermatitis. Take a high potency Vitamin B complex as directed and aim for levels of 50mg of Biotin daily.
Vitamin A   Has been shown to be deficient in seborrhoeic dermatitis sufferers. It can increase healing of the skin and may reduce scarring. Take 5000IU–10,000IU daily.

Acidophilus Helps to repopulate gut with 'good' bacteria and lessen bowel toxicity. Take 1–2 capsules daily that contain 1 billion of both *Bifidus* and *Lactobacillus acidophilus* strains.

Herbs

Detox Complete a gentle detox herbal programme and a parasite-cleansing programme to balance the internal body organs and prepare for a healthy start. Detox herbs should include **Burdock** (2g–6g of dried root daily) **Cleavers** (2g–4g daily) and **Red Clover** (2g–4g daily) to help cleanse the blood and clear the lymphatics. **Dandelion** (3g–5g of dried root daily) and **Milk Thistle** (9g–10g of seed daily) enhance bile flow and detoxify the liver.
Aloe Vera juice To aid proper digestion of food take 20ml–50ml with each meal.
Sarsaparilla A specific herb for treating skin conditions. Take 1g–4g daily.

Herbal rinses and scrubs

An infusion of **Chamomile, Thyme** and **Rosemary** as a skin rinse may be beneficial. Steep a handful of these herbs in a pot with just-boiled water for 20 minutes and then strain out the herbs. Add a pinch of **Ascorbic acid** (**Vitamin C** powder obtained from the chemist) to the rinse and dissolve. After shampooing and rinsing hair, use this as a secondary rinse carefully avoiding the eyes.

Use a skin scrub to loosen dead skin from the scalp, but avoid raw patches to allow healing to take place.

Shingles

Herpes zoster (shingles) is believed to come from the reactivation of the varicella (chicken pox) virus lying dormant in cells of a dorsal root ganglion (section of nerve). Chicken pox can occur at any age, but it's most common in children from 2–8 years old. Therefore shingles in adults may result from the herpes virus waiting to strike from childhood onward. This infection may become active in adult years in the form of shingles, sores or blisters and localised pain along the course of the sensory nerves. The shingles lesions are often preceded by three days of fever and burning or irritation of the skin. Herpes zoster symptoms are more likely to occur in people whose immune systems are suppressed.

Without treatment, viruses can be immortal. Many orthodox treatments are symptomatic but cannot penetrate the viral host's cell. Getting rid of symptoms related to the viral infection doesn't mean that the virus is eliminated. The virus can remain dormant and break out again when the host's immunity becomes compromised. Once a viral disease has invaded, the well-being of the host remains in danger of breaking down again.

Signs and symptoms

- Pain and tingling may precede (by several days) the re-emergence of the virus into the skin.
- It then produces characteristic vesicles (blisters), papules (a small solid elevation of the skin) or bulbous lesions throughout the skin.
- Secondary infection increases discomfort, and in an elderly person, intractable post-herpetic neuralgia may follow an attack of the shingles.
- Small ulcers sometimes appear on the face in association with cranial nerve involvement.
- Trigeminal nerve disease can lead to infection of the eye.

Warning: Patients with shingles may be infectious. The virus can be spread from fresh skin lesions by direct contact or by airborne transmission. Patients with shingles can be subject to complications and, therefore, must be **medically** monitored.

Complications: Postherpetic neuralgia
Postherpetic neuralgia is pain in the zone of the previous eruption; it occurs in some 10% of patients (often elderly). It is a burning, continuous pain that responds poorly to analgesics. Depression is almost universal. Treatment (orthodox) is unsatisfactory but there is a trend towards gradual recovery in two years.

Orthodox treatment includes drying, soothing creams like calamine lotion, antiseptic powders to limit secondary infection, acyclovir taken orally 5 times daily, and prednisolone.

Herbal Topical cream can be used by those who do not want to use chemicals or wish for a herbal or natural alternative. Try herbal creams with lysine and lemon balm herb, these may be available from health stores and some pharmacies.

Some creams may spread the blisters. Do try to avoid any creams that have this effect.

Naturopathic recommendations

Lifestyle hints
As a run-down condition can bring on shingles and the illness itself is extremely weakening, treatment aims to restore health and immune function.
- Avoid extreme weather changes.
- Apply ice to tingle if you feel a herpetic sore coming on.

Nutrition
- Eat fresh fruit and vegetables that have been thoroughly washed then boiled or steamed, or eat them raw. Choose green leafy vegetables and reduce consumption of tomatoes, potatoes and eggplant.
- Reduce consumption of all processed foods and eat foods that are prepared from scratch.
- Increase intake of yoghurt.
- Reduce consumption of protein as much as possible and eat only organic meats. Protein can encourage herpetic blisters and symptoms. If you do eat protein take the amino acid supplement lysine to counteract the arginine amino acid that is linked to shingles activation.
- These foods trigger the spread of shingles: chicken, eggs, salmon, tuna, bacon, beef, milk, stocks, almonds, peanuts, nuts, chocolate, brown rice, fried foods, corn and possibly foods containing gluten.

Supplements
Vitamin C Provides antioxidant protection against pollution and toxins. Take 1500mg daily.
Lysine An amino acid that may help reduce blisters and aid healing. Take up to 6g daily.
Zinc Helps the body fight off a range of viral infections from strep and influenza to herpes and the common cold. Take 45mg daily.

Herbs
Olive Leaf extract Has several antiviral properties that help to boost the immune system and may also help to eradicate viruses. Research shows that Olive Leaf extract with oleuropein can destroy the protein coating of the herpes virus, helping to reduce symptoms and ongoing infection. Take 270mg of Olive Leaf extract 3 times daily.

In 1969, Harold E. Renis, PhD, a virologist with The Upjohn Company of Kalamazoo,

Michigan, proved that calcium elenolate from oleuropein in the Olive Leaf is virucidal for all viruses against which it was tested. In particular, Dr. Renis showed that calcium elenolate kills the herpes virus, including the varicella zoster virus (VZ).
Astragalus The antiviral action of Astragalus is mainly due to increased immunity and interferon production. Take 500mg–10g daily.
Pau D'Arco Effective against viral activity including herpes 1 and 2 and influenza. Take 1.5g–3.5g daily.
St John's Wort Has antiviral action against cold sores and herpes outbreaks. Take the equivalent of 2g–5g of dried root daily.
Lemon Balm Add 1 handful of leaves to a pot of hot water. Cover with a plate and leave to steep for 15 minutes. You may drink this tincture or add to baths, as a gargle etc. Best to use as a preventative or when the first symptoms are felt or appear.

Pain
Capsaicin Derived from **Cayenne**, Capsaicin desensitises nerves. About 10% of all patients with herpes zoster experience postherpetic neuralgia about 30 days after herpetic infection. In 50% of cases, patients over the age of 60 may develop severe pain. Capsaicin cream is used to provide relief from postherpetic pain from shingles, phantom limb pain, cluster headaches, neuropathies, osteoarthritis and pain from skin conditions including psoriasis and puritis.[103,104] In one study patients suffering from postherpetic neuralgia found that a topical applications of Capsaicin cream (0.025%v Capsaicin) on painful areas was beneficial.[105] Should be continued for 4 weeks with a response expected at the end of the four weeks of treatment. Hands must be washed thoroughly to avoid contact within the eyes.
St John's Wort Has a specific effect on nerves, acting as a mild sedative, reducing pain, and is beneficial for mild depression, anxiety and nervousness associated with ongoing chronic pain. Take 2g–5g of dried herb or use topically (on the skin) as a tincture poultice, cream or oil on nerve pain sites.
Californian Poppy Has mild analgesic and sedative properties. It also exhibits a relaxing effect on the mind and has potential mood elevating actions without addictive side effects. Take 900mg daily.
Jamaican Dogwood Used for neuralgia and insomnia due to its anti-inflammatory and sedative effects. Take 2g–4g of dried root bark up to 3 times daily.

Sinusitis and Sore Throat
Many people experience these two conditions together as infection is normally involved. Viruses, fungal infections and bacterial infections often cause the sinuses to become inflamed with mucus build-up especially from colds or flus. The mucus is a perfect warm, moist breeding ground for infection, and transports it to the throat causing inflammation and reinstigating the infection.

Causes
- Acute viral respiratory infection.
- Bacterial infection including many resistant to common antibiotics. The bacteria *Streptococcus pneumoniae* and *Haemophilus influenzae* cause most of all sinusitis cases. *Staphylococcus aureus* is another bacterium that causes sinusitis.
- Dental infection.
- Allergies include hayfever, dairy and gluten (wheat, rye, barley and oats).

- Chronic sinusitis is normally caused by allergy although infection or even obstruction can lead to it.

Signs and symptoms
- Nasal congestion (possible nasal discharge intermittent with dryness)
- Headaches (frontal) are common
- Pain, tenderness, redness and swelling over involved sinus
- Postnasal drip
- Non-productive cough
- Fever and chills
- Putrid taste in mouth
- Itchy throat
- Swallowing is painful, especially if it is a throat infection caused by strep rather than a viral infection.

Naturopathic recommendations

Lifestyle hints
- Get regular sleep and bed rest.
- Local applications of heat have been shown to be very effective in alleviating both short-term and long-term sinus problems.

Nutrition
- Drink large amounts (2 litres) of purified water, diluted vegetable juices, soups and teas. Sage tea is very astringent and can soothe a sore throat.
- Limit simple sugar (maltose, glucose, white sugar, brown sugar, castor sugar, icing and even fruit sugars) consumption to 50g a day as sugar reduces the immune system function.
- Avoid airborne irritants such as tobacco smoke.
- Eliminate common food allergens (milk, gluten [wheat, rye, oats and barley], eggs, citrus, corn and peanut butter) until a more definite diagnosis can be made.
- Dairy products can produce excess mucus as can egg whites. Reduce dairy intake until symptoms subside.

Supplements
Acidophilus and **Bifidus** Beneficial bacteria that help to keep the digestive system healthy. If you have taken antibiotics as a treatment for secondary bacterial infection you will need to take 1 billion of the Acidophilus and Bifidus species in capsule form daily on an empty stomach to repopulate your digestive system after the antibiotic course.
Vitamin C Enhances white blood cell activity and immune support. Take 1500mg daily.
Zinc Requirements are increased during poor immunity. Take 45mg daily. Zinc gluconate lozenges (5mg–10mg) dissolved in the mouth every 2 hours help to coat the throat and mouth, improving Zinc levels and helping to inhibit viral replication.
Vitamin A or its precursor **Beta Carotene** Helps to heal any damage to the lining of the sinus and throat. Take 5000IU–8000IU daily.

Herbs
Olive Leaf extract The naturopathic treatment of choice as it can help eradicate antibiotic resistant bacteria. Rhinoviruses that precipitate colds and flus can progress into chronic sinusitis. Take 270mg 3 times daily.

Astragalus (500g–10g daily) and **Pau D'Arco** (1.5g–3.5g daily)   Help to enhance the body's resistance and are antiviral, effective for cold or flu viruses.

Echinacea   Improves the body's immune system. Echinacea is safe to take even while breastfeeding and helps to modulate and correct the immune system. Take a maximum of 1200mg daily if you are pregnant or breastfeeding. Take 1200mg–6g daily for 10–30 days for signs of viral, bacterial or fungal infection.

Myrrh and **Goldenseal**   These herbs are antiseptic and antimicrobial. Gargle with Myrhh and Goldenseal daily.

Castor oil   Massage the sinuses with Castor oil or apply a Castor oil pack. Pour Castor oil on a cloth and fold into a pack. Apply to sinus and place a heated flannel over the Castor oil pack. Be careful not to burn the skin. Reapply heated flannel until oil is absorbed.

Eucalyptus, Lavender and **Friars Balsam**   Add 2–3 drops of each in a bowl of hot water and inhale the steam to help clear the sinuses. Or add these essential oils to olive oil or popular bases such as almond or jojoba oils and massage into the feet and chest for congestion relief.

Homemade herbal teas   Simmer a handful of fresh **Sage** and **Thyme** herbs for 15 minutes. Strain the herbs and add manuka honey to sweeten. This tea helps relieve coughs and sore throats. Additionally simmer a handful of **Catnip** herb to help reduce fevers. **Lavender** and **Chamomile** tea help children calm down, especially if coughing or breathing is affected and they start to panic.

Sports Injuries

Every time I watch sports on the telly with a cuppa I grimace at the athletes who come off second best from sports injuries. I hope they employ natural therapies alongside physiotherapy to increase their rate of healing. Whether you're a professional sports person or experiencing a sport for the first time, chronic, acute or niggly injuries can respond really well to natural medicine, which helps get you back on your feet sooner rather than later.

Common injuries

Broken and **fractured bones** occur frequently in sport. A stress fracture is an overuse injury that can occur when muscles are unable to absorb added shock due to fatigue. The overload of stress is transferred to the bone causing a tiny crack.

Bruises or **haematomas** are clots of blood that have accumulated in the tissues after an injury or trauma to an area.

Bursitis is inflammation of the bursa, a fibrous sac that contains synovial fluid to lubricate the joints. Excessive friction, stress, forceful blunt trauma and even bacterial infection can cause bursitis, inflammation and swelling, and, if prolonged, calcified deposits on the bursa.

Cartilage injuries mainly involve tearing the menisci or knee cartilage by excessive twisting, which rips the joint capsule with the meniscus attached to it. As cartilage lacks blood supply it is difficult for it to nourish and heal itself.

Dislocation injuries happen when the bone is forced out of its joint socket or normal position, causing inflammation, pain and swelling.

Frozen shoulder is a shoulder joint with significant loss of its range of motion in all directions. Frozen shoulder can result from a strain leading to inflammation and possible scarring, thickening and shrinkage of the capsule that surrounds the normal shoulder joint. Any injury to the shoulder can lead to frozen shoulder, including tendonitis, bursitis and rotator cuff injury.

Overuse injuries involve repetitive or forceful movements or the maintenance of constrained or awkward postures. Discomfort and persistent pain are the main signs and symptoms involved.

Shin splints present as pain in front of the shin bone usually caused by a stress fracture or very small tears in the leg muscles at their point of attachment to the shin or inflammation of the sheath that protects the bone. It can be caused by overtraining, running on a hard surface and poor quality running or cross training shoes that do not provide support or perhaps aren't properly fitted.

Sprains occur when a ligament is overly stretched or tears.

Strains are a twist, pull and/or tear of a muscle and/or tendon.

Tendonitis is caused by trauma, a strain, stretching or overuse, which can lead to inflammation of the tendon (connects muscle to bone) and, if prolonged, calcified deposits can accumulate on the tendon.

The Achilles tendon connects muscles in the lower leg with the heel bone. Sports that tighten the calf muscles (or a blow to the foot, ankle or calf) can overstress this tendon and cause Achilles tendonitis.

Torn ligaments occur when the ligament is torn away from the bone. Too much tension can overstretch (over 6% of its length) the ligament, causing it to snap. Torn ligaments may involve the knee joints, groin, or Achilles tendon. Ligaments are fibrous and similar to tendons in tissue type and brace joints to keep them stable.

In the case of knee injuries, the anterior cruciate ligament (ACL) and the medial collateral ligament (MCL) are often injured in sports. The posterior cruciate ligament (PCL) also is frequently injured. A twisting motion is normally the cause of damage for knee injuries. Individuals who ski, play soccer, basketball, netball, hockey, tennis or rugby commonly tear their knee ligaments.

Tennis elbow is a condition where the outer part of the elbow becomes painful and tender, usually as a result of a specific strain, overuse or a direct bang. The outer part of the elbow is painful and tender to touch, and movements which involve lifting cause pain.

Naturopathic recommendations

Lifestyle hints

- Employ the RICE (rest, ice, compression and elevation) method. Rest the injured area by avoiding using it too much, or at all, when you first injure the site. To control swelling wrap ice in a tea towel and apply it onto or around the injured site for 30 minutes. Wait for 15 minutes then apply for another 30 minutes. Use a compressive elastic bandage applied snugly, but loose enough so that it does not cause pain and allows circulation. Finally, keep the injured site elevated above the level of your heart.
- Wear correct footwear. Replace athletic shoes as soon as the tread or heel wears out and make sure they support the arch of the foot and are designed for the type of sport you are participating in.
- Support the injury. Buy a brace from a sports shop or pharmaceutical supplier to immobilse the injured area and support recovery.
- Physiotherapy and/or ultrasound three times weekly aids recovery. See your local physiotherapist.
- Professional trainers can reduce injuries by showing you the correct techniques and can also take you through recovery or strengthening exercises.
- Warm up and stretch before any sports activity.
- Listen to your body. Don't overdo it. If pain is experienced or is more frequent or intense than normal, back off. Remember you still need time to regenerate, so it's a great excuse to get plenty of good quality rest, sleep and relaxation.

Nutrition

- Nightshade vegetables, such as eggplant, tomatoes, bell peppers, potatoes, onion and garlic, and tobacco, lamb and seafood can increase pain and inflammation in some people. It may be interesting to eliminate these foods while you are experiencing pain and inflammation to see if avoidance of these foods works for you. Other foods that can increase pain include instant coffee and red meat.
- Drink 1–2 litres of fresh water daily.
- Omega 3 and 6 are anti-inflammatory and increase the rate of healing. Increase intake of omega 3 oil by including deep-sea fish, such as tuna, salmon and sardines, in your diet on a daily basis or take 3g of omega 3 fish oil daily. Add 1 tsp–1 Tbsp of whole or crushed flaxseed (linseed) to your cereal in the morning to boost omega 3 and 6 dietary intake.
- Add ginger and turmeric to food to increase circulation and help reduce inflammation.
- Consume a lot of berries, cherries and blue, red, yellow and green fruit and vegetables to increase antioxidants and fibre in the diet.
- Make nourishing, hearty stews and soups that include cartilage from chicken, shark or beef to aid repair of your own joints, tendons and ligaments.
- Make sure you have adequate protein in your diet for muscle repair.

Supplements

Essential fatty acids or **Omega 3** and **6 oils**   Help to reduce inflammation within the joints. Take 3g–6g of **Evening Primrose oil** or **Fish oil** daily, or 1 Tbsp–2 Tbsp (13,000mg–26,000mg) of **Flax oil** daily. Essential fatty acids are important as they support the body's production of beneficial type 1 and type 3 prostaglandins, those which counteract pain and inflammation.

Antioxidant formulas   Those containing ProenOthera® (EPO Seed), Pine Bark, Green tea, Grape Seed, Ginkgo, Kelp, Beta 1.3 Glucan, Vitamins A, C, E, minerals Zinc and Selenium and amino acids Cysteine and Methionine are good antioxidant combinations to help reduce inflammation, further scarring and deposits to joints areas, enhance collagen repair and joint recovery, and inhibit damaging free radicals and excessive bone and joint-chewing enzymes. Strenuous exercise is known to produce an overload of harmful free radicals that damage healthy cells by oxidising the phospholipids in the cell membrane. Antioxidants neutralise the free radicals and limit their destructive impact, which is why athletes must make sure to get adequate amounts of antioxidants to protect themselves against stress injuries.

Vitamin C   Antioxidants such as Vitamins C and **E** may help prevent sports injuries by reducing the muscle damage caused by free radicals. Vitamin C is also a key player in the formation of the collagen that forms tendons and ligaments. Take 1500mg–5000mg daily.

Glucosamine and **Chondroitin**   These are anti-inflammatory and analgesic to joint areas, tendons, ligaments and connective tissue. They work by providing the ingredients required for these tissue types to the body. Research suggests that they heal damaged fissures within cartilage, and remodel and regenerate these damaged tissue areas. They are seen as an alternative therapy to anti-inflammatories, which inhibit growth regeneration. Take 1500mg of Glucosamine and 1200mg of Chondroitin daily.

MSM (methyl sulphonyl methane)   One of many organic sulphur compounds. Although it contains elemental sulphur (34%) it should not be confused with sulphur itself. MSM occurs naturally in minute amounts in food and the body. As a dietary supplement, it appears to inhibit pain impulses along nerve fibres, acting as an analgesic and anti-inflammatory. It also inhibits muscle spasms and increases blood flow. MSM is indicated for tendonitis, bursitis and tennis elbow to help regenerate healing and reduce inflammation and pain. Take 2g daily.

Magnesium Wards off muscle cramps, helps with muscular tension and the pain associated with it. As the muscles cushion themselves and isolate damaged areas with swelling, the Magnesium may help encourage relaxing of the muscles and therefore help the pain and inflammation. Take 450mg daily.
Bromelain and **Papain** These are enzymes found in pineapple and papaya. They effectively ease the inflammation, bruising and pain caused by strains and sprains. They speed up the healing process for relieving muscular pain. Dosage equates to 2000mg (1200mcu–1800mcu 'milk clotting units') per day divided into five doses taken on an empty stomach or 250mg–750mg 2 times daily.
Bone healing and **regeneration** Take supplements that include **Calcium** (**Citrate** and **Hydroxyapatite**), **Magnesium**, **Silica**, **Manganese**, **Zinc**, **Vitamin K**, **D** and **Boron**.

Herbs

Devil's Claw Contains two active ingredients, **Harpogoside** and **Betasitosterol**, with anti-inflammatory properties that help to reduce swelling and pain while also improving the mobility of the joints. One study found that its anti-inflammatory effects equalled those of the commonly prescribed anti-arthritic drug phenylbutazone.[106] Take 500mg of dried root daily.
Celery Seed Most widely used to help reduce pain and swelling associated with arthritic conditions and sports injuries. Celery Seed is a natural diuretic so it can be helpful in preventing fluid build-up. Take 500mg–3g daily.
White Willow Bark A natural pain reliever with an ingredient similar to aspirin. Take 1g–2g daily.
Other beneficial herbs Include **Ginger** and **Rue** to increase circulation. Rue also reduces spasms of contracted tight muscles and is popular as an anti-rheumatic remedy. **Wild Yam** and **Cramp Bark** normally associated with PMS-like conditions are also beneficial as anti-inflammatories and for muscle spasms. **Guaiacum** and **Jamaican Dogwood** are herbs used for chronic muscle pain.

External applications
Creams, ointments and gels to be used externally (topically).
Aloe Vera gel Mixed with oil of **Wintergreen**, **Menthol** or balms, such as **Tiger balm**, may increase circulation and heat to joints, relieving pain.
Arnica, Ginger, Basil and **Capsaicin** from capsicum Just a few examples of herbs that may be used topically on the skin over the joints to relieve pain and inflammation.
Calendula and **Tea Tree oil** Good for soothing cuts, scrapes, abrasions and help treat athlete's foot.
Arnica Liquid, creams or gels alleviate sore muscles and bruises. Arnica is also a capillary protector. When you do a lot of sports, it is common to have a bit of bleeding in the muscles. Arnica will help prevent that. Never use Arnica on an open wound.
St John's Wort May be better recognised by its Latin name *Hypericum perforatum*. Hypericum cream, oil or gel is fantastic for injuries that have a lot of nerve pain involvement, including sciatica.
Castor oil packs Have been known to help with pain, scar tissue and inflammation.

> How to make a Castor oil pack
>
> You will need: Castor oil (obtained from the chemist), a soft clean cotton cloth, plastic wrap, a plastic container to store the oil-laden cloth, and a hot water bottle. Directions: Soak the cloth in Castor oil. Place the folded cloth over the affected area after you have employed the RICE method for the acute inflammatory stage (normally 24–48 hours). Do not use on open wounds. Cover the cloth completely

with plastic wrap, both to avoid staining your clothes and to keep in the warmth. Place a towel over the plastic and put a hot water bottle on it. Leave it on overnight. Repeat this five nights in a row and rest for two nights. Do this for three weeks.

Broken or fractured bones Can be healed with a **Comfrey Leaf poultice**. I know most people will have their break immobilised or have a cast on, but this may be useful for areas such as fractured ribs after you have employed the RICE method for the acute inflammatory stage (normally 24–48 hours). A Comfrey poultice eases the pain.

> *How to make a Comfrey poultice*
> Place a handful of fresh or dried Comfrey leaves in a saucepan, cover with water and bring to the boil. Remove from the heat and place the leaves between 2 pieces of gauze. Allow to cool slightly and then place on the broken bone area. It should be hot but not burning. When the poultice cools maintain the warmth by putting a hot water bottle on top. Apply 3 times daily until you have relief then once daily for 2 weeks or more until bone break or fracture heals. You can also apply Comfrey cream on the site and take Comfrey homeopathic remedies to enhance healing.

Homeopathy

Homeopathic remedies taken externally or in this case internally as I've recommended below can make a world of difference to sports injury treatment and its success.

Sarcolactic acid Great for pain involving lactic acid build-up. Five pellets of the 12C or 30C potency is standard, and depending on the severity of the injury, this dose should be repeated every 15 or 30 minutes for four hours.

Arnica montana Treats sports injuries including bruises, nerve injuries, broken bones and fractures easing inflammation and pain. For best results, take Arnica internally immediately after sustaining an injury. Five pellets of the 12C or 30C potency is standard, and depending on the severity of the injury, this dose should be repeated every 15 or 30 minutes for four hours.

Broken bones or **fractures** *Calcarea phosphorica* and **Comfrey** (*Symphytum officinale*) help the bones to knit back together. In fact another name for Comfrey is knitbone. Five pellets of each in a 12C concentration taken in the morning and evening will lessen pain and greatly encourage bone regeneration.

Rhus Tox A wonderful homeopathic remedy for creaking, aching joints. Five pellets of the 12C or 30C potency is standard, and depending on the severity of the injury, this dose should be repeated every 15 or 30 minutes for four hours.

Ruta graveolens (**Rue**) Has long been used to help mend injured and stiff tendons (tendonitis) and ligaments. It's fantastic for shin splints and can work within a matter of minutes if chosen correctly for your type of injury. Five pellets of the 12C or 30C potency is standard, and depending on the severity of the injury, this dose should be repeated every 15 or 30 minutes for four hours. Rue is another homeopathic remedy specific for tendonitis.

Schuessler tissue salts

Homeopathically prepared minerals. Take every ½ hour until symptoms lessen or take more frequently, every 5 minutes, for a faster-working action.

Combination U Contains **Calc Phos**, **Calc Fluor**, **Silica** and **Nat Phos** to enhance absorption of Calcium and lay Calcium down where it is needed, such as fractures or broken bones.

Calc Phos Calcium phosphate can enhance Calcium uptake from food.

Other treatments
Massage, acupuncture, physiotherapy, osteopathy and a myriad types of other hands-on, therapeutic body work increase the rate of healing.
Bowen Technique Excellent for tennis elbow, frozen shoulder, bursitis and pain that will not respond to treatment. The Bowen Technique consists of a series of gentle rolling-type moves over muscle tissue on specific points, mainly on back, legs and neck. It is non-intrusive and is mostly performed over light clothing. Use an internet search engine for your nearest Bowen Practitioner.

Stress

Stress is a term widely used in today's society. Often daily demands build up to a point where we feel it is almost impossible to cope. We all know what it feels like, but what is stress?

Causes
Stress can stem from anything which creates a disturbance, including exposure to heat, cold or environmental toxins. We are geared to adapt to these stressors every day. However, if stress is extreme, unusual or long lasting, it may have a detrimental effect on health. Stress may be an expression of:
- Job pressures
- Deadlines
- Family arguments
- Relationship and financial pressures.

Signs and symptoms
- Tiredness, high blood pressure and cholesterol, and asthma.
- Immune suppression, leading to colds, flu and poor immunity against viruses and bacteria.
- Stomach ulcers, depression, insomnia, shingles, cold sores, headaches, migraines and PMS.
- Being prone to allergies and illnesses, weight gain and loss, blood sugar imbalances, dizziness, hot flushes, shaking, irritability, anxiety, increased perspiration, inability to concentrate, lack of energy in the morning and high energy at night, and depression.

How does the body combat stress?
First imagine yourself in a stressful situation. For instance, you're about to have a car accident. Your heart beats faster, your eyesight gets better as the pupils dilate and you might feel a sudden surge of strength. This happens as the adrenal glands that sit on top of the kidneys start to pump out adrenalin, blood rushes into our legs and arms, ready for us to flee the situation or stand up and fight — a primitive instinct. The fight or flight response is turned on and your body and mind are ready to spring into action.

This short-lived reaction can give way to the resistance reaction, which enables you to use up extra fat, glucose and protein as energy. After adrenalin has surged into the body the adrenal glands release cortisol for survival continuation. However, if this reaction is prolonged in response to long-term stress, it can develop into the signs and symptoms we mentioned above, such as high blood pressure.

Naturopathic recommendations

The key to stress recovery
It is important to have the right nutrients that repair and regenerate the adrenal glands as many of the disorders related to stress are not a direct result of stress itself, but a result of nutrient deficiencies caused by long periods of stress.

People experiencing and reacting to stress need to maintain a nutritious, well-balanced diet with special emphasis on replacing nutrients through supplementation to counteract the likelihood of deficiencies.

Lifestyle hints
- Avoid unnecessary stressors including (environmental) outside factors, e.g. processed foods, pollution, etc.
- Check for food sensitivities and thyroid gland dysfunction.
- Lymphatic and deep tissue massage can help release stress and tension.
- Learn how to relax by trying yoga, receiving a massage, or learning meditation or breathing techniques.
- Get plenty of restful sleep. Make sure the room is completely dark to help ensure sleep.
- Sexual intercourse helps to increase the 'feel good' hormones oxytocin and dopamine.
- Ring a counselling service or if appropriate seek spiritual or health professional guidance or communicate with helpful friends or family.

Exercise
- Exercise 3–4 times weekly for 20–40 minutes with a mixture of cardiovascular exercise (walking, gentle jogging, running) and resistance exercise (yoga, lunges, weights).

Nutrition
There are a few options to reduce the stress response and give the body time to repair.
- Potassium can be depleted during adrenal exhaustion, so a diet rich in potassium is critical. Foods rich in potassium include:
Fresh vegetables such as asparagus, avocado, raw carrots, corn, cooked lima beans, spinach, potatoes and raw tomatoes.
Fresh fruits like apples, dried apricots, bananas, oranges, peaches, plums and strawberries.
Unprocessed, cooked fish and meats, such as flounder, salmon, drained tuna, chicken (the white meat), pork, roast lamb and beef.
- The basic nutritional approach to stress management is to eat 5–6 times per day to keep blood sugar levels balanced.
- Eat good, wholesome food, especially potassium-rich food.
- Avoid stimulants such as caffeine (coffee, cola drinks, chocolate, black and green tea), alcohol, tobacco and recreational drugs.
- Take nutritional supplements to aid the adrenal glands and immune system.

Supplements
Stress symptoms can vary from irritation and anxiety to fatigue and insomnia. Adrenal exhaustion is the progressive decreased function of the adrenal glands. To reduce stress symptoms these glands need support.

Vitamin B5   The specific vitamin required for adrenal function. Take 50mg–100mg daily.
Vitamin B complex   Required for adrenal function. Take as directed.
Vitamin C   Vitamin C levels are reduced with stress which may lead to poor immunity

against disease. Take 1500mg daily.
Calcium and **Magnesium**   Deficiencies of these are common and may lead to muscle cramps, anxiety and depression. Take 1500mg of Calcium at night after a meal for better absorption and 450mg–900mg of Magnesium daily.

Herbs

Skullcap   Relaxes nervous tension, helps soothe the nervous system and combines well with the herb Valerian. Take 750mg 3–5 times daily.
Valerian   Has muscle relaxant and anti-anxiety effects. Take during the day for anxiety and/or at night for insomnia. There may, very rarely, be some people who find this herb stimulating. Take 1g–3g daily.
Kava   Has sedating and muscle relaxing effects, and aids anxiety symptoms for those who can't seem to slow down. Take 1.5g–3g of dried root daily.
Passionflower   Reduces nervousness, restlessness and digestive disturbances brought on by anxiety. Action magnified when combined with 5HTP. Take 4g–8g of dried herb daily.
Liquorice   Take 2g–4g daily or as prescribed.
Ginseng (*Panax*)   The specific herb for adrenal exhaustion. It also increases stamina and stress resistance. Take 600mg–10g of dried root daily unless otherwise prescribed.
St John's Wort   For mild depression, anxiety and nervousness. Take 2g–5g of dried herb daily.
Lemon Balm   A gentle relaxing herb with possible pain relieving effects. It may be taken as a tea and has a mint-lemon flavour. (Avoid taking in large doses if you have low thyroid function). Take 5g–10g of dried leaf daily.
Californian Poppy   Has a relaxing effect on the mind and potential mood elevating actions without addictive side effects. Take 900mg daily.

Sunburn

When skin is overexposed to ultraviolet (UV) rays it can burn. Excessive exposure to sun and UV rays is linked to skin cancers, and dermatologists are now beginning to agree that skin ages due to the effects of free radicals which reduce the skin's ability to heal and regenerate, resulting in loss of elasticity, slackness, discolouration and wrinkles.

Causes

- Overexposure to the sun during sports, gardening, sunbathing or even while driving a car.
- Sun beds may cause the skin to burn if not used properly and can cause long-term skin damage. Research also shows that people under the age of 30 who use tanning beds or sun lamps more than 10 times a year are 8 times more likely to develop skin cancers. Among all age groups skin cancer risk doubles among users of sun beds.

Signs and symptoms

- The skin will feel warm and tender to touch.
- Heat vapours may come off the skin.
- The skin will look flushed and red.
- After exposure the skin may become itchy and thin layers of skin may peel off.
- Depending on the severity of the sunburn the skin may even swell and blister. If the skin

has become raw or blisters and sores develop, there is an increased risk of infection and fluid loss.
- Chills, fever, nausea, blurred vision and a headache may accompany sunburn.
- Even sensitive areas including the eyes, eyelids and lips can become burnt; in fact any part of the body can be burnt if overexposed to UV rays.
- Sun spots and hyperpigmentation.
- Constantly sunburnt skin is linked to skin cancer.

Naturopathic recommendations

Lifestyle hints

If you are unsure what to do or if the severity of the burns is extreme, call your nearest medical centre for advice.
- Cool any burns with running cold water for at least 15–30 minutes.
- For minor sunburn, place an ice pack wrapped in a tea towel on the affected area. Use your imagination if you don't have any ice ready. You may use a chilly bin ice pack, frozen bag of peas or wheat bags on the area for 30 minutes to one hour. This can often prevent the skin peeling, resulting in a tan; however, the answer is to not burn your skin in the first place.
- If you have a headache associated with sunburn place the cold packs over your eyes and behind your neck.
- If the eyes are involved you can gently bandage them for 20 minutes.
- Avoid any more exposure to the sun or UV rays until healed. Afterwards give your skin protection by covering up, wearing a sun hat and protective eyewear.
- Use SPF 15+ suncream on exposed skin areas for protection.
- Have plenty of good quality sleep for regeneration and healing.

Nutrition

- Rehydrate your body by drinking 8–10 glasses of fresh water daily.
- Avoid dehydrating liquids such as tea, coffee and alcohol.
- Avoid smoking.
- Drink 50ml of aloe vera juice daily to encourage the body to heal itself.
- Eat plenty of watery fruits and vegetables including apples, melons, grapes, celery, tomatoes, citrus fruits and berries.
- Carrots and other vegetables that have yellow pigments carry compounds called carotenes, natural antioxidants that help protect the skin from sunray damage. Other vegetables and fruits rich in carotenes include apricots, mangoes, yams, squash and green leafy vegetables.
- Avoid any substances that may make your skin photosensitive (oversensitive to UV rays) including high doses of vitamin A (roaccutane or retinols) taken internally for acne, some antibiotics, bergamot essential oil used in perfumes and the herb St John's Wort taken in therapeutic doses over a long period of time.

Supplements

Antioxidant formula Free radical sources include sun overexposure and environmental toxins such as cigarette smoke and pollution. From as early as our mid-20s, our natural antioxidant defence system becomes depleted. Antioxidants are free radical neutralisers and these help our skin to regenerate, slowing the aging process. They also possess antimutagenic activity. Mutagenesis is one of the pathways involved in the initiation of cancer. Antioxidants prevent oxidative damage to skin as a result of UV radiation. Antioxidant formulas containing ProenOthera® (EPO Seed), Pine Bark, Green tea, Grape Seed, Ginkgo, Kelp, Beta 1.3 Glucan, Vitamins A (and Beta Carotene), C, E, minerals Manganese, Zinc and Selenium and amino acids Cysteine and Methionine are good combinations. Take a combined antioxidant formula as recommended.

Carotenoids and **Beta Carotene** Although **Vitamin A** itself has some antioxidant activity, the Vitamin A precursor, Beta Carotene, found in yellow and orange fruits is a more powerful antioxidant. Carotenoids are widely researched and represent the most widespread group of naturally occurring pigments in plant life. They can disarm reactive oxygen molecules generated by sunlight and air pollution and prevent free radical damage to skin, eyes and lungs. Recent evidence demonstrates that carotenes have a potent quenching effect on single-oxygen free radicals. If people go away on holiday and intend to sunbathe, I always recommend they take carotenoids 7–10 days before their holiday and to continue taking carotenoids during and 2 weeks after their holiday. For those with sunburn it is essential to take them for 2 weeks to 3 months after the burn to ensure healing and regeneration of the skin and to help lower the risk of skin cancer. Take 50,000IU–100,000IU of Beta Carotene or combined carotenoids daily.

Vitamin A Helps to heal damaged skin and acts as an antioxidant to protect the skin from free radical damage caused by UV rays. Free radical damage to the skin and mutagenic manifestation can continue well after the exposure. Take 8000IU–10,000IU daily. Avoid doses over 5000IU if pregnant.

Vitamin C Helps the collagen structures within the skin, and encourages healing and regeneration. Take 1g–3g daily.

Vitamin E Protects fatty components of the skin's makeup from becoming rancid by acting as an antioxidant and heals skin damage. Take 400IU daily and also apply Vitamin E oil onto the skin from a pierced capsule. To help de-stress your skin, use **Avocado oil**, **Rosehip oil** and **Vitamin E oil** on your face, neck and décolletage, and gently but firmly massage your forehead, jaw-line, the area over your sinuses and sunburnt areas when you've completed cooling the area properly.

Marine Collagen and **Lyophilised Marine Protein** To reach the skin nutritionally from a deep level we can deliver our body specific nutrients to support the formation of strong collagen bonds and help maintain skin hydration. This type of protein also contains natural polysaccharides that help to support the moisture within the skin, helping to regenerate and heal damaged skin. It also maintains natural, supple, fresh-looking skin. As we age, collagen becomes depleted, and fine lines and wrinkles appear on the skin's surface. Marine Collagen supports the action of collagen within our skin, replenishing this vital skin component. Take 440mg–1400mg daily of Lyophilised Marine Protein and 300mg of Marine Collagen daily.

Flaxseed oil and **Evening Primrose oil (EPO)** Provide essential fatty acids that can help heal the fatty components of the skin keeping it supple, elastic and youthful. Take 1 Tbsp of Flaxseed oil and/or 3g of EPO daily.

Herbs

Aloe Vera gel Aloe Vera is excellent for first aid and has a broad range of uses. Many people remember using Aloe Vera when they received a minor burn, and broke off a piece of Aloe Vera from the garden to smear the inner gel on the burn for relief. Aloe Vera has amazing soothing properties and has an ability to increase the skin's natural healing time 9-fold. Topically, Aloe is documented as supporting wound healing and aiding recovery from bruises and burns as it penetrates deeply into the skin. Aloe Vera has an enzymatic action, enhancing skin rehydration as it's rapidly absorbed through the pores into the skin.

Sun spot cream   Anti-neoplastic (anti-cancer) herbs, including **Sweet Violet Leaves**, **Pau D'Arco**, **Olive Leaf extract**, **Daisy** and **Calendula**, combined with **Castor oil** may help reduce the size of sun spots and the risk of cancer. Mix equal amounts into an aqueous cream and apply 1–2 times daily onto sun spots.

After sun care
Essential oils that have a reputation for after sun care include **Tea Tree** oil to help reduce itchiness for mild sunburns, **Lavender** oil and **Cajuput** oil.

Tinnitus

Tinnitus is a perceived sound or ringing in the ears without an external stimulus or cause. I've spoken to a few worried people over the years that have tinnitus. Apparently there used to be a lack of useful information on treating tinnitus and many were told there could be no positive change, they'd just have to live with it. I got quite excited when I started researching tinnitus because I found a marvellous, positive website (www.tinnitus.org). The message from the website was to learn how to change the perception of stress and tinnitus symptoms, leading to an acceptance of tinnitus through the use of a method called tinnitus retraining therapy (TRT).

Causes
- Ménière's disease, which is characterised by vertigo, tinnitus and deafness.
- Impacted earwax. The ear produces a waxy substance (cerumen) to clean the outer ear. Unsuccessful attempts to remove the wax can cause impaction, leading to tinnitus.
- Stimulants and medication, including aspirin, quinine (a drug used to treat malaria and, sometimes, night-time leg cramps), antibiotics and anti-inflammatory drugs can affect inner ear cells. Often the unwanted noise disappears when you discontinue the drugs. Smoking and caffeine can cause transient tinnitus.
- Food sensitivities, including some cheeses, red wine, artificial sugars and foods containing MSG (monosodium glutamate).
- Vitamin B12 deficiency has been found to cause tinnitus or make it worse.
- Overexposure to loud noise, rock bands, high-pitched sounds and high-decibel noises.
- Abnormal physiological hearing mechanisms may include abnormal firing of auditory receptors, transmission of signals and alterations in central processing of the signals.
- Broken or damaged hairs on auditory cells, turbulence in a carotid artery or jugular vein and temporomandibular joint problems.
- Changes in ear bones, such as stiffening of the bones in the middle ear (otosclerosis), may affect your hearing.
- Injury or trauma to your head or neck can damage your inner ear.
- Stress and perception of tinnitus can magnify or bring on tinnitus.
- Infection or obstruction caused by colds and flus or sinusitis.
- Head trauma.
- High blood pressure and atherosclerosis.
- High salt intake.

Signs and symptoms
- Hissing, roaring or ringing sound which may be intermittent, transient or constant.
- Buzzing, pulsing or whistling sound in the ears or head.

- It is fairly common for people with normal hearing to experience intermittent mild high-pitched sounds lasting for several minutes, especially when overexposed to loud continuous noise.
- Tinnitus is accompanied by hyperacusis in about 40% of the cases. Hyperacusis is a decreased tolerance of sound, leading to sound sensitivity and aggravation.

Naturopathic recommendations

Lifestyle hints

Because there are a range of causes for ringing in the ears, you should see your doctor for a full consultation and diagnosis. Your specialist needs to take a careful history, talking about the effect of tinnitus, the triggers and how it emerges and develops.
- Sometimes using external sounds to mask the tinnitus can be helpful, such as playing your favourite music, listening to nature sounds or using the television as background noise.
- Avoid overexposure to loud noise.
- Test for food sensitivities and check all medication for adverse effects that may include tinnitus.
- Tinnitus retraining therapy (TRT) is a method used to help those with tinnitus that includes using a combination of counselling and low-level, broad-band noise to distract the focus on the tinnitus symptoms, decrease the sensitivity to sound and to help the person deal with the stress associated with tinnitus.

Nutrition

- Eliminate common food and stimulant sensitivities including dairy products (milk, cheese, butter and yoghurt), gluten (wheat, rye, oats and barley), red wine, artificial sugars, aspirin, caffeine and smoking until a more definite diagnosis can be made. Reduce salt intake.
- Drink 8–10 glasses of fresh water daily. Avoid tonic water and artificial sugars, which may trigger tinnitus in some people.

Supplements

Vitamin B12 Deficiency is linked to tinnitus. B12 can be taken in two forms — the methylcobalamin is preferred over the cyanocobalamin form. Take 1g daily with **Folic acid** and a **Vitamin B complex** for better absorption if B12 deficiency is due to dietary lack. B12 deficiencies may need to be treated by intravenous injections by a doctor.
Magnesium Helps to reduce noise sensitivity. Take 450mg daily.
Manganese Deficiency is linked to tinnitus. Take 5mg daily.
Coenzyme Q10 May help with noise-induced tinnitus. Take 75mg–150mg daily.

Herbs

For tinnitus caused by congestion and poor circulation.
Ground Ivy Helps to remove catarrhal build-up. Take 1ml–4ml of tincture 3 times daily.
Goldenseal Improves the health of mucous membranes that line the ear canals, is effective against bacterial infections of the upper respiratory tract and reduces catarrhal deafness. Take 1.5g of dried root daily.
Black Cohosh Traditionally used for tinnitus. Take 0.5g–1g of dried root 3–4 times daily.
Wood Betony A cerebral relaxant which may help with catarrh build-up. Take 2ml of tincture 3 times daily.

Ginkgo Helps to increase cerebral circulation. Ginkgo may not be indicated for all tinnitus cases. It may help tinnitus where there is congestion of ear fluids. Ginkgo needs long-term (3–4 months) use to be effective. Do not take Ginkgo if you are taking strong blood thinners (warfarin), or before or too soon after surgery as it may have an increased blood-thinning effect.

Ulcers

Ulcers are open sores on the skin or tissues that are very slow to heal. Whether ulcers develop on the body from prolonged bed rest, circulatory problems in the legs (leg ulcers), stress or infections (mouth and stomach ulcers), the naturopathic treatment is fairly similar and very effective.

Causes
- Infection i.e. parasitic (*Helicobacter pylori*), viral, fungal or bacterial.
- Diabetes — lack of circulation and opportunistic infection.
- Poor circulation.
- Nutrient deficiencies in vitamin A, C, and E and poor diets.
- Prolonged bed rest.
- Smoking, aspirin, non-steroidal anti-inflammatories, alcohol and caffeine.
- Chronic health conditions, such as HIV and immunological problems.
- Varicose veins.
- Trauma or tissue and skin damage.
- Stress.

Signs and symptoms
- An exposed wound that may produce fluid or infective pus
- Red raw tissue
- Pain and discomfort.

Naturopathic recommendations

Lifestyle hints
- Remove any food sensitivities to improve the rate of healing and reduce inflammation.
- Avoid smoking, aspirin, non-steroidal anti-inflammatories, alcohol and caffeine.

Nutrition
- Avoid carbonated high-sugar drinks, sugary foods and refined carbohydrate intake.
- Ensure a well-balanced diet by eating plenty of raw and steamed green leafy vegetables, carrots, celery, broccoli and fresh fruit.
- Drink fresh juiced sprouted wheat grass, chickweed and cleavers. Add to fresh vegetable and fruit juices. Drink 3 times daily to help purify the blood and enhance wound healing. Drink 1–2 litres of fresh water daily.
- Decrease intake of saturated fats that contain arachidonic acid (AA), such as animal fats, animal meats and dairy products, to reduce the production of inflammatory chemicals that the AA promotes.
- Good oils and fats include unheated avocado, fish oil (3g daily), flaxseed oil (1 Tbsp

daily), olive oil and cold pressed vegetable oils. Eat a diet high in fish to provide essential fatty acids (EFA), aid healing and reduce inflammation.
- Fish provides omega 3, which reduces inflammation and promotes healing. Eat fish at least 3–4 times a week. This includes tuna, salmon, sardines and snapper. Sorry... this doesn't mean having fish and chips 4 times a week.

Supplements

If you are taking antibiotics and the treatment does not appear to be working, you may combine these herbs with antibiotic therapy.
Vitamin A (5000IU daily), **Vitamin C** (1500mg daily) and **Zinc** (45mg daily)   Help to increase the body's ability to resist infections and heal wounds.
Acidophilus and **Bifidus**   Replacement is needed for a healthy digestive system after medical antibiotic therapy. Take 1–2 capsules (active 1 billion) daily for at least 10–20 days.
Flax oil   Provides Omega 3 and 6, essential fatty acids that each cell uses for its membrane. A deficiency may lead to a reduction in the cell's ability to heal itself. Flax oil can also increase healing in the skin and stomach tissue (mucosa). Take 1 Tbsp daily.

Types of ulcers
Peptic or stomach ulcers

Often caused by a common bug found in the stomach called *Helicobacter pylori*.
Cabbage juice   Rich in glutamine, Cabbage juice helps to heal stomach ulcers and reduce the burning discomfort and pain they produce. Drink 1 litre of fresh juice throughout the day.
Aloe Vera juice   Heals the lining of the digestive tract. Take 50ml with meals.
Parasite-cleansing herbs   Take two 3-week courses of **Cloves** (1800mg daily) combined with **Wormwood** (2000mg daily) and **Black Walnut** (2000mg daily) to help eradicate *H. pylori*.
Bismuth (Bismuth subcitrate)   A mineral that coats the stomach ulcers, allowing them to heal. I find it a very effective treatment when taken with parasite-cleansing herbs. Take 240mg 2 times daily before meals. Obtain from your pharmacist and follow directions as prescribed.
Lugol's Iodine   Take 5 drops daily for 3 days to eradicate infections. Mix with 1 tsp of **Apple Cider Vinegar** and **Manuka honey** in a cup of hot water. Do not take without medical advice if you are allergic to Iodine or have a thyroid condition.

Bed and leg ulcers

Blood purifiers   Ulcers respond brilliantly to blood purifiers. I can't help but recommend two particular products for ulcers because I have had a lot of success with them. **Jamu No. 101 Gadong Gadok** and **No. 44 Bersih Darah** are Indonesian blood cleansing herbal formulas produced by an Indonesian herbal company Nonya Meneer. Try the internet to purchase these products. I admit it takes a while to get used to the taste, but they work wonders.
Detox   Complete a gentle detox herbal programme and a parasite-cleansing programme to balance the internal body organs and prepare for a healthy start. Detox herbs should include **Burdock** (2g–6g of dried root daily), **Cleavers** (2g–4g daily) and **Red Clover** (2g–4g daily) to help cleanse the blood and clear the lymphatics. **Dandelion** (3g–5g of dried root daily) and **Milk Thistle** (9g–10g of seed daily) enhance bile flow and detoxify the liver. **Olive Leaf extract** (270mg 6 times daily), **Goldenseal** (1500mg of dried root daily), **Myrrh** (30 drops of tincture daily) and **Echinacea** (1200mg–6g daily)   Help eradicate infections and strengthen the immune system.

External applications

For all types of wound healing take precautionary hygiene measures. To prevent the spread of bacteria or microbial infection, scrub hands, wear surgical gloves if necessary, use clean utensils and clean surfaces before preparing any herbs or poultices to be used on ulcers.

Wipe or swab area with **Lugol's Iodine**. If you have been advised not to swab inside the ulcer, just around the wound is adequate. If unsure confer with your doctor or nurse for approval and complete under supervision. Make sure you have no allergies to iodine in any form.

Mix crushed **Wormwood** herbs or use **Wormwood tincture**, **Black Walnut tincture**, **Manuka honey** and the fresh gel from an **Aloe Vera** plant with boiled water to make a paste. Apply directly onto ulcer and wrap a sterile bandage or a clean muslin cloth over the ulcer. Dress the ulcer twice daily until healed.

Massage the surrounding area. For instance if it's a leg ulcer massage both legs and torso to encourage healing. For the back or buttocks, massage down to the legs around hips and back.

Mouth ulcers

Small, painful ulcers that can occur singly or in groups, mouth ulcers take anywhere from 7–21 days to heal and are normally linked to low immunity, stress and food sensitivities.

Avoid gluten foods (wheat, rye, oats and barley), acidic fruits, including pineapple, acid tomatoes and citrus, and eat plenty of yoghurt.

Multi vitamin and **mineral formula**   Take a high potency Multi 2 times daily containing all the full spectrum vitamins and minerals including Vitamin A, Vitamin C, Zinc, Iron, Folic acid and Vitamin B12 to prevent deficiencies linked to mouth ulcers.

Myrrh or **Bee Propolis tincture**   Brush the tincture directly onto the ulcer, gargle and take internal amount as directed on the bottle. It will not taste very nice but, due to its antiseptic and astringent qualities, Myrrh is very effective for mouth ulcers.

Chamomile and **Sage tea**   Very astringent and soothing, the tea helps to tone the gums and mouth. Add 1 tsp of Sage leaves and Chamomile flowers (fresh or dried) to a cup of boiling hot water. Cover cup with a saucer to lock in oils of the herb and steep for 15 minutes. Drink 3 times daily.

Red Clover flowers (2g–4g daily), **Cleavers** (2g–4g daily) and **Burdock** (2g–6g of dried root daily)   Blood purifiers that help to clean out the toxins within tissues and the bloodstream.

Aloe Vera gel   Can be applied directly to the ulcer to help remove discomfort and pain and improve healing rate of the tissues.

Vaginitis (Gardnerella Vaginalis)

I speak to many women every year who suffer from gardnerella. It is characterised by irritation of the vagina and vaginal discharge that emits a fishy smell and is caused by an infection by bacteria called *Gardnerella vaginalis*. Although it is considered to be a sexually transmitted disease, it can stick around for years as a passive part of the vaginal flora, only to flare up unexpectedly.

Causes

Certain factors can change the protective acid pH level in the vagina, creating a favorable environment for opportunistic bacteria to grow. These factors include:

Vaginitis (Gardnerella Vaginalis)

- Lack of *Lactobacillus acidophilus* in the vagina
- Oral contraceptive pills
- Certain oral antibiotics
- Douching too frequently
- Wearing unbreathable nylon underwear
- Bubble baths or overzealous use of feminine hygiene sprays or deodorant tampons
- Low thyroid activity (check thyroid by seeing your GP)
- Anal intercourse
- Wiping the wrong way after bowel movement. (It is best to wipe from front to back.)
- Oral-genital contact
- Vaginal intercourse
- Irritants in scented toilet paper and condoms.

Signs and symptoms
- A white to greyish-white vaginal discharge which is fishy or foul smelling
- Vaginal itchiness
- Sexual intercourse may be uncomfortable or even painful.

Naturopathic recommendations

Lifestyle hints
If you have any unusual vaginal discomfort, discharge or notice any changes, see your medical health professional for an examination and testing. Follow your health professional's standard recommendations and combine with naturopathic treatment for chronic vaginitis that does not seem to respond totally to medical treatment.
- Douche with plain water with a few drops of iodine added to it. Douche for comfort every other day or so. Avoid excessive douching as this washes out both the normal and abnormal bacteria from the vagina. Washing out the normal bacteria can slow down your recovery.
- Live culture yoghurt, as both food and douches, helps the problem. Insert up to 1 tsp of plain yoghurt into the vagina once or twice a day, by putting the yoghurt into a tampon inserter and squeezing the yoghurt in as you would normally a tampon. This will help replace and fortify the normal bacteria of the vagina.
- Avoid sexual intercourse until the Gardnerella has been successfully treated. However, if you do have intercourse, use condoms, wash carefully and then douche afterwards.

Nutrition
- Follow the candida diet on page 102.
- Eat 300ml–500ml of acidophilus yogurt daily to reduce the risk of fungal and bacterial infection.

Supplements
Lactobacillus and **Bifidus acidophilus**   The vagina requires these flora to remain healthy. Take high potency 'beneficial bacteria' capsules with at least 40 million to 1 billion active species daily. Insert 1–2 capsules into the vaginal canal every day.
Vitamin C   Recommended to boost immunity and it is thought to increase the acidity of vaginal secretion. The vagina should have a slightly acidic pH to be healthy. Take 1g daily.
Multi vitamin and **mineral formula**   A high potency Multi with at least 50mg of each of the B vitamins should be taken daily to boost the immune system.
Vitamin E   Helps to heal vaginal tissues and reduce inflammation. Take 400IU daily.

Herbs

Parasite-cleansing herbs   Take two 3-week courses of **Cloves** (1800mg daily) combined with **Wormwood** (2000mg daily) and **Black Walnut** (2000mg daily) to help eradicate any Gardnerella infection and any other opportunistic microbial infections including *Trichomonas* and *Candida albicans*.

Detox   Complete a gentle detox herbal programme and a parasite-cleansing programme to balance the internal body organs and prepare for a healthy start. Detox herbs should include **Burdock** (2g–6g of dried root daily), **Cleavers** (2g–4g daily) and **Red Clover** (2g–4g daily) to help cleanse the blood and clear the lymphatics. **Dandelion** (3g–5g of dried root daily) and **Milk Thistle** (9g–10g of seed daily) enhance bile flow and detoxify the liver. **Olive leaf extract** (270mg six times daily), **Goldenseal** (1500mg of dried root daily) and **Echinacea** (1200mg–6g daily)   Help eradicate infections and strengthen the immune subsystem.

Varicose Veins

Varicose veins are bulging veins commonly located in the leg area that become enlarged and fail to circulate blood properly. Spider veins are much smaller and thinner, and appear under the surface of the skin. Both have a blue or pinkish appearance.

Causes

- Genetic weakness of the veins or venous valves.
- Excessive venous pressure due to straining during defecation from constipation, haemorrhoids, pregnancy and obesity.
- Long periods of standing and/or heavy lifting.
- Damage to the veins or venous valves.
- Decreased abilty to break down fibrin, leading to excessive fibrin deposit on the walls of the vein causing the skin to look hard and lumpy due to the presence of fibrin and fat.
- Interestingly, specialists now inform their clients that crossing the legs does not cause varicose veins as once thought.

Signs and symptoms

- The legs may feel heavy, ache or itch over the site of the veins.
- There may be an increase in lower leg volume and size of the ankles due to a build-up of fluid.
- The large veins can take on a bluish appearance as blood leaks through enlarged gaps between the walls of the vein.
- Varicose eczema or ulcers may develop.

Naturopathic recommendations

Lifestyle hints

Medical treatment of varicose veins may be necessary for cosmetic reasons or if there is severe discomfort. If individuals have medical treatment but do not address the cause of varicose veins (e.g. weak vein walls or constipation), it is highly likely they will develop more varicose veins within 2–3 years of treatment. Consider naturopathic treatment to maintain the appearance and health of normal veins.

- Raise the foot of the bed by about 25cm (10 inches) to help return blood.
- Lose weight if obese.
- Exercise or stretch the legs regularly.
- Put the feet up as often as possible.
- Avoid constricting garments.
- Avoid constipation by eating a high-fibre diet. Increasing fibre in the diet helps reduce straining during evacuation. Straining increases excessive venous pressure.
- Elevate your legs above your heart on cushions when resting.
- While standing next to a wall or a desk to support yourself, get on your tip-toes and lift your heels off the floor twenty times daily. This creates a pumping action within the muscles increasing upward circulation from the legs to the heart.
- Get plenty of rest and sleep.

Nutrition

- Don't smoke or drink coffee as these will cause the blood vessels to constrict, reducing oxygen to the tissues.
- Reduce or avoid alcohol to help the body heal.
- Antioxidants tone and protect veins from free radicals which cause damage to cells. Increase vitamin C and bioflavonoid foods in your diet, e.g. berries, cherries, citrus fruit, kiwifruit, green leafy vegetables and capsicums.
- Eat more garlic and ginger as these foods help to break down fibrin.
- Avoid saturated fats in the diet, such as animal fats, butter, cream, icecream, milk and heated vegetable and animal fats.
- Eat cold pressed oils, such as olive oil and flax oil, by adding them to your salad or vegetable dressings.
- Drink 1–2 litres of fresh water daily.

Supplements

Fibre supplements Help to soften the stool to reduce straining during defecation. As you increase your fibre intake your water intake must also be increased to avoid constipation. It is known that a diet high in fibre (traditionally from vegetables, grains, gums, etc.) can produce some benefits to general health. These particular fibres work by absorbing water and remain undigested as they pass through the body improving stool transit time and bulk. Take 1 tsp–2 tsp of **Flax fibre** or **Psyllium** daily.

Glucosamine and **Chondroitin** Supply the connective layer of veins with ingredients to strengthen and shrink relaxed veins that cause varicose veins. Additionally these ingredients enhance cartilage for arthritis or sports injuries in the joints, protect against glaucoma and may assist with cystitis and cellulite. Take 1500mg of Glucosamine and 1200mg of Chondroitin daily.

Vitamin C Helps to strengthen the vein walls. Take 1g–2g of Vitamin C daily.

Schuessler Tissue Salts **Calc Fluor** or **Combination G** are homeopathic minerals that provide strength to the relaxed, weakened veins that cause varicose veins. Take 1 tablet and dissolve in mouth every $1/2$ hour until vein redness or itchiness is reduced. Then take 2–3 tablets daily to maintain.

Grape Seed and **Bioflavonoids** Powerful antioxidants that protect cells and blood vessels from damage. Also help to tone small, broken capillaries and varicose veins. Take 50mg–400mg of mixed Bioflavonoids and 500mg–10g of Grape Seed extract daily.

Fish, Flaxseed and **Evening Primrose oil** Contain essential fatty acids important for cell membrane health maintenance. Take 3000mg daily.

Vitamin E   Prevents essential fatty acid oxidation and provides antioxidants that protect cells and blood vessels from damage. Take 200IU–400IU daily.

Vitamin B6   Helps maintain the balance of potassium and sodium, which regulates body fluids. Plays an important role as a coenzyme to help break down fats, carbohydrates and proteins. Take 15mg–50mg daily.

Herbs

Horse Chestnut extract   Has anti-inflammatory and anti-oedema properties. The unique actions of Horse Chestnut are on the vessel of the circulatory system. It increases the strength and tone of the veins in particular. It may be used for varicose veins, unsightly capillaries and inflammation in the veins. **Aescin** is the active constituent in Horse Chestnut and clinical trials confirm that 10mg of Aescin taken 3 times daily has a venotonic activity, demonstrating a positive effect for normalising varicose veins.

Gotu Kola   Has demonstrated impressive clinical results for venous insufficiency of the lower limbs and varicose veins. Normalises connective tissue and improves the blood flow through affected limbs. Take 30mg of Gotu Kola extract (Triterpenes) 3 times daily.

Ginkgo and **Hawthorn**   Improve peripheral blood circulation and also act as an antioxidant neutralising free radicals and preventing damage occurring to cell membranes. Take 1.5g–3g of dried Hawthorn flower, leaf or berry per day. Take 4g–8g of whole leaf or 24mg–30mg of standardised extract of Ginkgo flavone glycosides daily. Avoid with the prescribed medication warfarin, as Ginkgo in large amounts may magnify the drug's blood-thinning effect.

Turmeric   Has anti-inflammatory and antioxidant effects, and increases the effectiveness of other herbs through circulation. Take 900mg daily or add to your food.

Ginger   Helps circulation and breaks down fibrous and fatty deposits on blood vessels and varicose veins. Take 500mg 2–4 times daily, and add Ginger to foods and teas. Avoid with the prescribed medication warfarin, as Ginger in large supplement or herbal extract amounts may magnify the drug's blood-thinning effect. Ginger tea and adding to food should be fine.

Spider veins   If there are more than 7 clusters of spider veins the health of the liver may be implicated. **Dandelion** (3g–5g of dried root daily) and **Milk Thistle** (9g–10g of seed daily) enhance bile flow and detoxify the liver.

External applications

When massaging in oils or creams, work in an upward motion, massaging towards your heart, to help tone veins.

Apple Cider Vinegar (ACV)   ACV temporarily reduces unsightly veins and any itching or aching associated with varicose veins. This tip is not really related, but if you want beautiful-looking legs, rub the pores of your legs with ACV applied with a cotton bud as this can get rid of the appearance of those unsightly, dark pores caused by shaving.

Witch Hazel Cream or **Lotion**   Temporarily tones oedemic veins, lessening the appearance of (veinal oedemic blood colour) veins and capillaries.

Juniper and **Rosemary essential oils**   Act as diuretics to help remove excess water retention in the body and have a circulatory-stimulant effect on varicose veins.

Schuessler Tissue Salts   Calc fluor or **Combination G** help to tone varicose veins, and reduce aching or itchiness. Grind one tablet into a powder and mix into an aqueous-based cream. Massage into the legs morning and night. Calc fluor tissue salt creams are also available.

Warts

You've probably been told that if you touch frogs, you'll get warts. Myth surrounds the treatment of warts, too, which includes old folk remedies such as rubbing a wart with a piece of potato and burying the potato in the garden with the promise that the wart will transfer to the potato. Warts are small growths on the skin. If you have a wart, or even if you have a bunch of them, don't feel too bad because warts are a very common skin condition.

Over-the-counter medications (medicines that can be bought in a pharmacy without a prescription) contain acids that help remove the dead skin cells on the surface of the wart. The medicine is painted on, or it may come in a patch that sticks onto the wart. Eventually the wart crumbles away from the healthy skin. If these medicines don't work, your doctor may recommend freezing the wart so that it forms into a scab and eventually falls off, although this is fairly painful.

Causes

Warts are caused by human papilloma viruses, or HPV, which invade the skin and cause the cells to multiply rapidly. The wart virus likes small cuts or scratches on your hands or feet and may start to develop when it finds a moist, warm area. Wart symptoms can take years to develop or appear suddenly.

Picking up the HPV virus is so simple, especially for children who share many items, e.g. towels. Those who tend to bite their fingernails or pick at hangnails get warts more often than those who don't.

It's important to avoid touching, rubbing, or scratching a wart, whether it's on another person or on your own body. Warts may be passed from one area to another on the body or easily transferred to another person. People with depressed immune systems are more likely to contract warts and, although warts may occur at any age, they are most common in older children and are rarely seen in the elderly.

Signs and symptoms

- Common warts usually grow on fingers, hands, knees, and elbows. They are round, usually greyish-brown and have a rough surface with black dots.
- Verrucas, or plantar warts, are warts on the feet. The pressure from the body weight causes them to be flatter and to grow into the skin more, which can cause pain, rather like walking on a dried pea.
- Flat warts (juvenile warts) are pinhead small, smooth and have flat tops. They may look pink, light brown or yellow and are seen on the face, arms, knees or hands. Sometimes big groups of them cluster together.
- Filiform warts are commonly the larger wart seen on the face, finger-like in shape and usually flesh-coloured. They often grow on or around the mouth, eyes, or nose.
- Genital warts are soft, fleshy warts found around the vagina, scrotum, anus, penis or groin area. They are pink or reddish and resemble tiny cauliflower-like growths.
- Molluscum contagiosum is a skin growth similar to a wart that is pearly, flesh-coloured to translucent, small, round and often indented. They are caused by a virus called a poxvirus, which thrives on skin and is contagious. It can be spread to other parts of the body or to other people by direct contact with the lesion. In people who are generally healthy, molluscum contagiosum usually goes away on its own in 2–4 months, but some lesions may persist for years.

Naturopathic recommendations

Herbs
Warts can be difficult to get rid of because the thick layers of skin make it hard for medicine to reach the wart virus. Naturopaths work internally with antiviral herbs and externally with either natural anti-wart creams or paints.

Internally
Antiviral herbs such as Olive Leaf extract, Astragalus, Cloves, Wormwood and Black Walnut work internally on boosting the body's immune system while having a direct effect on the wart viruses. These are my favourite herbs to try first.

Olive Leaf extract Has several antiviral properties that help to boost the immune system and may also help to eradicate viruses. Research shows that Olive Leaf extract with oleuropein can destroy the protein coating of the wart virus, helping to reduce symptoms and ongoing infection. Take 270mg of Olive Leaf extract 3 times daily.

Astragalus The antiviral action of Astragalus is mainly due to increased immunity and interferon production. Take 500mg–10g daily.

Parasite-cleansing herbs Take two 3-week courses of **Cloves** (1800mg daily) combined with **Wormwood** (2000mg daily) and **Black Walnut** (2000mg daily) to help eradicate parasites.

Echinacea and **Thuja** herbal liquid combinations are similar in action to the herbs mentioned above, although they may need to be taken for longer periods to be effective.

Echinacea Helps improve the immune system. Take 1200mg–6g daily. See your health store for details to obtain Echinacea and Thuja combinations.

External applications
Make a paste of **Vitamin C** powder and water or **Vitamin E oil** and apply before bed and in the morning. Cover with gauze and socks.

For plantar warts apply either **Dandelion latex** (the milky juice from the stem) or **Banana Peel** (placed inner side directly on wart) and tape in place. Change 4 times daily for 2 weeks.

Castor oil, Lavender oil, Garlic oil or fresh crushed **Cloves** applied to the wart locally, especially if on the hands.

My favourite is **Thuja oil**. Apply lotion or cream to the wart every day for at least a month.

Appendices

Herb and supplement medicine and condition interaction list

If you have any doubts about your condition, or if you are taking medication, or are pregnant or breastfeeding, see a health professional before taking any herbs or supplements or following naturopathic recommendations. Health professionals, including specialists, doctors, herbalists and naturopaths, should have a better understanding after an individual consultation and can offer regular supervision while on supplements and drugs.

A lot of the interactions below are theoretical and dependent on dose. Some of these recommendations err on the side of caution and may be used with a drug or particular condition if under medical supervision. It would take another book to list every potential herb, drug and condition interaction, so I have only listed a common few here as a general guideline.

Herb or supplement and dose	Drug, condition or situation	Possible reaction
5HTP doses above 50mg daily	SSRI and MAO inhibitors e.g. paroxetine and prozac.	Patients should be monitored for serotonin syndrome.
Cascara sagrada doses above 50mg daily	Do not use if you are pregnant or lactating, or if you suffer from blocked bowels, impacted bowels, peritonitis or hernia.	May result in abortion and may be over-stimulating to the baby. Long-term use may result in dependence, diarrhoea and loss of needed electrolytes.
Comfrey Any dose	Do not take internally.	High doses can damage the liver by preventing bloodflow to this vital organ.
Echinacea purpurea doses above 25mg daily *Echinacea angustifolia* doses above 25mg daily	Organ transplant and autoimmune diseases – Echinacea is best thought of as an immune system modulator or enhancer, which does not mean that it will increase autoimmunity (the abnormal state of immune attack on the body's own tissues).	Rejection (theorised) None – pay attention to how you feel, and discontinue it if any autoimmune symptoms become worse.
Evening Primrose Oil (EPO) doses above 2000mg daily	Warfarin or coumadin blood thinners.	It may magnify the drugs' effects as EPO is a natural blood thinner.
	Epilim for epilepsy.	May stop the effectiveness of this drug. The GLA in EPO may interfere with drug conversion and increase risk of seizure.
	Some people with migraines.	Can trigger migraines in some and alternatively reduce frequency and pain for others.

Herb or supplement and dose	Drug, condition or situation	Possible reaction
Feverfew doses above 200mg daily	Warfarin, coumadin or blood thinners.	It may magnify the drugs' effects as feverfew is a natural blood thinner.
Fibre, e.g. Slippery Elm, Flaxseed, Marshmallow Root and Psyllium Seed doses above half a tsp or 2g daily affect the absorption of certain medications if taken at the same time. Take any fibre supplement 2–3 hours before or after medication. NEVER use when you have impacted constipation.	Lithium and antibiotics. Impacted constipation.	Absorbs antibiotics and lithium preventing their effectiveness. Exacerbates impacted bowel obstruction.
Fish oil doses above 2000mg daily	Warfarin, coumadin or blood thinners.	It may magnify the drugs' effects as fish oil is a natural blood thinner.
Flaxseed Oil doses above 2 tsp or 10,000mg daily	Warfarin, coumadin or blood thinners.	It may magnify the drugs' effects as flaxseed oil is a natural blood thinner.
Garlic doses above 300mg daily	Warfarin, coumadin or blood thinners.	It may magnify the drugs' effects as garlic is a natural blood thinner.
Ginkgo biloba doses above 200mg daily	Warfarin, coumadin or blood thinners.	It may magnify the drugs' effects as ginkgo is a natural blood thinner.
Ginseng doses above 50mg daily	MAOI antidepressasts.	May interfere with medication (e.g. phenelzine)
Glucosamine 1500mg daily	Diabetics and the elderly. Scleroderma — A rare excess collagen disease associated with thickened skin, body organs and excess collagen to joints.	In some extremely rare cases diabetics may have a rise in blood sugar levels and may substitute these nutrients with shark cartilage. Elderly with digestive disturbances should start on a low dose and build up slowly to prevent loose bowel motions occurring.
Goldenseal 2ml–4ml of tincture (for labels that read 1:10) or 0.3ml–1ml of Liquid Extract (for labels that read 1:1). Short-term use only; limit use from eight to ten days.	Do not use if you are pregnant or if you suffer from high blood pressure.	Not suitable if pregnant and in long-term use may increase blood pressure in some people.

Herb or supplement and dose	Drug, condition or situation	Possible reaction
Guarana doses providing more than 50mg of caffeine daily	High blood pressure. Beta adrenergic blockers, e.g. atenolol. Calcium channel blockers.	May increase blood pressure.
Iodine doses above 25mcg daily	Thyroxine. Hyperthyroidism.	May exacerbate hyperthyroidism.
Kelp doses providing more than 25mcg of iodine daily	Thyroxine. Hyperthyroidism.	May exacerbate hyperthyroidism.
Liquorice doses above 100mg daily	Oral prednisone and corticosteroids. High Blood Pressure. Spironolactone (diuretic) Digoxin	Liquorice slows the breakdown of corticosteroids, thus prolonging the anti-inflammatory effects of hormones such as cortisol. Clients should not add liquorice to steroid (glucocorticoid, for example prednisone) treatment unless they are under the supervision of a physician who can adjust their drug dosage. When taken continuously for several weeks, Liquorice can cause sodium and water retention as well as potassium loss, resulting in elevated blood pressure. Therefore, the duration should be limited to 3 weeks with constant blood pressure monitoring for doses over 100mg with hypertension (high blood pressure). More than 3g of Liquorice Root taken daily for more than six weeks may raise blood pressure and over-stimulate the adrenal glands.
Rhubarb Root any dose	Do not use if you are pregnant or lactating, or if you suffer from blocked bowels, impacted bowels, peritonitis or hernia.	May result in abortion and may be overstimulating to the baby. Long-term use may result in dependence, diarrhoea and loss of needed electrolytes.
St John's Wort doses above 1g daily	HIV protease inhibitors (Indinavir, nelfinavir, ritonavir, saquinavir). Photosensitivity. Roaccutane — Vitamin A. SSRI and MAO inhibitors e.g. paroxetine and prozac.	A clinical study demonstrated reduced blood levels of drugs with possible loss of HIV suppression. May cause photosensitivity. Patients should be monitored for a possible increased risk of serotonin syndrome.

Herb or supplement and dose	Drug, condition or situation	Possible reaction
Senna any dose	Do not use if you are pregnant or lactating, or if you suffer from blocked bowels, impacted bowels, peritonitis or hernia.	May result in abortion and may be overstimulating to the baby. Long-term use may result in dependence, diarrhoea and loss of needed electrolytes.
Vitamin E doses above 200IU daily	Warfarin, coumadin or blood thinners.	It may magnify the drugs' effects as Vitamin E is a natural blood thinner.
White Willow doses over 100mg daily	Warfarin, coumadin or blood thinners.	Although Aspirin (acetylsalic acid) has an anticlotting effect, White Willow, as once thought, does not have this blood thinning effect. White Willow contains salicin that does not carry the acetyl group responsible for blocking cyclooxygenase, inhibiting thromboxane synthesis.

Resources

The books listed below are valuable resources for answering questions about potential drug/herb interactions:

Blumenthal, Mark (Ed.). 1998. *The Complete German Commission E Monographs: Therapeutic Guide to Herbal Medicines.* American Botanical Council.

Brinker, Francis. 1998. *Herb Contraindications and Drug Interactions*, 2nd Edition. Eclectic Medical Publications.

Lininger, Skye (Ed.). 1999. *The A to Z Guide to Drug-Herb and Vitamin Interactions.* Prima Publishing.

McGuffin, Michael et al. 1997. *American Herbal Product Association's Botanical Safety Handbook.* CRC Press.

Herbs

List of common and latin plant names

Common Name	Latin Name
5-Hydroxy tryptophan, 5HTP (Compound)	*Griffonia simplicifolia*
Agrimony	*Agrimonia eupatoria*
Alderbuck or Alder buckthorn	*Rhamnus frangula*
Aloe Vera	*Aloe barbadensis*
American Cranesbill	*Geranium maculatum*
Aniseed	*Pimpinella anisum*
Arnica	*Arnica montana*
Artichoke or Globe Artichoke	*Cynara scolymus*
Astragalus	*Astragalus membranacaeus*
Baical Skullcap or Scullcap (Chinese)	*Scutellaria baicalensis*
Bearberry or Uva Ursi	*Arctostaphylos uva-ursi*
Bitter Melon	*Mormodica charanta*
Bitter Orange	*Citrus aurantium*
Bilberry	*Vaccinium myrtillus*
Bladderwrack or Kelp	*Fucus vesiculosus*
Black Cohosh	*Actaea (Cimicifuga) racemosa*
Black Haw	*Viburnum prunifolium*
Black Pepper	*Piper nigrum*
Black Walnut	*Juglans nigra*
Bupleurum	*Bupleurum falcatum*
Boswellia	*Boswellia serrata*
Buchu	*Barosma betulina*
Bugleweed or Gypsywort	*Lycopus virginicus*
Burdock	*Arctium lappa*
Butcher's Broom	*Ruscus aculeatus*
Calendula or Marigold	*Calendula officinalis*
Californian Poppy	*Eschscholtzia californica*
Capsicum or Cayenne	*Capsicum frutescens*
Cascara Sagrada	*Rhamnus purshiana*
Cayenne or Capsicum	*Capsicum frutescens*
Celery seed	*Apium graveolens*
Chamomile (German)	*Matricaria recutita*
Chamomile (Roman)	*Anthemis nobilis*
Chaste Tree or Chaste Berry	*Vitex agnus-castus*
Chinese Foxglove or Rehmannia	*Rehmannia glutinosa*
Cleavers or Clivers	*Galium aparine*
Cloves	*Eugenia caryophyllata*
Cola Vera	*Cola nitida*
Coleus	*Coleus forskohlii*
Coltsfoot	*Tussilago farfara*
Comfrey	*Symphytum officinale*
Corydalis	*Corydalis ambigua*
Cramp Bark	*Viburnum opulus*
Cranberry	*Vaccinium macrocarpon*
Daisy	*Bellis perennis*
Damiana	*Turnera diffusa*
Dandelion	*Taraxacum officinale*

Dan Shen	*Salvia miltiorrhiza*
Devil's Claw	*Harpagophytum procumbens*
Dong Quai	*Angelica sinensis*
Echinacea	*Echinacea angustifolia*
Echinacea	*Echinacea purpurea*
Elecampane	*Inula helenium*
Elder	*Sambucus nigra*
Evening Primrose	*Oenothera biennis*
Eyebright	*Euphrasia officinalis*
False Unicorn Root	*Chamaelirium luteum*
Fennel	*Foeniculum vulgare*
Fenugreek	*Trigonella foenum-graecum*
Feverfew	*Tanacetum parthenium*
Flaxseed or Linseed	*Linum usitatissimum*
Flax or Harakeke (New Zealand Native)	*Phormium tenax*
Garlic	*Allium sativum*
Gentian	*Gentiana lutea*
Ginger	*Zingiber officinale*
Ginkgo	*Ginkgo biloba*
Ginseng (American)	*Panax quinquefolius*
Ginseng (Korean)	*Panax ginseng*
Ginseng (Siberian)	*Eleutherococcus senticosus*
Globe Artichoke or Artichoke	*Cynara scolymus*
Goldenrod	*Solidago virgaurea*
Goldenseal	*Hydrastis canadensis*
Gotu Kola	*Centella asiatica*
Grapeseed	*Vitis vinifera*
Gravel Root	*Eupatorium purpureum*
Green Tea	*Camellia sinensis*
Ground Ivy	*Nepeta hederacea*
Guaiacum	*Guaiacum officinale*
Guarana	*Paullinia cupana*
Guggul	*Commiphora mukul*
Gymnema	*Gymnema sylvestre*
Gypsywort or Bugleweed	*Lycopus virginicus*
Hawthorn	*Crataegus oxycanthus*
Hops	*Humulus lupulus*
Horehound	*Marrubium vulgare*
Horse Chestnut	*Aesculus hippocastanum*
Horny Goat Weed	*Epimedium grandiflorum*
Hydrangea	*Hydrangea arborescens*
Hydroxycitric Acid (HCA) – a compound	*Garcinia cambogia*
Hyssop	*Hyssopus officinalis*
Irish Moss	*Chondrus crispus*
Jamaican Dogwood	*Piscidia piscipula*
Juniper	*Juniperus communis*
Kava	*Piper methysticum*
Kelp or Bladderwrack	*Fucus vesiculosus*
Kudzu	*Pueraria lobata*
Lady's Mantle	*Alchemilla vulgaris*
Lavender	*Lavandula angustifolia*

Lemon Balm	*Melissa officinalis*
Lime Blossom	*Tilia europaea*
Linseed or Flaxseed	*Linum usitatissimum*
Liquorice or Licorice	*Glycyrrhiza glabra*
Lobelia	*Lobelia inflata*
Maca	*Lepidium meyenii*
Marigold or Calendula	*Calendula officinalis*
Marshmallow	*Althea officinalis*
Meadowsweet	*Filipendula ulmaria*
Milk Thistle or St Mary's Thistle	*Silybum marianum*
Mullein	*Verbascum thapsus*
Myrrh	*Commiphora molmol*
Nettle	*Urtica dioica*
Oats	*Avena sativa*
Oatstraw	*Avena sativa*
Olive Leaf	*Olea europaea*
Oregano	*Oregano vulgare*
Oregon Grape	*Berberis aquifolium*
Parsley	*Petroselinum crispum*
Passionflower	*Passiflora incanarta*
Pau D'Arco	*Tabebuia avellanedae*
Peony	*Paeonia lactiflora*
Peppermint	*Mentha x piperita*
Perilla	*Perilla frutescens*
Pine	*Pinus radiata*
Pokeroot	*Phytolacca americana*
Pygeum	*Pygeum africanum*
Pysllium	*Plantago pysllium*
Queen's Delight	*Stillingia sylvatica*
Raspberry leaf	*Rubus idaeus*
Red Clover	*Trifolium pratense*
Rehmannia or Chinese Foxglove	*Rehmannia glutinosa*
Rhubarb	*Rheum palmatum*
Rosemary	*Rosmarinus officinalis*
Rue	*Ruta graveolens*
Sage	*Salvia officinalis*
St John's Wort	*Hypericum perforatum*
St Mary's Thistle or Milk Thistle	*Silybum marianum*
Sarsaparilla	*Smilax spp.*
Saw Palmetto	*Serenoa repens*
Scullcap (Chinese) or Baical Skullcap	*Scutellaria baicalensis*
Self Heal	*Prunella vulgaris*
Senna	*Cassia angustifolia*
Shepherd's Purse	*Capsella bursa pastoris*
Skullcap	*Scutellaria lateriflora*
Slippery Elm	*Ulmus rubra*
Soy beans	*Glycine max*
Sweet Clover	*Mellilotus officinalis*
Sweet Violet	*Viola odorata*
Tansy	*Tanacetum vulgare*
Tea Tree	*Melaleuca alternifolia*

Thuja	*Thuja occidentalis*
Thyme	*Thymus vulgaris*
Turmeric	*Curcuma longa*
Uva Ursi or Bearberry	*Arctostaphylos uva-ursi*
Valerian	*Valeriana officinalis*
Verbena	*Verbena officinalis*
Vervain	*Verbena officinalis*
White Kidney Bean	*Phaseolus vulgaris*
White Willow	*Salix alba*
Wild Indigo	*Baptisia tinctoria*
Witch Hazel	*Hamamelis virginiana*
Wood Betony	*Stachys betonica*
Wormwood	*Artemisia absinthium*
Wild Cherry bark	*Prunus serotina*
Wild Yam	*Dioscorea villosa*
Yarrow	*Achillea millefolium*
Yellow Dock	*Rumex crispus*
Yohimbe	*Pausinystalia yohimbe*
Yucca	*Yucca baccata*

Bibliography

Balch, J.F. and Balch P.A. 2000. *Prescription for nutritional healing: A practical A–Z reference to drug-free remedies using vitamins, minerals, herbs, and food supplements*. 3rd ed., Avery Publishing Group.

Bishop, P. and Lee, G. 1997. *Microbiology and infection control for health professionals*. Prentice Hall.

Bloomfield, M.M. and Stephens, L.J. 1996. *Chemistry and the living organism*. 6th ed., Wiley.

Bradley, P.R. (Ed.). 1992. *British herbal compendium*. British Medical Association.

Brody, T. 1999. *Nutritional biochemistry*. 2nd ed., Academic Press.

Bullock, B.L. 1996. *Pathophysiology: Adaptations and alterations in function*. 4th ed., Lippincott.

Cabot, S. 1998. *The liver cleansing diet*. Celestial Arts.

Clark, H.R. 1993. *The cure for HIV and AIDs*. Promotion.

Hoffman, D. 1994. *The new holistic herbal*. Element.

Kumar, K. and Clark, M. 1994. *Clinical medicine: A textbook for medical students and doctors*. 3rd ed., Bailliere Tindall.

McCance, K.L. and Huether, S.E. 1998. *Alterations of renal and urinary tract function. Pathophysiology: The biologic basis for disease in adults and children*. 3rd ed., Mosby-Year Book.

Marieb, E.N. 1992. *Human anatomy and physiology*. 2nd ed., Benjamin/Cummings.

Mills, S. 1993. *The essential book of herbal medicine*. Penguin.

Mills, S. and Bone, K. 2000. *Principles and practice of phytotherapy*. Churchill Livingston.

Murray, M. and Pizzorno, J. 1998. *Encyclopaedia of natural medicine*. Little Brown and Company.

Osiecki, H. 2001. *The physicians handbook of clinical nutrition*. 6th ed., Bioconcepts.

Porth, C.M. 1998. *Pathophysiology: Concepts of altered health states*. 5th ed., Lipincott.

Tillman, B.J. 1995. *The natural healing cookbook*. Ruda Press.

Vardaxis, N. 1995. *Immunology for the health sciences*. MacMillan.

References

1. New Zealand 1998, Consolidated food regulations, 13th Schedule, Permitted forms and RDI of vitamins and minerals.
2. Seow, A. et al. Dietary isothiocyanates, glutathione S-transferase polymorphisms and colorectal cancer risk in the Singapore Chinese Health Study. *Carcinogenesis*. 2002 Dec;23 (12):2055-61.
3. Walters, D.G. et al. Cruciferous vegetable consumption alters the metabolism of the dietary carcinogen 2-amino-1-methyl-6-phenylimidazo [4,5-b]pyridine (PhIP) in humans. *Carcinogenesis*. 2004 Apr 8. (Epub ahead of print, accessed internet pubmed 31/7/2004.)
4. Durak, I. et al. Effects of garlic extract consumption on blood lipid and oxidant/antioxidant parameters in humans with high blood cholesterol. *J Nutr Biochem*. 2004 Jun;15 (6):373-7.
5. Heber, D. Vegetables, fruits and phytoestrogens in the prevention of diseases. *J Postgrad Med*. 2004 Apr-Jun;50 (2):145-9.
6. Park, E.J. & Pezzuto, J.M. Botanicals in cancer chemoprevention. *Cancer Metastasis Rev*. 2002;21 (3-4):231-55.
7. Gao, C.M. et al. Protective effect of allium vegetables against both esophageal and stomach cancer: a simultaneous case-referent study of a high-epidemic area in Jiangsu Province, China. *Jpn J Cancer Res*. 1999 Jun;90(6):614-21.
8. Droge, W. Oxidative stress and aging. *Adv Exp Med Biol*. 2003;543:191-200.
9. Hughes, C.M. et al. The effects of antioxidant supplementation during Percoll preparation on human sperm DNA integrity. *Hum Reprod*. 1998 May;13(5):1240-7. Erratum in: *Hum Reprod* 1998 Nov;13(11):3284.
10. Murray, M. & Pizzorno. J. *A Textbook of Natural Medicine*. Bastyr University Publication, 1996.
11. Diesfeldt, H.F. & Diesfeldt-Groenendijk, H. Improving cognitive performance in psychogeriatric patients: the influence of physical exercise. *Age Ageing*. 1977 Feb;6(1):58-64.
12. Perrig, W.J., Perrig, P., & Stahelin, H.B. The relation between antioxidants and memory performance in the old and very old. *J Am Geriatr Soc*. 1997 Jun;45(6):718-24.
13. Cangiano, C. et al. Eating behavior and adherence to dietary prescriptions in obese adult subjects treated with 5-hydroxytryptophan. *American journal of clinical nutrition* (USA). (Nov 1992). v. 56(5) p. 863-867. 1992 0002-9165.
14. Cangiano, C. et al. Effects of oral 5-hydroxy-tryptophan on energy intake and macronutrient selection in non-insulin dependent diabetic patients. *Int J Obes Relat Metab Disord*. 1998 Jul; 22(7): 648-54 1998 0307-0565.
15. Cangiano, C. et al. Effects of 5-hydroxytryptophan on eating behavior and adherence to dietary prescriptions in obese adult subjects. *Adv Exp Med Biol*. 1991; 294: 591-3 1991 0065-2598.
16. Shoba, G, et al. Influence of piperine on the pharmacokinetics of curcumin in animals and human volunteers. *Planta Med*. 1998 May;64(4):353-6.
17. Jones, P.W. & Williams, D.R. The use and role of zinc and its compounds in wound healing. *Met Ions Biol Syst*. 2004;41:139-83.
18. Sandstead, H.H. Understanding zinc: Recent observations and interpretations. *J Lab Clin Med*. 1994;124:322–7.
19. Liszewski, R.F. The effect of zinc on wound healing: a collective review. *J Am Osteopath Assoc*. 1981;81:104–6.
20. Pories, W.J. et al. Acceleration of healing with zinc sulfate. Ann Surg 1967;165:432–6.
21. Pizzorno, J. & Murray, M. *Encyclopaedia of natural therapies*. 1999. pp., 201-210.
22. Rosenberg, C. Adding nutrients to the AIDS cocktail. *Nutrition Science News*. Penton Media Inc, Cleveland. 1998 Dec Issue.
23. Head, K. Nutritional supplementation for people with AIDS. *Natural foods Merchandiser*. Penton Media Inc, Cleveland. 1998 Sept Issue.
24. Bisignano, G. et al. On the in-vitro antimicrobial activity of oleuropein and hydroxytyrosol. *J Pharm Pharmacol*. 1999 Aug; 51 (8): 971-4.
25. Markin, D., Duek, L. & Berdicevsky, I. In vitro antimicrobial activity of olive leaves. *Mycoses*. 2003 Apr;46(3-4):132-6.

26. Lee-Huang, S. et al. Anti-HIV activity of olive leaf extract (OLE) and modulation of host cell gene expression by HIV-1 infection and OLE treatment. *Biochem Biophys Res Commun*. 2003 Aug 8;307(4):1029-37.
27. Walker, M. *Olive Leaf Extract*. Kensington Health, New York. 1997. pp 4-461.
28. www.keephope.net/v1996.html. Case report on Olive Leaf extract and HIV. (Accessed May 31, 2003).
29. Use of complementary therapies by people with HIV. 8th Conference on retroviruses and opportunistic infections. February 2001, Chicago, Illinois.
30. Takeuchi, T. et al. *Clinical experiences of administration of Spirulina to patients with hypochronic anemia*. Tokyo Medical and Dental Univ. Japan. 1978.
31. Bruyere, O. et al. Glucosamine sulfate reduces osteoarthritis progression in postmenopausal women with knee osteoarthritis: evidence from two 3-year studies. *Menopause*. 2004 Mar-Apr;11(2):138-43.
32. Einhorn, T.A. If it feels good, do it: use of glucosamine sulfate to prevent the progression of osteoarthritis in postmenopausal women. *Menopause*. 2004 Mar-Apr;11(2):134-5.
33. Christgau, S. et al. Osteoarthritic patients with high cartilage turnover show increased responsiveness to the cartilage protecting effects of glucosamine sulphate. *Clin Exp Rheumatol*. 2004 Jan-Feb;22(1):36-42.
34. Grahame, R. et al. Devil's Claw: Pharmacological and clinical studies. *Ann Rheum Dis*. 1 981; 40: 632.
35. Bruyere, O. et al. Glucosamine sulfate reduces osteoarthritis progression in postmenopausal women with knee osteoarthritis: evidence from two 3-year studies. *Menopause*. 2004 Mar-Apr;11(2):138-43.
36. Einhorn, T.A. If it feels good, do it: use of glucosamine sulfate to prevent the progression of osteoarthritis in postmenopausal women. *Menopause*. 2004 Mar-Apr;11(2):134-5.
37. Christgau, S. et al. Osteoarthritic patients with high cartilage turnover show increased responsiveness to the cartilage protecting effects of glucosamine sulphate. *Clin Exp Rheumatol*. 2004 Jan-Feb;22(1):36-42.
38. Grahame, R. et al. Devil's Claw: Pharmacological and clinical studies. *Ann Rheum Dis*. 1 981; 40: 632.
39. Grahame, R. et al. Devil's Claw: Pharmacological and clinical studies. *Ann Rheum Dis*. 1 981; 40: 632.
40. Baskaran, K. et al. Antidiabetic effect of a leaf extract from Gymnema sylvestre in non-insulin-dependent diabetes mellitus patients. *J Ethnopharmacol*. 1990 Oct;30(3):295-300.
41. Shanmugasundaram, E.R. et al. Use of Gymnema sylvestre leaf extract in the control of blood glucose in insulin-dependent diabetes mellitus. *J Ethnopharmacol*. 1990 Oct;30(3):281-94.
42. Vuksan, V. et al. American ginseng (Panax quinquefolius L.) attenuates postprandial glycemia in a time-dependent but not dose-dependent manner in healthy individuals. *Am J Clin Nutr*. 2001 Apr;73(4):753-8.
43. Gupta, A., Gupta, R. & Lal, B. Effect of Trigonella foenum-graecum (fenugreek) seeds on glycaemic control and insulin resistance in type 2 diabetes mellitus: a double blind placebo controlled study. *J Assoc Physicians*. India. 2001 Nov;49:1057-61.
44. Sharma, R.D., Raghuram, T.C. & Rao, N.S. Effect of fenugreek seeds on blood glucose and serum lipids in type I diabetes. *Eur J Clin Nutr*. 1990.
45. Madar, Z. et al. Glucose-lowering effect of fenugreek in non-insulin dependent diabetics. *Eur J Clin Nutr*. 1988 Jan;42(1):51-4.
46. De Swert, .LF., Cadot, P. & Ceuppens, J.L. Allergy to cooked white potatoes in infants and young children: A cause of severe, chronic allergic disease. *J Allergy Clin Immunol*. 2002 Sep;110(3):524-35
47. Brown, L. et al. A prospective study of carotenoid intake and cataracts among U.S. men. *Am J Epidemiol*. 1998;147:S54 (Abst. 213).
48. Quaranta, L. Effect of Ginkgo biloba extract on preexisting visual field damage in normal tension glaucoma. *Ophthalmology*. 2003 Feb;110(2):359-62; discussion 362-4.
49. Ritch, R. Potential role for Ginkgo biloba extract in the treatment of glaucoma. *Med Hypotheses*. 2000 Feb;54(2):221-35. Review.
50. Takano, H. et al. Extract of Perilla frutescens enriched for rosmarinic acid, a polyphenolic phytochemical, inhibits seasonal allergic rhinoconjunctivitis in humans. *Exp Biol Med*. (Maywood). 2004 Mar;229(3):247-54.
51. Peikert, A., Wilimzig, C. & Kohne-Volland, R. Prophylaxis of migraine with oral magnesium: results from a prospective, multi-center, placebo-controlled and double-blind randomized study. *Cephalalgia*. 1996 Jun;16(4):257-63.
52. Johnson, E.S. et al. Efficacy of feverfew as prophylactic treatment of migraine. *Br Med J*. 1985;291:569–573.

53. Nemoto, S. Plasma carnitine concentrations in patients undergoing open heart surgery. *Ann Thorac Cardiovasc Surg.* 2004 Feb;10(1):19-22.
54. Loster, H. et al. Prolonged oral L-carnitine substitution increases bicycle ergometer performance in patients with severe, ischemically induced cardiac insufficiency. *Cardiovasc Drugs Ther.* 1999 Nov;13(6):537-46.
55. Hepner, G., Fried, R. & St Jeor, S. et al. Hypocholesterolemic effect of yogurt and milk. *Am J Clin Nutr.* 1979;19-24.
56. Goldberg, A. et al. Multiple-dose efficacy and safety of an extended-release form of niacin in the management of hyperlipdemia. *Am J Cardiol.* 2000 May 1;85(9):1100-5.
57. Grodstein, F., Goldman, M.B. & Cramer, D.W. Infertility in women and moderate alcohol use. *Am J Public Health.* 1994;84:1429-32.
58. Florack, E.I.M., Zielhuis, G.A. & Rolland, R. Cigarette smoking, alcohol consumption, and caffeine intake and fecundability. *Prev Med.* 1994;23:175-80.
59. Joesoef, M.R. et al. Are caffeinated beverages risk factors for delayed conception? *Lancet.* 1990;335:136-7.
60. Fenster, L. et al. A prospective study of caffeine consumption and spontaneous abortion. *Am J Epidemiol.* 1996;143(11 suppl);525.
61. Hakim, R.B., Gray, R.H. & Zacur, H. Alcohol and caffeine consumption and decreased fertility. *Fertil Steril.* 1998;70:632-7.
62. Abell, A., Ernst, E. & Bonde, J.P. High sperm density among members of organic farmers' association. *Lancet.* 1994;343:1498.
63. Goverde, H.J.M. et al. Semen quality and frequency of smoking and alcohol consumption — an explorative study. *Int J Fertil.* 1995;40:135-8.
64. Prior, A. & Whorwell, P.J. Double blind study of ispaghula in irritable bowel syndrome. *Gut.* 1987;28(11):1510-3.
65. Annoni, F. et al. Venotonic activity of escin on the human saphenous vein. *Arzneim-Forsch.* 1979;29;672-5.
66. Weiss, R. *Herbal medicine.* Beaconsfield (UK): AB Arcanum; 1988. p 188.
67. Rudofsky, G. Improving venous tone and capillary sealing: effect of a combination of ruscus extract and hesperidine methyl chalcone in healthy probands in heat stress. *Fortschr Med.* 1989;107(19):52, 55-8.
68. Monteleone, P. et al. Blunting by chronic phosphatidylserine administration of the stress-induced activation of the hypothalamo-pituitary-adrenal axis in healthy men. *Eur J Clin Pharmacol.* 1992;42(4):385-8.
69. Maggioni, M. et al. Effects of phosphatidylserine therapy in geriatric patients with depressive disorders. *Acta Psychiatr Scand.* 1990 Mar:81(3):265-70.
70. Engel, R.R. Double-blind crossover study of phosphatidylserine vs. placebo in patients with early dementia of the Alzheimer type. *Eur Neuropsychopharmacol.* 1992;2:149-55.
71. Pepeu, G. et al. A review of phosphatidylserine pharmacological and clinical effects. Is phosphatidylserine a drug for the aging brain? *Pharmacol Res.* 1996;33:73-80.
72. Stenback, F., Weisburger, J.H. & Williams, G.M. Effect of lifetime administration of dimethylaminoethanol on longevity, aging changes, and cryptogenic neoplasms. *Mech Ageing Dev.* 1988 Feb; 42(2): 129-38.
73. Ferris, S.H. et al. Senile dementia: treatment with Deanol. *J Am Geriatr Soc.* 1977;25: 241-244.
74. Knobel, M. Approach to a combined pharmacologic therapy of childhood hyperkinesis. *Behav Neuropsychiatry.* 1974 Apr–1975 Mar;6:87-90.
75. Fisman, M., Mersky, H. & Helmes, E. Double-blind trial of 2-dimethylaminoethanol in Alzheimer's disease. *Am J Psychiatry.* 1981;138:970-972.
76. Casey, D.E. & Denney, D. Dimethylaminoethanol in tardive dyskinesia [letter]. *N Engl J Med.* 1974;291:797.
77. Meyer, J.S. et al. Neurotransmitter precursor amino acids in the treatment of multi-infarct dementia and Alzheimer's disease. *J Am Geriatr Soc.* 1977;7:289-98.
78. Banderet, L.E. & Lieberman, H.R. Treatment with tyrosine, a neurotransmitter precursor, reduces environmental stress in humans. *Brain Res Bull.* 1989;22:759-62.
79. Deijen, J.B. & Orlebeke, J.F. Effect of tyrosine on cognitive function and blood pressure under stress. *Brain Res Bull.* 1994;33:319-23.
80. Bolton-Smith, C. et al. Evidence for age-related differences in the fatty acid composition of human adipose

tissue, independent of diet. *Eur J Clin Nutr.* 1997;51:619-24.
81. Kalmijn, S. et al. Dietary fat intake and the risk of incident dementia in the Rotterdam Study. *Ann Neurol.*1997;42:776-82.
82. Terano,T. et al. Docosahexanoic acid supplementation improves the moderately severe dementia from thrombotic cerebrovascular diseases. *Lipids.* 1999;34:S345-46.
83. Morris, M.C. et al.Vitamin E and vitamin C supplement use and risk of incident Alzheimer disease. *Alzheimer Dis Assoc Disord.* 1998 Sep;12(3):121-6.
84. Bromberger, J.T. et al. Psychologic distress and natural menopause: a multiethnic community study. *Am J Public Health.* 2001 Sep;91(9):1435-42.
85. Warren, M.P. & Halpert, S. Hormone replacement therapy: controversies, pros and cons. *Best Pract Res Clin Endocrinol Metab.* 2004 Sep;18(3):317-32.
86. Yonehara, N. & Yoshimura, M. Influence of painful chronic neuropathy on neurogenic inflammation. *Pain.* 2001 May;92(1-2):259-65.
87. Ellison, N. et al. Phase III placebo-controlled trial of capsaicin cream in the management of surgical neuropathic pain in cancer patients. *J Clin Oncol.* 1997 Aug;15(8):2974-80.
88. Johnson, R.W. & Whitton,T.L. Management of herpes zoster (shingles) and postherpetic neuralgia. *Expert Opin Pharmacother.* 2004 Mar;5(3):551-9. Review.
89. Epstein, O. et al.Vitamin D, hydroxyapatite and calcium gluconate in Treatment of Cortical Bone Thinning in Post-menopausal Women with Primary Biliary Cirrhosis. *American Journal of Clinical Nutrition.*Vol. 36:426-30.
90. Nielsen, F.H. et al. Effect of Dietary Boron on Mineral, Estrogen and Testosterone Metabolism in Post-menopausal Women. *FASEB.* April, 1987.
91. Agnusdei, D. et al. A double blind, placebo-controlled trial of ipriflavone for prevention of postmenopausal spinal bone loss. *Calcif Tissue Int.* 1997 Aug;61(2):142-7.
92. Sesso, H.D., Paffenbarger, R.S. Jr. & Lee, I.M. Alcohol consumption and risk of prostate cancer: The Harvard Alumni Health Study. *Int J Epidemiol.* 2001 Aug;30(4):749-55.
93. Baskaran, K. et al.Antidiabetic effect of a leaf extract from Gymnema sylvestre in non-insulin-dependent diabetes mellitus patients. *J Ethnopharmacol.* 1990 Oct;30(3):295-300.
94. Shanmugasundaram, E.R. et al.Use of Gymnema sylvestre leaf extract in the control of blood glucose in insulin-dependent diabetes mellitus. *J Ethnopharmacol.* 1990 Oct;30(3):281-94.
95. Sesso, H.D., Paffenbarger, R.S. Jr. & Lee, I.M. Alcohol consumption and risk of prostate cancer: The Harvard Alumni Health Study. *Int J Epidemiol.* 2001 Aug;30(4):749-55.
96. De Stefani, E. et al. Tobacco, alcohol, diet and risk of prostate cancer. *Tumori.* 1995 Sep-Oct;81(5):315-20.
97. Koletzko, B. & Lehner, F. Beer and breastfeeding. *Adv Exp Med Biol.* 2000;478:23-8. Review.
98. Rugendorff, E.W. et al. Results of treatment with pollen extract (Cernilton N) in chronic prostatitis and prostatodynia. *Br J Urol.* 1993;71:433–8.
99. du Toit, P.J., van Aswegen, C.H. & du Plessis, D.J.The effect of essential fatty acids on growth and urokinase-type plasminogen activator production in human prostate DU-145 cells. *Prostaglandins Leukot Essent Fatty Acids.* 1996 Sep;55(3):173-7
100. Seville, R. H. "Psoriasis and Stress". *Br J Dermatol.* 97 (1977): page 297
101. Roberts, H.J. Spontaneous leg cramps and "restless legs" due to diabetogenic hyperinsulinism: observations on 131 patients. *J Am Geriatr Soc.*1965;13:602–8.
102. Roberts, H.J. Spontaneous leg cramps and "restless legs" due to diabetogenic (functional) hyperinsulinism. A basis for rational therapy. *JFMA.* 1973;60:29–31.
103. Yonehara, N. & Yoshimura, M. Influence of painful chronic neuropathy on neurogenic inflammation. *Pain.* 2001 May;92(1-2):259-65.
104. Ellison, N. et al. Phase III placebo-controlled trial of capsaicin cream in the management of surgical neuropathic pain in cancer patients. *J Clin Oncol.* 1997 Aug;15(8):2974-80.
105. Johnson, R.W. & Whitton,T.L. Management of herpes zoster (shingles) and postherpetic neuralgia. *Expert Opin Pharmacother.* 2004 Mar;5(3):551-9. Review.
106. Bisignano, G. et al. On the in-vitro antimicrobial activity of oleuropein and hydroxytyrosol. *J Pharm Pharmacol.* 1999 Aug; 51 (8): 971-4.

Index

5-hydroxytryptophan (5HTP); anxiety 79; ADD 91; depression 131; fibromyalgia 163; headaches and migraines 186; insomnia 211; multiple sclerosis 232; nerve pain 234; premenstrual syndrome 247; restless leg syndrome 256; seasonal affective disorder 258; weight loss 55
acidophilus (*lactobacillus acidophilus*); acne 65; AIDS 70; arthritis (rheumatoid) 84; bad breath 94; boils 95; candida 104; cellulitis 111; colds and flu 120; constipation 123; dandruff 128; detoxing 133; diarrhoea 140; eczema 147; endometriosis 153; fibromyalgia 163; food allergies and sensitivities 168; headaches and migraines 186; HIV 70; indigestion 205; irritable bowel syndrome 214; leaky gut syndrome 219; menopause 229; psoriasis 254; seborrhoeic dermatitis 260; sinusitis and sore throat 263; ulcers 277; vaginitis 279
acupuncture; sports injuries 269
aescin; lymphoedema 222; varicose veins 282
after sun care; sunburn 274
age-related macular degeneration (AMD); eye care 155
agrimony; diverticulosis 143; hiatus hernia 188; irritable bowel syndrome 215
alanine; prostate enlargement 251
alcohol 37; adverse effects and poisoning 71–73; angina and atherosclerosis 76; liver 48; weight loss 59
alder; constipation 124
allergies; eczema 145
allium, vegetables (onion family) 32
aloe vera cream; psoriasis 255
aloe vera gel; arthritis (osteo) 82; arthritis (rheumatoid) 85; hyperpigmentation of the skin 199; sports injuries 267; sunburn 273; ulcers 278
aloe vera juice; acne 65; alcohol poisoning and adverse effects 73; bad breath 94; Coeliac disease 116; constipation 123; cystitis 126; dandruff 129; detoxing 133; diverticulosis 143; fibroids 159; food allergies and sensitivities 169; gout 178; indigestion 205; irritable bowel syndrome 215; leaky gut syndrome 219; seborrhoeic dermatitis 260; ulcers 277
American cranesbill; endometriosis 153
American ginseng; diabetes mellitus 138; premenstrual syndrome 247
amino acids; (cysteine and methionine, see antioxidants)
amylase; Coeliac disease 116

anaphylactic reaction 167
androgens; acne 66–67
aniseed; diarrhoea 140
anthocyanidins; nerve pain 234
antibiotics; acne 66; colds and flu 119
antioxidant formula; AIDS 70; angina and atherosclerosis 77; arthritis (osteo) 82; arthritis (rheumatoid) 84; cataracts 108; detoxing 133; diabetes mellitus 137; eye care 154; food allergies and sensitivities 168; gallstones 174; gout 178; high cholesterol 195; HIV 70; hyperpigmentation of the skin 198; hyperthyroidism 200; liver 48; memory problems 224; multiple sclerosis 232; nerve pain 234; psoriasis 254; prostate enlargement 251; sports injuries 266; sunburn 272
antioxidants 30; bruises 101; chronic fatigue syndrome 114; dietary sources 31–33; eye care 155; infertility 209
apple cider vinegar (ACV) ; fungal infections 171; gum disease 179; varicose veins 282
apple cider vinegar and manuka honey; ulcers 277
arginine; infertility 209
arnica montana; sports injuries 268
arnica; arthritis (osteo) 83; arthritis (rheumatoid) 85; bruises 102; sports injuries 267
aromatherapy 20; bronchitis 99; cellulite 110; diverticulosis 141; emphysema 150
artichoke; angina and atherosclerosis 78; high cholesterol 196
artificial sweeteners 18
ascorbic acid; ear infection 144; seborrhoeic dermatitis 260
aspen; diverticulosis 143
Aspirin; anaemia 74; dandruff 128
astragalus; candida 105; cellulitis 111; chronic fatigue syndrome 115; colds and flu 119; cold sores 122; endometriosis 153; glandular fever 176; sinusitis and sore throat 264; shingles 262; warts 284
athlete's foot (see fungal infection)
autoimmune disease 83
avocado oil; sunburn 273;
AZT HIV drug therapy 70

Bach™ flower remedies, naturopathic therapies 19; ADD 91; bruises 102; candida 105; depression 131; diverticulosis 143; glandular fever 176; irritable bowel syndrome 215; premenstrual syndrome 246
bacopa; memory problems 226
banana peel; warts 284

barberry; constipation 124
basal metabolic rate (BMR) 50; hyperthyroidism 199; hypothyroidism 202
basil; arthritis (rheumatoid) 85; sports injuries 267
bearberry; cystitis 126; hyperpigmentation of the skin 199; kidney stones 218
bee propolis tincture; bad breath 94; gum disease 179; ulcers 278
beech; premenstrual syndrome 246
beta 1.3 glucan (see also antioxidants) 33; candida 105; cellulitis 111
beta carotene; bronchitis 99; cataracts 108; cervical dysplasia 112; colds and flu 119; cystitis 126; eczema 147; eye care 154; sinusitis and sore throat 263; sunburn 273
betaine; arthritis (rheumatoid) 84; bone spurs 97; fibromyalgia 163; food allergies and sensitivities 169
betasitosterol; sports injuries 267
bifidus; acne 65; AIDS 70; arthritis (rheumatoid) 84; bad breath 94; boils 95; candida 104; colds and flu 120; constipation 123; dandruff 128; detoxing 133; endometriosis 153; fibromyalgia 163; food allergies and sensitivities 168; HIV 70; indigestion 205; irritable bowel syndrome 214; leaky gut syndrome 219; menopause 229; sinusitis and sore throat 263; ulcers 277
bilberry; antioxidant 32; cataracts 108; diabetes mellitus 137; eczema 147; eye care 155; haemorrhoids 182
bioflavonoids (see also hesperidin, rutin and quercitin) 32; acne 65; angina and atherosclerosis 77; bruises 101; cellulite 109; eczema 147; eye care 155, 157; gum disease 179; haemorrhoids 181; lymphoedema 222; menopause 229; nerve pain 234; premenstrual syndrome 246; psoriasis 254; varicose veins 281
biotin; seborrhoeic dermatitis 259
bismuth (bismuth subcitrate); ulcers 277
bitter melon; diabetes mellitus 138; headaches and migraines 186; psoriasis 255
bitter orange 55
black cherry; kidney stones 218
black cohosh; fibromyalgia 164; headaches and migraines 186; hyperpigmentation of the skin 199; menopause 229, 230; polycystic ovary syndrome 242, 243; premenstrual syndrome 248; tinnitus 275
black haw; endometriosis 153; fibroids 161

Index

black heads 66
black pepper 55
black walnut; arthritis (osteo) 82; arthritis (rheumatoid) 85; ADD 91; bad breath 94; candida 105; constipation 124; detoxing 134; diabetes mellitus 138; diarrhoea 140; diverticulosis 143; endometriosis 152; fibroids 160; fibromyalgia 163; food allergies and sensitivities 168; infertility 207, 209; irritable bowel syndrome 215; lymphoedema 222; multiple sclerosis 233; polycystic ovary syndrome 242; premenstrual syndrome 246; prostate enlargement 252; psoriasis 255; ulcers 277; vaginitis 280; warts 284
bladderwrack; hypothyroidism 203
bleeding, excessive; endometriosis 153; fibroids 158
blood purifiers; ulcers 277
blood sugar level; low (anxiety) 78–79
blue bloater; emphysema 148
body mass index (BMI) 50–51
boldo; constipation 124
bone healing; sports injuries 267
bone regeneration; sports injuries 267
borage oil; anxiety 79; bruises 102; depression 131; diabetes mellitus 137; eczema 146; emphysema 149; endometriosis 152; eye care 155; infertility 207; polycystic ovary syndrome 242; premenstrual syndrome 247, 248; weight loss 56
boron; osteoporosis 238; sports injuries 267
boswellia; asthma 87; eczema 147; hayfever 183
bowel toxaemia 68; chronic fatigue syndrome 115; endometriosis 153
Bowen Technique; sports injuries 269
breast swelling and tenderness; premenstrual syndrome 248
broken bones (see sports injuries)
bromelain; AIDS 70; angina and atherosclerosis 77; asthma 87; bone spurs 97; bronchitis 99; carpal tunnel syndrome 106; emphysema 149; fibromyalgia 163; haemorrhoids 182; HIV 70; premenstrual syndrome 248; sports injuries 267
bruises (see also sports injuries) 100
buchu; cystitis 127
buckthorn; constipation 124
bugleweed; emphysema 150; high blood pressure 192; hyperthyroidism 201
bupleurum; arthritis (rheumatoid) 85; fibromyalgia 164; food allergies and sensitivities 168
burdock; boils 95; chronic fatigue syndrome 114; dandruff 129; detoxing 134; diabetes mellitus 138; eczema 147; endometriosis 153; gallstones 174; hyperpigmentation of the skin 198; infertility 207, 209; multiple sclerosis 233; nerve pain 235; premenstrual syndrome 246; prostate enlargement 252; psoriasis 255; seborrhoeic dermatitis 260; ulcers 277, 278; vaginitis 280

bursitis (see sports injuries)
Bush bitters; constipation 124
butcher's broom; bruises 102; haemorrhoids 182
Buteyko breathing 86; bronchitis 98; emphysema 148

cabbage juice; ulcers 277
caffeine 37; anxiety 79; weight loss 55
cajuput oil; sunburn 174
calc fluor; bruises 102; diverticulosis 143; emphysema 150; eye care 155; food allergies and sensitivities 168; haemorrhoids 181; hiatus hernia 188; leaky gut syndrome 220; varicose veins 281, 282;
calc phos; glandular fever 176; leaky gut syndrome 220; sports injuries 268
calc sulph; diverticulosis 143
calcium 28, 47; anxiety 79; asthma 87; depression 131; fibromyalgia 163; food allergies and sensitivities 168; headaches and migraines 185; high blood pressure 191; hyperthyroidism 200; insomnia 211; kidney stones 217; menopause 229; multiple sclerosis 232; nerve pain 234; sports injuries 267; stress 271
calcium hydroxyapatite; osteoporosis 238
calcium stones (see kidney stones)
calendula; acne 67–68; detoxing 134; eczema 146; fibroids 161; hyperthyroidism 201; lymphoedema 222; psoriasis 255; sports injuries 267; sunburn 274
Californian poppy; anxiety 80; insomnia 211; nerve pain 235; seasonal affective disorder 258; shingles 262; stress 271
candida; acne 66
caprylic acid; candida 104
capsaicin; arthritis (osteo) 83; arthritis (rheumatoid) 85; nerve pain 235; psoriasis 255; shingles 262; sports injuries 267
capsicum; arthritis (osteo) 83
carbohydrates 23; complex 23, 57; daily nutritional recommendations 35; liver 48; refined 76; simple 23; sources 23
carbonated drinks 37
carnitine 55; high blood pressure 191
carotenoids 31; eye care 154; sunburn 273
cartilage injuries (see sports injuries)
cartilage; arthritis (osteo) 80
cascara sagrada; constipation 124
castor oil; constipation 124; eye care 156; sinusitis and sore throat 264; warts 284
castor oil packs; fibroids 161; gallstones 174, nerve pain 236; sports injuries 267
catalase 33
catnip; colds and flu 119; sinusitis and sore throat 264
cayenne; detoxing 134; nerve pain 235; shingles 262
CD4+ cells 68–69
celery seed; arthritis (osteo) 82; arthritis (rheumatoid) 85; carpal tunnel syndrome 106; gout 178; sports injuries 267
cernilton; prostate enlargement 251, 252
chamomile; Coeliac disease 117; colds and flu 119; constipation 124; diarrhoea 141; diverticulosis (see German); eczema 146; fungal infections 171; hiatus hernia 188; indigestion 205; insomnia 212; irritable bowel syndrome 215; leaky gut syndrome 220; psoriasis 255; seborrhoeic dermatitis 260; sinusitis and sore throat 264
chamomile tea; ulcers 278;
charcoal tablets; diarrhoea 140;
chaste tree; acne 68; anxiety 80; candida 105; endometriosis 152; fibroids 161; headaches and migraines 186; infertility 207; menopause 230; polycystic ovary syndrome 242, 243; premenstrual syndrome 248
cherry plum; depression 131
Chinese foxglove; hyperthyroidism 201
chitosan; weight loss 56
chloasma 196
chlorella; bad breath 94; chronic fatigue syndrome 114
chloride 28
chlorophyll; bad breath 94; hyperpigmentation of the skin 197
cholesterol; angina and atherosclerosis 76; high cholesterol 194
choline; nerve pain 234
chondroitin; arthritis (osteo) 82; arthritis (rheumatoid) 84; bruises 102; haemorrhoids 181; leaky gut syndrome 219; sports injuries 266; varicose veins 281
chromium 29; acne 66–67; diabetes mellitus 137; headaches and migraines 186; polycystic ovary syndrome 241; premenstrual syndrome 247; psoriasis 255; restless leg syndrome 256; seborrhoeic dermatitis 259; weight loss 56
chronic obstructive pulmonary disease (COPD); emphysema 148
citrate; kidney stones 217
Clark, Professor Hulda (M.A., Ph.D., Physiology) 217
cleansing; bad breath 94
cleavers; arthritis (rheumatoid) 85; boils 95; cellulitis 111; cervical dysplasia 113; chronic fatigue syndrome 114; detoxing 134; diabetes mellitus 138; eczema 147; eye care 157; infertility 207, 209; lymphoedema 222; multiple sclerosis 233; nerve pain 235; premenstrual syndrome 246; prostate enlargement 252; psoriasis 255; seborrhoeic dermatitis 260; ulcers 278; vaginitis 280
cloves; arthritis (osteo) 82; arthritis (rheumatoid) 85; ADD 91; bad breath 94; candida 105; detoxing 134; diabetes mellitus 138; diarrhoea 140; diverticulosis 143; endometriosis 152; fibroids 160; fibromyalgia 163; food allergies and sensitivities 168; infertility 207,

209; irritable bowel syndrome 215; lymphoedema 222; multiple sclerosis 233; nerve pain 235; premenstrual syndrome 246; prostate enlargement 252; psoriasis 255; ulcers 277; vaginitis 280; warts 284
cod liver oil; ear infection 144; eczema 147
coenzyme Q10 (CoQ10); angina and atherosclerosis 77; antioxidant 33; bad breath 93; chronic fatigue syndrome 114; emphysema 149; gum disease 179; headaches and migraines 186; high blood pressure 191; hyperthyroidism 200; tinnitus 275
cola vera extract; cellulite 110
coleus; hypothyroidism 203
colloidal silver cream; fungal infections 171
colostrum; AIDS 70; alcohol poisoning and adverse effects 72; arthritis (rheumatoid) 84; candida 105; Coeliac disease 116; diarrhoea 140; eczema 147; fibromyalgia 163; food allergies and sensitivities 168; hiatus hernia 188; HIV 70; indigestion 205; irritable bowel syndrome 214; leaky gut syndrome 219; psoriasis 254
coltsfoot; bronchitis 99
combination G; varicose veins 281, 282
combination H; eye care 156
combination U; bone spurs 97; osteoporosis 238; sports injuries 268
comfrey; psoriasis 255; sports injuries 268
comfrey leaf poultice; sports injuries 268
compresses 43
copper 29
corydalis; endometriosis 153; fibroids 161; nerve pain 235
cosmetics 66–67
counselling, naturopathic therapies 20; anxiety 79
Cox-sackie B virus; chronic fatigue syndrome 113
crab apple; candida 105
cradle cap 127
cramp bark; arthritis (rheumatoid) 85; irritable bowel syndrome 215; sports injuries 267
cranberry; cystitis 126
cruciferous vegetables 31
curcumin; angina and atherosclerosis 78; high cholesterol 196
cysteine (see antioxidants) 32
cystine stones (see kidney stones)

dairy products; daily nutritional recommendations 35; acne 64–65
daisy; sunburn 274
damiana; depression 131; infertility 207; polycystic ovary syndrome 243
dan shen; angina and atherosclerosis 78; endometriosis 152
dandelion latex; warts 284
dandelion root 48; alcohol poisoning and adverse effects 72; candida 105; chronic fatigue syndrome 115;

constipation 124; dandruff 129; detoxing 134; diabetes mellitus 138; eczema 147; endometriosis 153; fibroids 160; fibromyalgia 164; food allergies and sensitivities 168; gallstones 174; hyperpigmentation of the skin 198; liver detoxing 45; memory problems 225; infertility 207, 209; multiple sclerosis 233; nerve pain 235; premenstrual syndrome 246; psoriasis 255; ulcers 277; vaginitis 280; varicose veins 282; weight loss 56
decoctions 42
demodex folliculorum 64
detoxing; detoxing observations 49, 134; liver 45–49; nerve pain 235; premenstrual syndrome 246, 247; prostate enlargement 252; seborrhoeic dermatitis 260
devil's claw; arthritis (osteo) 82; arthritis (rheumatoid) 85; carpal tunnel syndrome 106; fibromyalgia 164; gout 178; sports injuries 267
digestion enhancers 35
digestive enzymes; anaemia 74; asthma 87; bad breath 94; candida 104; constipation 123; diarrhoea 140; indigestion 205; irritable bowel syndrome 214; osteoporosis 238; psoriasis 254
diindolylmethane (DIM); fibroids 160; headaches and migraines 186; menopause 229; premenstrual syndrome 246
dislocation injuries (see sports injuries)
Disprin; dandruff 128
DMAE (2-dimethylaminoethanol); memory problems 225
docosahexaenoic acid (DHA); ADD 88; memory problems 226
dong quai; headaches and migraines 186; infertility 207; menopause 229, 230; polycystic ovary syndrome 243; premenstrual syndrome 248
dosages 43
dry scalp 128
dry skin brushing 20, 39; liver 49

echinacea; acne 68; asthma 88; bad breath 94; boils 95; bronchitis 99; cellulitis 111; colds and flu 119; cystitis 127; detoxing 134; diarrhoea 140; diverticulosis 143; ear infection 145; emphysema 149; endometriosis 153; eye care 157; fungal infections 171; gum disease 179; headaches and migraines 186; lymphoedema 222; multiple sclerosis 233; psoriasis 255; seasonal affective disorder 258; sinusitis and sore throat 264; ulcers 277; vaginitis; 280; warts 284
eicosapentaenoic acid (EPA); ADD 88
elder; hayfever 183
elecampane; bronchitis 99; colds and flu 119; emphysema 149
elimination diet 167
elm; depression 131
epsom salts; boils 95; diverticulosis 141; fibromyalgia 162

Epstein-Barr virus; chronic fatigue syndrome 113; glandular fever 175
Escherichia coli (*E. coli*); cystitis 125
essential fatty acids (EFA) 23, 35; alcohol poisoning and adverse effects 72; eczema 146; sports injuries 266; weight loss 56
essential oils 43; ADD 92; headaches and migraines 186
ethylene diamine tetra-acetic acid (EDTA); angina and atherosclerosis 77
eucalyptus; colds and flu 119; sinusitis and sore throat 264
euphorbia; bronchitis 99
evening primrose oil (EPO); acne 67; alcohol poisoning and adverse effects 72; anxiety 79; arthritis (osteo) 82; arthritis (rheumatoid) 84; asthma 87; bruises 102; carpal tunnel syndrome 106; cellulite 109; depression 131; diabetes mellitus 137; eczema 146; emphysema 149; endometriosis 152; eye care 155, 156; fibroids 160; fibromyalgia 163; food allergies and sensitivities 168; hiatus hernia 188; hyperpigmentation of the skin 198; infertility 207; leaky gut syndrome 219; memory problems 225, 226; multiple sclerosis 233; polycystic ovary syndrome 242; premenstrual syndrome 247, 248; prostate enlargement 251; psoriasis 254, 255; seborrhoeic dermatitis 259; sports injuries 266; sunburn 273; varicose veins 281
exercise 39; weight loss 50–54, 56
eye care; blood vessel damage 155; detoxing 131; droopy eyelids 156; dry eye 156; eye allergies 156; eye floaters 157; eye infections 157; yellow sclera 157
eyebright; asthma 87; ear infection 144; eye care 155, 156, 157; hayfever 183

false unicorn root; endometriosis 152; fibroids 161; headaches and migraines 186; infertility 207; menopause 230; polycystic ovary syndrome 243
fasting; liver fasts 46
fats 23; daily nutritional recommendations 35; essential fatty acids (EFA) 23, 35, 54; monounsaturated 76, 194; oxidised fats 34; polyunsaturated 23, 194; saturated 23, 66, 194; sources of fat 23, 35; trans fatty acids 34, 35, 76, 194; weight loss 58
fatty food; alcohol poisoning and adverse effects 72
fennel seeds; diarrhoea 141
fennel tea; indigestion 205; irritable bowel syndrome 215
fenugreek; asthma 88; bronchitis 99; diabetes mellitus 138; hayfever 183; leaky gut syndrome 220
ferr phos; anaemia 74; diverticulosis 143; emphysema 150; eye care 156; hiatus hernia 188; leaky gut syndrome 220
feverfew; bruises 102; fibromyalgia 164;

Index

headaches and migraines 186; infertility 207; nerve pain 235; premenstrual syndrome 248
fibre 24; angina and atherosclerosis 76–77; arthritis (rheumatoid) 84; bad breath 93; candida 104; constipation 123; detoxing 48, 134; diabetes mellitus 137; diarrhoea 140; diverticulosis 142; fibroids 160; gallstones 174; haemorrhoids 181; hiatus hernia 188; irritable bowel syndrome 214; memory problems 225; menopause 229; multiple sclerosis 233; nerve pain 235; polycystic ovary syndrome 241, 242; premenstrual syndrome 246; varicose veins 281; weight loss 56
fibrinogen; angina and atherosclerosis 77; high cholesterol 195
filiform warts (see warts)
fish oil; alcohol poisoning and adverse effects 72; angina and atherosclerosis 77; anxiety 79; arthritis (osteo) 82; arthritis (rheumatoid) 84; ADD 91; bruises 102; carpal tunnel syndrome 106; cellulite 109; Coeliac disease 116; dandruff 128; depression 131; diabetes mellitus 137; eczema 146; emphysema 149; endometriosis 152; eye care 155, 156; fibroids 160; fibromyalgia 163; gout 178; high blood pressure 191; high cholesterol 196; infertility 207; insomnia 211; leaky gut syndrome 219; memory problems 225, 226; multiple sclerosis 233; nerve pain 235; polycystic ovary syndrome 242; premenstrual syndrome 247, 248; psoriasis 254; sports injuries 266; varicose veins 281; weight loss 56
flat warts (see warts)
flavonoids ; dietary sources 32
flax root; constipation 124;
flaxseed fibre (see fibre)
flaxseed oil; acne 67; AIDS 70; alcohol poisoning and adverse effects 72; angina and atherosclerosis 76–77; anxiety 79; arthritis (osteo) 82; arthritis (rheumatoid) 84; asthma 87; ADD 91; bruises 102; candida 105; carpal tunnel syndrome 106; Coeliac disease 116; dandruff 128; depression 131; diabetes mellitus 137; eczema 146, 147; emphysema 149; endometriosis 152; eye care 155, 156; fibroids 160; fibromyalgia 163; food allergies and sensitivities 168; high cholesterol 196; HIV 70; indigestion 205; infertility 207; irritable bowel syndrome 214; leaky gut syndrome 219; menopause 229; nerve pain 235; polycystic ovary syndrome 242; premenstrual syndrome 246, 247, 248; prostate enlargement 251; psoriasis 254, 255; seborrhoeic dermatitis 259; sports injuries 266; sunburn 273; ulcers 277; varicose veins 281; weight loss 56–62
fluid; daily nutritional recommendations 35; extracts 42; retention, premenstrual syndrome 247

fluoride 29
folic acid 27; anaemia 73–75; angina and atherosclerosis 77; arthritis (rheumatoid) 84; bruises 101; cervical dysplasia 112; eczema 147; fibromyalgia 163; hyperpigmentation of the skin 198; infertility 207; leaky gut syndrome 219; osteoporosis 238; restless leg syndrome 256; tinnitus 275
food allergies; acne 64,66; addictive allergy 165; anaphylactic reaction 167; cyclic allergy 164; eczema 147; fixed allergy 164; liver 48; non-fixed allergy 164; masked allergy 164; testing 166
food; hygiene 139; preparation 37, 61; sensitivities (see also food allergies) 37
fractured bones (see sports injuries)
free radicals 30; sources of 33
friar's balsam; colds and flu 119; sinusitis and sore throat 264
frozen shoulder (see sports injuries)
fruit 31, 37; weight loss 57
fumaria officinalis; constipation 124
fungal infection 169

gall bladder flush fast 46; gallstones 173; nerve pain 236
garlic; angina and atherosclerosis 78; bruises 102; candida 105; cellulitis 111; fungal infections 171; high blood pressure 191; high cholesterol 196; seasonal affective disorder 258
garlic oil; warts 284
gential warts (see warts)
gentian; anaemia 75; depression 131; diarrhoea 140; food allergies and sensitivities 169; hyperthyroidism 201
German chamomile; diverticulosis 143
ginger; angina and atherosclerosis 78; arthritis (osteo) 83; arthritis (rheumatoid) 85; cellulite 110; constipation 124; detoxing 134; endometriosis 153; fibroids 161; fibromyalgia 164; fungal infections 171; gout 178; high blood pressure 191; high cholesterol 196; irritable bowel syndrome 215; kidney stones 218; premenstrual syndrome 248; sports injuries 267; varicose veins 282
ginkgo (see antioxidants) 32; angina and atherosclerosis 78; asthma 87; bruises 102; cataracts 108; depression 131; diabetes mellitus 138; eye care 155; high blood pressure 191; menopause 230; memory problems 225; tinnitus 276; varicose veins 282
ginseng; acne 68; anxiety 80; arthritis (rheumatoid) 85; candida 105; chronic fatigue syndrome (see Siberian and Korean); diabetes mellitus (see American); infertility 209; *Panax*, stress 271
glands (swollen) 175
glaucoma; eye care 155
globe artichoke; liver detoxing 49; gallstones 174; glandular fever 176
glucosamine; arthritis (osteo) 82; arthritis (rheumatoid) 84; bruises 102; cystitis 126; eye care 154; haemorrhoids 181; leaky gut syndrome 219;

sports injuries 266; varicose veins 281
glutamic acid; prostate enlargement 251
glutamine; Coeliac disease 116; hiatus hernia 188; leaky gut syndrome 219
glutathione 30
glycaemic index (GI) 136
glycerin; kidney stones 218
glycine; prostate enlargement 251
goldenrod; ear infection 145; eye care 157; headaches and migraines 186; kidney stones 218
goldenseal; boils 95; candida 105; cellulitis 111; cervical dysplasia 113; cystitis 127; eye care 157; fungal infections 171; gallstones 174; headaches and migraines 186; hiatus hernia 188; sinusitis and sore throat 264; tinnitus 275; ulcers 277; vaginitis 280
gorse; depression 131
gotu kola extract; bruises 102; cellulite 110; cystitis 127; emphysema 150; endometriosis 152; fibroids 160; haemorrhoids 181; memory problems 226; varicose veins 282
grape seed (see antioxidants); antioxidant 32; asthma 87; cellulite 109; haemorrhoids 181; varicose veins 281
grapefruit; hyperpigmentation of the skin 199
gravel root; kidney stones 218
green tea; angina and atherosclerosis 76; antioxidant 32; weight loss 56
ground ivy; tinnitus 275
guaiacum; sports injuries 267
guar gum; polycystic ovary syndrome 241
guarana 56
guggul; angina and atherosclerosis 78; high cholesterol 196; hypothyroidism 203
gymnema; headaches and migraines 186; premenstrual syndrome 247; weight loss 56

haematomas (see sports injuries)
hair rinse, how to make a 129
halitosis 92
harpogoside; sports injuries 267
hawthorn; angina and atherosclerosis 78; cellulite 110; emphysema 150; high blood pressure 191; hyperthyroidism 200; varicose veins 282
heart; murmurs (iron deficiency anaemia) 73
heavy metals 34; angina and atheroscerosis 75–78; toxin build-up, memory problems 225
herbal detoxing; ADD 91; cellulite 110; diabetes mellitus 137
herbal medicine 19, 41; creams and ointments 43; dosages 43; dry herbs 42; forms of herbs 41–43; herbal vinegars 43; sinusitis and sore throat 264; teas, ADD 92
hesperidin; bad breath 94; bruises 101; eye care 155
high cholesterol 192
high density lipoproteins (HDL) (see lipoproteins)

Index

hirsutism; polycystic ovary syndrome 243
histidine; hayfever 183
HIV (see human immunodeficiency virus) 68–71
holly; diverticulosis 143
homeopathy, naturopathic therapies 19; food allergies and sensitivities 169
homocysteine 75, 77
hops; polycystic ovary syndrome 242, 243
hormone balancing; acne 68; anxiety 80
hormone replacement therapy 227
horny goat weed; infertility 207
horse chestnut extract; bruises 102; cellulite 110; haemorrhoids 182; lymphoedema 222; varicose veins 282
human immunodeficiency virus (HIV) 68–71
human papilloma virus (HPV) (see warts)
hydrangea root; kidney stones 218
hydrochloric acid; arthritis (rheumatoid) 84; bone spurs 97; fibromyalgia 163; indigestion 205; low, insufficient 36, 64; osteoporosis 238; psoriasis 254; supplements 65
hydroxycitric acid (HCA) 56
hyssop; bronchitis 99; colds and flu 119
hysterectomy; fibroids 158

impatiens; premenstrual syndrome 246
indole-3-carbinole 35
infertility, female 206; male 207
inositol heaxaniacinate; high cholesterol 195
insomnia; anxiety 78–79
insulin dependent diabetes mellitus 135
intermittent claudication 75
intrinsic factor 73
in-vitro fertilisation (IVF); infertility 205
iodine 29; BP tincure 171; weight loss 56
IP6-Phytase; angina and atherosclerosis 77
ipriflavone; osteoporosis 238
Irish moss; detoxing 134
iron 29; anaemia 73–75; ADD 91; bruises 101; restless leg syndrome 256

Jamaica dogwood; endometriosis 153; insomnia 212; nerve pain 235; seasonal affective disorder 258; shingles 262; sports injuries 267
Jamu bersih darah; boils 95; ulcers 277
Jamu gadong gadok; boils 95; ulcers 277
jock itch (see fungal infection)
jojoba oil 67
juniper; cellulite 110; varicose veins 282

kali mur; eye care 157; hiatus hernia 188; lymphoedema 223
kali phos; ADD 91; depression 131; glandular fever 176
kava; anxiety 80; menopause 230; nerve pain 235; premenstrual syndrome 247; stress 271
kelp (see antioxidants); antioxidant 33

ketoacidosis 135
kidney stones 215
Korean ginseng; chronic fatigue syndrome 115
kudzu; menopause 229, 230
kumerahau; bronchitis 99

lady's mantle; endometriosis 153
lavender oil; acne 67; colds and flu 119; fungal infections 171; insomnia 212; sunburn 274; warts 284;
lavender tea; sinusitis and sore throat 264
laxative abuse, irritable bowel syndrome 213
lecithin 48; angina and atherosclerosis 77; ADD 91; cellulite 109; gallstones 174; high cholesterol 195; liver 48; memory problems 224; multiple sclerosis 232; nerve pain 235; weight loss 56
lemon balm; anxiety 80; cold sores 122; hyperthyroidism 200; leaky gut syndrome 220; shingles 262; stress 271
leutinising hormone (LH) reduction; polycystic ovary syndrome 242
libido; low (anxiety) 78–80
lifestyle recommendations, naturopathic therapies 20
light therapy; seasonal affective disorder 257
lime flower; high blood pressure 191
lipase; Coeliac disease 116
lipoic acid 70; diabetes mellitus 137
lipoproteins; angina and atherosclerosis 75–78; lipoprotein (a), angina and atherosclerosis 75–76; high cholesterol 192
liquorice; acne 68; AIDS 70; HIV 70; anxiety 80; arthritis (rheumatoid) 85; asthma 87; bronchitis 99; candida 105; Coeliac disease 117; chronic fatigue syndrome 115; constipation 124; detoxing 134; diverticulosis 143; eczema 147; emphysema 149; fibroids 161; fibromyalgia 164; food allergies and sensitivities 168; fungal infections 171; hyperpigmentation of the skin 199; infertility 207; leaky gut syndrome 220; polycystic ovary syndrome 242, 243; premenstrual syndrome 248; psoriasis 255; stress 271
liver; conditions 45; detoxing 45; detoxing nutrition 47–48; signs and symptoms 45; support 45; weight loss 56
lobelia; asthma 87; bronchitis 99; emphysema 149
low density lipoprotein (LDL) (see lipoproteins)
Lugol's iodine; boils 95; diarrhoea 140; fungal infections 171; hypothyroidism 203; ulcers 277, 278
lunaception, infertility 206
lutein; eye care 155
lymphatic massage; detoxing 134; lymphoedema 221
lysine; cold sores 121; shingles 261

maca; infertility 209
mag phos; ADD 91; diverticulosis 143; food allergies and sensitivities 168; leaky gut syndrome 220
magnesium 28; angina and atherosclerosis 77; anxiety 79; asthma 87; ADD 91; bone spurs 97; chronic fatigue syndrome 114; constipation 124; depression 131; emphysema 149; endometriosis 152; fibromyalgia 163; food allergies and sensitivities 168; gallstones 174; headaches and migraines 185; high blood pressure 191; infertility 207; insomnia 211; kidney stones 217, 218; liver 48; multiple sclerosis 232; nerve pain 234; osteoporosis 238; polycystic ovary syndrome 241; premenstrual syndrome 247, 248; restless leg syndrome 256; sports injuries 267; stress 271; tinnitus 275
major nutrients 22
manganese 30; dietary sources 30, 32; osteoporosis 238; sports injuries 267; tinnitus 275
manuka honey; menopause 230; ulcers 278
marigold; eye care 157
marine collagen; eye care 156; sunburn 273
marine protein (lyophilised); eye care 156; sunburn 273
marshmallow root; asthma 87; bronchitis 99; diarrhoea 141; diverticulosis 143; eczema 147; emphysema 149; hiatus hernia 188; kidney stones 218; leaky gut syndrome 220; psoriasis 255
massage 39; detoxing 49; sports injuries 269
meadowsweet; bruises 102; diarrhoea 140; hiatus hernia 188; indigestion 205
meat; red (anaemia) 74
melasma 196
melatonin; anxiety 78–79; cataracts 108; depression 131; insomnia 211
meningitis; colds and flu 118
mental strengthening 39
menthol; arthritis (osteo) 82; arthritis (rheumatoid) 85; sports injuries 267
mercury fillings; fibromyalgia 162
metabolism; weight loss 50
methionine (see antioxidants) 32
methyl sulphonyl methane (MSM); carpal tunnel syndrome 106; cystitis 126; fibromyalgia 163; headaches and migraines 186; nerve pain 234; sports injuries 266
migraines; acne 64
milk thistle; alcohol poisoning and adverse effects 72; angina and atherosclerosis 78; candida 105; chronic fatigue syndrome 115; dandruff 129; detoxing 134; diabetes mellitus 138; eczema 147; endometriosis 153; fibroids 160; fibromyalgia 164; food allergies and sensitivities 168; gallstones 174; glandular fever 176; high cholesterol 196; hyperpigmentation of

the skin 198; hyperthyroidism 201; hypothyroidism 203; infertility; 207, 209; liver detoxing 45; nerve pain 235; premenstrual syndrome 246; prostate enlargement 252; psoriasis 255; seborrhoeic dermatitis 260; ulcers 277; vaginitis 280; varicose veins 282; weight loss 56
mimulus; arthritis 80; irritable bowel syndrome 215
minerals 27; major 28–29, calcium 28, chloride 28, magnesium 28, phosphorus 28–29, potassium 29, sodium 28, sulphur 28; trace 29–30, chromium 29, copper 29, fluoride 29, iodine 29, iron 29, manganese 30, selenium 30, zinc 30
minor nutrients 24
molluscum contagiosum (see warts)
monounsaturated fats (see fats)
motherwort; hyperthyroidism 200; menopause 230
mouse ear; bronchitis 99
mullein; asthma 87; bronchitis 99; colds and flu 119; ear infection 144; emphysema 149
multi vitamin and mineral formulas; alcohol poisoning and adverse effects 72; anaemia 75; bruises 101; candida 104; Coeliac disease 116; chronic fatigue syndrome 114; detoxing 133; diabetes mellitus 137; diarrhoea 140; diverticulosis 142; ear infection 144; high cholesterol 196; hypothyroidism 203; irritable bowel syndrome 214; memory problems 225; ulcers 278; vaginitis 279
myrrh; bad breath 94; boils 95; cellulitis 111; fungal infections 171; gum disease 179; sinusitis and sore throat 264; ulcers 277

nail infections (see fungal infection)
nat mur; eye care 156; lymphoedema 223
nat phos; eye care 157; hiatus hernia 188; leaky gut syndrome 220
nat sulph; lymphoedema 223
natural fertility management; infertility 205
natural medicine 16
naturopath 17
nerve disorders; anaemia 73
nerve tonics; seasonal affective disorder 258
nerve-restoring herbs; menopause 230
nettle; nettle tea, anaemia 75; prostate enlargement 252
niacin (see vitamin B3)
non-insulin dependent diabetes mellitus 135
nut milk; how to make 146
nutrition 19, 22; daily nutrition guidelines 35–38; naturopathic therapies 19

oatmeal; eczema 146; hyperpigmentation of the skin 199
oats; depression 131
occupational overuse; carpal tunnel syndrome 105

oil infusion 42
olive leaf extract; acne 68; AIDS 70; asthma 88; bad breath 94; boils 95; bronchitis 99; candida 105; cellulitis 111; cervical dysplasia 112; chronic fatigue syndrome 114; colds and flu 119; cold sores 121; cystitis 127; diarrhoea 140; ear infection 145; emphysema 149; endometriosis 153; eye care 156; fibromyalgia 164; fungal infections 171; glandular fever 176; gum disease 179; headaches and migraines 186; HIV 70; multiple sclerosis 233; psoriasis 255; seasonal affective disorder 258; shingles 261; sinusitis and sore throat 263; sunburn 274; ulcers 277; vaginitis 280; warts 284
omega 3 23, 47; angina and atherosclerosis 77; high cholesterol 196
omega 6 23, 47; acne 66–67
oregano oil; fungal infections 171
orthodox medicine 17–18
osteoarthritis 80
osteopathy; sports injuries 269
overuse, injuries (see sports injuries)

pantethine; high cholesterol 196
papain; Coeliac disease 116; sports injuries 267
papaya; hyperpigmentation of the skin 199
parasite cleansing; acne 65
parsley; kidney stones 218; tea, how to make 248
passionflower; acne 68; angina and atherosclerosis 78; anxiety 80; candida 105; high blood pressure 191; hyperthyroidism 200; insomnia 212; menopause 230; premenstrual syndrome 247; seasonal affective disorder 258; stress 271
pau d'arco; candida 105; cellulitis 111; chronic fatigue syndrome 115; colds and flu 119; cold sores 122; glandular fever 176; shingles 262; sinusitis and sore throat 264; sunburn 274
pectin (see fibre)
peony; polycystic ovary syndrome 242, 243
peppermint capsules; gallstones 174
peppermint oil; irritable bowel syndrome 215
peppermint tea; constipation 124; diverticulosis 143; indigestion 205; irritable bowel syndrome 215
perilla; asthma 87; eczema 147; eye care 156; food allergies and sensitivities 168; hayfever 183
pesticides 33, 38
phosphatidylserine (PS); ADD 91; memory problems 224; multiple sclerosis 232; nerve pain 235
phosphorus 28–29
physiotherapy; sports injuries 269
pilosebaceous duct 66
pine; depression 131
pine bark (see antioxidants); antioxidant 32

pink puffer; emphysema 147
pityrosporum (see fungal infection)
plantar warts (verrucas) (see warts)
pokeroot; arthritis (rheumatoid) 85; cellulitis 111; detoxing 134; endometriosis 153; eye care 157; fibroids 161; hyperthyroidism 201; lymphoedema 222
policosanol; high cholesterol 196
pollution 33–34
polycystic ovarian disease (see polycystic ovary syndrome)
polycystic ovary syndrome 239
polysaccharides; sunburn 273
polyunsaturated fats (see fats)
potassium 29; high blood pressure 191
potassium rich foods; premenstrual syndrome 247
poultices 43; nerve pain 236; sports injuries 268
prescription medicine 38; combining prescription drugs and herbs 44
probiotics; Coeliac disease 116
processed foods 37
proenOthera (see antioxidants)
progesterone; premenstrual syndrome 246
protease; Coeliac disease 116
protein 22; complete proteins 22; daily nutritional recommendations 35; incomplete proteins 22; sources of protein 22; weight loss 56–62
psyllium (see fibre)
pumpkin seed oil; prostate enlargement 251
pygeum; infertility 209; prostate enlargement 252

queen's delight; detoxing 134
quercetin; asthma 87; bad breath 94; bruises 101; eczema 147; eye care 155, 156; hayfever 183; lymphoedema 222; psoriasis 254

radiation 33, 58
raspberry leaf; endometriosis 152; fibroids 161
recommended daily intake (RDI) 13, 24
recreational drugs 38
red clover; bad breath 94; boils 95; bruises 102; cervical dysplasia 113; chronic fatigue syndrome 114; dandruff 129; detoxing 134; diabetes mellitus 138; eczema 147; hyperthyroidism 201; infertility 207, 209; memory problems 225; menopause 229, 230; multiple sclerosis 233; nerve pain 235; premenstrual syndrome 246; prostate enlargement 252; psoriasis 255; seborrhoeic dermatitis 260; ulcers 277, 278; vaginitis 280
red raspberry leaf tea; infertility 207
reflexology, naturopathic therapies 19; bronchitis 100; diverticulosis 141; irritable bowel syndrome 215
rehmannia glutinosa; arthritis (rheumatoid) 85
relaxation techniques 39

Index

relaxing herbs; ADD 91
repetitive strain; carpal tunnel syndrome 105
rescue remedy 19; anxiety 80; bruises 102; depression 131; glandular fever 176; irritable bowel syndrome 215
rheumatoid arthritis 83
rhubarb root; constipation 124
rhus tox; carpal tunnel syndrome 107; sports injuries 268
RICE; sports injuries 268
ringworm (see fungal infection)
rock rose; depression 131
rosehip oil; acne and scarring 68; sunburn 273
rosemary; memory problems 225; menopause 229; seborrhoeic dermatitis 260;
rosemary essential oil; varicose veins 282;
rosmarinic acid; menopause 229
rotation diet; eczema 146
rue; sports injuries 267
ruta grav; carpal tunnel syndrome 107
ruta graveolens (rue); sports injuries 268
rutin; bad breath 94; bruises 101; eye care 155, 156; psoriasis 254

sage; menopause 230
sage tea; colds and flu 119; gum disease 179; sinusitis and sore throat 264; ulcers 278;
salt; acne (Celtic, herbal and iodised) 65–66
salve 43
sarcolactic acid; sports injuries 268
sarsaparilla; eczema 147; fungal infections 171; hyperpigmentation of the skin 199; hyperthyroidism 201; polycystic ovary syndrome 243; psoriasis 255; seborrhoeic dermatitis 260
saturated fats (see also fats); liver 48
saw palmetto; infertility 209; polycystic ovary syndrome 242, 243; prostate enlargement 252
scar tissue; sports injuries 267
scarring; acne 68
Schuessler tissue salts; anaemia 74; ADD 91; bone spurs 97; bruises 102; depression 131; diverticulosis 143; emphysema 150; eye care 155, 156, 157; food allergies and sensitivities 168; glandular fever 176; haemorrhoids 181; hiatus hernia 188; leaky gut syndrome 220; lymphoedema 223; sports injuries 268; varicose veins 281, 282
seaweed; fibroids 160
selenium (see antioxidants) 30; acne 67; asthma 87; cervical dysplasia 112; dandruff 128; dietary sources 30, 32; emphysema 149; seborrhoeic dermatitis 259
selfheal; lymphoedema 222
senna; constipation 124
serotonin; anxiety 78–79; weight loss 50, 55
shark cartilage; cystitis 126
shark liver oil; detoxing 133

Shepherd's purse; endometriosis 153; eye care 155; fibroids 161
shin splints (see sports injuries)
Siberian ginseng; chronic fatigue syndrome 115; infertility 207; menopause 230; premenstrual syndrome 247
signs 13
silica; ADD 91; diverticulosis 143; emphysema 150; eye care 157; food allergies and sensitivities 168; hiatus hernia 188; leaky gut syndrome 220; osteoporosis 238; sports injuries 267
sitz bath, infertility 208
skin; hygiene 67; white patches 169; red patches 169
skullcap; anxiety 80; hayfever 183; insomnia 212; irritable bowel syndrome 215; multiple sclerosis 233; nerve pain 236; psoriasis 255; seasonal affective disorder 258; stress 271
sleep 38
slippery elm; alcohol poisoning and adverse effects 72; angina and atherosclerosis 77; Coeliac disease 116; diarrhoea 141; diverticulosis 142, 143; hiatus hernia 188; indigestion 205; leaky gut syndrome 220
smoking (see also tobacco smoking) 38
sodium 28
soy; menopause 229, 230
spicy foods 64
spider veins; varicose veins 282
spirulina; anaemia 74; ADD 91; bad breath 94; Coeliac disease 116; chronic fatigue syndrome 114; dandruff 129; detoxing 133; diverticulosis 142; irritable bowel syndrome 214
sports injuries 264–265
sprains (see sports injuries)
St John's Wort; anxiety 80; AIDS 71; carpal tunnel syndrome 107; cold sores 122; controversy 44; depression 131; HIV 71; leaky gut syndrome 220; menopause 230; nerve pain 235; premenstrual syndrome 247; seasonal affective disorder 258; shingles 262; sports injuries 267; stress 271
St Mary's thistle; memory problems 225; psoriasis 255
standardised extract 42
staphylococcus aureus; boils 94
star of Bethlehem; diverticulosis 143
starch carbohydrate blockers 57
starflower oil; premenstrual syndrome 247
Stein Leventhal syndrome (see polycystic ovary syndrome)
strains (see sports injuries)
stress 39; acne 68; how does the body combat stress 269; recovery 270
struvite stones (see kidney stones)
subsyndromal SAD; seasonal affective disorder 257
sugar; angina and atherosclerosis 77; liver 38; weight loss 58
sulphoraphane 35
sulphur 28; dandruff 128
sun spot cream; sunburn 274
sundew; bronchitis 99

sunflower seed oil; prostate enlargement 251
superoxide dismutase 30
supplements, naturopathic therapies 19, 37
Swedish bitters; constipation 124; fibroids 159; food allergies and sensitivities 168
sweet clover; lymphoedema 222
sweet violet leaves; sunburn 274
symptoms 13
syrup simplex 42

tachycardia; anaemia (iron) 73
tansy; infertility 207
taurine (see antioxidants)
t-cells 68–70
tea; black, anaemia 74
tea bags; eye care 156
tea tree oil; acne 67; boils 95; dandruff 128; fungal infections 171; sports injuries 267; sunburn 274
tendonitis (see sports injuries)
tennis elbow (see sports injuries)
therapeutic body work, naturopathic therapies 20; therapeutic massage 39
thuja; endometriosis 153; fibroids 161; fungal infections 171; warts 284
thyme; bronchitis 99; colds and flu 119; seborrhoeic dermatitis 260; sinusitis and sore throat 264
thyroid glandular; hypothyroidism 203
thyroid hormones (T4-T3); hyperthyroidism 201
tiger balm; arthritis (osteo) 82; arthritis (rheumatoid) 85; sports injuries 267
tinctures 42
tinea (see fungal infection)
tinnitus retraining therapy 274, 275
tobacco smoking 33
torn ligaments (see sports injuries)
toxins 33–34, 38; acne 66–67
trans fatty acids (see fats)
tribulus; polycystic ovary syndrome 243
tub therapy 38
turmeric 49; AIDS 70; cellulite 110; detoxing 134; diabetes mellitus 138; gout 178; HIV 70; premenstrual syndrome 248; varicose veins 282
tyrosine; hypothyroidism 203; memory problems 225

ulcers, peptic or stomach 277; bed and leg 277; mouth 278
uric acid stones (see kidney stones)

valerian; angina and atherosclerosis 78; anxiety 80; arthritis (rheumatoid) 85; fibromyalgia 164; high blood pressure 191; hyperthyroidism 200; insomnia 211; irritable bowel syndrome 215; menopause 230; multiple sclerosis 233; nerve pain 236; premenstrual syndrome 247; psoriasis 255; stress 271
vegetables, organic 37; cleaning organic vegetables 37; weight loss 57
vegetarian diets; anaemia (iron) 73; premenstrual syndrome 246

Index

veins; acne (broken capillaries) 64–65
verbena; leaky gut syndrome 220
verrucas (plantar warts) (see warts)
vervain; depression 131
very low density lipoprotein (VLDL) (see lipoproteins)
vitamin A (see also antioxidants) 25; acne 65–67; arthritis (rheumatoid) 84; asthma 87; bad breath 93; boils 95; bronchitis 99; cataracts 108; cellulitis 111; cervical dysplasia 112; colds and flu 119; cystitis 126; ear infection 144; eczema 147; emphysema 149; eye care 154, 157; fibromyalgia 163; gum disease 179; hiatus hernia 188; hyperpigmentation of the skin 199; leaky gut syndrome 219; seborrhoeic dermatitis 259; sinusitis and sore throat 263; sunburn 273; ulcers 277
vitamin B complex (biotin, choline, folic acid, inositol, para-aminobenzoic acid [PABA], B13, B15, B17 25, 27); acne 65, 67–68; alcohol poisoning and adverse effects 72; anxiety 79; asthma 87; candida 105; carpal tunnel syndrome 106; cervical dysplasia 112; chronic fatigue syndrome 114; dandruff 128; depression 130; ear infection 144; emphysema 149; endometriosis 152; eye care 157; fibroids 160; gum disease 179; headaches and migraines 185, 186; high blood pressure 191; hyperpigmentation of the skin 198; infertility 206; irritable bowel syndrome 214; kidney stones 217, 218; menopause 229; multiple sclerosis 232; nerve pain 234; osteoporosis 238; polycystic ovary syndrome 241; premenstrual syndrome 246, 248; psoriasis 254; restless leg syndrome 256; seborrhoeic dermatitis 259; stress 270; tinnitus 275
vitamin B1 26; eye care 156; nerve pain 234
vitamin B2 26
vitamin B3 26; acne 62; high cholesterol 195
vitamin B5 26; anxiety 79; chronic fatigue syndrome 114; depression 130; gum disease 179; nerve pain 234; stress 270
vitamin B6 26; acne 66–67; angina and atherosclerosis 77; anxiety 80; carpal tunnel syndrome 106; cellulite 109; cervical dysplasia 112; dandruff 128; infertility 206; insomnia 211; kidney stones 217, 218; osteoporosis 238; polycystic ovary syndrome 242; premenstrual syndrome 248; varicose veins 282
vitamin B12 27; anaemia 73–75; angina and atherosclerosis 77; bruises 101; cervical dysplasia 112; infertility 207; multiple sclerosis 232; osteoporosis 238; tinnitus 275
vitamin C (see also antioxidants) 27; AIDS 70; anaemia 74; angina and atherosclerosis 77; anxiety 79; asthma 87; bad breath 93; boils 95; bronchitis 99;

bruises 101; carpal tunnel syndrome 106; cataracts 108; cellulitis 111; cervical dysplasia 112; chronic fatigue syndrome 114; colds and flu 119; cold sores 121; cystitis 126; depression 131; detoxing 133; diabetes mellitus 137; dietary sources 27, 31; diverticulosis 142; ear infection 144; eczema 147; eye care 154, 155; facial moisturiser 65; food allergies and sensitivities 168; glandular fever 176; gum disease 179; haemorrhoids 181; high blood pressure 191; high cholesterol 196; HIV 27; hyperpigmentation of the skin 199; memory problems 225; menopause 229; nerve pain 234; premenstrual syndrome 246, 248; seasonal affective disorder 258; seborrhoeic dermatitis 260; shingles 261; sinusitis and sore throat 263; sports injuries 266; stress 270; sunburn 273; ulcers 277; vaginitis 279; varicose veins 281; warts 284
vitamin D 25; multiple sclerosis 232; osteoporosis 238; sports injuries 267
vitamin E (see also antioxidants) 25; acne, essential oils, skin 67–68; AIDS 70; angina and atherosclerosis 77; asthma 87; ADD 91; bruises 102; cataracts 108; cervical dysplasia 112; diabetes mellitus 137; eczema 147; emphysema 149; endometriosis 152; eye care 154; fibroids 160; gout 178; hiatus hernia 188; high blood pressure 191; HIV 70; hyperpigmentation of the skin 199; infertility 207, 209; irritable bowel syndrome 214; leaky gut syndrome 219; memory problems 225, 226; menopause 230; multiple sclerosis 232; nerve pain 235; premenstrual syndrome 246, 247, 248; restless leg syndrome 256; sports injuries 266; sunburn 273; vaginitis 279; varicose veins 282; oil, warts 284
vitamin K 25; bruises 101; sports injuries 267
vitamins 24; fat soluble 24; water soluble 25
von Willebrand's disease; bruises 100

warts 283
water 24, 48; infusions 42; retention, cellulite 109
weight loss 50–62; food, exercise and supplement planning chart 62; exercise 52–54; four step success plan 51; hormonal imbalance 50; mental commitment and goal setting 51–52; nutrition 54–62; nutritional deficiencies 50; psychological factors 50
whey protein shakes (see protein) 57–62; AIDS and HIV 70
white heads 66
white horehound; bronchitis 99
white kidney bean extract 57
white willow; arthritis (osteo) 82; arthritis (rheumatoid) 85; bronchitis 99; bruises 102; carpal tunnel syndrome 106; fibromyalgia 164;

headaches and migraines 186; sports injuries 267; weight loss 57
wild cherry bark; bronchitis 99
wild indigo; bronchitis 99; cellulitis 111; diarrhoea 140; ear infection 145
wild yam; Coeliac disease 117; constipation 124; diverticulosis 143; fibromyalgia 164; headaches and migraines 186; leaky gut syndrome 220; menopause 229, 230; polycystic ovary syndrome 243; sports injuries 267
wine; red (anaemia) 74
wintergreen; arthritis (osteo) 82; arthritis (rheumatoid) 85; sports injuries 267
witch hazel; eye care 155
witch hazel cream or lotion; bruises 102; varicose veins 282; haemorrhoids 182
wood betony; bronchitis 99; tinnitus 275
wormwood; arthritis (osteo) 82; arthritis (rheumatoid) 85; bad breath 94; candida 105; detoxing 134; diabetes mellitus 138; diarrhoea 140; diverticulosis 143; endometriosis 152; fibroids 160; fibromyalgia 163; food allergies and sensitivities 168; infertility 207, 209; irritable bowel syndrome 215; lymphoedema 222; multiple sclerosis 233; polycystic ovary syndrome 242; premenstrual syndrome 246; prostate enlargement 252; psoriasis 255; ulcers 277, 278; vaginitis 280; warts 284
wormwood tincture; ulcers 278;

yarrow; bronchitis 99; endometriosis 153; fibroids 161; fibromyalgia 164; infertility 207; polycystic ovary syndrome 243
yellow dock; constipation 124; detoxing 134; eczema 147; liver detoxing 48
yoghurt, how to make your own 104

zeaxanthin; eye care 155
zinc (see also antioxidants) 30; acne 67; arthritis (rheumatoid) 84; ADD 91; bad breath 93; boils 95; bronchitis 99; cellulitis 111; cervical dysplasia 112; colds and flu 119; cold sores 121; cystitis 126; dandruff 128; ear infection 144; eczema 147; fibromyalgia 163; glandular fever 176; hiatus hernia 188; infertility 207, 209; leaky gut syndrome 219; polycystic ovary syndrome 241; prostate enlargement 251; seasonal affective disorder 258; seborrhoeic dermatitis 259; shingles 261; sinusitis and sore throat 263; sports injuries 267; ulcers 277
zinc oxide; eczema 146